Benson &
t Kennedy

D1396815

HONOLULU, WAIKIKI & O'AHU

CONTENTS

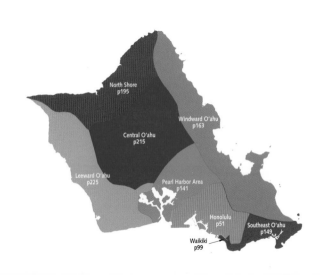

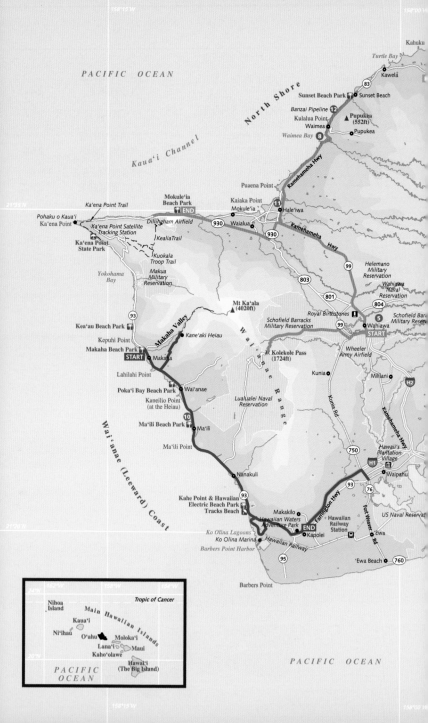

BEST O'AHU EXPERIENCES

O'ahu is the *ali'i* (chief) of the Hawaiian Islands. Most locals say they've got the best of both worlds here. There's the big city of Honolulu, encompassing the kinetic streets of Chinatown, downtown high-rises filled with power brokers next to Victorian-era historical sites and, of course, the classic beaches of Waikiki. Then there's the other side of the island – the 'country' – where rural farms and dirt roads lead deep into a Hawaiian heartland. On some wild, rugged and nearly deserted beaches, sea turtles still outnumber the surfers. Who says you can't have it all here? Not us, and definitely not O'ahuans.

The following pages showcase, in no particular order, our recommendations for the most unforgettable and in-depth experiences on O'ahu right now.

❶ BEST ISLAND-STYLE NIGHTLIFE: Waikiki (p135)

Waikiki is back, baby. Hawaii's most famous beach resort may still be a haven for tacky plastic leis, coconut-shell bikini tops and motorized hip-shaking hula dolls, but real aloha has returned to this prototypical paradise. Nightly at beachfront hotels, bars and even shopping malls you can stumble upon famous Hawaiian musicians strumming their slack key guitars and ukuleles, singing *ha'i* (a style of falsetto) or traditional Hawaiian chants, and shaking *ipu* (gourds) while performing the subtle hand movements and patterned footsteps of ancient and contemporary hula dances. At sunset, watch the tiki torches get lit and the conch shell blown at Kuhio Beach Park, where you can spread out a blanket in front of the hula mound, where dancers sway nightly. Then wander over to the courtyard of the Moana Surfrider, the House Without a Key in the Halekulani Hotel, or a dozen more venues for live contemporary Hawaiian music and hula that's not strictly for tourists – it's also a way of keeping island traditions alive. And with such a gorgeous beachfront setting, it's irresistible and pure magic.

1

❷ BEST PLACE TO FIND OUT WHAT HAWAII IS ALL ABOUT:
Bishop Museum (p74)

From the time the first Protestant missionaries stepped ashore to the onset of mass tourism after WWII, Hawaiian culture and traditions have come under pressure from what one 19th-century commentator described as 'a tide of foreign invasion.' While a rich polyglot mix of immigrants is part of what makes Oʻahu unique, sometimes it can be hard to find the lifeblood of ancient Hawaiian ways that took root here over 1000 years before Captain Cook arrived. That's what makes the Bishop Museum such a valuable treasure house of Hawaiian cultural and natural history. Here you can see rare island artifacts such as the feathered cloak worn by Kamehameha the Great and fearsome *ki'i akua* (carved temple images) that once commanded the respect of ancient *kahuna* (priests) and *maka'ainana* (commoners) alike. This multidisciplinary educational campus is also a fantastic place to gaze at the stars – the same ones that guided ancient Polynesian voyagers to this remote archipelago – inside Oʻahu's only planetarium. No doubt, when you walk out of this place, you'll know more about Hawaii than ever before.

❸ **BEST BEACH:** Kailua Beach Park (p173)

On a Polynesian island that has over 125 beaches, choosing the very best one is a tricky proposition. If you judge by numbers, Waikiki is packed with more bodies than anywhere else on O'ahu. Still, biggest isn't necessarily best. It's Kailua Bay that really deserves the gold star. For starters, it has jaw-dropping scenery, with tempting offshore islands that practically beg you to jump in the ocean, launch your kayak and paddle over to do a little sunbathing and snorkeling. Or look down at the beach itself and wonder at the soft, golden sand nestling between your toes, while waves wash gently over your *rubbah slippah* (flip-flops) or your bare feet. Come in the early morning for sunrise yoga or a meditative swim. For an adrenaline-charged afternoon, show up when windsurfers and kitesurfers launch their rigs into the surf. Kailua Bay proves that yes, a beach really can be all things to all people. Don't forget to stop at the 1930s landmark Kalapawai Market beforehand for a fast java fix and to fill your beach cooler with a gourmet deli lunch.

RICHARD CUMMINS

Kailua Bay deserves the gold star

O'ahu is
an unsung
destination for
adventurous
hikers

4

❹ BEST HIKING TRAIL NETWORK:
Mt Tantalus area (p77)

With its lofty mountain ranges, Oʻahu is an unsung destination for adventurous hikers. While many visitors think the Neighbor Islands possess all the best trails, that's just not true. You don't even have to go outside Honolulu to find incredible routes winding into the lush Koʻolau Range, especially around Mt Tantalus, aka Puʻu ʻOʻhia. Take the kids on a pint-sized trek up to Manoa Falls, or press on up a steep ladder of tree roots to the head-spinning Nuʻuanu Valley Lookout, where you can peer through a gap in the mountains to the emerald Windward Coast. Or join the locals back below on the thickly forested Makiki Valley Loop trail, which grants sweeping views of Honolulu and its protected harbor. No matter which trail you choose, you'll also get a free lesson in Hawaiian natural history along the way, walking past hulking banyan trees, fragrant guava, musical bamboo and delicate honeycreepers that flutter through the air. Without doubt, these interconnected trails are the best escape from urban traffic jams and the concrete high-rises of Waikiki. Getting back to nature is rarely so easy.

KARL LEHMANN

5

❺ BEST UNEXPECTED GREENERY:
Wahiawa Botanical Garden (p221)

While Oʻahu was built on a reputation of green fields, lush rainforests and sparse population, sadly too many tourists remain city bound and never experience the island's nature. Time to buck the trend and get out of the city and see what Oʻahu is really all about. All it takes to escape the urban jungle is a little bit of effort and a point in the right direction. There is little excuse not to get among the greenery here. The perfect rest stop on the way to the North Shore, the town of Wahiawa has a hidden gem in this historical and aesthetic garden, camouflaged among the suburbs. Founded by pineapple farmers nearly 90 years ago, the 27 acres are home to massive unkempt trees, manicured lawns and examples of both native and imported plants. The pathways weave a twisted tale through the trees and offer a sublime journey through the maintained wilderness. You can take a picnic, go for a jog or simply wander – this place is the perfect midisland location for a return to nature and a deep breath of solitude.

En route, pull over at romantic coves and dramatic lookouts

❻ BEST SCENIC DRIVE: Southeast Coast (p162)

The Pali Hwy over the mountains from Honolulu gets all the fame, while the day-trippers' fave remains the Kamehameha Hwy that snakes up the Windward Coast all the way to the North Shore. But for the biggest dose of drive-by beauty, our vote goes to the Southeast Coast, starting at crescent-shaped Hanauma Bay and curving around Makapu'u Point over to Waimanalo (which boasts O'ahu's longest beach). En route, pull over at lava-rock blowholes, romantic coves and dramatic lookouts. You can even hike out to a windswept lighthouse and still get back to Waikiki in time for sunset mai tais.

RICHARD CUMMINS

❼ BEST SHOP FOR FILLING YOUR SUITCASE:
Bailey's Antiques & Aloha Shirts (p123)

Nothing makes you look more like a tourist here than *not* wearing an aloha shirt, at least for guys. Fellas, as soon as you land in Waikiki, take yourself down Kapahulu Ave to this veritable museum of aloha wear, stocking everything from vintage prints to modern reproductions and everything in between, including neon designs of Don Ho–worthy taste from the 1960s and '70s. Prices start at just $10, so you've got no excuse for not giving your everyday wardrobe a little vacation. There are plenty of vintage tiki goods to peruse, too.

❽ BEST SPLIT-PERSONALITY BEACH: Waimea Bay (p204)

Waimea is one of those beaches that can either be your worst fear or your wildest dream. The massive expansive sand is a year-round feature – it's the water that has a life all its own. In summer, when the swell switches to the south side of the island, the bay is a placid place to lounge by the sea. There is good snorkeling to be found and even the kiddies can enjoy a swim. Come winter, everything is very, very different. When the big winter swells pick up Waimea becomes a place of legend. The waves jack up to heights that would make even the boldest waterman quake in his boots. Wave heights of 20-plus feet are not uncommon and the rumble of the crashing mountains of water shakes the sand on the beach. Top-level surfers import from all around the world to test their mettle on the legendary break. If you know what you're doing Waimea is one of the best big-wave surf breaks on the planet – if not, stay away. Heroes are born here, legends have died and the rest of us stand in awe at the power of mother ocean.

ANN CECIL

MERTEN SNIJDERS

❾ BEST NEIGHBORHOOD FOR WALKING: Chinatown (p64)

An anchor's throw from Honolulu Harbor, the crowded streets of Chinatown possess more history, block for block, than any other place on O'ahu. Nineteenth-century whalers whooped it up in bars and brothels, while plantation-era immigrants made their way into island society after putting down roots here. Despite suffering through plague, fire and discrimination, Chinatown residents built a community that has endured. Today the neighborhood just keeps on evolving, with emerging art galleries, epicurean restaurants and hipster nightspots. Conveniently, it's small enough to leisurely walk around in a morning or afternoon, with a tasty break for dim sum.

❿ BEST SECRET SUNSET SPOT:
Ma'ili Beach Park (p234)

Shhh, don't tell anyone, but this could be the best spot on the island to watch the sunset. Sure Waikiki, the North Shore and other more tourist-oriented spots get most of the attention, but isn't the best part about a good sunset having the beach to yourself? Forget fighting the crowds here – located halfway up the Wai'anae (Leeward) Coast, this uncluttered and under-populated beach is popular with locals and the odd tourist who's looking to escape the masses. There's a vast stretch of sand from which to choose your sunset-watching spot – all of it is front-row center to watch the sun dip below the Pacific. If you're feeling energetic, the soft-sand beach is perfect for a sun-kissed stroll with your sweetie on your arm or a jog in the creeping surf. Those keen for a more relaxed session are in luck too – the swaying palms of the beach park make for fine photo props and even better back rests as you sit, reflect on the day that's been and hatch plans for the next day of adventure.

RAY LASKOWITZ

SCOTT KENNEDY

LINDA CHING

⓫ BEST SHAVE ICE:
Matsumoto's (p210)

It's a big call – the best is a pretty large claim. Some will say the softer, smoother shave ice found elsewhere is the way to go. Others prefer the crunchier style of Matsumoto's shave ice, though some say that Matsumoto's is the victim of its own popularity, with lines out the door and sticky floors all around. Perhaps the best plan is to decide for yourself – try them all. Savor all the sticky goodness you can handle before reaching sweetness saturation point. Debate the subtle differences in sweetness, texture and flavor with the ferocity of a wine connoisseur.

Pipeline offers a glimpse of the rock stars of the ocean

⑫ BEST BEACH TO WATCH THE WORLD'S BEST SURFERS:
Pipeline (p202)

When the waves are crashing huge all around the North Shore and you want to get a glimpse of the rock stars of the ocean, where do you go? In a word: Pipeline. Not only does it have best and most consistent break on the North Shore, it is by far the most spectator-friendly surfing spot on the island. With the waves breaking mere yards offshore you get a great view from the beach. Forget having to pull out the camera lens larger then a howitzer; here you can look the surfers in the eye as they paddle into the monster surf.

ANN CECIL

ISLAND
ITINERARIES

See the itineraries at the beginning of each regional chapter for more detailed routes.

IN THREE DAYS *This leg: 40 miles*

❶ WAIKIKI (p99) Bronze your bod on the world-famous beach-resort strip, stretching from the windsurfing waves of **Fort DeRussy Beach (p106)** all the way south to the hideaway swimming and snorkeling spot of **Sans Souci Beach Park (p108)**.

❷ KUHIO BEACH TORCH LIGHTING & HULA SHOW (p137) After you've put up your surfboard for the day and the sun starts to lazily sink over the Pacific, spread out your beach mat by the hula mound at Kuhio Beach Park (p107).

❸ DOWNTOWN HONOLULU (p59) On your second day, take a bus downtown to the Victorian-era 'Iolani Palace (p59) then browse the Hawai'i State Art Museum (p61) and Hawai'i Maritime Center (p64), near the landmark Aloha Tower (p63).

❹ CHINATOWN (p64) Walk in the steps of 19th-century whalers from Honolulu's breezy harbor over to this vibrant neighbor-

hood, full of fresh **markets and lei shops (p65)**, eclectic **art galleries (p96)** and a tasty panoply of pan-Asian **eateries (p83)**.

❺ UPPER MANOA VALLEY (p72) In the afternoon, shake off that urban grit by heading for the hills above downtown Honolulu. Wander among tropical plants in the **Lyon Arboretum (p72)**, then hike the family-friendly trail to **Manoa Falls (p76)** or **Nu'uanu Valley Lookout (p77)**.

❻ PEARL HARBOR (p141) On your third day, get up early to visit O'ahu's dramatic WWII-era sites, starting with the sunken **USS Arizona Memorial (p144)** and finishing at the **Pacific Aviation Museum (p145)**. Stuff yourself silly with *manapua* (Chinese-style steamed buns) from **Chun Wah Kam Noodle Factory (p147)**.

❼ ALA MOANA BEACH PARK (p58) Finish off with a dip at Honolulu's favorite city beach, then take a sunset stroll around **Magic Island (p58)**.

IN FIVE DAYS *This leg: 60 miles*

8 DIAMOND HEAD (p153) Start your fourth day with a sunrise hike up this ancient volcanic crater, now a state monument (p154), then ride the waves of Kuilei Cliffs Beach Park (p153) below.

9 HANAUMA BAY NATURE PRESERVE (p158) If you're jonesing to go face to mask with schools of rainbow-colored fish and gentle sea turtles, head straight to this crescent-shaped bay with hands-on, kid-friendly educational exhibits.

10 KOKO HEAD REGIONAL PARK (p160) Roadside stops through this coastal park include the Halona Blowhole (p161), next to idyllic Halona Cove (p161) and the bodysurfers' mecca of Sandy Beach (p161). Further along the highway is the lighthouse trail out to windy Makapu'u Point (p162).

11 WAIMANALO (p170) Rounding the southeast tip of the island brings you to the rural farming community on 'Nalo, boasting the island's longest beach (p170), a white-sand beauty with gentle waves beloved by families. This really feels like the countryside.

12 KAILUA (p172) Grab dinner, then bed down in a beachfront cottage B&B in this laid-back surf-style town. Don't leave the Windward Coast's adventure-sports capital without kayaking (p173) to offshore islands, windsurfing (p174) or doing sunrise yoga (p175) at Kailua Beach Park (p173).

13 KANE'OHE (p180) The next morning, take off early for a leisurely drive up the Windward Coast. Stop off at Ho'omaluhia Botanical Garden (p180) and Byōdō-In (p180) temple, both with the misty Ko'olau Mountains as a dramatic backdrop.

14 KUALOA (p184) Continue the classic drive up the Windward Coast to the North Shore, passing fruit stands like Tropical Farms (p185) along the way. Kualoa Regional Park (p184) is an incredibly scenic spot for a swim, just across the highway from historic Kualoa Ranch (p184), a famous movie and TV location.

15 LA'IE (p190) All the tour buses stop at the Polynesian Cultural Center (p192), but just north of town you'll find an irresistibly wild, rugged beach at Malaekahana State Recreation Area (p190), where you can pitch a tent. Kahuku's shrimp trucks (p194) are just up the road.

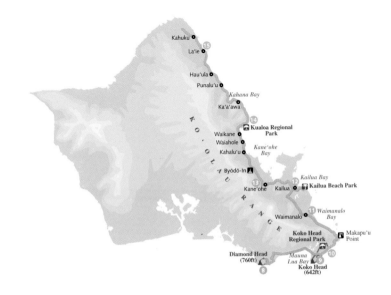

IN SEVEN DAYS *This leg: 50 miles*

16 **WAHIAWA (p220)** On your sixth day venture into the vast interior of the island and stop off at the **Wahiawa Botanical Garden (p221)**. These luscious gardens are home to hundreds of native and imported species. They're a sanctuary for flora, nature lovers and those escaping the hustle of the south. Just to the east is **Kolekole Pass (p219)**. Weave your way through Schofield Barracks and climb the steep hill to this historic pass. During the attack on Pearl Harbor, Japanese fighter planes soared through here to reach their targets. These days it offers a nice walk with great views. Finally, head north to the **Dole Pineapple Plantation (p222)**. Want to learn everything you ever needed to know about pineapples? Here is your chance. It's sickly sweet and prepackaged fun – do the maze, ride the train, buy the T-shirt.

17 **WAIMEA BAY (p204)** On day seven head to the North Shore. If you're an experienced surfer it's a great place to catch some big winter waves. If it's summer, bring your snorkeling gear.

18 **TED'S BAKERY (p203)** Ted's is a legendary place to grab a bite on the North Shore. The chocolate coconut pie is as good as it sounds and the savory delights are a perfect first course.

19 **HALE'IWA (p207)** Get the sand out of your shorts and head to Hale'iwa – the largest town on the North Shore – filled with cool shops, yummy restaurants and some great galleries. Be sure to stop off at **Matsumoto's (p210)** – you can't come to the North Shore and not get some shave ice. Like a snow cone on steroids, this could be the best 1000 calories of your day.

20 **MOKULE'IA BEACH PARK (p212)** Finish the day by visiting one of the more secluded beaches on the island. If you're a windsurfer, this is a great place to catch some wind and waves. If you're more of a land lover, go for a stroll on the deserted beach.

IN EIGHT DAYS *This leg: 23 miles*

㉑ MAKAHA (p235) For your last day head to the Leeward Coast and experience the quiet side of the island. The heart and soul of little Makaha is classic **Makaha Beach Park (p235)**. If the surf is up, it can be way up – winter brings monster waves here. Summer is a quiet time, with gentle rollers and infrequent visitors. Or take a break from the beach and get cultured at **Kane'aki Heiau (p238)**, just up the hill. This ancient site is a great spot to see what the old Hawaii was all about. Finish up with a scrummy smoothie from nearby **Surfah Smoodeez (p234)**. It's one of the best tropical treats on the island – on a hot day a bucket of fresh berry smoothie is like a gift from the gods. Stick around for a nice, no-nonsense lunch.

㉒ MA'ILI (p234) Time to head back to the beach – grab a bodyboard and hit the beach break at Ma'ili Beach Park, where microtubes are a go-go when the swell is in. If that sounds too juvenile, hit the sand and tuck into your book.

㉓ TRACKS (p233) If Ma'ili was going off, then Tracks will be pumping. Forget the bodyboard, pull out the short-board and rip it up. The shore is the opposite of aesthetic, but the waves are great.

㉔ KO OLINA LAGOONS (p229) Mellow out and go for a swim in some placid waters. Pull out the snorkeling gear and see what you can see – try near the rocks; the goods are hidden out there. When hunger strikes head to **Poke Stop (p232)**. Good food at a strip mall? Believe it; this little shop has some of the best eats around. Take away a plate of poke, or devour it on the picnic table out front. Finish up with some waterslide action at **Hawaiian Waters Adventure Park (p230)** – fun for kids of all ages.

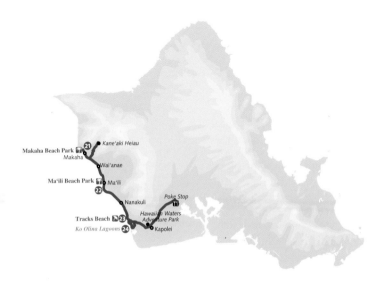

KICKIN' IT WITH THE KEIKI

❶ KUHIO BEACH PARK (p107) Kids love a day at the beach, so start off on Waikiki's most popular stretch of sand, with two walled-off pools and screamin' bodyboarding.

❷ KAPI'OLANI PARK (p108) Take an ocean-front amble or hop on a bus to the **Waikiki Aquarium (p109)** and **Honolulu Zoo (p110)**.

❸ DIAMOND HEAD STATE MONUMENT (p154) Scramble through spooky tunnels and up twisted staircases to summit an ancient volcanic crater.

❹ HANAUMA BAY NATURE PRESERVE (p158) This outdoor fishbowl has great snorkeling spots for little 'uns to get their feet and face masks wet.

❺ BISHOP MUSEUM (p74) Take a mini-submarine dive or walk through an exploding mock volcano at Hawaii's top natural and cultural history museum.

❻ HAWAI'I MARITIME CENTER (p64) See traditional Polynesian canoes and 19th-century sailing ships, then climb nearby **Aloha Tower (p63)** for aerial views.

❼ HAWAIIAN WATERS ADVENTURE PARK (p230) It's got wild rides on all sorts of chutes and slides – some geared for youngsters, others for speed riders.

❽ KO OLINA RESORT (p228) Even if you don't stay overnight, stop by for a swim in the calm, waveless **Ko Olina Lagoons (p229)**.

GO GREEN

❶ MT TANTALUS (p77) Where Honolulu-ans go to hike in the cool upland forests of the misty Ko'olau Range.

❷ HANAUMA BAY (p158) Protected as the state's first underwater park, this is O'ahu's premier snorkeling and diving spot.

❸ KAILUA (p172) This adventure-sports hub has cozy vacation rentals and B&Bs, yoga on the beach and ecofriendly eateries.

❹ HO'OMALUHIA BOTANICAL GARDEN (p180) The Windward Coast doesn't get more lush than inside this county park, which also has pretty campsites.

❺ MALAEKAHANA STATE RECREATION AREA (p190) Another opportunity for camping or renting a rustic cabin, along with all kinds of family-friendly water sports.

❻ WAIMEA VALLEY (p205) Explore some ancient Hawaiian archeological sites, go bird-watching or waterfall-pool swimming.

❼ DEEP ECOLOGY (p209) North Shore dive shop with strong environmental ethics that runs whale-watching tours in winter.

❽ KA'ENA POINT STATE PARK (p239) This feels about as far away from urban civilization as you can get on O'ahu, especially if you approach from the Mokule'ia side.

SURF'S UP

❶ CENTRAL WAIKIKI BEACH (p107) It doesn't matter if you're an old pro or a grommet, you have to start your surfing adventure under the watchful eyes of Duke. Central Waikiki Beach is the ancestral home of surfing and where most O'ahu surfers catch their first wave. Pull out the long-board and ride a few.

❷ LEEWARD COAST (p225) Off the radar for most travelers and a hidden gem. This coast is chockablock with great surf breaks. **Tracks (p233)** is a local classic and can have some great waves. **Ma'ili (p234)** is a ferocious beach break and is perfect for a bodysurf. End the day in **Makaha (p235)**, where the waves can be massive and the vibe is always mellow.

❸ NORTH SHORE (p195) This is the day you've been waiting for. From the east, surf **Sunset Beach Park (p201)**, **Pipeline (p202)**, **Waimea Bay (p204)** and **Hale'iwa Ali'i (p208)**. All are classic breaks and must-dos on any surfer's itinerary.

❹ SOUTHEAST COAST (p149) Finish up the circle and surf some of the southeast classics. **Diamond Head Beach (p153)** often has good waves even when other breaks are playing the fickle card.

TAKE A HIKE

❶ DIAMOND HEAD STATE MONUMENT (p154) Do the classic O'ahu hike and walk to the top of this beautiful lookout. You won't have it to yourself, but the views are unreal and it's a great way to get a feel for the island's geography.

❷ UPPER MANOA VALLEY (p76) An awesome place for a hike and, best yet, it's only a few steps from Honolulu. It doesn't take a huge effort to get here, and the walks are some of the island's best.

❸ MAUNAWILI TRAIL SYSTEM (p168) Trek this southeast O'ahu classic, with panoramic views of the mountains and Windward Coast that are a feast for the photographic eye.

❹ LEEWARD COAST (p225) Hike this wild, rarely visited coast and you'll likely have it all to yourself. The **Ka'ena Point Trail (p240)** takes in great beaches and explores the island's wild northwest corner.

❺ KAWELA (p199) On the island's northeast corner is this little pocket of trails. Most people head here to surf, but there are great walks, beaches to explore and bays to discover.

❻ KEALIA TRAIL (p214) Go to the island's northwest for this gem of a track. Get lost on the set of *Lost* and take in the views from the ridge – classic.

OUTDOOR ACTIVITIES & ADVENTURES

Oʻahu – the land of surf, sand, sun and adventure. When people think of Oʻahu, many assume that their sporting options amount to surfing and beach lounging. But that's just the tip of the tropical iceberg – all you need to do is wrestle yourself away from the opulence of your beach towel and discover what's happening around the island.

As you'd expect, surfing is king on the island. There are world-class surf breaks, revered for their enormous and nearly perfect barreling waves, but there are also great beginner surf spots.

If you're more of a landlubber, there are picturesque hiking trails, numerous horseback options and even the opportunity to leap out of a perfectly good airplane with a parachute.

Oʻahu is a dream destination for those keen to get outside – whether you're searching for action and adventure or just a leisurely stroll, you can do it all here.

AT SEA

Water, water everywhere – a trip to Oʻahu wouldn't be complete without venturing into the ocean. There's a host of aqueous activities to be sampled from the mundane to the mad.

BODYSURFING & BODYBOARDING

Bodysurfing is a great way to catch some waves, sans equipment. There's a bit of a knack to it, but once you've found the groove, its good times ahead. There are quite a few good spots around the island to catch some waves – the ideal locations are sandy shorebreaks where inevitable wipe outs aren't that painful.

If you're someone who knows your way around the surf, head to Sandy Beach Park (p161) and Makapuʻu Beach Park (p162) in the southeast, and

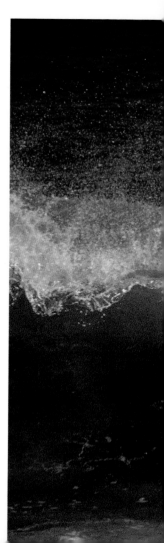

O'AHU ACTIVITIES

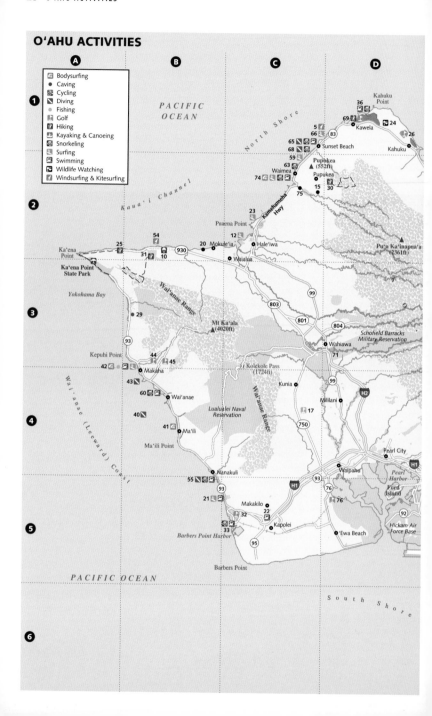

A **B** **C** **D**

- 🏄 Bodysurfing
- ● Caving
- 🚴 Cycling
- 🤿 Diving
- ● Fishing
- ⛳ Golf
- 🥾 Hiking
- 🛶 Kayaking & Canoeing
- 🤿 Snorkeling
- 🏄 Surfing
- 🏊 Swimming
- 🦅 Wildlife Watching
- 🏄 Windsurfing & Kitesurfing

PACIFIC OCEAN

North Shore

Kaua'i Channel

Ka'ena Point

Ka'ena Point State Park

Yokohama Bay

Wai'anae Range

Mt Ka'ala ▲(4020ft)

Kolekole Pass (1724ft)

Kepuhi Point

Makaha

Wai'anae

Ma'ili

Ma'ili Point

Lualualei Naval Reservation

Wai'anae Range

Wai'anae (Leeward) Coast

Nanakuli

Makakilo

Kapolei

Barbers Point Harbor

Barbers Point

PACIFIC OCEAN

South Shore

Kamehameha Hwy

Puaena Point

Mokule'ia

Hale'iwa

Waialua

Sunset Beach

Waimea

Pupukea ▲(552ft)

Pupukea

Kahuku Point

Kawela

Kahuku

Pu'u Ka'inapua'a ▲(2361ft)

Schofield Barracks Military Reservation

Wahiawa

Kunia

Mililani

Waipahu

Pearl City

Pearl Harbor

Ford Island

Hickam Air Force Base

'Ewa Beach

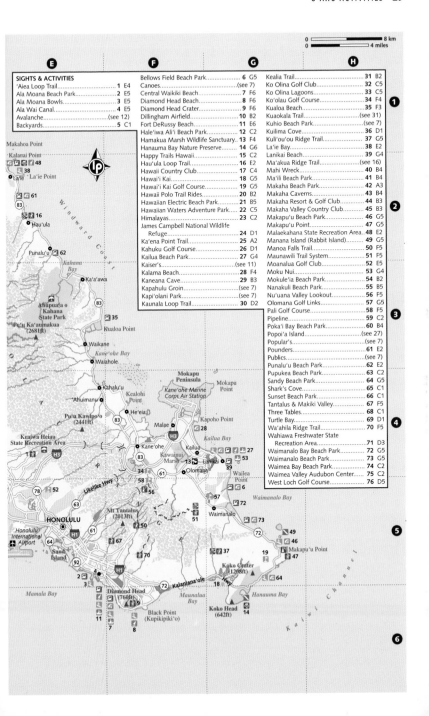

SIGHTS & ACTIVITIES

'Aiea Loop Trail	1 E4
Ala Moana Beach Park	2 E5
Ala Moana Bowls	3 E5
Ala Wai Canal	4 E5
Avalanche	(see 12)
Backyards	5 C1
Bellows Field Beach Park	6 G5
Canoes	(see 7)
Central Waikiki Beach	7 F6
Diamond Head Beach	8 F6
Diamond Head Crater	9 F6
Dillingham Airfield	10 B2
Fort DeRussy Beach	11 E6
Hale'iwa Ali'i Beach Park	12 C2
Hamakua Marsh Wildlife Sanctuary	13 F4
Hanauma Bay Nature Preserve	14 G6
Happy Trails Hawaii	15 C2
Hau'ula Loop Trail	16 E2
Hawaii Country Club	17 C4
Hawai'i Kai	18 G5
Hawai'i Kai Golf Course	19 G5
Hawaii Polo Trail Rides	20 B2
Hawaiian Electric Beach Park	21 B5
Hawaiian Waters Adventure Park	22 C5
Himalayas	23 C2
James Campbell National Wildlife Refuge	24 D1
Ka'ena Point Trail	25 A2
Kahuku Golf Course	26 D1
Kailua Beach Park	27 G4
Kaiser's	(see 11)
Kalama Beach	28 F4
Kaneana Cave	29 B3
Kapahulu Groin	(see 7)
Kapi'olani Park	(see 7)
Kaunala Loop Trail	30 D2
Kealia Trail	31 B2
Ko Olina Golf Club	32 C5
Ko Olina Lagoons	33 C5
Ko'olau Golf Course	34 F4
Kualoa Beach	35 F3
Kuaokala Trail	(see 31)
Kuhio Beach Park	(see 7)
Kuilima Cove	36 D1
Kuli'ou'ou Ridge Trail	37 G5
La'ie Bay	38 E2
Lanikai Beach	39 G4
Ma'akua Ridge Trail	(see 16)
Mahi Wreck	40 B4
Ma'ili Beach Park	41 B4
Makaha Beach Park	42 A3
Makaha Caverns	43 B4
Makaha Resort & Golf Club	44 B3
Makaha Valley Country Club	45 B3
Makapu'u Beach Park	46 G5
Makapu'u Point	47 G5
Malaekahana State Recreation Area	48 E2
Manana Island (Rabbit Island)	49 G5
Manoa Falls Trail	50 F5
Maunawili Trail System	51 F5
Moanalua Golf Club	52 E5
Moku Nui	53 G4
Mokule'ia Beach Park	54 B2
Nanakuli Beach Park	55 B5
Nu'uana Valley Lookout	56 F5
Olomana Golf Links	57 G5
Pali Golf Course	58 F5
Pipeline	59 C2
Poka'i Bay Beach Park	60 B4
Popoi'a Island	(see 27)
Popular's	(see 7)
Pounders	61 E2
Publics	(see 7)
Punalu'u Beach Park	62 E2
Pupukea Beach Park	63 C2
Sandy Beach Park	64 G5
Shark's Cove	65 C1
Sunset Beach Park	66 C1
Tantalus & Makiki Valley	67 F5
Three Tables	68 C1
Turtle Bay	69 D1
Wa'ahila Ridge Trail	70 F5
Wahiawa Freshwater State Recreation Area	71 D3
Waimanalo Bay Beach Park	72 G5
Waimanalo Beach Park	73 G5
Waimea Bay Beach Park	74 C2
Waimea Valley Audubon Center	75 C2
West Loch Golf Course	76 D5

Makaha Beach Park (p235) and Ma'ili Beach Park (p234) in Leeward O'ahu.

Other top shorebreaks are at Waimea Bay Beach Park (p204) on the North Shore; Kalama Beach (p175) in Kailua; and Malaekahana State Recreation Area (p190) and Pounders Beach (p190) in La'ie.

If you're just getting started, Waimanalo Beach Park (p170) and nearby Bellows Field Beach Park (p170) in Windward O'ahu have gentle shorebreaks good for beginner bodysurfers.

Bodyboarding is the bridge between bodysurfing and surfing – with that in mind, you're spoilt for break choices. If you're keen for shorebreaks, try the aforementioned bodysurfing waves. If you want something a bit bigger, have a look at the surfing spots (p33). If you want to see and be seen, the island's most popular bodyboarding site is Kapahulu Groin (p107) in Waikiki.

DIVING

O'ahu is a great place to head down under and experience the marine world. The water temperatures are perfect for diving with yearly averages from 72°F to 80°F. Even bet-ter then the bathwater temperatures is the visibility, which is usually excellent – perfect for seeing the plethora of fish, coral and other sea creatures.

Of the 700 fish species that live in Hawaiian waters, nearly one-third are found nowhere else in the world. In addition to all those tropical fish, divers can often see spinner dolphins, green sea turtles and manta rays. The waters hold all sorts of hard and soft corals, waving anemones, unusual sponges and a variety of shellfish. Because of its volcanic origins, O'ahu also has some cool underwater caves and caverns.

Whether you're an old pro or a beginner, O'ahu has plenty to offer: boat dives, shore dives, night dives, reef dives, cave dives and wreck dives. Experienced divers needn't bring anything other than a swimsuit and their certification card. Two-tank boat dives average $120 and include all gear.

If you want to experience diving for the first time, several dive operators offer a short beginners' 'try scuba' course, which includes a brief instruction followed by a shallow beach or boat dive. The cost is generally around $120, depending on the operation and whether a boat is used.

DIVING & SNORKELING OUTFITTERS

Company	Page	Tours	Price	Departs
Aaron's Dive Shop (☎ 262-2333, 888-847-2822; www.hawaii-scuba.com; 307 Hahani St)	p175	sea caves, lava tubes, coral gardens and WWII-era shipwrecks; courses also offered	$115-125 (2-tank), $450 (3-day open-water course)	Kailua
Deep Ecology (☎ 637-7946, 800-578-3992; www.deepecologyhawaii.com; 66-456 Kamehameha Hwy)	p209	dive sites around the island, courses and an ecofriendly approach	$139 (2-tank)	Hale'iwa
Island Divers (☎ 423-8222, 888-844-3483; www.oahuscubadiving.com; Hawai'i Kai Shopping Center, 377 Keahole St)	p157	boat dives for all levels, including expert-level wreck dives	$50 (snorkel), $125-160 (2-tank)	Hawai'i Kai
Waikiki Diving Center (☎ 922-2121; www.waikikidiving.com; 424 Nahua St)	p111	small-group boat dives and open-water PADI-certification courses	$35 (snorkel), $115 (2-tank), $125 (wreck), $350 (open-water course)	Waikiki

RESPONSIBLE DIVING

The popularity of diving is placing immense pressure on many sites. Please consider the following tips when diving to help preserve the ecology and beauty of reefs.

- Do not use reef anchors and take care not to ground boats on coral. Encourage dive operators to establish permanent moorings at popular sites.

- Avoid touching living marine organisms with your body or dragging equipment across the reef. Polyps can be damaged by even the gentlest contact. Never stand on coral. If you must hold on to the reef, only touch exposed rock or dead coral.

- Be conscious of your fins. Even without contact, the surge from heavy fin strokes near the reef can damage delicate organisms. When treading water in shallow reef areas, take care not to kick up clouds of sand. Settling sand can easily smother the delicate organisms of the reef.

- Practice and maintain proper buoyancy control. Major damage can be done by divers descending too fast and colliding with the reef. Make sure you are correctly weighted and that your weight belt is positioned so that you stay horizontal. Be aware that buoyancy can change over the period of an extended trip: initially you may breathe harder and need more weight; a few days later you may breathe more easily and need less weight.

- Take care in underwater caves. Spend as little time within them as possible, as your air bubbles may be caught within the roof and thereby leave previously submerged organisms high and dry.

- Resist the temptation to collect or buy coral or shells. Aside from the ecological damage, taking home marine souvenirs depletes the beauty of a site and spoils the enjoyment for others.

- Ensure that you take home all your rubbish and any other litter you may find. Plastics in particular are a serious threat to marine life. Turtles can mistake plastic for jellyfish and eat it.

- Do not feed fish. You may disturb their normal eating habits, encourage aggressive behavior or feed them food that is detrimental to their health.

- Minimize your disturbance of marine animals. It is illegal to approach endangered marine species too closely; these include whales, dolphins, sea turtles and the Hawaiian monk seal. In particular, do not ride on the backs of turtles, as this causes them great anxiety.

A number of shops offer full open-water certification courses, which can sometimes be completed in as little as three days and cost around $450. The **Professional Association of Diving Instructors** (PADI; ☎ 800-729-7234; www.padi.com) certifies scuba divers.

O'ahu's top summer dive spots include the caves and ledges at Three Tables (p205) and Shark's Cove (p205) on the North Shore, and the Makaha Caverns off Makaha Beach (p235). For wreck diving, the sunken 165-foot ship *Mahi*, also off Makaha Beach, is a prize. Numerous spots between Honolulu and Hanauma Bay provide good winter diving.

For detailed diving information, pick up a copy of Lonely Planet's *Diving & Snorkeling Hawaii*.

Divers Alert Network (www.diversalertnetwork.org) gives divers advice on diving emergencies, insurance, decompression services, illness and injury.

FISHING

Why order dinner when you can catch it? There are a number of sport-fishing operations around the island that'll take you out on the sea for the day and help you land the big one. While having the taxidermist on speed dial was the done thing back in the day, do respect the ocean and practice catch and release if you can. Some of the recommended outfitters are found in Hawai'i Kai (p156) and Makaha (p235) and you can go freshwater fishing at the Wahiawa Freshwater State Recreation Area (p223).

KAYAKING

Who says you need an engine to get around the sea? Paddle power is the way to go. Kayaking is not only a great workout, but it's an enjoyable way to explore the surface of the Hawaiian turquoise waters. The top spot is undoubtedly Kailua Beach

BUT WHERE IS EDDIE GOING?

'Eddie Would Go,' say the bumper stickers on half the cars in O'ahu that sport surfboards on top. Eddie who? Go where?

Eddie Aikau was a full-blooded native Hawaiian who got turned on to surfing as a teenager, learning the ropes as he moved up from Waikiki's tame surf to the monster waves of the North Shore. He so loved surfing that in 1968 he took a job as a lifeguard working at the North Shore beaches from Waimea Bay to Sunset Beach. Even though the North Shore has the most dangerous waves on O'ahu, no one was ever lost when Eddie was on duty. It's estimated he saved hundreds of lives during his decade-long career. Not only was he undaunted by 30-foot waves, but he was also a master at maintaining the peace between local surfers and upstart outsiders competing for the best breaks.

In an effort to get more in tune with his Hawaiian heritage, in 1978 Eddie joined a rediscovery trip aboard the *Hokule'a,* the double-hulled canoe that replicated the boats the first Polynesians used to reach Hawaii. It was to be the second journey for the *Hokule'a,* which, in 1976, had followed the ancient migrations from O'ahu 2400 miles to Tahiti and back again.

For this second journey, more than 10,000 people gathered at the tip of Magic Island to see the canoe off. On the way out, the boat had to go through the Moloka'i Channel, the roughest waterway in the Hawaiian Islands, and the *Hokule'a* capsized. Unable to right it, Eddie jumped on his surfboard and set out to paddle 12 miles across the treacherous channel to the island of Lana'i to get help. In the meantime a Hawaiian Air pilot spotted the capsized boat and rescuers were sent to pick up the crew. Eddie, however, was never seen again.

His brave life and tragic death became the stuff of legends. The excellent biography *Eddie Would Go,* by Stuart Holmes Coleman, details not only Eddie's life, but also the Hawaiian renaissance of the 1960s and '70s. Today the Quiksilver in Memory of Eddie Aikau surf competition is held at Waimea Bay in winter – but only when waves reach monstrous heights.

(p173), which has three uninhabited islands within the reef to which you can paddle. Landings are allowed on two of the islands: Moku Nui, which has a beautiful beach good for sunbathing and snorkeling; and Popoi'a Island (Flat Island), where there are some inviting walking trails. And it's all so easy – with advance reservations, you can rent a kayak right at Kailua Beach Park (see p173). If you're new to the sport several of the operations run guided tours for around $120. Waikiki doesn't have the same *Robinson Crusoe* element, but kayak rentals are also readily available at Fort DeRussy Beach (p106). Single and tandem kayaks are available and cost around $50 a day.

KITESURFING

Just a few years ago, nobody had heard of kitesurfing (also sometimes called kiteboarding). Fast-forward to today and, on a windy day, you'll see more kites over the water then the land. Combine a wakeboard with a giant kite and add water, stir in the mentality of a windsurfer and the water knowledge of a surfer, and you have kitesurfing. It's amazing to watch and hard to master – if you're keen to learn on O'ahu, the place to try your hand is Kailua (p174). The cost for a package of lessons that should get you on your way is $480.

OUTRIGGER CANOEING

There's not much in Hawaii that's more traditional then outrigger canoeing. First popularized by native Hawaiians as a means to get around the Pacific it has since become an activity popular with tourists, hard-core watermen and recreational ocean goers. The best place to give it a crack is Kuhio Beach Park (p107), where you can ride right from the sand and surf the waves back in. The round trip will cost around $25 and is very popular with kids.

SNORKELING

There really isn't much of an excuse to not go snorkeling in O'ahu. The water is warm, the currents are generally gentle and the underwater visibility is awesome. As activities go, it's about as cheap as it gets, with mask and snorkel rentals available nearly everywhere for around $10 a day.

The shallow reefs and nearshore waters are awash with fish and colorful corals. You can expect to spy large rainbow-colored parrotfish munching coral on the sea floor, schools of silver needlefish glimmering near the surface, brilliant yellow tangs, odd-shaped filefish and ballooning puffer fish.

The island's year-round snorkeling mecca is scenic Hanauma Bay Nature Preserve (p158), which has a protected bay and is easily accessible from Waikiki. When waters are calm on the North Shore, Waimea Bay (p204) and Pupukea Beach Park (p205) provide excellent snorkeling in pristine conditions with far less activity than at Hanauma. These North Shore sites are great in summer, but forget it in winter when the monster waves make them definite no-go zones.

STAND UP PADDLE SURFING

The latest craze in surfing is taking the O'ahu scene by storm. Stand up paddle surfing is a derivative of the sport where the rider, instead of stroking with his arms, stands on the board and uses a long paddle. It can be done on flat water and, for those who know what they're doing, in the surf. It's a great workout and a fun alternative when the surf is flat. Most surf shops rent the oversized boards and paddles and many also offer lessons.

SURFING

O'ahu is known the world over for surfing – and rightfully so. The island boasts 594 defined surfing sites, nearly twice as many as any other Hawaiian island. Whether you're a seasoned board rider or brand new to the sport, you'll find the appropriate break for your taste here. See the boxed

O'AHU SURF BEACHES & BREAKS *Jake Howard*

Hawaiian for 'the gathering place,' O'ahu has become a hub for the islands' surf economy. Because O'ahu has some of the most diverse surf breaks in the islands, boarders of all skill levels can find what they're looking for.

In Waikiki, slow and mellow combers (long curling waves) provide the perfect training ground for beginners. Board rentals abound on **Central Waikiki Beach** (p107) and local beachboys are always on hand for lessons at spots like mellow **Queens**, mushy left- and right-handed **Canoes**, gentle but often crowded **Populars** and ever-popular **Publics**. In Honolulu proper, **Ala Moana** (p58) offers a heavy tubing wave – it's *not* a learning locale. Waves in this area are best during summer, when south swells arrive from New Zealand and Tahiti.

Reckon yourself a serious surfer? A pilgrimage to the famed North Shore is mandatory. In winter, when the waves can reach heights of more than 30ft, spots like **Waimea Bay** (p204), **Pipeline** (p202) and **Sunset Beach** (p201) beckon to the planet's best professional surfers.

While home to some great waves, the **Wai'anae Coast** (p233) has turf issues; the locals who live and surf here cherish this area and are trying to hold onto its last vestiges of Hawaiian culture and community. In winter, large west swells can make for big surf at places like **Makaha Beach Park** (p235), but tread lightly: the locals know each other here, so there will be no question that you're from out of town.

If you're looking for a multipurpose wave, **Diamond Head Beach** (p153) is friendly to short-boarders, long-boarders, windsurfers and kitesurfers. And for a good day of bodysurfing, **Sandy Beach Park** (p161) and **Makapu'u** (p162), on the island's southeast shore, are ideal. If you go out here, do so with caution: the pounding waves and shallow bottom have caused some serious neck and back injuries.

For surf reports, call **Surf News Network** (☎ 596-7873; www.surfnewsnetwork.com), a recorded surf-condition telephone line that reports winds, wave heights and tide information, or check out **Wavewatch** (www.wavewatch.com) or **Surfline** (www.surfline.com) online.

Jake Howard is a senior writer at Surfer *magazine and lives in San Clemente, CA.*

Take a dive (if you dare) at Kuhio Beach Park (p107), Waikiki

RICHARD I'ANSON

text, p33, for more information on this popular sport.

SWIMMING

If you want to go for a dip, O'ahu is the place for you. The island is ringed with beautiful white-sand beaches, ranging from crowded resort strands to quiet, hidden coves. There are more than 50 beach parks, most with restrooms and showers; about half are patrolled by lifeguards.

O'ahu has four distinct coastal areas, each with its own peculiar seasonal water conditions. When it's rough on one side, it's generally calm on another, which means you can find places to swim year-round. As a general rule, the best places to swim in winter are along the south shore, and in summer, the North Shore.

The south shore, which extends from Barbers Point to Makapu'u Point, encompasses some of the most popular beaches on the island, including legendary Waikiki Beach. The North Shore has spectacular waves in winter but can be as calm as a lake during summer. The leeward Wai'anae Coast typically has conditions similar to those of the North Shore, with big surf in winter and suitable swimming conditions in summer, but you'll find protected year-round swimming at Poka'i Bay Beach Park (p234) in Wai'anae. Or go south to the calm waters of Ko Olina Lagoons (p229).

If you prefer your water chlorinated there are a few good options for year-round aqua fun. The best place for kids is the Hawaiian Waters Adventure Park (p230), where there are water slides, a wave pool and all sorts of other fun aqueous things to do.

Top Picks

BEACHES FOR KEIKI (KIDS)

- **Ko Olina Lagoons** (p229)
- **Kuhio Beach Park, Waikiki** (p107)
- **Hanauma Bay Nature Preserve** (p158)
- **Hawaiian Waters Adventure Park** (p230)

WHALE WATCHING

Catching a view of a whale in O'ahu isn't a fluke – and no, we're not talking about people watching on Waikiki Beach. Between late December and mid-April, humpback whales and their newly birthed offspring visit the harbors of northern and western O'ahu. Hawaiian spinner dolphins are year-round residents of the Wai'anae Coast. Well regarded for its environmental stewardship, the North Shore's Deep Ecology (p209) offers whale- and dolphin-watching boat tours. For details about swimming with dolphins, see p43.

WINDSURFING

O'ahu has the perfect combination of conditions for epic windsurfing. Warm water, steady winds and a thriving local scene – it's the board-sailing place to be. If you're an old hand, you'll know the reputation for stellar conditions – if you're new to the sport, what better place to learn?

The windsurfing action centers on Kailua (p174), where you'll find persistent year-round trade winds and some top-notch shops renting gear and offering instruction. Kailua Bay has superb conditions for all levels from beginner to pro, with flat-water and wave conditions in different sections of the bay. It's never a slacker but the very best winds typically occur in summer, when east-to-northeast trades run at eight to 15 knots. And when high-pressure systems

come in, they can easily double that, which makes for awesome speed.

Other good windsurfing spots include Diamond Head (p153) for speed and jumps; Malaekahana State Recreation Area (p190) for open-water cruising; Mokule'ia Beach Park (p212) for consistent North Shore winds; and Backyards (p201), off Sunset Beach, with the island's highest sailable waves. In Waikiki, Fort DeRussy Beach (p106) is the main windsurfing spot. Windsurfing gear rents for around $25 an hour. A three-hour introductory lesson that ends up with sailing costs around $65.

ON LAND

Think O'ahu is just about the water? Think again. There are plenty of land-based activities to keep aquaphobes more than occupied. Biking, hiking, golfing, running – you name it, you'll find it.

BIRD-WATCHING

Most islets off O'ahu's Windward Coast are sanctuaries for seabirds, including terns, noddies, shearwaters, Laysan albatrosses, boobies and 'iwa (great frigate birds). Moku Manu (Bird Island), off the Mokapu Peninsula near Kane'ohe, has the greatest variety of species, including a colony of 'ewa'ewa (sooty terns) that lays its eggs in ground scrapes. Although visitors are not allowed on Moku Manu, birders can visit

O'ahu has the perfect combination of conditions for windsurfing   KARL LEHMANN

Island Insights

Ten days after the full moon, jellyfish swim into the shallow waters of leeward beaches, including Waikiki, usually for a one-day stay.

Moku'auia (Goat Island; p190), offshore from Malaekahana State Recreation Area, north of La'ie.

Further north along the Windward Coast, the James Campbell National Wildlife Refuge (p194) encompasses a native wetland habitat protecting some rare and endangered waterbird species. In Kailua, just over the *pali* (mountains) from Honolulu, the Hamakua Marsh Wildlife Sanctuary (p175) is another place to see Hawaiian waterbirds in their natural habitat.

Hikers who tackle O'ahu's many forest-reserve trails, especially around Mt Tantalus (p77), can expect to see *'elepaio* (Hawaiian monarch flycatcher), a brownish bird with a white rump, and *'amakihi,* a yellow-green honeycreeper, the most common endemic forest birds on O'ahu. The *'apapane,* a bright-red honeycreeper, and the *'I'iwi,* a scarlet honeycreeper, are rarer.

Watch for the red-footed booby DAVE LEVITT

For birding checklists and group field trips, contact the ✿ **Hawaii Audubon Society** (Map pp60-1; ☎ 528-1432; www.hawaiiaudubon.com; 850 Richards St, Honolulu).

CAVING

Nobody has ever accused O'ahu of being a spelunking destination of choice, but if you want to dip your head underground there is one good option. Kaneana Cave (p239), at the northern end of the Leeward coast, is both easy to get to and aesthetic.

CYCLING & MOUNTAIN BIKING

O'ahu by bike is the way to go – the roads are in good nick and once you get out of the urban areas the traffic is generally light. Cycling is gaining popularity on the island, so you'll likely have some fellow riders on the road. Keep an eye out for the handy and free *Bike O'ahu* map – it shows which roads are recommended for novices and which are for experienced cyclists. All public buses have bike racks, making it easy to head out one way by bike and return by bus.

Mountain biking is still an emerging sport on the island and there are limited opportunities to get off the pavement with your bike. Having said that, there are some trails worth seeking out. Hau'ula Loop Trail (p189) is a fun track, if only it was a little bit longer. Just around the corner is the Maunawili Trail System (p168), a scenic 10-mile ride that connects the mountain crest at the Nu'uanu Pali Lookout with Waimanalo in windward O'ahu. In the southeast check out the Kuli'ou'ou Ridge Trail (p157) for great views and a staunch climb. Another popular mountain-bike trail is the 'Aiea Loop Trail (p148) in Kea'iwa Heiau State Recreation Area above Pearl Harbor.

The ✿ **Hawaii Bicycling League** (☎ 735-5756; www.hbl.org) holds bike rides around O'ahu nearly every weekend, ranging from 10-mile jaunts to 60-mile treks. Some outings are geared strictly to road riding and others include off-road sites. Rides are free and open to the public. The league's website has some great interactive cycling maps and is a good resource for ride ideas.

For information on getting around O'ahu by bike, including bicycle rentals, see p288.

Cycling by Sunset Beach (p201) ANN CECIL

GOLF

Some say that a round of golf is the perfect way to ruin a good walk, but if you disagree, O'ahu could very well be paradise. With over 40 courses to choose from, you're spoiled for golfing choice. You'll find PGA-level private clubs with the snooty demeanor of members-only private clubs. But don't despair; there are plenty of public courses that offer reasonable green fees, a relaxed atmosphere and the same spectacular surrounds. High-rated public courses include the Ko'olau Golf Club (p182) in Kane'ohe, which claims to be the island's toughest 18; Ko Olina Golf Club (p230) in Kapolei; and Turtle Bay Golf (p200) at Turtle Bay Resort at the island's northern tip. The green fees at these courses are about \$135 to \$165 for 18 holes, but if you don't mind teeing off in the afternoon, ask about twilight discounts that can lower the fees to less than \$100.

The City and County of Honolulu, which encompasses all of O'ahu, maintains six municipal golf courses (☎ 296-2000; www.honolulu .gov/des/golf/golf.htm; 9/18 holes \$21/42, incl cart rental

\$29/58). Reservations for out-of-state visitors are accepted up to three days in advance, with tee times starting at 6:30am.

HIKING

O'ahu is an unlikely hikers' paradise with trails spread out over much of the island. There are placed strolls just steps from the city, to more adventuresome undertakings further afield.

Trails

Even if you don't have a plethora of time, there are plenty of hikes that can be accessed near Honolulu and Waikiki. The classic hike, and the most popular, is the short but steep trail to the summit of Diamond Head Crater (p154), which is easy to reach from Waikiki and ends with a panoramic city view.

The less-trodden Manoa Falls Trail (p76) is a steep and rewarding excursion. The views are great and the reward of ending at a waterfall is a fine reason to give this one a go. Nearby is the Nu'uanu Valley Lookout (p77), which has a similar flavor and makes for a good double shot.

Only 2 miles from the madness of downtown Honolulu, the Tantalus and Makiki Valley area (p77) is like an oasis of forested glory. The extensive trail network, with fine views of Honolulu and surrounding valleys, makes for great walking only steps from the city. The lesser-known Wa'ahila Ridge Trail (p78), on the east side of Manoa Valley, offers a different perspective on the area and good birding possibilities.

There is a great multi-use trail in the Pearl Harbor area. Popular with both hikers and mountain bikers, the 'Aiea Loop Trail (p148), in Kea'iwa Heiau State Recreation Area, has great views of Pearl Harbor and the surrounding area.

In the island's southeast corner, investigate the Kuli'ou'ou Ridge Trail (p157). It's a sturdy climb, but the views are worth the effort.

The Maunawili Trail System (p168) is an interesting and varied walk that covers a lot of different territory in its 10 miles of travel. Also on O'ahu's windward side, a pleasant hour-long hike to Makapu'u lighthouse (see p162) often rewards hikers with a view of

Hiking up Diamond Head (p154)   CHRISTINA LEASE

frolicking whales in winter. For a hardier walk on the windward coast, the 2.5-mile Hau'ula Loop Trail (p189) takes you deep into the forest.

Those wanting to really escape the crowds should head up the Leeward Coast to the Ka'ena Point Trail (p240). The stunning coastal hike passes through a windswept natural reserve on the uninhabited northwestern tip of O'ahu.

On the North Shore there are some good hikes around Turtle Bay. The Kaihalulu Beach Trail (p199) and the Kawela Bay Trail (p199) are both pleasant excursions, taking in the beach, coastline and rocky surrounds. In Waimea the Kaunala Loop Trail (p206) was considered sacred by Hawaiian royalty – it's no wonder, since the view is awesome. On the northwest tip of the island the Kealia Trail (p214) is a fine reason to venture out to the furthest corner of the island. Infrequently visited and a challenging ridge walk, the altitude-induced panorama is apt reward for the energetic.

Na Ala Hele Trail & Access Program (☎ 587-0062; www.hawaiitrails.org) coordinates public access to hiking trails, as well as historical trail preservation and maintenance. Its excellent website contains useful maps, guidelines for safe hiking and announcements of recently developed or reopened trails.

Guided Hikes

A guided hike is a great way to meet some new friends and get a bit more insight into the local flora and fauna. It's also a great way to get into the backcountry if you don't have your own transport. Be sure to come prepared with the proper equipment: food, water and sturdy boots or shoes. It's always a good idea to check to see what is provided for you.

Hawaii Audubon Society (☎ 528-1432; www.hawaii audubon.com; suggested donation $2) Leads bird-watching hikes once a month, usually on a weekend, meeting at a trailhead. The website is a great resource for birders.

Hawaiian Trail & Mountain Club (http://htmclub .org/index.html; donation $3) Leads informal hikes every weekend. It doesn't provide transport so you'll have to make your own way to the trailhead.

Mauka Makai Excursions (☎ 896- 0596; www .hawaiianecotours.net; hiking tours $50-80) A Hawaiian-owned cultural ecotour company offering full- and half-day field trips to cultural and archaeological sites around O'ahu.

Nature Conservancy (www.nature.org/hawaii) Offers guided hikes, including one on O'ahu. Protects Hawaii's rarest ecosystems by buying up tracts of land.

O'ahu Nature Tours (☎ 924-2473; www.oahunature tours.com; tours $20-50) Offers tours to all sorts of stops around the island. The focus is on self-powered adventure to some of the more scenic locations around the island. They are a good choice for bird-watchers, with many tours focusing on our feathered friends.

Sierra Club (www.hi.sierraclub.org; per person $5) Leads hikes and other outings on weekends.

Hiking Safety

Overall, O'ahu is a very safe place to go for a hike. You won't find any poison oak, snakes, poison ivy or many wild animals to contend with. There is the rare chance you might encounter a wild boar – as exciting and death defying as that sounds, unless cornered they are rarely a problem.

What is a concern are flash floods. Many of the hikes cross streams, and after a sudden rain these waterways can swell to dangerous levels. If you hear a distant rumble, notice the smell of fresh earth or experience a sudden rise in water level, seek high ground immediately.

Be alert to the possibility of landslides, falling rocks and exposed tree roots that are easy to trip over. Be wary of swimming under waterfalls, as rocks can dislodge from the top, and be careful on the edge of steep cliffs, since cliff-side rock in Hawaii tends to be crumbly.

Darkness falls fast in Hawaii once the sun sets, and ridge-top trails are no place to be caught unprepared at night. Always carry a flashlight just in case. Long pants offer protection from overgrown parts of the trail, and sturdy footwear with good traction is a must. It's advisable to hike with at least one other person or, at the very least, tell a reliable person where you are going and when you are expected back. Pack four pints of water per person for a day hike, carry a whistle to alert rescuers should the need arise, wear sunscreen and, above all, start out early.

HORSEBACK RIDING

Saddle up cowboy! There are some great options for seeing the island on horseback – whether you want to gallop along the beach or mosey through the rainforest, there is a ride and a steed to suit any taste. The North Shore is the equine area of choice. For beach-bound rides go for Hawaii Polo Trail Rides (p214) in Mokule'ia or Turtle Bay Resort (p200). If you want to ride in the mountains, Happy Trails Hawaii (p2070), above Waimea, is the place; it's also very kid-friendly.

Trail rides typically cost $50 to $75.

RUNNING

Perhaps it's the warm weather or the clean air; whatever the reason, running in O'ahu is huge. In the early hours of the morning you'll see joggers aplenty in parks, on footpaths and on beaches all around the island. Kapi'olani Park (p108), Ala Moana Beach Park (p58) and the Ala Wai Canal are favorite jogging spots in the Waikiki area.

O'ahu has about 75 road races each year, from 1-mile fun runs and 5-mile jogs to competitive marathons, biathlons and triathlons. For an annual schedule of running events

with times, dates and contact addresses, check out the **Running Room** (www.running roomhawaii.com) and click on 'Races.'

O'ahu's best-known race is the Honolulu Marathon, which has mushroomed into the third-largest marathon in the US. Held in mid-December, it's an open-entry event, with an estimated half of the 25,000 entrants running in their first marathon. For information, contact **Honolulu Marathon Association** (www.honolulumarathon.org); entry forms can be downloaded from its website.

SPAS

Is all this outdoor activity wearing you out? How about a spa treatment to re-boot the system? Waikiki (see the boxed text, p111) has many options.

TENNIS

O'ahu has 181 public tennis courts at county parks throughout the island. If you're staying in Waikiki, the most convenient locations are the courts at Ala Moana Beach Park (p58); at the Diamond Head Tennis Center (p112), at the Diamond Head end of Kapi'olani Park; and at the Kapi'olani Park (p112) courts, opposite the Waikiki Aquarium. Court time is free and on a first-come, first-served basis.

YOGA

The healthy lifestyle of O'ahu is a perfect setting for yoga. Regardless of whether you have a long-established practice or are looking to get started, there are classes to suit. Many hotels that have indoor gyms have yoga programs and there is a handful of good studios scattered throughout the island. Kailua (p175) has a host of yoga options, many of which take advantage of the sunrise. On the North Shore head to Waialua where Jasmine Yoga (p212) will help you stretch it out.

GREEN

OʻAHU

Oʻahu is a lush, green wonderland almost everywhere you look. The Hawaiian Islands chain, 2500 miles from the nearest continent, is the most geographically isolated land mass in the world. That fact alone gives Oʻahu one of the most astounding natural environments on earth, not to mention Hawaii's unique cultural heritage, which draws on Polynesia, Asia, Europe and the Americas. With the rise of both the ecotourism trend and an ongoing Hawaiian cultural renaissance, environmentally and culturally responsible businesses are sprouting up all around the island and conservation efforts, both state-funded and grassroots, are gaining strength. From marine biologists to Hawaiian cultural practitioners to land-loving locals, the *aloha ʻaina* (love for the land) is running strong. Now you too can join the island's 'green' party, starting even before you land on Oʻahu.

OʻAHU GOES GREEN

Environmental consciousness has taken root on Oʻahu, the most densely populated and heavily touristed of the Hawaiian Islands. These days, more and more locals are thinking about and enacting plans for how Oʻahu can build a more sustainable future.

A wide coalition of scientists, activists and residents has made island conservation efforts a slow, but steady success. There are dozens of environmental groups on Oʻahu, running the gamut from chapters of international organizations fighting to save endangered species and swaths of native forest to neighborhood groups working to protect local beaches against development. Laws have been passed banning jet skis in waters used by humpback whales, and stopping the killing of sea turtles by the longline fishing industry. Legal action has also been able to halt development in some agricultural areas.

Meanwhile, private businesses have started applying the principles of social entrepreneurship to effect change. Take, for example, the North Shore shop Country Feeling Surfboards (p202), which fashions

🌺 SUSTAINABLE ICON

It seems like everyone's going green these days, but how can you know which O'ahu businesses are actually ecofriendly and which are simply jumping on the sustainability bandwagon? Throughout this book, our sustainable icon indicates listings that we are highlighting because they demonstrate an active sustainable-tourism policy. Some are involved in environmental conservation and/or education, others maintain and preserve Hawaiian identity and culture, and many are owned and operated by local and indigenous operators. For quick reference, these listings are compiled in the GreenDex (p303).

ecofriendly surfboards using hemp and cotton, and allies with antidevelopment groups like Keep the North Shore Country (www.keepthenorth shorecountry.org). Another O'ahu-based company, Styrophobia (www.styrophobia.com), sells compostable and biodegradable takeout containers made from corn, potato and sugarcane as an alternative to Styrofoam and other petroleum-based products, such as plastic, that are choking local landfills.

Even the government has gotten into the swing of things with an ambitious Hawai'i 2050 (www.hawaii2050.org) sustainability plan. This evolving statewide program combines community input with a governmental task force to formulate economic, social and environmental policies that focus on renewable energy, living sustainably within the bounds of the islands' natural resources and striking a balance between profitable tourism and Hawaiian cultural preservation. After decades of controversy, O'ahuans voted in 2008 to build a light-rail commuter transit system rather than another elevated multilane highway. A state-wide electric network is on the drawing board, too.

The island's future really is looking greener.

SUSTAINABLE O'AHU

Hawaii's natural ecosystem has been ravaged by non-native plants and animals ever since the first foreign ships arrived. Seeds caught in the soles of your own shoes or bugs left hiding out in the bottom of your backpack can potentially be a threat too. Before arriving on O'ahu, carefully clean your shoes and wipe down your luggage.

Practice *aloha 'aina*. When hiking, stay on trails; when snorkeling, stay off the coral. Respect any 'No Trespassing – *Kapu*' signs that you'll see around the island, unless a trustworthy local says it's actually OK. Respect the privacy of island residents, whose quality of life is continually being encroached upon by tourist development.

Do not approach or otherwise disturb any endangered creatures, especially marine species such as whales, dolphins, seals and sea turtles. Doing so not only harms wildlife, but is also illegal and trespassers are subject to hefty fines. Many beach parks have recycling bins for aluminum cans and glass bottles, although recycling is not always available at hotels. Even though bottled water is convenient, the tap water on O'ahu is perfectly fine to drink, so bring along a refillable container instead.

Try to buy local, and bring reusable shopping bags. Every product not made on O'ahu has to be imported here by boat or plane, which contributes to the worldwide greenhouse effect. You can follow foodie trends by eating local, too. Farmers markets are booming on O'ahu, and many restaurants now feature island-grown produce such as 'Nalo greens, North Shore grass-fed beef and locally caught seafood on the menu.

Any plane trip to Hawaii, no matter how much carbon offsetting you do (see p267), increases the amount of CO_2 in the earth's

Top Picks

HAWAIIAN CULTURAL TOURISM

- Kuhio Beach Torch Lighting & Hula Show (p137)
- Hawai'i State Art Museum (p61)
- Bishop Museum (p74)
- Hawai'i Maritime Center (p64)
- Native Books/Nā Mea Hawai'i (p95)
- Ono Hawaiian Foods (p121)
- Na Lima Mili Hulu No'eau (p124)
- Kumu Kahua Theatre (p94)
- Kane'aki Heiau (p238)
- Aloha Festivals (p273)

atmosphere. While you're on O'ahu, you can reduce your carbon footprint by riding TheBus (p289). Alternatively, consider renting a car for only part of your trip, especially if you're staying in Waikiki, where overnight parking can be an expensive hassle anyway.

ON THE GROUND

One of the best things about traveling more sustainably on O'ahu is that it often means saving money. Camping and rental cabins (p269) are among the cheapest accommodations on the island, while locally owned B&Bs and vacation rentals (p269) often charge less than resort hotels. Riding TheBus (p289) not only cuts down on air pollution, but a four-day pass costs just $20 – less than a one-day car rental. At farmers markets you'll save money while supporting organic farms and earth-friendly food vendors.

It costs nothing to spend all day at the beach, because all of O'ahu's beaches are free for public access. Although private property blocks access to some hiking trails, Na Ala Hele (www.hawaiitrails.org) recommends 40 routes on O'ahu that are freely open to hikers (and sometimes mountain bikers). For more about outdoor activities and adventures on land and at sea, from traditional Hawaiian paddle surfing to sunrise yoga on the beach, see p26. For O'ahu's best parks, nature preserves and gardens, see p50. Finally, for our recommended 'Green O'ahu' travel itinerary, see p24.

Helpful online resources for sustainable travel on O'ahu (just watch out for some advertorial content):

Alternative Hawaii (www.alternative-hawaii.com) Focuses on Hawaii's natural and cultural beauty, with hundreds of ecofriendly tourism listings.

Hawaii Ecotourism Association (www.hawaiiecotourism.org) Offers ecotravel tips, a 'green' business directory and downloadable self-guided touring brochures.

HELPFUL ORGANIZATIONS

All around O'ahu, locals are working on ways to make island life 'greener' and more sustainable, from ecofriendly businesses that promote recycling and use only biodegradable takeout containers to activists

---

DOLPHIN SWIMS

Think twice before signing up for a dolphin swim on O'ahu, even when these for-profit programs claim to be 'ecofriendly' or 'educational.'

- In the wild, acrobatic spinner dolphins are nocturnal feeders that come into sheltered bays during the day to rest. Although it may look tempting to swim out and join them, these intelligent animals are very sensitive to human disturbance, so it's illegal to approach them. Some tour boats on O'ahu allow swimmers to approach closer than the recommended guideline of 50 yards. Even if wild dolphins appear 'happy' to see you and frolicsome, encountering humans tires them out, according to many marine biologists, so the dolphins may not have enough energy later to feed or defend themselves. Repeated encounters with humans have driven some dolphins out of their natural habitats into less-safe resting places.

- In captivity, dolphins (usually the Atlantic bottlenose species) may be trained to perform for a human audience through food-deprivation techniques, while other places use positive reinforcement. The only way you can know is to ask. Instead of encouraging natural behaviors, holding dolphins in captivity subjects them to artificial routines that are painful and cause the animals to exhibit signs of stress. Programs that let children or even adults 'ride' the dolphins by hanging onto their dorsal fins are the most irresponsible; some captive dolphins in Hawaii have had to undergo surgery to repair their damaged fins. Regardless of training techniques and treatment, captive dolphins die much faster than wild ones, mostly due to exposure to human-borne illnesses and bacteria.

- Through a domino effect, the overwhelming success of dolphin-swim programs in the US has led to copycat programs worldwide, in which wild dolphins may be 'harvested' and forced into captivity. The 2008 documentary *The Cove,* directed by a former dolphin trainer, takes a hard-hitting look at the 'dolphinarium' biz and the global industry now invested in keeping dolphins in captivity.

Find exotic foods at the Oʻahu Market (p65), Chinatown   LINDA CHING

aiming to protect endangered species, promote alternative-energy projects and limit development. You too can get in on the act and give something back to Hawaii during your trip by volunteering just a few spare hours, whether for pulling invasive plants, counting migratory whales, restoring ancient Hawaiian archaeological sites or rebuilding hiking trails. There's no better way to connect with locals and their tradition of *aloha ʻaina*.

If you'd like to volunteer in Oʻahu, check out the volunteer listings in the free tabloid **Honolulu Weekly** (www.honoluluweekly.com /calendar). Many of the following organizations also offer volunteer opportunities:

Fair Catch Hawaii (www.faircatchhawaii.org) Encourages sustainable fishing practices and protection of coral reefs and native fish.

Hawaii Audubon Society (www.hawaiiaudubon.com) Publishes environmental news and a monthly newsletter; also offers birding field trips.

Hawaiʻi Nature Center (www.hawaiinaturecenter.org) Offers voluntourism opportunities in Honolulu to help the environment and community development.

Kahea (www.kahea.org) Environmental alliance to protect sensitive shorelines and Native Hawaiian cultural sites.

Malama Hawaiʻi (www.malamahawaii.org) A volunteer-oriented network of environmental groups and other community organizations.

Nature Conservancy (www.nature.org/hawaii) Protects Hawaii's rarest ecosystems by buying up tracts of land; also offers guided hikes.

Oʻahu Invasive Species Committee (www.hawaii invasivespecies.org) Runs monthly volunteer projects and an invasive **pest-sighting hotline** (☎ 643-7378).

Sierra Club (www.hi.sierraclub.org/oahu) Activities range from political activism to group hikes and environmental clean-up projects.

Slow Food Oʻahu (http://slowfoodoahu.org) Organizes social events and provides agrotourism links to organic island farms.

Surfrider Foundation (www.surfrider.org/oahu) Grassroots advocates for clean water, better beach access and responsible tourism development.

ENVIRONMENTAL ISSUES

Hawaii's ecosystem is fragile – so fragile, in fact, that 25% of all the endangered species in the US are endemic to the Hawaiian Islands. These native species are highly sensitive to habitat degradation. Over the past century, many species have become extinct, including dozens of native forest birds. Today several hundred of Hawaii's estimated 10,000 endemic species of flora and fauna are threatened, endangered or already extinct. For more about O'ahu's wildlife, see p47.

Vast tracts of native forest have long been cleared to give way to the monocrop industries of sugarcane and pineapple. In the 1960s the advent of mass tourism posed new challenges to the environment, most worryingly in the rampant development of land-hungry and water-thirsty golf courses. In recent decades the number of golf courses on O'ahu has jumped from just a handful to over 40, and the total acreage given over to these golf courses now rivals that used for agriculture.

When it comes to air quality, O'ahu has no polluting heavy industry. However, Honolulu, being on the dry and less-windy leeward side of the island, occasionally sees increased levels of vehicle-related pollution. As for scenery aesthetics, roadside billboards are prohibited by law, although littering along highways and at beaches is a pervasive problem. Landfill waste is another pressing concern on O'ahu. Finding new places to bury trash without contaminating groundwater is nearly impossible. Other hot-button political issues include water pollution caused by golf-course and agricultural runoff; whether GMOs (genetically modified organisms) should be allowed; and how the US military presence on O'ahu, as well as the cruise ships docked at Honolulu Harbor, may have a negative impact on the environment.

For the latest environmental issues facing the island, check the investigative journal Environment Hawaii (www.environment-hawaii.org).

Mass tourism
has posed new
challenges to the
environment

MERTEN SNIJDERS

Harvesting salad greens at Nalo Farms, Waimanalo (p170)

LINDA CHING

THE ENVIRONMENT

THE LAND

Hawaii is the northernmost point of the triangle of Pacific islands known as Polynesia ('many islands'); the other points are New Zealand and Easter Island. With a total land area of 594 sq miles, O'ahu is the third-largest Hawaiian island. Though it accounts for less than 10% of Hawaii's total land mass, over 70% of state residents call O'ahu (nicknamed 'the Gathering Place') home. The City and County of Honolulu also includes the Northwestern Hawaiian Islands, which comprises dozens of small, unpopulated islands and atolls stretching more than 1200 miles across the Pacific.

All of the Hawaiian Islands are actually the tips of massive mountains formed over a crack in the earth's mantle, called a 'hot spot,' that has been actively spewing out molten rock for more than 70 million years. The hot spot is stationary now, but

the ocean floor is part of the Pacific Plate, which is moving northwest at the rate of over 3 inches a year. (The eastern edge of this plate is California's San Andreas Fault.) As weak spots in the earth's crust pass over the hot spot, molten lava pierces upward, creating underwater volcanoes. If these underwater seamounts build up enough mass, they eventually emerge above the ocean's surface as islands. The Big Island of Hawai'i sits over the hot spot as you are reading this today.

Each new volcano slowly creeps northward past the hot spot that created it. The further from the source the volcano is, the lower the volcanic activity, until it is cut off completely. Then the forces of erosion – wind, rain and waves – add more geologic character to the newly emerged islands, cutting valleys, creating beaches and turning a mound of lava into paradise. All of this plate-tectonic activity can cause earthquakes and tsunami on the islands, although Honolulu tends to be safely distant from the epicenter and feels only minor shocks. Keep in mind that a local tsunami can also be caused by seismic events elsewhere in the world, such as Alaska.

The island of Oʻahu is really two separate shield volcanoes that arose about two million years ago and formed Oʻahu's two mountain ranges: Waiʻanae in the northwest and Koʻolau in the southeast. Oʻahu's last gasp of volcanic activity occurred between 10,000 and one million years ago, creating the tuff cone of Diamond Head (p153), Oʻahu's most famous geographical landmark. Oʻahu's highest point, Mt Kaʻala (4020ft), is in the central Waiʻanae Range.

WILDLIFE

It has been said that if Darwin had arrived in Hawaii first, he would have developed his theory of evolution in a period of weeks instead of years. Almost all the species carried by wind and waves across the vast Pacific – for example, seeds clinging to a bird's feather, or fern spores that drifted thousands of miles through the air – adapted so uniquely to these remote volcanic islands that they evolved into new species endemic to Hawaii.

Before human contact, a new species managed to take hold in the Hawaiian Islands – which were born barren – only once every 70,000 years. But the final results of this slow process of adaptive radiation can be amazing. For instance, it's believed that many of Hawaii's birds evolved from a single species, as is thought to have been the case with the islands' 30-plus species of honeycreeper. Today, over 90% of Hawaii's endemic flora and fauna are found nowhere else on earth.

This is both a blessing and its curse. Having evolved with limited competition and few predators, native species generally fare poorly among more aggressive introduced flora and fauna. They are also highly sensitive to habitat destruction and human disturbance. Today, Hawaii has the highest rate of extinction of any US state.

Whose fault is it? Well, the first Polynesian settlers imported food and medicinal plants, chickens, dogs, rats and pigs. The pace of introducing exotic (aka alien) species escalated with the arrival of Europeans, starting with Captain Cook, who dropped off goats and left melon, pumpkin and onion seeds. The introduction of pigs, cattle and goats, which grazed and foraged at will, along with invasive ground covers, devastated Hawaii's fragile ecosystems and spelled extinction for many native plants. Released songbirds and game birds spread avian diseases to native Hawaiian birds, which did not have the immunity to fight off foreign pathogens.

The invasion of exotic species continues today. Most environmentalists agree

LET SLEEPING SEA DOGS LIE

One of the Pacific's most endangered creatures is the Hawaiian monk seal, named both for the monastic cowl-like fold of skin at its neck and for its solitary habits. The Hawaiian name for the animal is *ilio holo kai,* meaning 'the dog that runs in the sea.'

- The species has remained nearly unchanged for 15 million years, though in the past century it has been in danger of dying out completely. The annual birth rate for Hawaiian monk seals hovers around 200 pups, but due to shark attacks and other predators, many pups don't reach maturity. Human disturbance of beaches where monk seals haul out further endangers the species.

- Conservation efforts, including relocation of overly aggressive male seals to protect juveniles and reproductive females, seemed to be bringing Hawaii's remaining monk seals back from the edge of extinction, although recently Hawaii's total population of 1200 monk seals has been declining by around 4% each year.

- Their prime habitat is the uninhabited Northwestern Hawaiian Islands, but monk seals do occasionally haul up on Oʻahu's more remote beaches. Please report any monk seal sightings by calling the **hotline** (☎ 220-7802). Also, keep at least 150ft from any monk seal, limit your observation time to 30 minutes, and never get between a mother and her pup.

that the biggest threat on Oʻahu is from the brown tree snake, which has led to the extinction of all native birds on the Pacific island of Guam. This tree-climbing snake has been found several times in arriving planes at Honolulu International Airport and Hickam Air Force Base, though it's not known if any have yet escaped into the wild.

Animals

Oʻahu's nearshore waters harbor hundreds of tropical fish, including rainbow-colored parrotfish, moray eels and ballooning puffer fish, to name just a few species, as well as *honu* (green sea turtles), manta rays, sharks and dolphins (see also the boxed text, p43). Of all the whales that frequent Hawaiian waters, it's the migratory North Pacific humpback, known for its leaping breaches and tail flips, that everyone wants to see. Whale-watching cruises (p35) are offered from late December until mid-April.

Native waterfowl include the graceful Hawaiian stilt *(aeʻo),* a black-necked wading bird with a white underbelly and long pink legs, which feeds along the marshy edges of ponds; the Hawaiian coot *('alae keʻa),* usually black and grey except for its white bill; the secretive Hawaiian moorhen *('alae 'ula),* mostly black with white feathers and a red-and-yellow bill; and the mottled, brown Hawaiian duck *(koloa maoli),* with short orange legs. All four of these endangered species can be spotted at Hamakua Marsh Wildlife Sanctuary (p175) and James Campbell National Wildlife Refuge (p194) in Windward Oʻahu.

Most of the islets off Oʻahu's Windward Coast are sanctuaries for seabirds, including terns, noddies, shearwaters, Laysan albatrosses and boobies. Moku Manu (Bird Island), off the Mokapu Peninsula in Kaneʻohe, has the greatest variety of species, including a colony of *'ewa'ewa* (sooty terns) that lays its eggs in ground scrapes. Because the nesting birds are sensitive to human disturbance, visitors are not allowed on Moku Manu. To protect other seabirds, human visitors are also restricted on many other islands.

Hikers who tackle Oʻahu's mountain trails, especially around Mt Tantalus (p77) above downtown Honolulu, can expect to see some colorful forest birds. The *'elepaio* (Hawaiian monarch flycatcher), a brownish bird with a white rump, and the *'amakihi,* a small yellow-green honeycreeper, are the most common endemic forest birds on Oʻahu. The *'apapane,* a bright-red honeycreeper, and the *'i'iwi,* a scarlet honeycreeper, are less common but also sometimes spotted.

Prior to human contact, the Hawaiian Islands had no native mammals, save for monk seals (see the boxed text, p47) and *'ope'ape'a* (hoary bats), which are rarely seen on Oʻahu. Introduced island species include pigs, which are commonly hunted in Oʻahu's forests, and mongoose, originally imported to control rats in the sugarcane fields. Egg-eating mongoose have now decimated Oʻahu's native-bird populations. As for those pesky mosquitoes, you can blame 19th-century whaling ships for first importing them into Honolulu Harbor.

Oʻahu has an endemic genus of tree snail, the endangered *Achatinella.* In former days the forests were loaded with these colorful snails, which clung like gems to the leaves of trees. They were too attractive for their own good, however, and up until the early 20th century people collected them by the handful. Deforestation and the introduction of a cannibal snail and predatory ro-

Spot spinner dolphins year-round (p35)

dents like mongoose have been even more devastating.

Plants

O'ahu blooms year-round. For travelers, perhaps no flower is more closely identified with the islands than hibiscus, the blossoms of which are often worn by women (tucked behind the left ear if married, the right if not). Other exotic tropical flowers commonly seen include blood-red anthurium, brilliant orange bird-of-paradise, showy bougainvillea and various heliconia (lobster claw) with bright orange-and-red bracts. Countless varieties of cultivated and native wild orchids also abound on O'ahu.

The native 'ohia lehua has bright-red pompom flowers and grows in barren volcanic areas as a shrub, and on more fertile land as a tree. Noteworthy among O'ahu's other flowering trees are monkeypod, a common shade tree with puffy pink flowers and longish seed pods; and plumeria, the fragrant pink and white blossoms of which are often used in lei making.

Flowering native coastal plants include *pohuehue* (beach morning glory), with its glossy green leaves and pink flowers, found just above the wrack line along the coast throughout O'ahu; beach *naupaka*, a shrub with oval green leaves and a small pinkish-white, five-petal flower that looks as if it's been torn in half; and the low-growing *'ilima,* which has delicate yellow-orange blossoms.

The most revered of the native Hawaiian forest trees is koa, found at higher elevations on O'ahu. Koa grows up to 60ft high and is unusual in that the young saplings have fernlike leaves, while mature trees have flat, crescent-shaped phyllodes. Koa's rich hardwood was traditionally used to make canoes, surfboards and ukuleles, while today it's most often used to carve exquisite ornamental bowls.

Brought to O'ahu by early Polynesian settlers, the *kukui* (candlenut) tree has silvery light-green foliage and oily nuts that ancient Hawaiians burned for light, hence its common name. Two trees found along the coast that were also well utilized in ancient Hawaii are hala (screwpine or pandanus), easily recognized by its prop-root support system, and whose spiny leaves were used for thatching and weaving; and the *niu* (coconut palm), which thrives in O'ahu's blazing sun and high humidity. Although it was the Polynesians who also first planted *ko* (sugarcane), most of O'ahu's other agricultural products, including pineapples, macadamia nuts and coffee, were imported during the 19th century.

KARL LEHMANN

An exotic member of the mesquite family, kiawe is useful for making charcoal but is a nuisance for beachgoers as its sharp thorns easily pierce rubbah slippahs. Also plentiful in coastal areas are stands of ironwood, a conifer with drooping needles that act as natural windbreaks and prevent beach erosion. The pesky and intrusive mangrove has a twisted root system that has choked natural ponds and done a nasty job on O'ahu's ancient fishponds, weakening stone walls with its winding roots.

NATIONAL, STATE & COUNTY PARKS

O'ahu has no national parks, but the Hawaiian Islands Humpback Whale National Marine Sanctuary (www.hawaiihumpbackwhale.noaa.gov) encompasses waters off O'ahu's north and south shores. The federal government also manages the USS Arizona Memorial (p144) at Pearl Harbor, as well as coastal wetlands at James Campbell National Wildlife Refuge (p194), a prime bird-watching venue. From Diamond Head, near Waikiki, to Ka'ena Point, on the remote northwestern tip of the island, a rich system of state parks and forest reserves are loaded with diverse opportunities for outdoor activities, especially hiking. Dozens of county beach parks offer all kinds of aquatic adventures.

About 25% of the island's land is protected, although tensions exist between the government and a few rural communities that want more land for affordable housing and farming, especially on the Windward Coast (see the boxed text, p184). For more information, Hawaii's Department of Land & Natural Resources (Map pp60-1; DLNR; ☎ 587-0400; www.state.hi.us/dlnr; Kalanimoku Bldg, 1151 Punchbowl St, Honolulu) posts useful news online. DLNR also oversees the following divisions, which have offices in the same building:

Division of Forestry & Wildlife (DOFAW; ☎ 587-0166; www.dofaw.net) Manages Hawaii's forests and natural area reserves; public outreach focuses on outdoor recreation and conservation.

Division of State Parks (☎ 587-0300; www.hawaii stateparks.org) Provides free downloadable brochures online and issues state-park camping permits (see p270).

O'AHU'S TOP 10 PROTECTED AREAS

Natural area	Features	Activities	Page
Diamond Head State Monument	remnants of a volcanic crater and tuff cone	hiking	p154
Hanauma Bay Nature Preserve	Hawaii's only state-run underwater park, coral reefs, tropical fish, sea turtles	snorkeling, diving	p158
Ho'omaluhia Botanical Garden	artificial reservoir, native trees and shrubs	hiking, camping	p180
James Campbell National Wildlife Refuge	wetland habitat with natural, spring-fed marshlands, native birds	bird-watching, walking	p194
Ka'ena Point State Park	O'ahu's westernmost tip, accessible on foot	hiking, surfing, swimming, snorkeling	p239
Koko Head Regional Park	lava sea cliffs, beaches, natural blowholes, lookouts and lighthouse	bodysurfing, hiking, hang gliding	p160
Malaekahana State Recreation Area	sandy beach, Moku'auia (Goat Island) bird sanctuary	swimming, snorkeling, bird-watching, camping	p190
Mt Tantalus	arboretum, forest reserve, waterfalls, native birds, trees and shrubs	hiking	p72
Wahiawa Botanical Garden	tropical rainforest, arboretum of grand old trees	hiking	p221
Waimea Valley	nature preserve with ancient Hawaiian archaeological sites, native plants	hiking, bird-watching, swimming in a waterfall pool	p205

HONOLULU

A boisterous Polynesian capital, Honolulu delivers a tasty mixed plate of experiences. Eat your way through the pan-Asian alleys of Chinatown, where 19th-century whalers once brawled and immigrant traders thrived. Amble around Victorian-era buildings – including the USA's only royal palace – still standing beside downtown's sleek, modern high-rises. Watch Pacific breezes rustle palm trees along the harborfront, then head up into the cool, mist-shrouded Ko'olau Range, where forested hiking trails offer panoramic city views. Here in Honolulu, away from the touristy haunts of Waikiki, is where you can get to know the real Hawaii – both its future and its colorful past.

HONOLULU ITINERARIES

IN TWO DAYS *12 miles*

❶ CHINATOWN (p64) Poke around fragrant flower lei stands and animated markets, then do some antique-store and art-gallery hopping after joining the locals at a savory dim-sum palace.

❷ HAWAI'I STATE ART MUSEUM (p61) Satiate your artistic side with a full-on visual experience of Hawaii's multicultural society and heritage, then stop downstairs for a gourmet plate lunch at **Downtown (p82)**.

❸ LYON ARBORETUM (p72) Head up into the hills to take a walk on the wild side (literally – the paths are mostly unmanicured) at this verdant tropical flora–lovers' paradise, with a hidden waterfall at the back.

❹ MANOA FALLS & NU'UANU VALLEY LOOKOUT (p76) Although the Tantalus–Round Top scenic drive looks tempting, those waterfall and mountaintop views are best earned with your own two feet.

❺ HONOLULU ACADEMY OF ARTS (p67) The next morning, get a dose of culture at this prestigious art museum, which also sponsors film screenings and community events. Fork into market-fresh fare at the **Pavilion Café (p86)** for lunch and make advance reservations for an excursion to **Shangri La (p155)**.

❻ ALA MOANA BEACH PARK (p58) Head to Honolulu citizens' favorite beach park to swim laps or simply laze on the golden sands. Then take a sunset walk around **Magic Island (p58)**.

❼ ALA MOANA CENTER (p94) End the day at O'ahu's biggest shopping mall with superbly executed Hawaii Regional cuisine at **Alan Wong's Pineapple Room (p87)**. Then head upstairs to the boisterous **Mai Tai Bar (p91)** for live island-style music.

Hawai'i State Art Museum (p61)

FOR HISTORY HOUNDS

❶ 'IOLANI PALACE (p59) Start your journey through time at the USA's only royal palace, today a symbol for Native Hawaiian sovereignty activists.

❷ KAMEHAMEHA THE GREAT STATUE (p62) Pay your respects to the great *ali'i* (chief) who was the first to unify the Hawaiian Islands after 20 years of warfare.

❸ MISSION HOUSES MUSEUM (p61) Take a guided tour of Hawaii's first Protestant settlement, which set off tidal waves of foreign arrivals across the islands throughout the 19th century.

❹ KAWAIAHA'O CHURCH (p62) A solid, imposing, Gothic-style church made of priceless coral rock signaled that the missionaries were here to stay – Hawaiian society would never be the same. Look for royal and colonial ghosts in the cemetery out back.

❺ ALOHA TOWER (p63) Stroll over to the harborfront and take the elevator up this 1926 landmark, which welcomed all tourists to O'ahu before the jet age arrived in 1935.

❻ HAWAI'I MARITIME CENTER (p64) Take a sweeping look at Hawaiian history, from the arrival of ill-fated Captain Cook and hurly-burly whaling ships to modern cruise liners. Clamber aboard the *Falls of Clyde,* a floating national historic landmark.

❼ BISHOP MUSEUM (p74) This museum is aimed at kids, but everyone will enjoy the ancient Hawaiian artifacts on display, including *kahili* (feathered royal staffs) and feathered capes once worn by royalty.

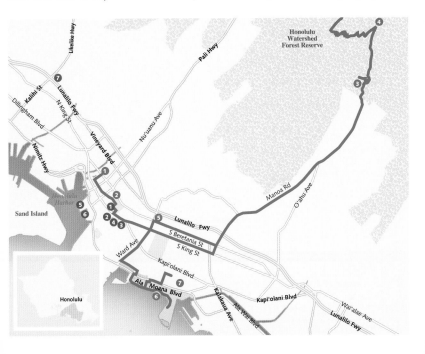

HONOLULU

HONOLULU & AROUND

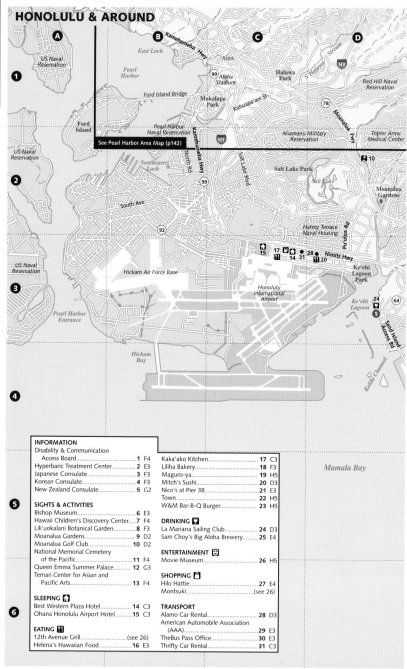

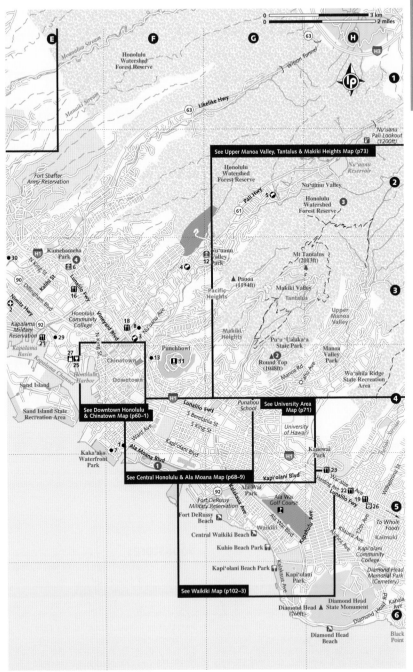

See Upper Manoa Valley, Tantalus & Makiki Heights Map (p73)

See Downtown Honolulu & Chinatown Map (p60–1)

See University Area Map (p71)

See Central Honolulu & Ala Moana Map (p68–9)

See Waikiki Map (p102–3)

HIGHLIGHTS

❶ **BEST BEACH:** Ala Moana Beach Park (p58)
❷ **BEST VIEW:** Pu'u 'Ualaka'a State Park (p74)
❸ **BEST ACTIVITY:** Hiking in the Ko'olau Range (p76)
❹ **BEST HAWAIIAN HISTORY LESSON:** Bishop Museum (p74)
❺ **BEST TIKI BAR:** La Mariana Sailing Club (p91)

Highlights are numbered on the map on pp54–5.

pop 375,570

HISTORY

In 1793 the English frigate *Butterworth* became the first foreign ship to sail into what is now Honolulu Harbor. In 1809 Kamehameha the Great moved his royal court from Waikiki to Honolulu (Sheltered Bay) to control the vigorous international trade already taking place there.

In the 1820s Honolulu's first bars and brothels opened to crews of whaling ships. Hotel St, a lineup of bars and strip joints a few blocks from the harbor, remains the city's red-light district. Christian missionaries began arriving around the same time, presumably for different purposes. Today, Hawaii's first missionary church is just a stone's throw from the royal palace.

Sugar plantations, established in the 1830s, soon became O'ahu's major industry. Contract workers from Asia, North America and Europe were brought in to fill the labor shortage, a surge in immigration exemplified by today's ethnic diversity. Honolulu replaced Maui as the official capital of the Kingdom of Hawai'i in 1845.

By the late 19th century, Western expatriates dominated Hawaiian affairs. It's no coincidence that the names of Honolulu's rich and powerful – Alexander, Baldwin, Cooke and Dole – read like rosters from the first mission ships. In 1893 a small group of these new Hawaiian citizens seized control of the kingdom from Queen Lili'uokalani and declared it a republic. In 1898 Hawaii was formally annexed by the USA, although statehood wasn't finally achieved until 1959.

For more of O'ahu's history, see p242.

ORIENTATION

The City and County of Honolulu sprawls along the south shore of O'ahu. The city proper is generally considered to extend west to the airport and east to Kaimuki.

Two major thoroughfares run the length of the city: Ala Moana Blvd (Hwy 92) skirts the coast from the airport to Waikiki, and the H1 runs east–west between the beach and the mountains. In between are several grids bisected by one-way streets overlapping at irregular angles, making navigation within central Honolulu difficult.

King St (one-way heading southeast) and Beretania St (one-way heading northwest) are primary conduits into downtown Honolulu, which contains O'ahu's government buildings, including the state capitol and 'Iolani Palace.

Chinatown is immediately north of downtown Honolulu, roughly bounded by the harbor, Bethel St, Vineyard Blvd and River St. The landmark Aloha Tower and cruise-ship terminals sit *makai* (ocean side) of Chinatown.

Kapi'olani Blvd and University Ave are the main thoroughfares connecting the Ala Moana area and University of Hawai'i campus, situated in Manoa Valley beneath the southern Ko'olau Range.

The tourist epicenter of Waikiki is southeast of downtown Honolulu via Ala Moana Blvd, past the Ala Moana Center. Waikiki is contained within the boundaries of Honolulu, but this area is covered in a separate chapter (p99).

INFORMATION

Bookstores

Bestsellers (Map pp60-1; ☎ 528-2378; 1003 Bishop St; ☽ 7:30am-5:30pm Mon-Fri, 9am-3pm Sat) Good selection of travel guides, novels and maps.
Borders (Map pp68-9; ☎ 591-8995; Victoria Ward Center, 1200 Ala Moana Blvd; ☽ 10am-11pm Mon-Thu, 10am-midnight Fri, 9am-midnight Sat, 9am-10pm Sun; ⓧ) Extensive news, magazine and travel sections.
Native Books/Nā Mea Hawai'i (Map pp68-9; ☎ 597-8967; www.nativebookshawaii.com; Ward

Warehouse, 1050 Ala Moana Blvd; ☺ 10am-9pm Mon-Sat, 10am-6pm Sun) Specializes in Hawaiiana titles and hosts readings, performances and classes (see p80).

Rainbow Books & Records (Map p71; ☎ 955-7994; www.rainbowbookshawaii.com; 1010 University Ave; ☺ 10am-10pm Sun-Thu, 10am-11pm Fri & Sat) Carries new and used books, CDs and records.

Emergency

Police (☎ 529-3111) For nonemergencies.

Police, Fire & Ambulance (☎ 911) For emergencies.

Internet Access

FedEx Office (www.fedex.com; per hr $6-12; ☞) Ala Moana (Map pp68-9; ☎ 944-8500; 1500 Kapi'olani Blvd; ☺ 7am-11pm Mon-Thu, 7am-9pm Fri, 9am-9pm Sat & Sun); Downtown (Map p60-1; ☎ 528-7171; 590 Queen St; ☺ 7am-11pm Mon-Fri, 8am-7pm Sat, 7am-7pm Sun); University area (Map p71; ☎ 943-0005; 2575 S King St; ☺ 24hr) Self-serve computer terminals, pay-as-you-go wi-fi and digital photo–printing and CD-burning stations.

Hawaii State Library (Map pp60-1; ☎ 586-3500; www.librarieshawaii.org; 478 S King St; ☺ 10am-5pm Mon & Wed, 9am-5pm Tue, Fri & Sat, 9am-8pm Thu; ☞) Free wi-fi and internet terminals; reservations available.

Netstop Cafe (Map p71; ☎ 955-1020; 2615 S King St; per hr $6; ☺ 7:30am-midnight; ☞) Cybercafe near the university offers pay-as-you-go wi-fi and computer terminals.

Media

NEWSPAPERS & MAGAZINES

O'ahu's biggest daily newspapers are the morning *Honolulu Advertiser* (www.honoluluadvertiser.com) and afternoon *Honolulu Star-Bulletin* (www.starbulletin.com). For the entertainment scene, pick up the tabloid *Honolulu Weekly* (http://honoluluweekly.com), available free around the island. Glossy monthly *Honolulu Magazine* (www.honolulumagazine.com) covers the arts, culture, fashion and cuisine scenes.

RADIO & TV

Radio station Da KINE (105.1FM) plays contemporary Hawaiian music. National Public Radio (NPR) and the University of Hawai'i are at the lower end of the FM dial. For more local flavor, KHON's Channel 2 evening news broadcast ends with slack key guitar music by Keola and Kapono Beamer and clips of people waving the *shaka* (Hawaii hand greeting) sign.

Medical Services

Hyperbaric Treatment Center (Map pp54-5; ☎ 851-7030/2; www.hyperbaricmedicinecenter.com; 275 Pu'uhale Rd) Divers with the bends come here.

Longs Drugs (Map p71; ☎ 947-2651; 2220 S King St; ☺ 24hr) Convenient pharmacy near the university campus.

Queen's Medical Center (Map pp60-1; ☎ 538-9011;

Seeing double on Ala Moana Blvd

MERTEN SNIJDERS

www.queens.org; 1301 Punchbowl St) O'ahu's best-equipped hospital offers 24-hour emergency services.
Straub Clinic & Hospital (Map pp68-9; ☎ 522-4000; www.straubhealth.org; 888 S King St) Operates a 24-hour emergency room here, as well as neighborhood clinics around O'ahu.

Money

Banks with convenient branches and ATMs around the city, and the entire island:
Bank of Hawaii (☎ 888-643-3888; www.boh.com) Ala Moana (Map pp68-9; ☎ 942-6111; Ala Moana Center, 1441 Kapi'olani Blvd); Chinatown (Map pp60-1; ☎ 532-2480; 101 N King St); University Area (Map p71; ☎ 973-4460; 1010 University Ave)
First Hawaiian Bank (☎ 844-4040; www.fhb.com) Chinatown (Map pp60-1; ☎ 525-6888; 2 N King St); Downtown (Map pp60-1; ☎ 525-6340; First Hawaiian Center, 999 Bishop St); University area (Map p71; ☎ 525-7841; 2411 S King St)

Post

For more post office locations and hours, dial ☎ 800-275-8777 or visit www.usps.com.
Ala Moana Post Office (Map pp68-9; ground fl, Ala Moana Center, 1450 Ala Moana Blvd; ⊙ 8:30am-5pm Mon-Fri, 8:30am-4:15pm Sat)
Chinatown Post Office (Map pp60-1; 100 N Beretania St; ⊙ 9am-4pm Mon-Fri)
Downtown Post Office (Map pp60-1; ground fl, 335 Merchant St; ⊙ 8am-4:30pm Mon-Fri) In the Old Federal Building.
Mo'ili'ili Post Office (Map p71; 2700 S King St; ⊙ 9:30am-4:15pm Mon-Fri) Near the University of Hawai'i.

DANGERS & ANNOYANCES

Drug dealing and gang activity are prevalent on the north side of Chinatown along the Nu'uanu Stream, so the neighborhood, including the River St pedestrian mall, should be avoided after dark. Exercise extra caution around the university campus in the Manoa neighborhood, where violent thefts and sexual assaults have been reported.

BEACHES

ALA MOANA BEACH PARK
Map pp68-9; 1201 Ala Moana Blvd; P
Opposite the Ala Moana Center, this fave is fronted by a broad, golden-sand beach,

---

Don't Miss

- A **walking tour of Chinatown** (p81)
- Brothers Cazimero at **Chai's Island Bistro** (p92)
- **Helena's Hawaiian Food** (p89)
- **La Mariana Sailing Club** (p91)
- **Prince Lot Hula Festival** (p273)
- **TheBoat** (p289)

---

nearly 1 mile long, which is buffered from passing traffic noise by statuesque shade trees. This is where Honolulu residents go to jog after work, play volleyball and enjoy weekend picnics. It's popular, yet big enough so it never feels crowded. The park has full facilities, including tennis courts. It's also an ideal choice for distance swimmers. However, at low tide the deep channel that runs the length of the beach can be a hazard – a former boat channel, it drops off suddenly to overhead depths.

MAGIC ISLAND
Map pp68-9; P
Jutting out from the east end of Ala Moana Beach Park is 'Aina Moana State Recreation Area, a peninsula better known as Magic Island. During the school year you can often find high-school outrigger canoe teams training here in the late afternoon. In summer it's a hot surf spot. Any time of year there's an idyllic walk around the perimeter of the peninsula, and sunsets can be picture-perfect, with sailboats pulling in and out of the adjoining Ala Wai Yacht Harbor.

KAKA'AKO WATERFRONT PARK
Map pp54-5; 677 Ala Moana Blvd; P
Near downtown Honolulu, just off Ala Moana Blvd at the end of Cooke St, little Kaka'ako Waterfront Park feels far away from the urban jungle. This hilly park attracts experienced surfers in the morning and picnickers in the afternoon. It's not a safe swimming beach, but the tricky Point Panic surf break is near the shore, making Kaka'ako a great place to watch surfers up close. Rollerbladers cruise along the rock-fringed promenade, which offers clear views of Diamond Head and Honolulu Harbor.

SIGHTS
Downtown Honolulu

This surprisingly compact area was center stage for the political intrigue and social upheavals that changed the fabric of Hawaii in the 19th and 20th centuries. Major players ruled here, revolted here, worshipped here and still rest, however restlessly, in the graveyards. Today, stately Victorian-era buildings are reflected in the black glass of modern high-rises, all just a lei's throw from the harbor.

'IOLANI PALACE

our pick Map pp60-1; ☎ info 538-1471, reservations & tickets 522-0832/23; guided tour adult/child 5-12yr $20/5, self-guided audio tour $12/5, basement galleries $6/3; ☷ guided tours every 15min 9am-11:15am Tue-Sat, self-guided tours every 10min 11:45am-3:30pm Tue-Sat, basement galleries 9am-5pm Tue-Sat

No other place evokes a more poignant sense of Hawaii's history than 'Iolani Palace. The palace was the official residence of King Kalakaua and Queen Kapi'olani from 1882 to 1891, and of Queen Lili'uokalani after that. Following the overthrow of the Hawaiian kingdom in 1893, the palace became the capitol. Two years after the coup, Lili'uokalani was convicted of treason and spent nine months as a prisoner in her former home.

It wasn't until 1969 that Hawaii's state government moved out of its cramped palace quarters. Until that time the Senate had met in the dining room, and the House of Representatives in the throne room. By the time they left, 'Iolani Palace was a shambles and the grand koa staircase termite-ridden. In the intervening years, many royal artifacts had been lost or stolen by persons unkown. After a decade of renovations, the restored palace finally reopened as a museum. In 2008, small groups of Native Hawaiian sovereignty activists occupied the palace grounds twice, bringing media attention to their cause.

You must take a docent-led or self-guided tour (children under five aren't allowed) to see 'Iolani's grand interior, including re-creations of the throne room and residential quarters upstairs. The palace was

'Iolani Palace, once the official residence of Hawaii's royalty   ANN CECIL

HONOLULU

DOWNTOWN HONOLULU & CHINATOWN

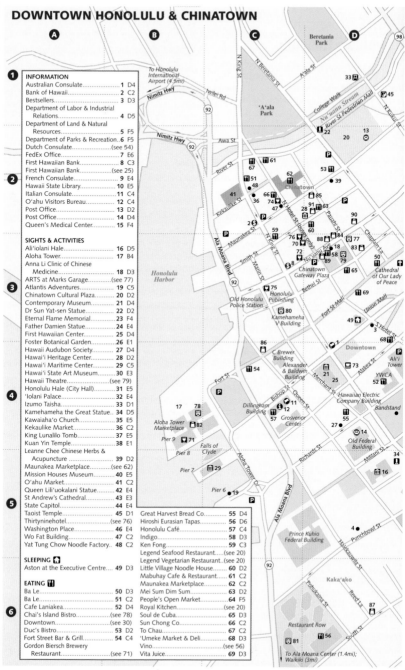

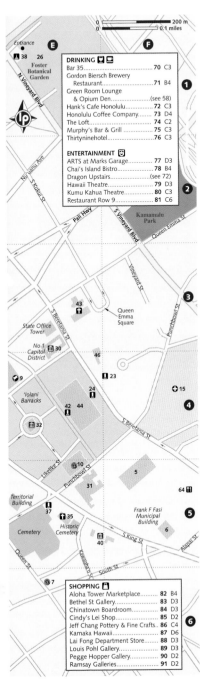

quite modern by Victorian-era standards. Every bedroom had its own bathroom with hot running water, and electric lights replaced the gas lamps years before the White House in Washington DC installed electricity. You can independently browse the historical exhibits in the basement, including priceless royal regalia and reconstructions of the kitchen and chamberlain's office.

The palace grounds are open during daylight hours and free of charge. The former barracks of the Royal Household Guards, a building that looks oddly like the uppermost layer of a medieval fort, now houses the palace ticket booth. Nearby, a domed pavilion, originally built for the coronation of King Kalakaua in 1883, is still used for governor inaugurations. Swing by the huge banyan tree between noon and 1pm on Friday to hear the Royal Hawaiian Band (p93) play.

Call ahead to confirm tour schedules and reserve tickets during peak periods.

🎨 HAWAI'I STATE ART MUSEUM

our pick Map pp60-1; ☎ 586-0900; www
.hawaii.gov/sfca; No 1 Capitol District Bldg, 250 S
Hotel St; admission free; ⏲ 10am-4pm Tue-Sat,
5-9pm 1st Friday of month

HiSAM fulfills a 35-year effort by the Hawai'i State Foundation on Culture and the Arts to find a permanent home for its vibrant, multimedia collection of works by Hawaiian artists. Some of the artists are island-born, while others arrived from far-flung places. All capture the soul of the islands and the heart of the people. Artworks are displayed around themes, such as the islands' Polynesian heritage, social issues and the natural beauty of land and sea. Hawaii's complex confluence of Asian, Pacific Rim and European cultures is evident throughout. Dating from 1928, the grand Spanish mission–style building is itself a work of art, now a nationally registered historic site. Drop by at noon on the last Tuesday of the month for free 'Art Lunch' lectures.

MISSION HOUSES MUSEUM

Map pp60-1; ☎ 447-3910; www.missionhouses
.org; 553 S King St; grounds admission free, temporary exhibit galleries $6, guided tours adult $10,
student & child 6-18yr $6; ⏲ 10am-4pm Tue-Sat,
tours usually 11am, 1pm & 2:45pm

The old headquarters of the Sandwich Islands Mission has been set aside as a quaint museum. Although it may look modest, this Protestant mission's influence permanently reshaped 19th-century island society and the eventual fate of the Kingdom of Hawai'i. Walking around the grounds, you'll see that the first missionaries packed more than their bags when they left Boston – they brought a prefabricated wooden house, called the Frame House, with them around the Horn. Erected in 1821, it's the oldest wooden structure in Hawaii. The coral-block Chamberlain House served as the mission's storeroom, while the printing office housed a lead-type press used to painstakingly print the Bible in Hawaiian.

KAWAIAHA'O CHURCH

Map pp60-1; ☎ 522-1333; 957 Punchbowl St; admission free; 🕒 8am-4pm daily, worship service 9am Sun

O'ahu's oldest church was built on the site where the first missionaries constructed a grass thatch church. Completed in 1842, this typical New England Congregational church with simple Gothic influences is made up of 14,000 coral slabs, each weighing about 1000lb, which Hawaiian divers chiseled out of O'ahu's underwater reefs – a task that took four years. The clock tower was donated by Kamehameha III, and the old clock, installed in 1850, still keeps accurate time. The rear seats of the church, marked by *kahili* (feathered staffs) and velvet padding, are still reserved for royal descendants. The tomb of King Lunalilo, the short-lived successor to Kamehameha V, is at the main entrance to the church grounds. The cemetery to the rear of the church is a bit like a who's who of colonial history. You'll find the gravestones of early missionaries buried alongside other important figures of the day, including the infamous Sanford Dole, who became the first territorial governor of Hawai'i after overthrowing Queen Lili'uokalani.

ALI'IOLANI HALE

Map pp60-1; ☎ 539-4994; 417 S King St; admission free; 🕒 8am-4pm Mon-Fri

The first major government building constructed by the Hawaiian monarchy in 1874, the 'House of Heavenly Kings' was designed by Australian architect Thomas Rowe to be a royal palace, although it was never used as such. Instead, the Italianate

St Andrew's Cathedral   LINDA CHING

building houses Hawaii's Supreme Court and was once home to Hawaii's legislature. It was on the steps of Ali'iolani Hale, in January 1893, that Sanford Dole proclaimed the establishment of a provisional government and the overthrow of the Hawaiian monarchy. Peek inside to find displays on Hawaii's judicial history dating back to the time of Kamehameha the Great.

Outside, a bronze statue of Kamehameha the Great stands in front of Ali'iolani Hale, facing 'Iolani Palace. On June 11, a state holiday honoring Kamehameha I, the statue is ceremonially draped with layers of flower lei. The statue was cast in 1880 in Florence, Italy, by American sculptor Thomas Gould. The current statue is actually a recast, as the first statue was lost at sea near the Falkland Islands. The original statue, which was recovered from the ocean floor after the second version was dedicated here in 1883, now stands in Kohala on the Big Island of Hawai'i, where Kamehameha was born.

STATE CAPITOL

Map pp60-1; ☎ 586-0178; 415 S Beretania St; admission free; ☻ 8am-5pm Mon-Fri, tours usually 1:30pm Mon, Wed & Fri

Built in the 1960s, Hawaii's state capitol is not your standard gold dome. It's a grandiose, themed design: its two legislative chambers have sloping walls to represent volcanoes; the supporting columns symbolize palm trees; the rotunda is open to let trade winds blow through; and the whole structure is encircled by a pool representing the Pacific. Visitors are free to walk through the rotunda and peer through viewing windows into the legislative chambers.

In front of the capitol is a highly stylized statue of Father Damien, the Belgian priest who lived and worked with victims of Hansen's disease who were exiled to the island of Moloka'i in the late 19th century, before dying of the disease himself.

Standing between the capitol and 'Iolani Palace is a life-sized bronze statue of Queen Lili'uokalani, Hawaii's last reigning monarch. She holds a copy of the Hawaiian constitution, which she wrote in 1893 in an attempt to strengthen Hawaiian rule; Aloha 'Oe, a patriotic hymn she composed; and Kumulipo, the traditional Hawaiian chant of creation.

HONOLULU HALE

Map pp60-1; ☎ 768-4385; 530 S King St; admission free; ☻ 8:30am-4:30pm Mon-Fri

City Hall was designed and built in 1927 in the style of a Spanish mission by CW Dickey, Honolulu's then-famous architect. On the National Register of Historic Places, it has a tiled roof, decorative balconies, arches and pillars, some ornate frescoes and an open-air courtyard sometimes used for concerts and art exhibits. On the front lawn, an eternal-flame memorial honors the victims of the September 11 terrorist attacks on the US mainland.

WASHINGTON PLACE

Map pp60-1; ☎ 586-0248; http://hawaii .gov/gov/washington_place; 320 S Beretania St; donations welcome; ☻ tours Mon-Fri

Formerly the governor's official residence, this colonial-style mansion was built in 1846 by US sea captain John Dominis. The captain's son became the governor of O'ahu and married the Hawaiian princess who

later became Queen Lili'uokalani. After the queen was dethroned, she lived at Washington Place in exile until her death in 1917. A plaque near the sidewalk on the left side of Washington Place is inscribed with the lyrics to Aloha 'Oe, the anthem she composed. For tour reservations, call at least two days in advance. Note that tourists may not carry anything larger than a purse onto the property, and should bring photo ID.

ST ANDREW'S CATHEDRAL

Map pp60-1; ☎ 524-2822; 229 Queen Emma Sq; admission free; ☻ 9am-5pm, tours 11am Sun

King Kamehameha IV, attracted by the royal trappings of the Church of England, decided to build his own cathedral in Hawaii. He and his consort, Queen Emma, founded the Anglican Church in Hawaii in 1861. The cathedral's cornerstone was laid by King Kamehameha V in 1867, four years after the death of Kamehameha IV, who died on St Andrew's Day – hence the church's name. The architecture is French Gothic, using stone and glass shipped from England. Historical tours usually meet by the pulpit after the 10am worship service on Sunday. At 12:15pm on Wednesday, the largest pipe organ in the Pacific is sonorously played.

FIRST HAWAIIAN CENTER

Map pp60-1; ☎ 526-1322; www.tcmhi.org; 999 Bishop St; admission free; ☻ 8:30am-4pm Mon-Thu, 8:30am-6pm Fri

The headquarters of the First Hawaiian Bank also houses the downtown gallery of the Contemporary Museum (p73), featuring fascinating rotating exhibits of Hawaiian art. Docent-guided tours usually meet at noon on the third Thursday of the month while exhibitions are being held. Honolulu's tallest high-rise features some of its own artwork, including a four-story glass wall that incorporates 185 prisms.

ALOHA TOWER

Map pp60-1; ☎ 537-9260; Pier 9; admission free; ☻ 9am-5pm

Built in 1926 at the edge of downtown, this 10-story tower is a Honolulu landmark that for years was the city's tallest building. In the days when all tourists arrived by ship, this prewar icon – with its four-sided clock tower inscribed with 'Aloha' – greeted every visitor to the islands. These days cruise ships disembark at the terminal beneath the tower. Take the elevator to the top of the tower, where an observation deck offers 360-degree views of Honolulu and the waterfront, then peek inside the cruise-ship terminal to see nostalgic murals depicting the harborfront's bygone days.

HAWAI'I MARITIME CENTER

ourpick Map pp60-1; ☎ 523-6151; www.bishop museum.org; Pier 7; adult/senior/child 4-12yr incl audio tour $8.50/7/5.50; ☼ 9am-5pm; **P** $5

A great place to get a sense of Hawaii's history, this maritime museum covers everything from the arrival of Captain Cook to modern-day windsurfing. The whaling section masterfully conveys a sense of the era as it affected Hawaii. Interesting displays on early tourism include a reproduction of a Matson liner stateroom and photos of Waikiki in the days when just the Royal Hawaiian and the Moana Hotels shared the shore with Diamond Head. The centerpiece is *Hokule'a*, a traditional double-hulled sailing canoe that has sailed to and from the South Pacific, retracing the routes of Hawaii's original Polynesian settlers using only ancient navigation methods that rely on the sun, stars, wind and wave patterns. Outside, you can board the *Falls of Clyde*, the world's last four-masted, four-rigged ship. Built in 1878, the ship once carried

---

OODLES OF NOODLES

If you look inside one of the half-dozen noodle factories in Chinatown, you'll see clouds of white flour hanging in the air and thin sheets of dough running around rollers and coming out as noodles. The Lilliputian **Yat Tung Chow Noodle Factory** (Map pp60-1; ☎ 531-7982; 150 N King St; ☼ 6am-3pm Mon-Sat, 6am-1pm Sun) makes almost a dozen sizes of noodles, from skinny golden thread to fat udon (75¢ to $1.50 per pound).

---

sugar and passengers between Hilo and San Francisco; it's now a floating National Historic Landmark. The museum announced a temporary closure just as this book went to press, so call ahead before you visit.

Chinatown

The location of this mercantile district is no accident. Between the port and what was once the countryside, enterprising businesses selling to city folks and visiting ship crews sprang up. Many were established in the 1860s by Chinese laborers who had completed their sugarcane-plantation contracts. The most successful immigrant families have long since moved out of the low-rent district

Making noodles at Yat Tung Chow Noodle Factory, Chinatown

LINDA CHING

of Chinatown to wealthier suburbs, making room for newer waves of immigrants: Vietnamese, Laotians and Filipinos.

Today, the scent of burning incense still wafts through Chinatown's buzzing markets, fire-breathing dragons spiral up the columns of buildings and steaming dim sum awakens even the sleepiest of appetites. Take time to explore: wander through nouveau art galleries and antiques stores, consult with a herbalist, rub shoulders with locals over a bowl of noodles and take a meditative stroll in Foster Botanical Garden.

KEKAULIKE & MAUNAKEA STREETS
our pick Map pp60-1

The commercial heart of Chinatown revolves around the markets and food shops on Kekaulike St. Noodle factories, pastry shops and produce stalls line the street, which is crowded with hobbling grandmothers and errand-running families. An institution since 1904, the O'ahu Market (cnr Kekaulike & N King Sts; 7am-5pm) sells everything a Chinese cook needs: ginger root, fresh octopus, quail eggs, slabs of tuna, jasmine rice, long beans and salted jellyfish. You owe yourself a bubble tea if you spot a pig's head in the market.

Between King and Hotel Sts, at the start of a pedestrian mall, is the newer, but just as vibrant, Kekaulike Market (Kekaulike St; 7am-5pm). At the top of the pedestrian mall is Maunakea Marketplace (1120 Maunakea St; 7am-5pm), where food supplies, prepared meals and Chinatown souvenirs are sold under one roof. The popular food court (p84) is full of mom-and-pop stalls, many Filipino-run.

At the nearby intersection of Maunakea and N Beretania Sts, you'll find clusters of lei shops, where lei makers deftly string flowers and the heady fragrances of plumeria and jasmine fill the air. Further south, on the corner of Maunakea and N Hotel Sts, is one of Chinatown's oldest structures, the Wo Fat Building (1900), with its ornate facade resembling a Chinese temple. The Chinese characters in the building's name signify peace and prosperity.

HAWAI'I HERITAGE CENTER
Map pp60-1; 521-2749; 1040 Smith St; 9am-2pm Mon-Sat

Local volunteers with family ties to the community run this friendly gallery that displays changing historical and cultural exhibitions about O'ahu's Chinese and other ethnic communities. For interesting, docent-led historical walking tours of Chinatown, see p81.

HAWAII THEATRE
Map pp60-1; 528-0506; 1130 Bethel St; tours $5; tours usually 11am Tue

This neoclassical theatre first opened in 1922 with silent films playing to the tunes of a pipe organ. Dubbed the 'Pride of the Pacific,' it ran continuous shows during WWII, but the development of Waikiki cinemas in the 1960s and '70s brought down the curtain. Thanks to multimillion-dollar restorations, this nationally registered historic site once again has trompe-l'oeil mosaics and bas-relief scenes of Shakespearean plays. Call ahead to confirm current schedules of the one-hour guided tour, which offers insights about the history and architecture of the place and a demonstration of the old organ.

CHINATOWN CULTURAL PLAZA
Map pp60-1

This open-air shopping mall, covering the better part of a block, doesn't have the character of Chinatown's older shops, but it's still quintessentially Chinatown, with tailors, acupuncturists and calligraphers working alongside travel agencies and dim-sum restaurants. In the small courtyard, elderly Chinese come daily to light incense at a statue of Kuan Yin. Outside,

FOR WHATEVER AILS YOU

Chinatown herbalists are both physicians and pharmacists, with walls full of small wooden drawers filled with different herbs. They'll size you up, feel your pulse and listen to you describe your ailments before deciding what drawers to open, mixing herbs and flowers and wrapping them for you to take home and boil together. You'll find herbalists in the Chinatown Cultural Plaza and at **Leanne Chee Chinese Herbs & Acupuncture** (Map pp60-1; 533-2498; 1159 Maunakea St) and **Anna Li Clinic of Chinese Medicine** (Map pp60-1; 537-1133; 1121 Nu'uanu Ave).

HONOLULU

a bronze statue of Dr Sun Yat-sen stands watch near the start of the River St pedestrian mall, where senior citizens play checkers and mah-jongg on shady benches alongside Nu'uanu Stream.

🌺 FOSTER BOTANICAL GARDEN
Map pp60-1; ☎ 522-7066; www.co.honolulu .hi.us/parks/hbg/fbg.htm; 180 N Vineyard Blvd; adult/child 6-12yr $5/1; ☼ 9am-4pm daily, guided tour 1pm Mon-Sat; 🚌 4; 🅿

If you need a reprieve from the city, this impressive garden, which first took root in 1850, reveals O'ahu's exotic natural heritage. Among its rare specimens are the Hawaiian *loulu* palm and the East African *Gigasiphon macrosiphon,* both thought to be extinct in the wild. Several of the garden's towering trees are the largest of their kind in the USA. Oddities include a double coconut palm capable of producing a 50lb nut – watch your head! Follow your nose through fragrant vanilla vines and cinnamon trees in the spice and herb gardens. Don't miss the blooming orchids either. Limited free parking is available for visitors.

KUAN YIN TEMPLE
Map pp60-1; ☎ 533-6361; 170 N Vineyard Blvd; admission free; ☼ sunrise-sunset

This brightly adorned Chinese temple is Honolulu's oldest. The richly carved interior overflows with the sweet, pervasive scent of burning incense. The temple is dedicated to Kuan Yin, goddess of mercy, whose statue is the largest in the prayer hall. Devotees burn paper 'money' for prosperity and good luck, and offerings of fresh flowers and fruit are placed at the altar. The large citrus fruit stacked pyramid-style is the pomelo, considered a symbol of fertility because of its many seeds. Honolulu's multiethnic Buddhist community worships at the temple. Respectful visitors are welcome.

TAOIST TEMPLE
Map pp60-1; 1315 River St

Founded in 1889, the Lum Sai Ho Tong Society was one of more than 100 societies started by Chinese immigrants in Hawaii to help preserve their cultural identity. This one was for the Lum clan, which hails from west of the Yellow River. The society's Taoist temple honors the goddess Tin Hau, a

DETOUR ➡

LILI'UOKALANI BOTANICAL GARDEN
A hidden waterfall in downtown Honolulu? You bet; right in the heart of this **city park** (Map pp54-5; ☎ 522-7060; 123 N Kukini St; admission free; ☼ 9am-4pm) that follows Nu'uanu Stream. Although slightly run-down these days, it was once tended by Queen Lili'uokalani as her private garden. To get here from Chinatown, take Nu'uanu Ave north and after crossing over the H1 Fwy, turn left onto Kuakini St.

Lum child who rescued her father from drowning and was later deified. Some claim to see her apparition when they travel by boat. The temple is not open to the general public, but you can still admire the colorful exterior.

IZUMO TAISHA
Map pp60-1; ☎ 538-7778; 215 N Kukui St; admission free; ☼ 9am-4pm

Across the river from the Taoist temple, this wooden Shinto shrine was built by Japanese immigrants in 1906. It was confiscated during WWII by the city and wasn't returned to the community until the early 1960s. The 100lb sacks of rice that sit near the altar symbolize good health, and ringing the bell placed at the shrine entrance is considered an act of purification for those who come to pray. Thousands of good-luck amulets are sold here, especially on January 1, when the temple heaves with people seeking New Year's blessings.

Central Honolulu & Ala Moana
Ala Moana means 'Path to the Sea' and its namesake road, Ala Moana Blvd (Hwy 92), connects the coast between Waikiki and Honolulu. Although most people think of Ala Moana only for shopping (see the boxed text, p94), Ala Moana Beach Park (p58) has few rivals anywhere else on the island.

HONOLULU

HONOLULU ACADEMY OF ARTS

our pick Map pp68-9; ☎ 532-8700; www
.honoluluacademy.org; 900 S Beretania St; adult
$10, senior & student $5, child under 13yr free, all
free 1st Wed & 3rd Sun of month; ⊙ 10am-4:30pm
Tue-Sat, 1-5pm Sun; ⊟ B, 2 & 13

This exceptional fine arts museum, with
solid Asian, European and Pacific collections, houses nearly 40,000 pieces of art.
The museum, dating to 1927, has a classical
facade that's invitingly open and airy, with
galleries branching off a series of garden and

ISLAND VOICES

NAME: STEPHEN LITTLE
OCCUPATION: DIRECTOR, HONOLULU
ACADEMY OF ARTS
RESIDENCE: HONOLULU

What drew you to living on O'ahu? I grew up in Asia, but I've
been coming to Hawaii since before statehood; I saw Waikiki
grow through the 1960s and '70s. I've lived an itinerant life, but
I love Hawaii because it reminds me of Asia. I feel very at home
here.

**How would you describe Honolulu to someone who has
never been here?** It's spiritual, beautiful and complex. Honolulu
may also be the most ethnically diverse city in America. Cultur-
ally, it's a remarkable place. It also has hidden complexities, especially politically. It's not
really what first-time visitors see – it's just not that simple.

What's the best and worst thing about living here? In some ways, we suffer from being
removed from the world, but I also look at that as a gift. It's a kind of strength, to be this
remote. Being so far away from anywhere gives us freedom. It makes this a place of opportunity. Here at the museum, it enables us to take risks with our exhibitions and
programming.

Tell me more about the museum's mission. It was founded in 1927 by Anna Rice Cooke,
who wanted to create an art collection that would reflect the diversity of the local population. She wanted this to be a place where children who are born here could come and
examine their own cultural roots through the window of works of art – and, just as importantly, to discover something about their neighbors. Although she had no formal training
in art, she had an amazing curiosity about people and cultures.

Why should first-time visitors come to Hawaii? One of our aims is to ask challenging
questions, for example about identity, which has real relevance in Hawaii, where identity is
particularly fluid and complex. Visitors who come here can see things that they may never
get to see back home – paintings by Van Gogh, Picasso and Gauguin; galleries of antiqui-
ties and Italian renaissance paintings; major works of modern American art; and one of the
country's top collections of Asian art. Here you can learn something new about yourself,
and the world. We're also the gateway to Shangri La (p155).

Where else should visitors go to get off the beaten path? Find any kind of authentic
hula. Traditionally it was a ritual of sacred expression, not performed on a stage, and it can
be very moving. Also, go see a heiau (stone temple), such as Ulupo Heiau (p173) on the
other side of the *pali* (cliffs).

HONOLULU

CENTRAL HONOLULU & ALA MOANA

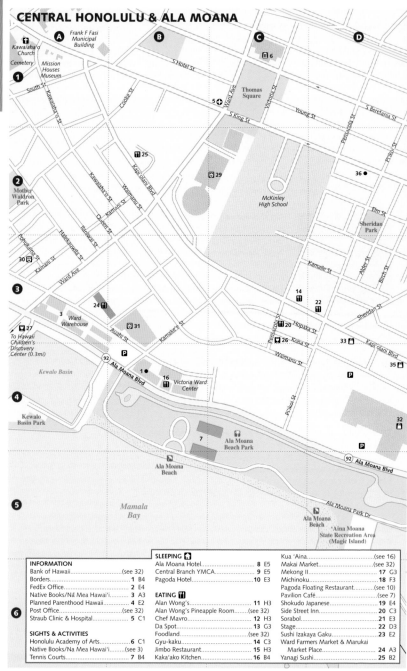

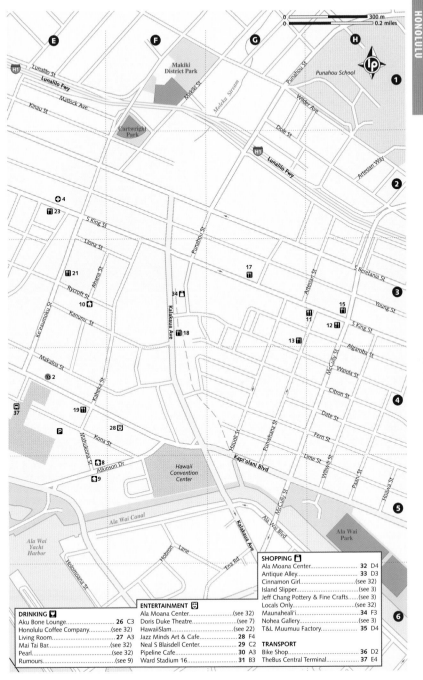

DRINKING 🍸
Aku Bone Lounge	**26** C3
Honolulu Coffee Company	(see 32)
Living Room	**27** A3
Mai Tai Bar	(see 32)
Pearl	(see 32)
Rumours	(see 9)

ENTERTAINMENT 🎭
Ala Moana Center	(see 32)
Doris Duke Theatre	(see 7)
HawaiiSlam	(see 22)
Jazz Minds Art & Cafe	**28** F4
Neal S Blaisdell Center	**29** C2
Pipeline Cafe	**30** A3
Ward Stadium 16	**31** B3

SHOPPING 🛍
Ala Moana Center	**32** D4
Antique Alley	**33** D3
Cinnamon Girl	(see 32)
Island Slipper	(see 3)
Jeff Chang Pottery & Fine Crafts	(see 3)
Locals Only	(see 32)
Maunaheali'i	**34** F3
Nohea Gallery	(see 3)
T&L Muumuu Factory	**35** D4

TRANSPORT
Bike Shop	**36** D2
TheBus Central Terminal	**37** E4

HONOLULU

Le Grande Penelope by Antoine Bourdelle, Honolulu Academy of Arts (p67)

LINDA CHING

water-fountain courtyards. Exhibits, which reflect the various cultures that make up contemporary Hawaii, include one of the USA's finest Asian art collections, featuring everything from Japanese woodblock prints by Hiroshige and Ming dynasty porcelain paintings to Indonesian woven textiles to temple carvings from Cambodia and India. Another highlight is the striking contemporary wing with Hawaiian works on its upper level, and modern art by such luminaries as Henry Moore and Georgia O'Keeffe below. Pacific and Polynesian artifacts include ceremonial carvings, war clubs, masks and bodily adornments. This is a place to relax and move slowly, perhaps combining your visit with lunch at the museum's courtyard Pavilion Café (p86) or a guided tour of Shangri La (p155).

University Area

In the foothills of Manoa Valley, the pedestrian-friendly university area has a pretty happening scene, with a collection of cool cafes, ethnic restaurants and bargain-basement shops. You'll pass through here en route to Manoa Falls and the university's Lyon Arboretum (p72).

UNIVERSITY OF HAWAI'I AT MANOA

Map p71; ☎ 956-8111; www.uhm.hawaii.edu; cnr University Ave & Dole St; P $3, free after 4pm & all day Sat & Sun; 🚌 4 & 6

Two miles north of Waikiki, the main campus of the statewide university system was born too late to be weighed down by the tweedy academic architecture of the mainland. Today, the university has strong programs in astronomy, geophysics, marine sciences and Hawaiian and Pacific studies. Its breezy, tree-shaded campus is crowded with students from islands throughout Polynesia.

Staff at the UH Information & Visitor Center (☎ 956-7235/6; room 212, Campus Center; 🕑 8:30am-4:30pm Mon-Fri) offer campus maps and free one-hour walking tours of the campus, emphasizing history and architecture. Tours leave at 2pm Monday, Wednesday and Friday; to join, show up 10 minutes beforehand. The *Campus Art* brochure, available at the information center, provides a self-guided walking tour of outdoor sculptures and other works by distinguished Hawaii artists.

Downhill, the John Young Museum of Art (☎ 956-8866; Krauss Hall, 2500 Dole St; admission free; 🕑 11am-2pm Mon-Fri, 1-4pm Sun) features 20th-century Hawaiian painter John Young's collection of artifacts from Pacific islands,

Africa and Asia, mostly ceramics, pottery and sculpture. Although it's just two rooms, it's worth a quick visit.

On the east side of campus is the **East-West Center** (☎ 944-7111; www.eastwestcenter.org; 1601 East-West Rd), an internationally recognized education and research organization that promotes mutual understanding among the peoples of Asia, the Pacific Rim and the US. Thought-provoking temporary exhibits are displayed in the center's **art gallery** (Burns Hall; admission free; ⏰ 8am-5pm Mon-Fri, noon-4pm Sun). The center occasionally hosts multicultural programs that are open to the public, including films, lectures, music concerts and dance performances.

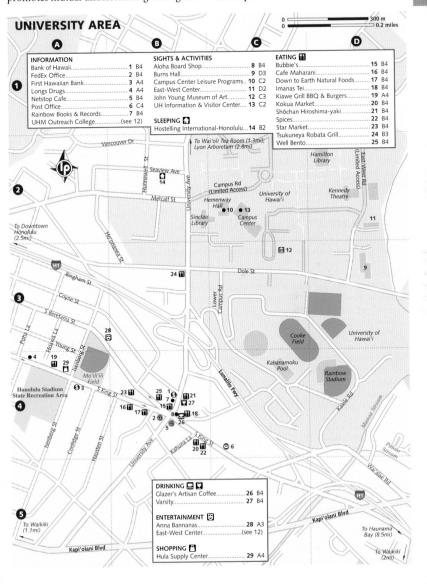

UNIVERSITY AREA

0 _____ 300 m
0 _____ 0.2 miles

INFORMATION	
Bank of Hawaii	1 B4
FedEx Office	2 B4
First Hawaiian Bank	3 A4
Longs Drugs	4 A4
Netstop Cafe	5 B4
Post Office	6 C4
Rainbow Books & Records	7 B4
UHM Outreach College	(see 12)

SIGHTS & ACTIVITIES	
Aloha Board Shop	8 B4
Burns Hall	9 D3
Campus Center Leisure Programs	10 C2
East-West Center	11 D2
John Young Museum of Art	12 C3
UH Information & Visitor Center	13 C2

SLEEPING	
Hostelling International-Honolulu	14 B2

EATING	
Bubbie's	15 B4
Cafe Maharani	16 B4
Down to Earth Natural Foods	17 B4
Imanas Tei	18 B4
Kiawe Grill BBQ & Burgers	19 A4
Kokua Market	20 B4
Shōchan Hiroshima-yaki	21 B4
Spices	22 B4
Star Market	23 B4
Tsukuneya Robata Grill	24 B3
Well Bento	25 B4

To Waiʻoli Tea Room (1.3mi);
Lyon Arboretum (2.8mi)

Vancouver Dr

Seaview Ave

Campus Rd
(Limited Access)

Hamilton Library

Hemenway Hall

University of Hawaiʻi

Kennedy Theatre

Sinclair Library

Campus Center

Metcalf St

To Downtown Honolulu (2.5mi)

Dole St

Bingham St

Coyne St

S Beretania St

Young St

S King St

Moʻiliʻili Field

Honolulu Stadium State Recreation Area

Cooke Field

University of Hawaiʻi

Kahanamoku Pool

Rainbow Stadium

Lunalilo Fwy

Kūhiō Ave

Kapiʻolani Blvd

To Waikiki (1.1mi)

To Haunama Bay (8.5mi)

To Waikiki (2mi)

Waiʻalae Rd

Mānoa Stream

Pālolo Stream

DRINKING	
Glazer's Artisan Coffee	26 B4
Varsity	27 B4

ENTERTAINMENT	
Anna Bannanas	28 A3
East-West Center	(see 12)

SHOPPING	
Hula Supply Center	29 A4

HONOLULU

Upper Manoa Valley, Tantalus & Makiki Heights

Welcome to Honolulu's green belt. The verdant Upper Manoa Valley climbs beyond the university through residential neighborhoods into forest reserve high in the Ko'olau Range above Honolulu. It's a peaceful place to commune with nature. For hiking trails, including walks to Manoa Falls and the head-spinning Nu'uanu Valley Lookout, see p76.

Further west, a narrow, switchbacking road cuts its way up the forest reserve of Tantalus and the Makiki Valley. The scenic drive climbs almost to the top of Mt Tantalus (2013ft), passing swank homes along the way. Although the road is one continuous loop, the western side is called Tantalus Dr and the eastern side, Round Top Dr. This 8.5-mile Tantalus–Round Top circuit is the city's most popular scenic drive (and an athletic cycling route), offering dizzying skyline views. Branching off the loop road, there's a network of forested hiking trails (see p76).

🌿 LYON ARBORETUM

Map p73; ☎ 988-0456; 3860 Manoa Rd; suggested donation $5; ☽ 9am-4pm Mon-Fri, 9am-3pm Sat; 🚍 5

Managed by the University of Hawai'i, this hilly arboretum tempts with wildly unkempt walking paths through O'ahu's most accessible tropical rainforest. Its seminatural state is such a relief from the touristy, manicured tropical flower gardens so common elsewhere in the islands.

Key plants in the Hawaiian ethnobotanical garden include *'ulu* (breadfruit) and *kalo* (taro); *ko,* the sugarcane brought by early Polynesian settlers; *kukui,* which was used to produce lantern oil; and *ti,* which was used for medicinal purposes during ancient times and for making moonshine after Westerners arrived. It's a short walk to Inspiration Point, or keep walking uphill for about 1 mile along a jeep road, then a narrow, tree root–ridden path to visit seasonal 'Aihualama Falls, a lacy cliff-side cascade. No swimming, sorry.

MR OBAMA'S NEIGHBORHOOD

During the race to elect the 44th President of the United States, Republican vice presidential candidate Sarah Palin kept asking the country, 'Who is Barack Obama?' It was Obama's wife, Michelle, who had an answer ready: 'You can't really understand Barack until you understand Hawaii.'

Obama, who grew up in Makiki Heights, has written that 'Hawaii's spirit of tolerance…became an integral part of my world view, and a basis for the values I hold most dear.' The local media and many *kama'aina* (those who were born and grew up in Hawaii) agree that Hawaii's diverse multiethnic social fabric helped shape the leader who created a rainbow coalition during the 2008 US election.

Obama has also said Hawaii is a place for him to rest and recharge, as he did with his family just before assuming office. Back in 1999 he wrote: 'When I'm heading out to a hard day of meetings and negotiations, I let my mind wander back to Sandy Beach, or Manoa Falls… It helps me, somehow, knowing that such wonderful places exist and [that] I'll always be able to return to them.'

If you want to walk in Obama's footsteps on O'ahu, here are places you can visit:

- **Manoa Falls** (p76)
- **Rainbow Drive-In** (p120)
- **Kapi'olani Beach Park** (p108)
- **Hanauma Bay** (p158)
- **Makapu'u Point** (p162)
- **Sandy Beach** (p161)
- **Olomana Golf Links** (p171)
- **Island Snow** (p177)

To learn more about President Obama's childhood in Hawaii, read *The Dream Begins: How Hawaii Shaped Barack Obama* by Stu Glauberman and Jerry Burris.

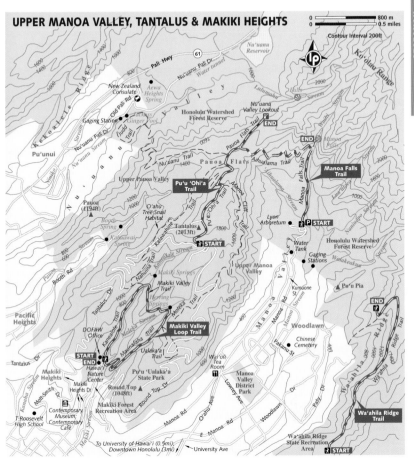

UPPER MANOA VALLEY, TANTALUS & MAKIKI HEIGHTS

On public transit, catch TheBus 5 from the Ala Moana Center toward Manoa Valley and get off at the last stop, from where it's a half-mile walk uphill. If you're driving, follow University Ave north onto O'ahu Ave, then turn right and follow Manoa Rd to its end.

CONTEMPORARY MUSEUM

Map p73; TCM; ☎ 526-1322; www.tcmhi.org; 2411 Makiki Heights Dr; adult $5, senior & student $3, child under 13yr free, all free 3rd Thu of month; ☼ 10am-4pm Tue-Sat, noon-4pm Sun, tours 1:30pm Tue-Sun; Ⓟ ⊜ 15

With tropical sculpture gardens, this engaging art museum occupies an estate house constructed in 1925 for Anna Rice Cooke,

an influential newspaper heiress and patron of the arts. Here the main galleries feature changing exhibits of paintings, sculpture and other contemporary artwork from the 1940s through today by international and national artists, including those who were born in Hawaii. A lawn pavilion holds the museum's most prized piece, an environmental installation by David Hockney based on sets for *L'Enfant et les Sortilèges*, Ravel's 1925 opera. A delightful courtyard cafe (p86) serves drinks and lunch, including romantic picnic baskets for two.

If you're driving, follow Makiki St north of S Beretania St in central Honolulu, then turn left onto Makiki Heights Dr. On public transit, take TheBus 2 or B CountryExpress!

HONOLULU

from Waikiki towards downtown Honolulu and get off at the corner of Beretania and Alapaʻi Sts; walk one block towards the ocean along Alapaʻi St and transfer to TheBus 15, which stops outside the museum.

PUʻU ʻUALAKAʻA STATE PARK
Map p73; admission free; ⏰ 7am-7:45pm Apr-Aug, 7am-6:45pm Sep-Mar

For a remarkable panorama of Honolulu, visit this tiny roadside state park. The entrance is about 2.5 miles up Round Top Dr from Makiki St; then it's another half-mile to the lookout, bearing left when the road forks. The sweeping view extends from Kahala and Diamond Head on the far left, across Waikiki and downtown Honolulu, to the Waiʻanae Range on the far right. To the southeast is the University of Hawaiʻi, easily recognizable by its sports stadium; to the southwest you can see clearly into the green mound of Punchbowl Crater. The airport is visible on the edge of the coast, and Pearl Harbor beyond that.

TheBus does not stop near the park, so you'll have to drive or cycle here.

Greater Honolulu

🌺 BISHOP MUSEUM

our pick Map pp54-5; ☎ 847-3511; www.bishop museum.org; 1525 Bernice St; adult $16, senior & child 4-12yr $13; ⏰ 9am-5pm; 🅿 🚌 2

Like Hawaii's version of the Smithsonian Institute in Washington, DC, the Bishop Museum showcases a remarkable array of cultural and natural history exhibits. It is often ranked as the finest Polynesian anthropological museum in the world.

The main gallery, the Hawaiian Hall, dedicates three floors of a Victorian-era building to the cultural history of Hawaii. First-floor displays from the pre-Western contact era include a full-sized *pili* grass-thatched house, carved *kiʻi akua* (temple images) and shark-tooth war clubs. The foremost treasure is a feather cloak worn by Kamehameha the Great and created entirely of the yellow feathers of the now-extinct *mamo* – around 80,000 birds were caught and plucked to create this cloak. Meanwhile, the hall's upper floors cover the importance of land and nature to Native Hawaiians and the diversity of the islands' modern multiethnic society.

DETOUR ➡

MOANALUA GARDENS

A former vacation haunt for Hawaiian royalty, this off-the-beaten-path **park** (Map pp54-5; ☎ 833-1944; www.mgf-hawaii .org; admission free; ⏰ sunrise-sunset) hints at its regal past, including King Kamehameha V's gingerbread-trimmed summer cottage overlooking an ancient taro pond. But what all those tour buses are stopping by to see is the gigantic Hitachi Tree, a monkeypod used in Japanese corporate marketing promotions since the 1970s. Traditional Hawaiian culture is celebrated here every July during the Prince Lot Hula Festival (p273), one of the biggest festivals of its kind in Hawaii. To find the park, take the Puʻuloa Rd/Tripler Hospital exit off Hwy 78, then make an immediate right turn into the gardens.

The Kahili Room, off the main hall, features portraits of Hawaiian royalty and a display of *kahili*, the feathered staffs used at coronations and royal funerals. The fascinating two-story exhibits of the Polynesian Hall delve into the myriad island cultures of Polynesia, Micronesia and Melanesia. Many astounding and rare ritual artifacts, from elaborate dance masks and ceremonial costumes to carved canoes and tools of warfare, are on display.

The eye-popping, state-of-the-art multisensory Science Adventure Center lets kids walk through an erupting volcano, take a mini-submarine dive and play with all sorts of interactive gadgets. The Bishop Museum is also home to Oʻahu's only planetarium (☎ 848-4136), which highlights traditional Polynesian methods of wayfaring (navigation), using wave patterns and the position of the stars to travel thousands of miles across the open ocean in traditional outrigger canoes. Show schedules vary, so call ahead.

By public transit from Waikiki or downtown Honolulu, take bus 2 School St-Middle St or B CityExpress! bus to Kapalama St, then walk toward the ocean for one block, turning right on Bernice St. By car, take exit

20A off the eastbound H1 Fwy, merge onto the Likelike Hwy (Hwy 63) northbound and then turn right on Bernice St.

NATIONAL MEMORIAL CEMETERY OF THE PACIFIC

Map pp54-5; ☎ 532-3720; 2177 Puowaina Dr; admission free; ☼ 8am-5:30pm Sep 30-Mar 1, 8am-6:30pm Mar 2-Sep 29; Ⓟ

A mile north of downtown Honolulu sits the bowl-shaped remnant of a long-extinct volcanic crater, now nicknamed the Punchbowl. Ancient Hawaiians called the crater Puowaina (Hill of Human Sacrifices). Once there was probably a heiau (temple) here with the slain bodies of *kapu* (taboo) breakers ceremonially cremated upon the altar.

Today the remains of Hawaiians sacrificed to appease the gods share the crater floor with the bodies of nearly 50,000 soldiers, many of whom were killed in the Pacific during WWII. The remains of Ernie Pyle, the distinguished war correspondent who fought in WWI and was hit by machine-gun fire on Ie-shima during the final days of WWII, lie in section D, grave 109. Five stones to the left, at grave D-1, is the marker for astronaut Ellison Onizuka, the Big Island native who perished in the 1986 *Challenger* space-shuttle disaster.

Even without the war sights, Punchbowl would be worth the drive up for the view. After entering the cemetery, bear left and go to the top of the hill, where there's a lookout offering sweeping views clear out to Diamond Head and the Pacific beyond.

If you're driving, take the H1 Fwy westbound to the Pali Hwy; there's a marked exit on your right almost immediately as you start up the Pali Hwy. From there, just follow the signs through winding, narrow streets. On public transit, take TheBus 2 or B CountryExpress! from Waikiki toward downtown Honolulu and get off at Beretania and Alapa'i Sts. Walk one block toward the ocean along Alapa'i St and transfer to TheBus 15 to the cemetery entrance, then walk uphill for 15 minutes.

QUEEN EMMA SUMMER PALACE

Map pp54-5; ☎ 595-6291; www.daughtersof hawaii.org; 2931 Pali Hwy; adult/child $6/1; ☼ 9am-4pm; Ⓟ 🚌 4

In the heat of the summer, Queen Emma, the royal consort of Kamehameha IV, used to slip away from her formal downtown Honolulu home to this cooler hillside retreat. The exterior resembles an old Southern plantation mansion, with a columned porch, high ceilings and island-style louvered windows to catch the breeze. Inside you'll find a repository of regal memorabilia and period furniture collected from five of Emma's homes. Gracious, sharp-witted docents from the Daughters of Hawai'i society will show you the cathedral-shaped koa cabinet displaying a set of china from Queen Victoria and the feather cloaks and capes once worn by Hawaiian royalty. Look for the entrance on the northbound side of the Pali Hwy (Hwy 61), near the 2-mile marker.

National Memorial Cemetery of the Pacific   ANN CECIL

ACTIVITIES

The University of Hawai'i at Manoa's Campus Center Leisure Programs (p80) offers a variety of public water-sports classes and group activities, from snorkeling excursions around O'ahu ($25) and half-day introductory bodyboarding ($20) or learn-to-sail classes ($130) to intensive week-long PADI certification courses for scuba divers.

Swimming & Surfing

For Honolulu's best ocean swimming, head to Ala Moana Beach Park (p58). There are intermediate-level surf breaks just off Ala Moana Beach Park, while those off Kaka'ako Waterfront Park (p58) are for advanced surfers. In the university area, you can rent surfboards from Aloha Board Shop (Map p71; ☎ 955-6030; www.alohaboardshop .com; Puck's Alley, 2600 S King St; 3-day/weekly rental $60/100; ⏲ 10am-7pm Mon-Sat, 11am-5pm Sun).

Whale Watching

From late December through mid-April, Atlantis Adventures (Map pp60-1; ☎ 973-1311, 800-548-6262; www.atlantisadventures.com; Pier 6, Aloha Tower Dr; 2½hr tour incl buffet lunch adult/child $65/33) offers naturalist-led whale-watching cruises aboard the *Navatek I*, a sleek, high-tech catamaran designed to minimize rolling, usually departing at noon daily.

Hiking

You can spend days enjoying the solitude of the mountains surrounding the city. Some

of the most lightly trodden trails in the lush Ko'olau Range are just above downtown Honolulu. For guided hikes around the island, many of which depart from Honolulu, see p38.

UPPER MANOA VALLEY
❀ MANOA FALLS TRAIL
Map p73

Maybe Honolulu's most rewarding short hike, this trail runs for 1300 yards above a rocky streambed before ending at a pretty little cascade. The trail is often a bit muddy and, if it has rained recently, the packed clay will be slippery. Many of the tall swamp mahogany trees and flowering orange African tulip trees that line the path were planted by the nearby Lyon Arboretum (p72). Wild purple orchids and red ginger grow around the falls, which drop 100ft into a small pool (not deep enough for swimming). Falling rocks and the risk of leptospirosis – a waterborne bacteria found in many of Hawaii's freshwater streams, which can cause seri-

It's no fluke: you can see humpback whales off O'ahu in winter   KARL LEHMANN

ous illness – make even wading dangerous, so don't venture beyond the established viewing area.

To reach the trailhead, drive almost to the end of Manoa Rd, where locals will demand you pay $5 for parking. On public transit, take TheBus 5 Manoa Valley service from the Ala Moana Center to the end of the line; from there, it's a 10-minute walk uphill to the trailhead.

NU'UANU VALLEY LOOKOUT

Map p73

About 50ft before reaching Manoa Falls (see left), the inconspicuous 'Aihualama Trail starts to the west of a chain-link fence and scrambles over some boulders. The trail soon enters a bamboo forest with some massive old banyan trees, then contours around the ridge, offering broad views of Manoa Valley. Another mile of gradual switchbacks brings hikers to an intersection with the Pauoa Flats Trail, which ascends to the right for 900 yards over muddy tree roots to the spectacular Nu'uanu Valley Lookout. Here, atop the Ko'olau Range, with O'ahu's steep *pali* (cliffs) visible all around, it's possible to peer through a gap over to the Windward Coast. The round-trip distance from the Manoa Falls trailhead is just over 5.5 miles.

TANTALUS & MAKIKI HEIGHTS

Map p73

Presided over by Mt Tantalus, the fertile Makiki Valley was once the site of an ancient Hawaiian settlement. The archaeological remains of stone walls and evidence of a 19th-century coffee plantation can still be seen. Today the area is part of the Honolulu Watershed Forest Reserve, which is crisscrossed by the Honolulu Mauka Trail System.

Inside the Makiki Forest Recreation Area, the Hawai'i Nature Center (Map p73; ☎ 955-0100, 888-955-0104; www.hawaiinaturecenter.org; 2131 Makiki Heights Dr) conducts family programs and hikes on many weekends, costing $4 to $18 per parent-child pair (reservations recommended). Further up the same service road, the Division of Forestry & Wildlife (Dofaw; Map p73; ☎ 973-9778; www.hawaiitrails.org; 2135 Makiki Heights Dr; ☺ 7:45am-4:30pm Mon-Fri) distributes free trail maps. Beside the office there's a soda-vending machine and a drinking fountain.

To reach the forest baseyard, where the Dofaw office and the trailheads are located,

Top Picks

FREE STUFF

- Magic Island (p58)
- Hawai'i State Art Museum (p61)
- Royal Hawaiian Band (p93)
- Manoa Falls & Nu'uanu Valley Lookout (opposite)
- Chinatown's First Friday Gallery Walk (p96)

turn right onto Makiki St from S Beretania St in central Honolulu, then turn left onto Makiki Heights Dr and go 900 yards uphill. Where the road makes a sharp bend, keep driving straight ahead through a gate into the Makiki Forest Recreation Area. By public transit, take TheBus 15 from downtown Honolulu, then get off near the intersection of Mott-Smith and Makiki Heights Drs and walk downhill on Makiki Heights Dr for about 1 mile. From Waikiki, take TheBus 4 Nu'uanu–Dowsett/Pauoa to the intersection of Wilder Ave and Makiki St, from where it's a 1-mile walk up Makiki St.

MAKIKI VALLEY LOOP

Map p73

Starting inside the Makiki Forest Recreation Area baseyard, three Tantalus area trails can be combined into the popular 2.5-mile Makiki Valley Loop. A favorite hike for Honolulu residents, the loop wends through a lush tropical forest, made up mainly of nonnative species grown to replace the 'iliahi (sandalwood) trees leveled here during the 19th century (see p245).

The Maunalaha Trail begins at the restrooms near the Hawaii Nature Center. After crossing over a small stream and a few tame switchbacks, the trail makes a no-holds-barred ascent of the Makiki Valley's east ridge over a giant staircase of tree roots, passing Norfolk pines, banyans and taro patches along the way. Behind are views of Honolulu's skyscrapers and harbor.

After 0.7 miles, you'll come to a four-way junction. Follow the Makiki Valley Trail straight ahead and proceed uphill. The 1.1-mile trail traverses small gulches and across gentle streams bordered with patches of ginger. Edible yellow guava and strawberry guava also grow along the trail.

The Kanealole Trail begins as you cross Kanealole Stream and then follows the stream back to the baseyard, 0.7 miles away. The trail leads down through a field of Job's tears; the beadlike seed bracts of the female flowers of this tall grass are often used for lei. The trail is usually muddy, so wear shoes with good traction.

PU'U 'OHI'A (MT TANTALUS)
Map p73

Along the Tantalus–Round Top loop drive a network of trails littered with fragrant *liliko'i* (passion fruit) encircles Mt Tantalus, offering contemplative forest hikes with city views.

The Pu'u 'Ohi'a Trail, in conjunction with the Pauoa Flats Trail, leads up to Nu'uanu Valley Lookout. It's nearly 2 miles each way and makes a hardy hike. The trailhead is at the very top of Tantalus Dr, about 3.6 miles up from its intersection with Makiki Heights Dr. The trail begins with reinforced log steps and leads past fragrant ginger, groves of bamboo that rustle musically in the wind and lots of eucalyptus. About 0.5 miles up, the trail summits Mt Tantalus (2013ft), also called Pu'u 'Ohi'a.

From Mt Tantalus, the trail leads back onto a service road that ends at a telephone company building, behind which you can pick up the trail again. Continue to the intersection with the Manoa Cliff Trail and go left. At the next intersection, turn right onto the often-muddy Pauoa Flats Trail, which leads to the Nu'uanu Valley Lookout, with its sweeping view of Windward O'ahu.

You'll pass two more trailheads before reaching the lookout. The first is the Nu'uanu Trail, on the left, which runs 0.75 miles along the western side of Upper Pauoa Valley and offers broad views of Honolulu and the Wai'anae Range. The second is the 'Aihualama Trail, on the right, which leads east to Manoa Falls (see p76).

GREATER HONOLULU
WA'AHILA RIDGE TRAIL

Popular even with novice hikers, this boulder-strewn, 4.8-mile round-trip trail starts deep inside Wa'ahila Ridge State Recreation Area (Map p73; ☎ 587-0062; www.hawaiistateparks .org; Ruth Pl; ☼ sunrise-sunset). Marked by a Na Ala Hele sign, the trailhead is just past the picnic tables.

Bear left and immediately start climbing the ridge, continuing uphill on a rutted dirt road past a water tank. Watch for a small arrow pointing to the left where the trail leaves the road and enters the forest reserve. Scattered with soft ironwood needles, it contours before sliding steeply downhill to a dry and rocky area. Only partly shaded, it rolls up and down along a series of small saddles and knobs. At one point, a series of boulders requires a little kid-friendly scrambling. The final climb leads to a grassy clearing with bird's-eye views of the Manoa Valley and Honolulu.

To reach the park, turn north off Wai'alae Ave onto St Louis Dr. Turn right near the top onto Peter St, then left onto Ruth Pl, which runs west into the park. From Waikiki, TheBus 14 St Louis Heights stops at the intersection of Peter and Ruth Sts, about a 15-minute walk from the trailhead.

Cycling

The Bike Shop (Map pp68-9; ☎ 596-0588; 1149 S King St; per day $20-40; ☼ 9am-7pm Mon-Fri, to 5pm Sat, 10am-5pm Sun) rents a variety of high-quality bicycles and can give you a map showing suggested cycling routes to match your interest. Diehards often head up to the Tantalus–Round Top loop road (p72); expect a good workout, but the scenery is ample reward.

Golf

The oldest golf course in Hawaii and, for that matter, the oldest gold course west of the Rockies, is Moanalua Golf Club (Map pp54-5; ☎ 839-2411; http://moanaluagolfclubhawaii.com; 1250 Ala Aolani St; green fees $25-40; ☼ by appointment Mon-Fri). Built in 1898 by a missionary family, it's a fairly quick course, with an elevated green, straight fairways and nine holes that are played twice around (par 72).

Tennis

Ala Moana Beach Park (p58) has 10 free first-come, first-served public tennis courts. If you hit them during the day, you can cool off with a dip in the ocean afterwards; if you come at night, the courts are lit.

WALKING TOUR

Forget your car. Instead, set off on foot to explore Honolulu's history-laden downtown district, wandering past Victorian-era and early-20th-century buildings and the Aloha Tower, an icon of Honolulu's bygone days, still standing by the breezy harborfront.

❶ 'IOLANI PALACE (p59)

The heart of old Honolulu, both historically and geographically speaking, is Hawaii's royal palace. If you've got time to spare, join a guided palace tour for a glimpse into the Kingdom of Hawai'i's royal past. At least take a stroll around the grand grounds.

❷ MISSION HOUSES MUSEUM (p61) & KAWAIAHA'O CHURCH (p62)

Follow in the footsteps of O'ahu's first Protestant missionaries, who started arriving in 1820. The coral-rock church is still in use today, including by descendants of Hawaiian royalty.

❸ LANIAKEA YWCA

This Mediterranean-style jewel at 1040 Richards St, open 5am to 7pm weekdays, 7am to 2pm weekends, was built in 1927 by Julia Morgan, the renowned US mainland architect who designed William Randolph Hearst's San Simeon estate in California. For lunch, grab a courtyard table at Café Laniakea (p82).

WALK FACTS

Start 'Iolani Palace
End Hawai'i Maritime Center
Distance 1.5 miles
Duration Two to four hours

---

❹ HAWAI'I STATE ART MUSEUM (p61)

Inside the elegant five-story No 1 Capitol District Building, two floors of light and airy art galleries delve into Hawaii's rich multicultural heritage. On the ground floor, Downtown (p82) elevates the island-style plate lunch to a level sophisticated enough for haute urbanites and city power brokers.

❺ ALEXANDER & BALDWIN BUILDING

En route to the harborfront, stop in front of this 1929 building at 822 Bishop St. Its stone-and-tile facade incorporates tropical fruit, Hawaiian fish and the Chinese characters for prosperity and longevity. The building itself is named after sons of missionaries who became wealthy sugar-plantation owners.

❻ JEFF CHANG POTTERY & FINE CRAFTS (p95)

Do a little window-shopping along the pedestrian-only Fort St Mall, where this renowned island art gallery displays eye-catching jewelry, koa wood carvings and Japanese *raku* pottery, all Hawaii-made.

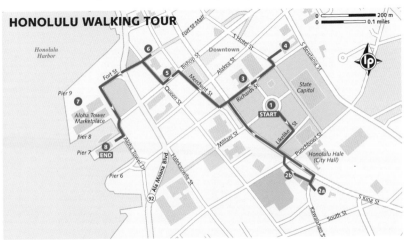

HONOLULU WALKING TOUR

⑦ ALOHA TOWER (p63) This 1926 landmark still welcomes cruise-ship passengers to O'ahu, just like it did in the golden age before jet travel. It was also once Honolulu's tallest building, and today the views from the 4th-floor observation deck still impress.

⑧ HAWAI'I MARITIME CENTER (p64) Let yourself drift back to Hawaii's old whaling days or to when ancient Polynesian voyagers first arrived on O'ahu in their double-hulled outrigger canoes. After exploring the museum, you could keep walking north to Chinatown (p64) or catch a convenient bus south to Ala Moana Beach Park (p58).

COURSES

Campus Center Leisure Programs (Map p71; ☎ 956-6468; www.hawaii.edu/cclp; Room 101, Hemenway Hall, 2445 Campus Center Rd; courses $20-210) The University of Hawai'i at Manoa offers a variety of value-priced classes open to the public. Some courses, like the bodyboarding class, finish in a day, though most others, including hula, yoga and slack-key guitar classes, meet once or twice a week during a month-long session. For the university's continuing-education and college credit classes, see p276.

Native Books/Nā Mea Hawai'i (Map ppp68-9; ☎ 596-8885; www.nativebookshawaii.com; Ward Warehouse, 1050 Ala Moana Blvd) Bookstore, art gallery and gift shop hosts free classes, workshops and demonstrations in hula dancing, Hawaiian language, traditional feather lei making and ukulele playing.

Temari Center for Asian and Pacific Arts (Map pp54-5; ☎ 536-4566; www.temaricenter.com; 1754 Lusitana St; courses $25-60) Make your own colorful souvenir to take home at this nonprofit center that perpetuates traditional Pacific Rim arts. The community-oriented center offers one-day courses in subjects like paper-making, lei making and fabric stenciling; many classes are family-friendly.

HONOLULU FOR KIDS

For grassy picnicking lawns, endless sand and calm waters, take the kids to Ala Moana Beach Park (p58); it's convenient to Waikiki, and there are lifeguards and outdoor showers to wash the sand off little feet. The Bishop Museum (p74) has plenty of entertainment for kids of all ages; a planetarium chronicles star-guided navigational systems that guided ancient Polynesians to Hawaii; and the Science Adventure Center lets you walk through an erupting volcano. In the basement of the Honolulu Academy of Arts (p67) you'll find an interactive arts-and-crafts center made specially for families. At the harborfront Hawai'i Maritime Center (p64), older kids can climb down into the hull of the *Falls of Clyde*, a 19th-century ship that once plied the Pacific trading routes. If you crave a fresh breath of the outdoors, drive up into the Upper

Water garden at the Lyon Arboretum (p72), Manoa Valley
LINDA CHING

Manoa Valley to visit Lyon Arboretum (p72) or make the family-friendly hike to Manoa Falls (p76). For little arts-and-crafters, check out the Temari Center for Asian and Pacific Arts (opposite).

HAWAII CHILDREN'S DISCOVERY CENTER

Map pp54-5; ☎ 524-5437; www.discoverycenter hawaii.org; 111 'Ohe St; adult/senior $10/6, child 1-17yr $6.75; ☽ 9am-1pm Tue-Fri, 10am-3pm Sat & Sun; P 🚍 19, 20 & 42

With plenty of aloha, this hands-on kiddie zone designed for tots and young students is an entertaining diversion on a rainy day. The 'Fantastic You' exhibit explores the human body, where kids can walk through a mock-up of a human stomach. In the 'Your Town' section, kids can drive an interactive fire engine or become a TV interviewer, while the 'Hawaiian Rainbows' and 'Rainbow World' sections touch on multicultural life in historical and contemporary Hawaii, letting kids pretend to be farmers or ship captains. The museum is near Kaka'ako Waterfront Park (p58).

TOURS

For a self-guided walking tour of downtown Honolulu, see p79. Guided walking tours of Chinatown are peppered with historical insights and often take you into a few places that you'd be unable to visit by yourself. Myriad sunset sails, dinner cruises and party boats leave daily from Kewalo Basin, just west of Ala Moana Beach Park. Many provide transport to/from Waikiki and advertise various specials; check out the free tourist magazines for the latest offers.

Atlantis Adventures (Map pp60-1; ☎ 973-1311, 800-548-6262; www.atlantisadventures.com; Pier 6, Aloha Tower Dr) Offers daytime lunch-buffet and sunset dinner cruises aboard *Navatek I*, a sleek, high-tech catamaran designed to minimize rolling.

Hawaii Food Tours (☎ 926-3663, 800-715-2468; www.hawaiifoodtours.com; tours incl transportation $99-$149) Former chef and restaurant critic for the *Honolulu Advertiser* designs a four-hour lunchtime tour sampling Chinatown's ethnic holes-in-the-wall, while a three-hour evening tour delves into traditional Hawaiian and contemporary island cuisine.

Hawai'i Heritage Center (Map pp60-1; ☎ 521-2749; 1117 Smith St; tours $10; ☽ 9:30-11.30am Wed & Fri)

CRUISING FOR ART

Smartly dressed professionals now flock to once-seedy Nu'uanu Ave in Chinatown for art, socializing, music and barhopping. The city's **First Friday Gallery Walk** (☽ 5-9pm 1st Friday of month) is prime time for Chinatown's art galleries, which set out free *pupu* (snacks) and host live entertainment to lure browsers. You can pick up a gallery walking map from any of two dozen art galleries (see the boxed text, p96), mostly clustered in a two-block area radiating out from the landmark Hawaii Theatre (p65). Grab dinner at a nearby restaurant (p83) before hitting the nightlife scene (p91) that cranks up later in the evening.

Leads walking tours of Chinatown, beginning at the center's storefront gallery.

FESTIVALS & EVENTS

For more island-wide festivals and events, see p272.

Chinese New Year (☎ 533-3181; www.chinatownhi .com) Between late January and mid-February, festivities include a downtown parade with lion dances and crackling firecrackers.

Great Aloha Fun Run (www.greataloharun.com) Popular 8.15-mile fun run from Honolulu Harbor's Aloha Tower to Aiea's Aloha Stadium on Presidents' Day (third Monday in February).

Honolulu Festival (☎ 926-2424; www.honolulufesti val.com) Two days of Asian-Pacific cultural exchange with a crafts fair and music, dance and drama performances at various venues in mid-March.

Pan-Pacific Festival (p115) Three days of Hawaiian, Japanese and South Pacific live entertainment in early June, with music, dancing and *taiko* drumming at the Ala Moana Center.

King Kamehameha Hula Competition (☎ 586-0333; http://hawaii.gov) One of Hawaii's biggest hula contests, with around 500 dancers competing at the Neal S Blaisdell Center (Map pp68–9) in early June.

Queen Lili'uokalani Keiki Hula Competition (☎ 521-6905; http://web.mac.com/kpca) Children's hula troupes from throughout Hawaii perform at the Neal S Blaisdell Center (Map pp68–9) in mid-July.

Prince Lot Hula Festival (☎ 839-5334; www.mgf -hawaii.org) Held at Moanalua Gardens (p74) on the third Saturday of July, this major hula event features Hawaii's leading hula schools.

HONOLULU

Hawaii Dragon Boat Festival Colorful Chinese dragon boats race to the beat of island drummers at Ala Moana Beach Park (p58) in late August.

Talk Story Festival (☎ 768-3003; www.co.honolulu .hi.us/parks/programs) Storytellers gather at Ala Moana Beach Park (p58) over a long weekend in mid-October; Friday is usually spooky stories.

our pick **Hawaii International Film Festival** (www .hiff.org) This celebration of celluloid packs the city's movie theaters with homegrown and imported Pacific Rim and Asian films for 10 days in late October.

King Kalakaua's Birthday Festive Victorian-era decorations and a concert of traditional monarchy-era music by the Royal Hawaiian Band at 'Iolani Palace (p59) on November 16.

Honolulu Marathon (☎ 734-7200; www.honolulu marathon.org) The USA's third-largest marathon starts at Ala Moana Beach Park on the second Sunday of December (see also p116).

EATING

While the city may not be widely known as a chowhound capital, Honolulu has an unmatched variety of restaurants that reflects O'ahu's multiethnic mosaic. The key is to get out of the touristy areas (ahem, Waikiki Beach) and eat where locals do.

Downtown Honolulu

Downtown Honolulu, once the domain of only bland quick-lunch stops, has blossomed into a dining destination in its own right. Cheerful weekday cafes for office workers abound downtown, while the Aloha Tower Marketplace has breezy waterfront tables.

GREAT HARVEST BREAD CO
Bakery $

Map pp60-1; ☎ 587-0017; 233 Merchant St; items $1-7; ⏱ 6:30am-4:30pm Mon-Fri

Never mind that this is a franchise chain when the whole-grain goodies (hello, vegans!) are this good: tropical coconut-banana-pineapple bars, peanut-butter cookies, Tuscan chicken sandwiches laden with tomatoes. It's mostly brown-bag service, but there's a small counter with a half-dozen stools by the street-front windows.

🌿 VITA JUICE
Takeout $

Map pp60-1; ☎ 526-1396; 1111-C Fort St Mall; snacks $4-6; ⏱ 7am-5pm Mon-Fri, 9am-3pm Sat

Top Picks
LATE-NIGHT EATS
- **Shokudo Japanese** (p86)
- **Side Street Inn** (p86)
- **Yanagi Sushi** (p87)
- **Liliha Bakery** (p89)
- **Sorabol** (p87)

Flooded with students from nearby Hawai'i Pacific University, this orange-walled juice and smoothie bar takes the concept of 'brain food' seriously. Healthy, alt-minded ingredients on the menu range from Amazonian *açai* and Tibetan *goji* berries to green tea and ginseng. Homemade cookies and hard-boiled eggs are also good-for-you fuel. On hot, sticky days order a 'Big Island Snow Bowl' of shave ice.

HONOLULU CAFÉ
American $

Map pp60-1; ☎ 533-1555; Pacific Guardian Center, 741 Bishop St; mains $4-10; ⏱ 7:45am-4pm Mon-Fri

This chef-owned courtyard cafe is inside the old Dillingham Transportation Building, one of the hubs of US 'robber barons' who once ruled Hawaii's economy. The light fare features hot grilled panini sandwiches and entree salads with citrus dressing; daily specials are more adventurous. It's an easy walk from the Aloha Tower Marketplace.

🌿 DOWNTOWN
Island Contemporary $$

Map pp60-1; ☎ 536-5900; 1040 Richards St; mains $6-15; ⏱ lunch Mon-Fri, dinner 1st Fri of month

Hidden on the ground floor of the Hawai'i State Art Museum, this arty cafe is a downtown outpost of Kaimuki's trendy Town (p90) restaurant. 'Local first, organic whenever possible' is still the theme, with fresh salads, soups and sandwiches that break through culinary barriers – think cantaloupe sorbet, lotus-root chips and ginger chicken sandwiches. Make reservations or grab a haute plate lunch to go from the 'ASAP' takeout counter.

🌿 CAFE LANIAKEA
Island Contemporary $$

our pick Map pp60-1; ☎ 538-7061; 1040 Richards St; mains $8-12; ⏱ lunch Mon-Fri

Highlights at this classy courtyard cafe in the Julia Morgan–designed YWCA include organic 'Nalo salads, North Shore free-range beef burgers and fresh ocean-catch club sandwiches with Maui onions and Wailalua tomatoes, along with chocolate cream puffs and 'passionberry' iced tea. Health-conscious and committed to local ingredients, this chic spot attracts a very different crowd from your average YWCA mess hall.

VINO
Italian/Tapas $$

Map pp60-1; ☎ 524-8466; Restaurant Row, 500 Ala Moana Blvd; dishes $7-19; ☻ 5:30-9:30pm Wed & Thu, 5:30pm-12:30am Fri, 5:30-10:30pm Sat

Drop by for some seasonally inspired Italian tapas – crispy fried octopus, roasted wild-mushroom chowder and butternut-squash lasagna – wrapped up in a sleek, modern, date-worthy setting that's also great for boisterous groups. The world-ranging, sommelier-picked wine list gets an enthusiastic nod from *Wine Spectator*.

FORT STREET BAR & GRILL
Island Contemporary $$

Map pp60-1; ☎ 523-1500; Topa Financial Center, 745 Fort St Mall; mains $8-15; ☻ lunch Mon-Fri, dinner Wed-Fri

For dressed-down contemporary American fare with an island twist, this unpretentious spot is Colin Nishida's latest addition to the Side Street Inn (p86) family. Office workers roll in after work for island *pupu* platters and karaoke. The chef's famous pork chops are usually served here on Wednesday.

HIROSHI EURASIAN TAPAS
Eurasian $$$

our pick Map pp60-1; ☎ 533-4476; Restaurant Row, 500 Ala Moana Blvd; mains $22-37; ☻ dinner

A longtime player on the Honolulu culinary scene, Hiroshi Fukui, the former chef at L'Uraku, has emerged with his own restaurant. Look for a Japanese twist on reigning Pacific Rim fusion styles, from crab cannelloni with miso sauce to smoked *hamachi* (yellowtail) with a garlicky habanero pepper kick, served with refreshing real fruit-puree sodas and foamy tropical vodka martinis. Reservations recommended.

Also recommended:

People's Open Market (Map pp60-1; ☎ 522-7088; City Hall parking lot deck, cnr Alapa'i & Beretania Sts; ☻ 10-11am Wed) Farmers market sells fresh bounty from the land and sea.

'Umeke Market & Deli (Map pp60-1; ☎ 522-7377; 1001 Bishop St; ☻ 7am-4pm Mon-Fri) Fresh, organic island produce, natural-food groceries and a vegan-friendly takeout deli.

Gordon Biersch Brewery Restaurant (Map pp60-1; ☎ 599-4877; Aloha Tower Marketplace, 1 Aloha Tower Dr; mains $10-28; ☻ 10am-11pm Sun-Thu, 10am-midnight Fri & Sat) Waterfront chain matches decent microbrews with island-style *pupu*; live music on weekends.

Chai's Island Bistro (Map pp60-1; ☎ 585-0011; Aloha Tower Marketplace, 1 Aloha Tower Dr; dinner mains $28-48; ☻ 11am-10pm Tue-Fri, 4-10pm Sat-Mon) Hit-or-miss contemporary Pacific Rim cuisine is overshadowed by famous-name live entertainment (p92).

Chinatown

With its crowded, boisterous markets (p65) overflowing with fresh produce, meat and fish, it's no surprise that this neighborhood has Honolulu's best dining deals. Chinese restaurants are plentiful, but the cavalcade doesn't stop there – you'll find dishes from all across Asia and the Pacific Rim cooked up here.

ROYAL KITCHEN
Chinese $

Map pp60-1; ☎ 524-4461; Chinatown Cultural Plaza, 100 N Beretania St; snacks $1; ☻ 5:30am-4pm Mon-Fri, 6:30am-4:30pm Sat, 6:30am-2pm Sun

A simple takeout shop, Royal Kitchen is worth fighting Chinatown's traffic headaches for. It's famous for its baked *manapua* (Chinese-style steamed buns) with a tantalizing selection of fillings: *char siu* (barbecued pork), chicken curry, sweet potato, *kalua* (cooked in a pit) pig, sugary coconut and more.

SUN CHONG CO
Bakery $

Map pp60-1; ☎ 537-3525; 127 N Hotel St; snacks around $1.50; ☻ 7am-5pm

You'd better come early to buy Chinese baked goods like almond cookies and other pastries at bargain prices. It's also the place to buy dried and sugared foods – everything from candied ginger and pineapple to dried squash and lotus root. It's like an experimental museum for the senses.

MEI SUM DIM SUM
Chinese $

Map pp60-1; ☎ 531-3268; 65 N Pauahi St; dim sum dishes $2-4, mains $6-12; ☻ 7am-8:45pm

Where else can you go to satisfy that crazy craving for dim sum in the afternoon or evening? For over 10 years, this no-nonsense little corner shop has been cranking out a multitude of cheap, delectable little plates. It's also got a full spread of Chinese mains – ask for the secret garlic eggplant that's not on the menu.

LEGEND VEGETARIAN RESTAURANT
Chinese/Vegetarian $

Map pp60-1; ☎ 532-8218; Chinatown Cultural Plaza, 100 N Beretania St; mains $8-13; ⏰ 10:30am-2pm Thu-Tue

This 100%-vegetarian Buddhist Chinese dining spot offers savory, imaginative dishes (vegetarian butterfish! sweet-and-sour vegetarian pork!) that creatively use tofu and wheat gluten to duplicate the flavors of meat and seafood. The menu is extensive.

LEGEND SEAFOOD RESTAURANT
Chinese $

Map pp60-1; ☎ 532-1868; Chinatown Cultural Plaza, 100 N Beretania St; dim sum dishes $2.50-4, mains $8-20; ⏰ 10:30am-2pm Mon-Fri, 8am-2pm Sat & Sun, 5:30-9:30pm daily

Brightly lit and busy, this impersonal banquet restaurant is best known for peddling dim sum. Spinach and scallop dumplings get wheeled around on the steam cart, followed by the pan-fried cart (turnip cakes and BBQ pork pastries) and then the dessert cart (egg custard, anyone?). The variety of tasty morsels here is greater than at other dim sum restaurants, but you've also got more competition from savvy locals.

BA LE
Vietnamese $

Map pp60-1; ☎ 521-3973; 150 N King St; mains $3-9; ⏰ 6am-5pm Mon-Sat, 6am-3pm Sun

This fluorescent-lit bakery-cafe is part of a Hawaii-wide chain established by a Vietnamese immigrant. Best known for its chewy baguette sandwiches, you can also scratch that spring-roll itch here. For a caffeine jolt, there's an equally chewy coffee, either hot or iced, served with loads of sugar and milk. There's another downtown branch at 1154 Fort St Mall.

TO CHAU
Vietnamese $

Map pp60-1; ☎ 533-4549; 1007 River St; mains $5-8; ⏰ 8:30am-2:30pm

Always packed, this Vietnamese restaurant holds fast to its reputation for serving Honolulu's best *pho* (Vietnamese noodle soup). Beef, broth and vegetables – the dish is a complete meal in itself, but the menu includes other Vietnamese standards. It's so popular that even at 10am you may have to queue for one of the 16 tables.

KEN FONG
Chinese $

Map pp60-1; ☎ 537-6858; 1030 Smith St; mains $5-12; ⏰ 10:30am-3pm & 5-9pm Mon-Sat

Blithely ignore the fashionably chic Chinatown art scene at this home-style storefront that the art-gallery hipsters don't know about yet. Feast on savory roast duck or ginger chicken atop a mountain of jasmine rice, or tuck into a spicy lamb hot-pot casserole. The family that cooks here, eats here – now that's a real vote of confidence.

MAUNAKEA MARKETPLACE
Pan-Asian $

Map pp60-1; 1120 Maunakea St; meals from around $6; ⏰ 7am-3:30pm

For island-style local grinds, head to the food court of this open-air marketplace, where you'll find about 20 stalls dishing out home-style Chinese, Filipino, Thai, Vietnamese, Korean and Japanese fare. You can chow down at tiny wooden tables crowded into the central walkway.

MABUHAY CAFE & RESTAURANT
Filipino $

Map pp60-1; ☎ 545-1956; 1049 River St; mains $6-12; ⏰ 10am-10pm

The red-and-white checked tablecloths, well-worn counter stools and jukebox should clue you in that this is a mom-and-pop joint. In fact, they've been cooking up pots full of succulent, garlic-laden pork adobo and *kare-kare* (oxtail stew) on this same corner by the river since the 1960s.

LITTLE VILLAGE NOODLE HOUSE
Chinese $

our pick Map pp60-1; ☎ 545-3008; 1113 Smith St; mains $8-15; ⏰ 10:30am-10:30pm Sun-Thu, 10:30am-midnight Fri & Sat

If you live for anything fishy in black bean sauce, this is the gold standard for Honolulu. With special attention paid to the northern provinces, highlights on the eclectic pan-Chinese menu include spicy shrimp, plump Shanghai noodles and sizzling butterfish. For a cross-cultural combo, try the roasted pork with island-grown taro.

Lavish buffet table at Indigo   ANN CECIL

contemporary tastes of Hawaii and Asia. Creative dim sum appetizers such as 'ahi tempura rolls and goat cheese wontons appear at lunchtime. Dinners include Malaysian beef *rendang*, Pacific fish topped with cocoa-bean curry wrapped in a banana leaf, and pork ribs with pineapple chutney. An award-winning wine list matches the inspired menu, while serious martinis fuel the late-night bar scene (p91).

Central Honolulu & Ala Moana

Shopping malls are ground zero for this neighborhood, but many of the tastiest places are spread out along east–west thoroughfares or hidden on dumpy-looking side streets.

Reservations recommended. Free parking behind the restaurant.

SOUL DE CUBA   Cuban $$
Map pp60-1; ☎ 545-2822; 1121 Bethel St; mains $7-22; ⊙ 11:30am-10pm Mon-Thu, 11:30am-11pm Fri & Sat

Nowhere in Honolulu can you sate that craving for Afro-Cuban food, along with cocktails and live music, except at this hip resto-lounge near the Chinatown art galleries. Stick with the family-recipe classics like *ropa vieja* (shredded beef in tomato sauce) and black bean soup. The *mojitos* are out of this world.

DUC'S BISTRO   Eurasian $$$
Map pp60-1; ☎ 531-6325; 1188 Maunakea St; lunch mains $12-19, dinner $16-32; ⊙ lunch Mon-Fri, dinner Mon-Sat

Honolulu's bigwigs hang out after work at this swank French-Vietnamese bistro with a tiny Manhattan-like bar. Ignore the surrounding seedy streets and step inside for flat-iron steaks, buttery escargot, pan-fried fish with green mango relish, and fire-roasted eggplant with spicy lime dressing. A small jazz combo performs most evenings.

INDIGO   Eurasian $$$
Map pp60-1; ☎ 521-2900; 1121 Nu'uanu Ave; dinner mains $18-30; ⊙ 11:30am-2pm Tue-Fri, 6-9:30pm Tue-Sat

Hobnob with the Hawaii Theatre crowd at this smart, chef-driven eatery serving up

MAKAI MARKET   Food Court $
Map pp68-9; ground level, Ala Moana Center, 1450 Ala Moana Blvd; meals $6-12; ⊙ 9am-9pm Mon-Sat, 9am-7pm Sun

Bringing the Asian-style marketplace indoors, this above-average mall food court is a circus of neon signs, hundreds of tiny tables crowded together and dozens of fast-food stalls. Search out Yummy Korean BBQ, CoCo Curry House for Japanese-style curries, Donburi Don-Don for Japanese rice bowls, and island-flavored Lahaina Chicken Company and Ala Moana Poi Bowl.

DA SPOT   Eclectic/Takeout $
Map pp68-9; ☎ 941-1313; 908 Pumehana St; smoothies around $5, plate lunches $7-10; ⊙ 10am-9:30pm Mon-Wed, Fri & Sat, 10am-4pm Thu

You'll find this enterprising duo of chef-owners setting up shop at farmers markets and on the UH campus, but this neighborhood storefront is still home base for takeout smoothies and plate lunches, both world fusion and local island–flavored. The Egyptian chicken, Southeast Asian curries and homemade baklava get rave reviews.

KAKA'AKO KITCHEN   Island Contemporary $
Map pp68-9; ☎ 596-7488; Victoria Ward Center, 1200 Ala Moana Blvd; meals $7-12; ⊙ 8am-9pm Mon-Thu, 8am-10pm Fri & Sat, 8am-5pm Sun

Although it's not as 'ono (delicious) as it once was, this takeout joint still serves functional plate-lunch meals with brown rice and organic salad. For a gastronomic edge,

HONOLULU

order a gourmet plate with crispy sweet-chili chicken or a seared 'ahi sandwich on a taro bun. Daily specials may disappoint. Also at Airport Industrial Park (Map pp54–5).

MEKONG II
Thai $

Map pp68-9; ☎ 941-6184; 1726 S King St; mains $8-12; ⏱ 11am-2pm Mon-Fri, 5-9pm daily

One of Honolulu's oldest Thai restaurants, famed for its spicy 'Evil Jungle Prince' curry, this hole-in-the-wall may not have the most authentic tastes in town, but it's a filling lunch stop. The artfully presented *pad thai* is also worth detouring for.

GYU-KAKU
Japanese $$

Map pp68-9; ☎ 589-2989; 1221 Kapi'olani Blvd; shared plates $4-21; ⏱ 5-11pm Sun-Thu, 5pm-midnight Fri & Sat

Everybody loves a good grill-it-yourself barbecue place. So round up your entourage and settle in at this crowd-pleasing chain for Kobe rib eye steak, *kalbi* short ribs, garlic shrimp, *enoki* mushrooms or grilled beef tongue, served with plentiful sweet and spicy marinades and dips. Enter off Hopaka St.

SHOKUDO JAPANESE
Japanese $$

Map pp68-9; ☎ 941-3701; Ala Moana Pacific Center, 1585 Kapi'olani Blvd; shared plates $7-17; ⏱ 11:30am-1am Sun-Thu, 11:30am-2am Fri & Sat, last call 1hr before closing

This sleek, modern Japanese restaurant (*shokudō* means 'dining room') is always filled to the rafters, especially with late-night diners. A mixed traditional Japanese and island fusion menu lists dizzying dozens of small plates, from *mochi* cheese gratin to lobster dynamite rolls, as well as more traditional noodle and sushi options and house-made tofu. Reservations recommended. Validated parking in the rear off Kona St.

SIDE STREET INN
Island Contemporary $$

our pick Map pp68-9; ☎ 591-0253; 1225 Hopaka St; plate lunches $6-8, shared plates $8-18; ⏱ 10:30am-1:30pm Mon-Fri, 4pm-midnight daily

The outside looks like hell, and the sports-bar atmosphere surely wouldn't rate on a Zagat's survey, but this late-night mecca attracts Honolulu's best chefs after their own kitchens close, along with a faithful following of locals and foodies who come for hearty portions of *kalbi* short ribs and

famous pan-fried pork chops. At lunch, join the line-up of construction workers ordering plate lunches at the counter.

SUSHI IZAKAYA GAKU
Japanese $$

Map pp68-9; ☎ 589-1329; 1329 S King St; dishes $8-25; ⏱ 5-11pm Mon-Sat

Known by word-of-mouth, this *izakaya* (Japanese pub serving food) beats the competition with its adherence to tradition and supremely fresh sushi and sashimi – no fusion novelty rolls named after caterpillars or California here. A spread of savory and sweet, hot and cold dishes include such hard-to-find specialties as *chazuke* (tea-soaked rice porridge) and even *natto* (fermented soybeans). Reservations recommended.

JIMBO RESTAURANT
Japanese $$

Map pp68-9; ☎ 947-2211; 1936 S King St; mains $9-14; ⏱ 11am-3pm daily, 5-10pm Sun-Thu, 5-10:30pm Fri & Sat

Jimbo is famous across the island for making its own silky soba and thick udon noodles fresh daily, always flavorful and chewy. You can slurp your way to happiness with hot noodle soup on rainy days, or in a cold dish on summer afternoons. For even more Japanese comfort food, order *donburi* (rice bowls). Cash only.

✿ PAVILION CAFÉ
Island Contemporary $$

Map pp68-9; ☎ 532-8734; Honolulu Academy of Arts, 900 S Beretania St; mains $9-15; ⏱ 11:30am-1:30pm Tue-Sat

Market-fresh salads and sandwiches made from island produce, a decent wine selection and tempting desserts make this an indulgent way to support the arts. Romantic tables facing the courtyard fountains are equally suited to dates or power-broker lunches. Reservations recommended, especially if a special exhibit or event is taking place.

MICHINOKU
Japanese $$

Map pp68-9; ☎ 942-1414; 1614 Kalakaua Ave; mains lunch $9-15, dinner $12-20; ⏱ lunch & dinner Tue-Sun

Step behind the tea-green curtain into this cozy country kitchen, which looks as if it belongs in the Japanese Alps. You may be flustered by the Japanese menu, but all you really need to know is that this little shop is famous for its *donburi* (rice bowls) topped with anything from broiled *unagi* (eel) or salmon with *ikura* (fish roe) to *chirashizushi* (assorted sashimi). Order a *teishoku* (set meal) with rice, miso soup and veggies.

SORABOL
Korean $$$

Map pp68-9; ☎ 947-3113; 805 Ke'eaumoku St; mains $10-37; 🕑 24hr

Sorabol feeds lunching ladies by day and bleary-eyed clubbers before dawn. Detractors often sniff that its reputation is undeserved, but the rest of the city has undying gratitude for this around-the-clock Korean joint, most often visited in a drunken stupor. Barbecued *kalbi* short ribs and steamed butterfish are specialties. Warning: watch out for the late-night service charge of 20% tacked onto your bill.

YANAGI SUSHI
Japanese $$$

Map pp68-9; ☎ 597-1525; 762 Kapi'olani Blvd; à la carte sushi from $4, lunch $9-23, dinner $15-31; 🕑 11am-2pm daily, 5:30pm-2am Mon-Sat, 5:30-10pm Sun

From the outside, it may look like a tumbledown shack that has seen way better days. But you can join the clubbing crowd here for 'late bird' specials on average sushi and other standard Japanese fare after 10:30pm (avoid Sunday nights, though, which tend to be oddly deserted).

PAGODA FLOATING RESTAURANT
Buffet $$$

Map pp68-9; ☎ 948-8356; Pagoda Hotel, 1525 Rycroft St; buffet breakfast adult/child $11/9, brunch $24/12, dinner $28/15; 🕑 6:30-10am & 5-9:30pm Wed-Fri, 6:30-10:30am & 5-9:30pm Sat, 6:30-9:30am, 10am-2pm & 5-9:30pm Sun

A vaguely tropical atmosphere draws elderly crowds to the kitschy Pagoda Hotel (p97). The so-so breakfast buffet includes local favorites like Portuguese sausage. Dinner is a fancier spread of prime rib, crab legs, Hawaiian *poke* and sashimi. It's overpriced but there are worse buffets in Waikiki.

ALAN WONG'S PINEAPPLE ROOM
Hawaii Regional $$$$

Map pp68-9; ☎ 945-6573; www.alanwongs .com; 3rd fl, Macy's, Ala Moana Center, 1450 Ala Moana Blvd; prix-fixe lunch $22, dinner mains $19-35; 🕑 11am-8:30pm Mon-Fri, 8am-8:30pm Sat, 9am-3pm Sun

Though Honolulu foodies may disagree, we prefer this dressed-down cafe inside a high-end department store to Alan Wong's eponymous dining room (below) on King St. All the star chef's classics are made here in an open exhibition kitchen, plus the menu shows off some haute twists on island comfort food like the kalua-pig BLT sandwich and *loco moco* (rice, fried egg and hamburger patty) made with *kiawe*-grilled North Shore beef burgers. Desserts are killer, especially the five-sorbet sampler with knock-out pairings of fresh fruit and sweets.

🍴 ALAN WONG'S
Hawaii Regional $$$$

Map pp68-9; ☎ 949-2526; www.alanwongs .com; 1857 S King St; mains $27-52; 🕑 dinner

From the creative genius of Alan Wong, this special-occasion dining destination emphasizes fresh seafood and local produce, especially at bimonthly 'farmers series' dinners. The ginger-crusted *onaga* (red snapper) and twice-cooked *kalbi* short ribs are Wong's time-honored signature dishes. You can safely skip the multicourse tasting menus, which are both too experimental and too blasé, although the whimsical soup-and-sandwich combo with foie gras is delish. Reservations essential; ask for a window table with city views.

STAGE
Hawaii Regional $$$$

Map pp68-9; 2nd fl, Honolulu Design Center, 1250 Kapi'olani Blvd; 3-course prix-fixe lunch $25, dinner mains $29-49; 🕑 11:30am-1:30pm Mon-Fri, 6-8:30pm Mon-Sat

High-concept cuisine is matched by chic interior design and artwork at this ambitious dining room inside the ultramodern Honolulu Design Center. The dinner menu is crazily adventurous and the desserts amusing, but it's really only worth showing up for the prix-fixe lunch menu. Next door is the artful Amuse wine bar.

CHEF MAVRO
Hawaii Regional $$$$

Map pp68-9; ☎ 944-4714; www.chefmavro.com; 1969 S King St; 4-course dinner with/without wine pairings $108/69; 🕑 6:30-9:30pm Tue-Sun

Every foodie on O'ahu has heard of maverick George Mavrothalassitis, who may be Hawaii's most inventive chef. But this high-flying foodie mecca crashes and burns as often as it hits the mark with its whimsical, extremely experimental cuisine. You'll either have the meal of your life here or hate every dish you try, and either way the backhanded service and half-empty atmosphere often fall short.

For groceries and quick eats:

Ward Farmers Market & Marukai Market Place (Map pp68-9; ☎ 593-9888; Ward Gateway, 1020 Auahi St; ✆ 7am-8pm Mon-Sat, 7am-6pm Sun) Hawaiian and Asian dishes and ingredients, from local produce to prepared meals.

Foodland (Map pp68-9; ☎ 949-5044; Ala Moana Center, 1450 Ala Moana Blvd; ✆ 6am-10pm Mon-Fri, 7am-10pm Sat, 7am-8pm Sun) Full-service supermarket at Hawaii's biggest mall, with free parking.

Kua 'Aina (Map pp68-9; ☎ 591-9133; Victoria Ward Center, 1200 Ala Moana Blvd; mains $5-9; ✆ 10:30am-9pm Mon-Sat, 10:30am-8pm Sun) Outpost of Hale'iwa's gourmet burger joint, serving crispy matchstick fries.

University Area

The area around the University of Hawai'i's Manoa campus is packed with affordable ethnic restaurants, coffee shops and health-food stores. Most are a short walk from the three-way intersection of University Ave and S King and Beretania Sts.

WELL BENTO
Vegetarian/Takeout $$
Map p71; ☎ 941-5261; 2nd fl, 2570 S Beretania St; meals $7-13; ✆ 10:30am-9pm
This inconspicuous little takeout kitchen specializes in Zen macrobiotic meals free of refined sugar and dairy products. Tahini sauce and brown rice accompany anything from sliced tempeh and grilled tofu to blackened swordfish and steak, always fresh.

SHŌCHAN HIROSHIMA-YAKI
Japanese $$
Map p71; ☎ 947-8785; Puck's Alley, 1035 University Ave; mains $8-12; ✆ 11:30am-10pm (last order 9pm) Wed-Mon
Talk about a niche market: this sunny cafe grills up Hiroshima-style *okonomiyaki* (savory Japanese pancakes) layered with cabbage and barbecue-sauced *yakisoba* or udon noodles instead of flour and topped off by a crepe-thin fried egg, just like *obāchan* (grandma) used to make.

KIAWE GRILL BBQ & BURGERS
Fast Food $$
Map p71; ☎ 955-5500; 2334 S King St; mains $8-12; ✆ 10am-9pm Mon-Sat, 10am-8pm Sun

Enter a 1950s time warp inside this takeout joint, where green Formica tables heave with plastic plates of exotic venison, ostrich, buffalo and Kobe beef burgers piled high with heaping steak fries or spicy Korean vegetables (*kim chi* is just the beginning). After chowing down here, you'll smell like barbecue smoke for the rest of the day.

CAFE MAHARANI
Indian $$
Map p71; ☎ 951-7447; 2509 S King St; dishes $9-15; ✆ dinner
Although the original owners have packed up and left, this family-run restaurant still serves up some spicy standards like tandoori chicken and lamb curry, along with excellent true vegetarian dishes, such as eggplant tikka masala. Order 'em any way you want, from mild to tongue-searing hot. The free parking lot is usually full.

SPICES
Pan-Asian $$
Map p71; ☎ 949-2679; 2671-D S King St; mains $11-14; ✆ 11:30am-2pm Tue-Fri, 5:30-9:30pm Tue-Sat & 5-9pm Sun
This Southeast Asian restaurant has spiced up the university dining scene with Thai curries, Lao soups and Burmese noodles. The chefs sets a modern but neighborhood-friendly table, free of extraneous ethnic kitsch. Prices are higher than the norm, though.

TSUKUNEYA ROBATA GRILL
Japanese $$$
Map p71; ☎ 949-0390; 1442 University Ave; shared plates $4-38; ✆ 5pm-midnight Sun, Mon, Wed & Thu, 5pm-1am Fri & Sat
Imported from Nagoya, this sleek modern Japanese *robatayaki* skewers, grills and deep fries every carnivore's delight, including signature *tsukune* (meatballs) done in a dozen different styles. Kahuku shrimp from O'ahu's Windward Coast and spicy Hawaiian *'ahi* on a hot lava-rock platter are unique specialties of the house.

IMANAS TEI
Japanese $$$
our pick Map p71; ☎ 941-2626; 2626 S King St; shared plates $5-30; ✆ 5-11:30pm Mon-Sat
Look for the orange sign outside this long-standing *izakaya*, where staff all shout their welcome (*'Irrashaimase!'*) as you make your way inside to a low-slung tatami-mat table. Sake fans come here first for the liquid ver-

sion of rice, then graze their way through the menu of sushi and crowd-pleasing DIY *nabemono* (clay-pot meat and vegetable soups). The restaurant is tucked behind Puck's Alley.

For snack, groceries and takeout meals:

Bubbie's (Map p71; ☎ 949-8984; Varsity Center, 1010 University Ave; dishes $3-6; noon-midnight Mon-Thu, noon-1am Fri & Sat, noon-11:30pm Sun) Homemade ice cream in tropical flavors like papaya ginger and chocolate mochi.

Down to Earth Natural Foods (Map p71; ☎ 947-7678; 2525 S King St; 7:30am-10pm) Natural-food grocery store with a veg salad bar and deli, across the street from 24-hour Star Market.

Kokua Market (Map p71; ☎ 941-1922; 2643 S King St; 8:30am-8:30pm) Hawaii's only natural-food co-op has an organic salad bar and vegan-friendly deli.

Upper Manoa Valley, Tantalus & Makiki Heights

Although hiking boots may look out of place at these genteel cafes, they're conveniently close to the Upper Manoa Valley and Mt Tantalus trail networks.

CONTEMPORARY CAFÉ
Island Contemporary $$

Map p73; ☎ 523-3362; Contemporary Museum, 2411 Makiki Heights Dr; mains $8-10; lunch Tue-Sun

In the shady foothills of the Ko'olau Range high above downtown Honolulu, this elegant museum cafe spills out onto the lawn. Country club–worthy salads and sandwiches come with artisan breads, from focaccia to multigrain loaves, with cheesecake and chocolate gâteau for dessert. Call ahead to order a picnic basket lunch (wine corkage fee $5) to enjoy on woven *lauhala* mats in the sculpture gardens.

WAI'OLI TEA ROOM
Bakery/Cafe $$

Map p73; ☎ 988-5800; 2950 Manoa Rd; mains $6-13, high tea $19; 10:30am-3:30pm Mon-Fri, 8am-3:30pm Sat & Sun, high tea 10:30am-3:30pm daily

If author Robert Louis Stevenson were still hanging around Honolulu today, this is where you'd find him; the grass shack in which he lived during the late 1800s stood here until just a few years ago. This restaurant set in the verdant Manoa Valley still exudes period charm. Its open-air dining room looks onto gardens of red ginger and birds-of-paradise. Light eats like cinnamon-apple waffles and chicken-curry sandwiches are served, but the real event is afternoon high tea (by reservation only).

Greater Honolulu

On the east side of the city, along Wai'alae Ave, Kaimuki is making its mark on Honolulu's cuisine scene with an increasing number of trendy urban restaurants. It's also where you'll find **Whole Foods** (Map pp54-5; ☎ 738-0820; 4211 Wai'alae Ave; 7am-10pm), an organic grocery store with a takeout deli. More off-the-beaten-path eateries are scattered around the metro area, from the waterfront to the hills.

LILIHA BAKERY
Coffee Shop $

Map pp54-5; ☎ 531-1651; 515 N Kuakini; snacks from $1.50, mains $6-10; 6am-midnight Tue, 24hr Wed-Sat, midnight-8pm Sun

Not too far from downtown Honolulu, this old-school island bakery and diner causes a neighborhood traffic jam for its coco-puff cream pastries, which also come in a rainbow of other flavors, including green tea. Still hungry? Grab a counter seat and order a hamburger steak or other hearty lumberjack faves in the coffee shop.

HELENA'S HAWAIIAN FOOD
Hawaiian $

Map pp54-5; ☎ 845-8044; 1240 N School St; dishes $2-10; 10:30am-7:30pm Tue-Fri

Walking through the door is like stepping into another era. Even though long-time owner Helena Chock has passed away, her grandson still commands the family kitchen. Most people order à la carte. Start with *poi* (fermented taro paste) and rice and add a couple of small plates of smoky *pipi kaula* (beef jerky), *kalua* pig, fried butterfish or squid cooked in coconut milk, and you've got a mini luau for just over $10.

NICO'S AT PIER 38
Seafood $

Map pp54-5; ☎ 540-1377; 1133 N Nimitz Hwy; mains $4-10; 6:30am-5pm Mon-Fri, 6:30am-2:30pm Sat

Chef Nico was inspired by the island cuisine scene to merge his classical French training with the humble island plate lunch. French standards like *steak frite* appear alongside market-fresh fish sandwiches and local belly-fillers such as chicken *katsu* and hoisin BBQ chicken. Casual tables are near the waterfront and Honolulu's fish auction.

MAGURO-YA
Japanese $$
Map pp54-5; ☎ 732-3775; 3565 Wai'alae Ave; dinner mains $17-20; 11am-1:45pm Tue-Sat, 5-9:30pm Tue-Thu & Sun, 5-10pm Fri & Sat

Japanese tourists make the trek out to the 'Tuna Shop' for a taste of home, so you know you're in good hands here. Jostle for a spot at the sushi bar, or savor the traditional *teishoku* (combination) meals including tempura, sashimi and sushi, *hijiki* (seaweed), rice and delicate *chawanmushi* (savory egg custard).

12TH AVENUE GRILL
Island Contemporary $$$
Map pp54-5; ☎ 732-9469; 1145-C 12th Ave; mains $18-29; dinner Mon-Sat

Hidden on a side alley south of Wai'alae Ave, this neighborhood bistro with dark wood booths and low lighting looks like it belongs in San Francisco, not Honolulu. Nouveau takes on comfort food include porter-braised short ribs and BBQ-rubbed, grass-fed Big Island rib-eye steak or gnocchi with locally caught abalone. Not everything on the menu hits the mark, but there's a value-priced wine list.

🍽 TOWN
Island Contemporary $$$
our pick Map pp54-5; ☎ 735-5900; 3435 Wai'alae Ave; mains breakfast & lunch $6-15, dinner $15-22; 6:30am-9:30pm Mon-Thu, 6:30am-10pm Fri & Sat

At this hip modern bistro, one of O'ahu's hottest foodie destinations, you can watch the Kaimuki action buzz past. Its motto –

Top Picks
LOCALS' HANGOUTS
- Ala Moana Beach Park (p58)
- Hank's Cafe (p92)
- Movie Museum (p94)
- Makiki Forest Recreation Area (p77)
- Side Street Inn (p86)

'local first, organic whenever possible, with aloha always' – characterizes the daily-changing menu. Even elemental burgers and steaks are made from cattle raised hormone-free on the North Shore. An oh-so-casual atmosphere and urban-coffee-shop decor – imagine stainless steel and dark wood tables and original artwork – belie the serious goodness of the boldly flavored cooking. Neighborhood yoga teachers and surfers don't even blink when the stars of *Lost* drop by.

Also worth a detour:

W&M Bar-B-Q Burger (Map pp54-5; ☎ 734-3350; 3104 Wai'alae Ave; snacks $2-5; 10am-4:30pm Wed-Fri, 9am-4:30pm Sat & Sun) Old-school burger joint grilling 'em up with secret sauce since the 1940s.

Mitch's Sushi (Map pp54-5; ☎ 837-7774; 524 Ohohia St; meals $50-100; 11:30am-7:30pm) A 13-seat sushi bar near the airport is for cashed-up connoisseurs only; reservations essential.

DRINKING & ENTERTAINMENT
For current listings of live music gigs, DJ clubs, theaters, movies and cultural events, check out the free tabloid *Honolulu Weekly*, which comes out every Wednesday, and *Honolulu Advertiser's* TGIF section, published on Friday.

Inside thirtyninehotel art gallery and nightclub   ANN CECIL

Cafes

GLAZER'S ARTISAN COFFEE

Map p71; ☎ 391-6548; 2700 S King St;
⏲ 6:30am-11pm Mon-Thu, 6:30am-9pm Fri,
9am-11pm Sat & Sun; 🛜

Nobody in Honolulu is more serious about brewing the perfect lineup of espresso drinks than this university hangout, with comfy living-room sofas, jazzy artwork on the walls and plentiful electrical outlets to revive your laptop. Free wi-fi.

HONOLULU COFFEE COMPANY

Map p60-1; ☎ 521- 4400; 1001 Bishop St;
⏲ 6am-5:30pm Mon-Fri, 7am-noon Sat; 🛜

Overlooking Bishop Sq with city skyline views, here you can take a break for a java jolt brewed from hand-picked, hand-roasted 100% Kona estate-grown beans. Also at Ala Moana Center (Map pp68–9). Free wi-fi.

Bars, Lounges & Clubs

Every self-respecting bar in Honolulu has a *pupu* (snack) menu. Locals often call happy hour *pau hana* (literally, 'stop work'). For watering holes in Waikiki, see p135.

GREEN ROOM LOUNGE & OPIUM DEN

Map pp60-1; ☎ 521-2900; Indigo, 1121 Nu'uanu Ave; ⏲ 4-11:30pm Tue & Wed, 4pm-2am Thu-Sat

A small army of martinis are found at this bar and lounge inside Indigo restaurant (p85). Being on the edge of Chinatown and near the Hawaii Theatre, a mixed crowd gravitates here, with live music and DJs some nights spinning everything from funk and jazz to house and techno.

THE LOFT

Map pp60-1; ☎ 688-8813; 115 N Hotel St;
⏲ usually 9pm-2am Wed-Sun

On a seedy-looking stretch of Hotel St, where dive bars are usually the order of the day, this fashion-forward ultralounge, upstairs from a bakery, is a hip retreat, with glowing paper lanterns and a vivacious bar scene. DJs spin mostly down-tempo house and techno.

THIRTYNINEHOTEL

Map pp60-1; ☎ 599-2552; www.thirtyninehotel .com; 39 N Hotel St; ⏲ 4pm-2am Tue-Sat

More arty than clubby, this multimedia space is a gallery by day and low-key dance scene at night. Guest DJs from the mainland don their best aloha wear for special weekend appearances, while rock bands test the acoustics some weeknights.

BAR 35

Map pp60-1; ☎ 537-3535; 35 N Hotel St;
⏲ 4pm-2am Mon-Fri, 6pm-2am Sat

Nudging against Chinatown's happening thirtyninehotel, this urban bar has a dizzying 100 domestic and international bottled beers to choose from, and addictive chef-made gourmet fusion pizzas to go along with all the brews. There's live music most Saturday nights.

MAI TAI BAR

Map pp68-9; ☎ 947-2900; Ho'okipa Terrace, Ala Moana Center, 1450 Ala Moana Blvd;
⏲ 4pm-midnight

A happening bar in the middle of a shopping center? We don't make the trends, we just report 'em. During afternoon and late-night happy hours, this enormous circular bar is packed with a see-and-flirt crowd. Island-style live music plays nightly.

LIVING ROOM

Map pp68-9; ☎ 779-1421; Fisherman's Wharf, 1009 Ala Moana Blvd; cover Fri & Sat after 10pm $10; ⏲ 4:30pm-2am Tue & Wed, 4:30pm-4am Thu & Fri, 10pm-4am Sat

The laid-back, island-style nightclub upstairs, where DJs spin everything from reggae to house and hip-hop, is jumpin' Thursday to Saturday nights. The joint is even more popular during weekday happy hours, especially for its panoramic harborfront views.

LA MARIANA SAILING CLUB

our pick Map pp54-5; ☎ 848-2800; 50 Sand Island Access Rd; ⏲ 11am-9pm Sun-Thu, 11am-midnight Fri & Sat

Who says all the great tiki bars have gone to the dogs? Irreverent and unbelievably kitschy, this 1950s joint by the lagoon is filled with yachties and long-time locals. The classic mai tais are as killer as the other signature tropical potions, complete with tiki-head swizzle sticks. Grab a table by the water and fantasize about sailing to Tahiti.

HANK'S CAFE HONOLULU
Map pp60-1; ☎ 526-1410; 1038 Nu'uanu Ave;
🕙 3pm-1am
You can't get more low-key than this neighborhood bar on the edge of Chinatown. Owner Hank Taufaasau is a jack-of-all-trades when it comes to the barfly business: the walls are decorated with Polynesian-themed art, live music rolls in most nights and regulars practically call it home.

MURPHY'S BAR & GRILL
Map pp60-1; ☎ 531-0422; 2 Merchant St;
🕙 11:30am-10pm
Honolulu's version of a *Cheers* bar, this downtown pub pours Irish stouts and Hawaii-brewed beers. Just a block from the waterfront, the site hails back to the days of the whalers and lays claim to being the city's oldest saloon. There's an over-abundance of Irish pubs in the same neighborhood, most featuring live local bands on weekends.

VARSITY
Map p71; ☎ 447-9244; 1015 University Ave;
🕙 10am-2am
Even though Magoo's has changed its name, University of Hawai'i students still hang out at this open-air sidewalk bar, with plenty of cheap microbrews from Hawaii and the US mainland on tap (and $1 Pabst Blue Ribbon!). Thursday nights are really buzzing.

AKU BONE LOUNGE
Map pp68-9; ☎ 589-2020; 1201 Kona St;
🕙 5pm-2am
This down-home dive bar with a tasty *pupu* menu, cold Bud Light and a rubbah-slippah crowd is 'keeping Old Hawaii alive, one beer at a time.' Weekend nights are for karaoke, which are sung by patrons from

the comfort of their own tables, while live Hawaiian music takes over other nights.

For dance divas who just can't get enough:
Pearl (Map pp68-9; ☎ 944-8000; Ho'okipa Terrace, Ala Moana Center, 1500 Ala Moana Blvd; 🕙 4:30pm-2am Mon-Thu, 4:30pm-4am Fri, 7pm-4am Sat) Thirtysomething hotties crowd the pop and hip-hop dance floor and chandelier-lit terraces; expect bouncers with attitude.
Rumours (Map pp68-9; ☎ 955-4811; Ala Moana Hotel, 410 Atkinson Dr; 🕙 9pm-3:30am Fri & Sat) Top-40, '70s and '80s DJs spin for baby boomers and ironical twentysomethings.

Live Music
Waikiki is O'ahu's hub for traditional and contemporary Hawaiian sounds (p137). For more bars and clubs with live music, see also Bars, Lounges & Clubs (p91).

CHAI'S ISLAND BISTRO
Map pp60-1; ☎ 585-0011; Aloha Tower Marketplace, 1 Aloha Tower Dr; 🕙 11am-10pm Tue-Fri, 4-10pm Sat-Mon
Nobody really comes here for the food. But every night when the sun sets over the harbor, folks from all walks of life gather at this shopping-mall restaurant to hear some of the greatest contemporary Hawaiian musicians in the islands play. Show up when the Brothers Cazimero or Jerry Santos are playing.

JAZZ MINDS ART & CAFE
Map pp68-9; ☎ 945-0800; http://honolulu jazzclub.com; 1661 Kapi'olani Blvd; 🕙 9pm-2am Mon-Sat
Intimate and subdued, this jazz lounge with almost a speakeasy ambience pulls in the city's best talent, ranging from big band and bebop to fiery salsa and cutting-edge mini-

---

ALOHA, BEER GEEKS!
If you're searching for that perfect Hawaii-made pint glass from the westernmost state in the USA, you can round out your collection at the Big Island's **Kona Brewing Company** (p157) in southeast O'ahu, or stop by these Honolulu brewpubs:

■ **Sam Choy's Big Aloha Brewery** (Map pp54-5; ☎ 545-7979; 580 N Nimitz Hwy; 🕙 10:30am-9:30pm Sun-Thu, 10:30am-10pm Fri & Sat) Down microbrews next to shiny metal vats and blaring sports TVs; skip the pricey *pupu*.
■ **Gordon Biersch Brewery Restaurant** (Map pp60-1; ☎ 599-4877; 1st fl, Aloha Tower Marketplace, 1 Aloha Tower Dr; 🕙 10am-11pm Sun-Thu, 10am-midnight Fri & Sat) Fresh lagers made according to Germany's centuries-old purity laws; live music on weekends.

malist. Just don't let all the Asian tourist-oriented strip clubs nearby turn you off.

DRAGON UPSTAIRS
Map pp60-1; ☎ 526-1411; http://thedragonup stairs.com; 2nd fl, 1038 Nu'uanu Ave; ☽ usually evenings Wed-Sat

Right above friendly Hank's Cafe Honolulu (opposite), this little hideaway with a sedate older vibe and lots of funky artwork and mirrors hosts a rotating lineup of cool local jazz cats, from funk bands to bop trios and piano or vocal soloists.

PIPELINE CAFE
Map pp68-9; ☎ 589-1999; http://pipelinecafe hawaii.com; 805 Pohukaina St; ☽ schedule varies

A gargantuan warehouse in an industrial side street, this place has a punk-rock heart but also showcases hip-hop and heavy metal bands. You don't need multiple face piercings to blend in, but it doesn't hurt. There's often an admission charge, depending on the band.

ANNA BANNANAS
Map p71; ☎ 946-5190; 2440 S Beretania St; ☽ 9pm-2am Thu-Sat

A reliable college dive bar that's part road-house and part art house, Anna Bannanas goes beyond its retro-1960s atmosphere to feature alt-rock, reggae, Jawaiian, punk and metal bands. Now, if only they'd bring back those hookah pipes – sigh.

Performing Arts
Over a dozen community theater groups around the Honolulu metro area perform everything from David Mamet satires to Hawaiian pidgin fairy tales.

HAWAII THEATRE
Map pp60-1; ☎ 528-0506; www.hawaiitheatre .com; 1130 Bethel St

Beautifully restored, this grand dame of O'ahu's theater scene is a major venue for dance, music and theater. Performances include top Hawaii musicians like the Brothers Cazimero, contemporary plays, international touring acts and film festivals.

ARTS AT MARKS GARAGE
Map pp60-1; ☎ 521-2903; www.artsatmarks .com; 1159 Nu'uanu Ave

CHEAP THRILLS
Although Waikiki (p99) has the most free island-style entertainment in Honolulu, there's plenty going on elsewhere in the city, if you know where to look.

■ **Royal Hawaiian Band** (☎ 922-5331; www.royalhawaiianband.com; admission free) The Royal Hawaiian Band, which dates back to the days of the Hawaiian monarchy, still performs as it did a century ago in the bandstand outside 'Iolani Palace (Map pp60–1); check the website for more scheduled appearances around O'ahu.

■ **Ala Moana Center** (Map pp68-9; ☎ 955-9517; www.alamoanacenter.com; 1450 Ala Moana Blvd) The shopping center's Centerstage courtyard area is the venue for all sorts of free local entertainment, including island-born keiki hula shows every Sunday morning.

■ **Mayor's Office of Culture & the Arts** (MOCA; ☎ 768-6622; www.honolulu.gov/moca) Free city-sponsored hula shows, art exhibits and musical events at various venues; call for a recorded list of upcoming events.

■ **HawaiiSlam** (Map pp68-9; ☎ 387-9664; www .hawaiislam.com; Cupola Theatre, 2nd fl, Honolulu Design Center, 1250 Kapi'olani Blvd; admission $3-5; ☽ 8:30pm 1st Thu of month) One of the biggest poetry slams in the country, with international stars, artists, musicians and DJs sharing the stage.

At the cutting edge of the Chinatown arts scene, this community gallery (p96) and performance space puts on a cornucopia of live shows, from youth poetry slams and conversations with island artists to live jazz and Hawaiian music or Shakespearean plays.

NEAL S BLAISDELL CENTER
Map pp68-9; ☎ 591-2211; www.blaisdellcenter .com; 777 Ward Ave

This modern complex hosts concerts ranging from island artists to visiting rock stars. It's also the venue for Broadway shows, concerts by the Honolulu Symphony, Hawaii Opera Theatre performances, Hawaii Ballet recitals and more family-friendly events.

KUMU KAHUA THEATRE
Map pp60-1; ☎ 536-4441; www.kumukahua
.org; 46 Merchant St

This little 100-seat treasure in the restored
Kamehameha V Post Office building is
dedicated to premiering works by Hawaii's
playwrights, with themes focusing on contemporary multicultural island life, often
richly peppered with Hawaiian pidgin.

Smaller live-performance venues:
Doris Duke Theatre (Map pp68-9; ☎ 532-8768; www
.honoluluacademy.org; 900 S Beretania St) Multicultural
performing arts, chamber music concerts and
art lectures happen at the Honolulu Academy of
Arts (p67).
East-West Center (Map p71; ☎ 944-7111; www
.eastwestcenter.org; 1601 East-West Rd) Occasionally hosts
multicultural theater, concerts and films on the University
of Hawai'i campus (see p71).

Cinemas
For more theater locations, showtimes and
ticketing, check **Fandango** (☎ 800-326-3264; www
.fandango.com).
Doris Duke Theatre (Map pp68-9; ☎ 532-8768; www
.honoluluacademy.org; 900 S Beretania St; ⌚ schedules
vary) Shows experimental, alternative and art-house films,
especially ground-breaking documentaries, at the Honolulu
Academy of Arts (p67).
Movie Museum (Map pp54-5; ☎ 735-8771; www
.kaimukihawaii.com; 3566 Harding Ave; ⌚ noon-8pm
Thu-Sun) Screens classic oldies, foreign flicks and indie
films, with two dozen comfy Barcaloungers; reservations
recommended.
Restaurant Row 9 (Map pp60-1; ☎ 526-4171;
500 Ala Moana Blvd) Multiplex shows first-run movies.
Ward Stadium 16 (Map pp68-9; ☎ 593-3000; 1044
Auahi St) Multiplex screens new Hollywood releases.

SHOPPING
Antiques & Souvenirs
ANTIQUE ALLEY
Map pp68-9; ☎ 941-8551; 1347 Kapi'olani Blvd;
⌚ 11am-5pm

This cooperative shop is delightfully
crammed full of rare collectibles and other
cast-off memorabilia from Hawaii through
the decades. Vendors sell everything from
poi pounders and carved wooden bowls
to vintage hula dolls, Matson cruise-liner
artifacts and estate jewelry.

MALL ROLL CALL
Overlooking Honolulu Harbor, the
Aloha Tower Marketplace (Map pp60-1;
☎ 528-5700; 1 Aloha Tower Dr; ⌚ 9am-9pm
Mon-Sat, 9am-6pm Sun) has 50 shops of
varying quality, with barely an off-island
chain among them. **Ala Moana Center**
(Map pp68-9; ☎ 955-9517; 1450 Ala Moana Blvd;
⌚ 9:30am-9pm Mon-Sat, 10am-7pm Sun) is
Hawaii's largest shopping mall, boasting
nearly 300 department and mostly chain
stores, but also a few island specialty
shops like the Crack Seed Center. Nearby,
the open-air **Ward Centers** (Map pp68-9;
☎ 591-8411; cnr Ala Moana Blvd & Kamake'e St;
⌚ 10am-9pm Mon-Sat, 10am-6pm Sun), which
include the Ward Warehouse, offer a smaller,
more one-of-a-kind collection of island-
born shops.

LAI FONG DEPARTMENT STORE
Map pp60-1; ☎ 781-8140; 1118 Nu'uanu Ave;
⌚ 9am-7:30pm Mon-Sat

This family-owned shop sells a variety of
antiques and knickknacks, including Chinese silk and brocade clothing, imported
porcelain and vintage postcards of Hawaii
from the early 20th century. Tailor-made
clothing can still be ordered here.

HILO HATTIE
Map pp54-5; ☎ 535-6500; 700 Nimitz Hwy;
⌚ 9am-7pm

You can't escape ads for this warehouse
of kitschy Hawaiiana, built to process gigantic busloads of tourists. If you need a
cheap aloha shirt, matching muumuu or
plastic puka shell necklace, Waikiki's ubiquitous ABC Stores are probably cheaper,
however.

Top Picks
MUSEUM SHOPS
- Bishop Museum (p74)
- Hawai'i State Art Museum (p61)
- Honolulu Academy of Arts (p67)
- Queen Emma Summer Palace (p75)
- Hawaii Maritime Center (p64)

Cindy of Cindy's Lei Shop weaving flowered leis

LINDA CHING

Art & Crafts

NATIVE BOOKS/NĀ MEA HAWAI'I

Map pp68-9; ☎ 597-8967; Ward Warehouse, 1050 Ala Moana Blvd; ☺ 10am-9pm Mon-Sat, 10am-6pm Sun

So much more than just a bookstore stocking Hawaiiana titles and a rainbow array of CDs and DVDs, this cultural gathering spot also sells beautiful silk-screened fabrics, koa wood bowls, Hawaiian quilts and fish-hook jewelry. Pack your bags with Hawaii-made gourmet foodstuffs – Big Island honey, Maui sea salts, lavosh flatbread crackers – for all your friends and family back home.

JEFF CHANG POTTERY & FINE CRAFTS

Map pp60-1; ☎ 599-2502; 808 Fort St Mall; ☺ 10am-5pm Mon-Fri

Not everything at this beautiful downtown gallery is island-made, but it is all hand-crafted. The striking *raku* pottery is made by Chang himself. You'll also find exquisite hand-turned bowls of Hawaiian hardwoods, art jewelry and blown glass by some of Hawaii's finest artisans. There's another branch at Ward Warehouse (Map pp68–9).

NOHEA GALLERY

Map pp68-9; ☎ 596-0074; Ward Warehouse, 1050 Ala Moana Blvd; ☺ 10am-9pm Mon-Sat, 10am-6pm Sun

A soothing space amid the shopping-mall madness, this high-end gallery sells handcrafted jewelry, glassware, pottery and woodwork, the vast majority of it made in Hawaii. Island artisans occasionally give demonstrations of their craft on the sidewalk outside.

CINDY'S LEI SHOP

Map pp60-1; ☎ 536-6538, 877-536-0007; 1034 Maunakea St; ☺ 6am-8pm Mon-Sat, 6:30am-6pm Sun

At this inviting little corner shop, a Chinatown landmark, you can watch aunties craft flower lei made of orchids, plumeria, twining maile, lantern *'ilima* and ginger. Several more lei shops nearby will also pack lei for you to carry back home on the plane.

KAMAKA HAWAII

Map pp60-1; ☎ 531-3165; 550 South St; ☺ 8am-4pm Mon-Fri

Dozens of shops sell cheap plastic and wood ukuleles around Waikiki and Chinatown. But this legendary instrument maker near Restaurant Row specializes in the real thing: handcrafted ukuleles made on O'ahu, with prices starting around $500. In business since 1916, its signature instrument is a 'pineapple' ukulele with an oval-shaped body that produces a less twangy sound.

HULA SUPPLY CENTER

Map p71; ☎ 941-5379; 2338 & 2346 S King St; ☺ 9am-5:30pm Mon-Fri, 9am-5pm Sat

For 60 years, Hawaiian musicians and dancers have come here to get their *kukui*-nut lei, calabash drum gourds, Tahitian-style hula skirts, nose flutes and more.

Kapa-print aloha shirts and Hawaiiana CDs, DVDs and books are nifty souvenirs for nondancers.

Clothing & Shoes

MANUHEALI'I
Map pp68-9; ☎ 942-9868; 930 Punahou St; ⌚ 9:30am-6pm Mon-Fri, 9am-4pm Sat, 10am-3pm Sun

Island fashionistas look to this homegrown shop for original and modern designs. The flowing rayon dresses lightly take inspiration from the traditional muumuu, but are transformed into contemporary looks that are fresh and sassy. Silk aloha shirts for men show off big, bold tropical prints often worn by island musicians.

MONTSUKI
Map pp54-5; ☎ 734-3457; 1148 Koko Head Ave; ⌚ 9:30am-5pm Tue-Sat

In the Kaimuki neighborhood, the mother-daughter designer team of Janet and Patty Yamasaki refashion classic kimono and obi designs into modern dresses. East-West wedding dresses, formal attire or sleek day wear can all be custom-crafted.

ISLAND SLIPPER
Map pp68-9; ☎ 593-8229; Ward Warehouse, 1050 Ala Moana Blvd; ⌚ 10am-9pm Mon-Sat, 10am-6pm Sun

There are dozens of stores selling rubbah slippahs across Honolulu, but nobody else carries such large sizes – 'we have to fit the local people,' a clerk says – let alone such ultracomfy suede and leather styles, some made right here on the islands.

CINNAMON GIRL
Map pp68-9; ☎ 947-4332; Ala Moana Center, 1450 Ala Moana Blvd; ⌚ 9:30am-9pm Mon-Sat, 10am-7pm Sun

Flirty rayon dresses that are cool, contemporary and island-made hang on the racks of this trendy shop designed by O'ahu resident Jonelle Fujita. Sandals, bejeweled necklaces and sweet, old-fashioned accessories like floppy hats line the shelves.

LOCALS ONLY
Map pp68-9; ☎ 942-1555; Ala Moana Center, 1450 Ala Moana Blvd; ⌚ 9:30am-9pm Mon-Sat, 10am-7pm Sun

The brand name, which has been around since 1981, says it all. It's a casual place to pick up rayon reproductions of vintage aloha shirts and T-shirts that represent island lifestyles, such as a Rastafarian-colored *shaka* sign with the logo 'Keep Hawaii Green.'

T&L MUUMUU FACTORY
Map pp68-9; ☎ 941-4183; 1423 Kapi'olani Blvd; ⌚ 9am-6pm Mon-Sat, 10am-4pm Sun

---

CHINATOWN GALLERY HOPPING

Chinatown is bursting with dozens of art galleries, best visited during the **First Friday Gallery Walk** (p81):

- **ARTS at Marks Garage** (Map pp60-1; ☎ 521-2903; 1159 & 1161 Nu'uanu Ave; ⌚ 11am-6pm Tue-Sat) Eclectic works by up-and-coming island artists in all types of media.
- **thirtyninehotel** (Map pp60-1; ☎ 599-2552; 39 N Hotel St; ⌚ gallery 4-9pm Tue-Sat) Cool local multi-media art gallery also hosts theater performances; see p91.
- **Pegge Hopper Gallery** (Map pp60-1; ☎ 524-1160; 1164 Nu'uanu Ave; ⌚ 11am-4pm Tue-Fri) Prints and paintings of voluptuous Hawaiian women by a transplant from California.
- **Ramsay Galleries** (Map pp60-1; ☎ 537-2787; 1128 Smith St; ⌚ 10am-5pm Mon-Fri, 10am-4pm Sat) Finely detailed pen-and-ink drawings of Honolulu, plus changing exhibitions by well-known Hawaii artists.
- **Bethel St Gallery** (Map pp60-1; ☎ 524-3552; 1140 Bethel St; ⌚ 11am-6pm Tue-Fri, 11am-4pm Sat) A mixed plate of Hawaiian and international artists; abstract paintings to blown-glass sculptures.
- **Louis Pohl Gallery** (Map pp60-1; ☎ 521-1812; 1111 Nu'uanu Ave; ⌚ 11am-6pm Tue-Sat) Paintings by a former 'living treasure' of Hawaii, along with multimedia works by contemporary artists.
- **Chinatown Boardroom** (Map pp60-1; ☎ 585-7200; 1160 Nu'uanu Ave; ⌚ 11am-4pm Tue-Sat) Customized, one-of-a-kind surfboards and surf-themed 'lowbrow' art exhibitions.

A rainbow of hula skirts at T&L Muumuu Factory   LINDA CHING

So much flammable aloha wear in one space – it's worth a visit for the kitsch factor alone. This is a shop for *tutu* (grandmothers), where polyester still represents progress. Bold-print muumuus run in sizes from supermodel-skinny to Polynesian-island-queen.

SLEEPING

Most tourists stay in Waikiki, where you'll find the bulk of O'ahu's visitor accommodations (see p125). If you need to be next to the airport (though you probably don't), there are a couple of nondescript chain hotels nearby.

HOSTELLING INTERNATIONAL – HONOLULU   Hostel $
Map p71; ☎ 946-0591; www.hostelsaloha.com; 2323-A Seaview Ave; dm $20-23, r $50-56; ⌚ reception 8am-noon & 4pm-midnight; P ⌨ ⌂

Along a residential side street near the university campus, this tidy, low-lying house feels miles away from the hustle and bustle of Waikiki, although it's just a short bus ride to the beach. Same-sex dorms are kept cool by the trade winds, plus there are two basic private rooms. Some students use this as a landing pad before finding an apartment, so it's often full at the beginning of the semester. Limited free parking.

CENTRAL BRANCH YMCA   Hostel $
Map pp68-9; ☎ 941-3344; www.ymcahonolulu .org; 401 Atkinson Dr; s with shared/private bath $37/45; ⌂ ⌨ ⌂

On the east side of the Ala Moana Center, the 'Y' offers the best budget deal in town, as long as you're not too fussy. Basic rooms with shared bathroom (reserved for men only) are as small and spare as a Jesuit monastery. Rooms with teensy private bathrooms are available to both sexes. Bonus guest privileges include free use of an indoor Olympic-sized swimming pool and a modern, fully equipped gym.

PAGODA HOTEL   Independent Hotel $$
Map pp68-9; ☎ 923-4511, 800-472-4632; www .pagodahotel.com; 1525 Rycroft St; r $95-169, 1br $105-185; P ⌨ ⌂ ⌂ ⌂

North of the Ala Moana Center, the retro Pagoda Hotel is a mid-20th-century survivor with terribly outdated decor. This no-frills place is divided into a 12-story hotel tower and an apartment complex with kitchenette units. Although it has seen far better days, the hotel remains popular with Neighbor Island families as an alternative to the hectic Waikiki scene. Still, the price is steep for such thin towels, scratchy sheets and nonstop noise. Surcharge applies for in-room wired high-speed internet access and lobby and poolside wi-fi.

ALA MOANA HOTEL   International Hotel $$$
Map pp68-9; ☎ 955-4811, from US & Canada 800-367-6025, from Neighbor Islands 800-446-8990; www.alamoanahotel.com; 410 Atkinson Dr; r $149-330, ste $299-579; P $16/day ⌨ ⌂ ⌂ ⌂

Looming over the Ala Moana Center and convenient to the convention center, this 35-story condo-hotel high-rise offers bland,

HONOLULU

fairly identical-looking hotel rooms without much island flavor. Rooms on upper floors may have straight-on views of Ala Moana Beach Park. Down below, expect to share the check-in line with jet-lagged executives and airline crews. Wired high-speed internet in all guest rooms is free, but wi-fi in the hotel lobby costs extra. Access to a well-equipped fitness room is complimentary.

ASTON AT THE EXECUTIVE CENTRE HOTEL   International Hotel $$$$
Map pp60-1; ☎ 539-3000, 877-997-6667; www
.astonhotels.com; 1088 Bishop St; ste $250-270, 1br
$300-320; 🅿 $16/day 🔀 💻 🖳 🛜
On the upper floors of a modern high-rise, Honolulu's only downtown hotel is decked out exclusively for business travelers. Large, modern suites are outfitted with all necessary electronic gadgets to run mobile empires, while one-bedroom units have full kitchens and washer/dryer. A fitness center, heated lap pool and business center offering laptop rentals round out the executive-class amenities. There's free wired high-speed internet in all guest suites and free wi-fi in the hotel lobby.

These hotels offer free 24-hour airport shuttle services and continental breakfast:

Best Western Plaza Hotel (Map pp54-5; ☎ 836-3636, 800-800-4683; www.bestwesternhawaii.com; 3253 N Nimitz Hwy; r $129-159; 🅿 $5/day 🔀 💻 🖳 🛜) Top pick among airport-area hotels; noisy rooms front the highway.

Ohana Honolulu Airport Hotel (Map pp54-5; ☎ 836-0661, 866-968-8744; www.ohanahotels.com; 3401 N Nimitz Hwy; r $139-209; 🅿 $15/day 🔀 🖳 🛜) Also near the airport, with free lobby wi-fi and wired high-speed internet in guest rooms.

GETTING THERE & AROUND

For information on flights into Honolulu International Airport, see p284. For details on transportation to/from the airport, see p287. For taxis, see p292.

If you're visiting downtown Honolulu or Chinatown on a weekday, consider riding TheBus instead of driving. Not only will you avoid heavy traffic and expensive, hard-to-find parking, but it can be more convenient. You can start touring anywhere you like, then hop on the next bus back to your hotel without having to circle back to where you've parked.

Bus

From the Ala Moana Center (Map pp68–9), the central terminal for TheBus (p289) network, you can catch public buses to many points around the island. Route A City Express! connects downtown Honolulu with the Ala Moana Center and the University of Hawai'i at Manoa.

To reach downtown Honolulu from Waikiki, there are several direct bus routes that don't require transferring at the Ala Moana Center. If you're heading to the 'Iolani Palace or Chinatown, the most convenient routes are TheBus 2 or 13 or B CityExpress!. To go directly to waterfront locales, including Ala Moana Beach Park and the Aloha Tower, take TheBus 19 or 20 or E CountryExpress!.

Private trolley buses also connect Honolulu with Waikiki (see p134).

Car & Motorcycle

Major car-rental companies are located at Honolulu International Airport (see p290).

Downtown Honolulu and Chinatown have street-side metered parking; it's reasonably easy to find an empty street-side space on weekends but nearly impossible on a weekday. Brings lots of quarters to feed the meters.

Chinatown is full of one-way streets, traffic is thick and parking can be tight. Note that N Hotel St is open to bus traffic only. Public parking garages, including these at the Chinatown Gateway Plaza and the ARTS at Marks Garage, are crowded.

Parking is also available at several municipal lots in the downtown Honolulu area. On the outskirts of the downtown core, the private Neal S Blaisdell Center (Map pp68–9) offers all-day parking for around $6, depending on special-events schedules.

Most major shopping centers offer free parking for customers. The Aloha Tower Marketplace has validated public parking; make sure you have your ticket stamped after making a purchase inside. On weekdays after 3pm and all day on weekends and holidays, a validated flat rate of $2 applies; on weekdays before 3pm, validated parking costs $2 for the first three hours. Otherwise, it's a steep $3 per 30 minutes.

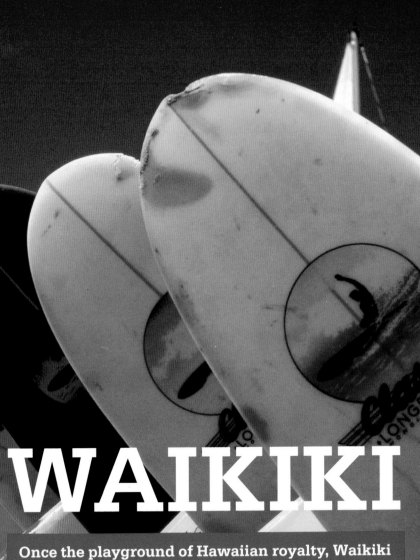

WAIKIKI

Once the playground of Hawaiian royalty, Waikiki has reinvented itself. No longer just a plasticky beach destination for package tourists, this famous strand of sand is flowering again with a renaissance of Hawaiian music and hula. Oceanfront resorts now aim for boutique intimacy, while Waikiki Beach Walk, with its diverting shops, restaurants and bars, keeps evolving on lower Lewers St. Find whispers of the past here, from the chanting of hula troupes to the legacy of Olympic gold medalist Duke Kahanamoku. Take a surfing lesson from a bronzed beachboy, sip a mai tai as the sun drops into the sea and just enjoy life. It's for good reason that everyone's here.

WAIKIKI
ITINERARIES

IN ONE DAY *7.5 miles*

① EGGS 'N THINGS (p116) Sometimes all the tourists really are headed in the right direction: this diner serves just about the best bang-for-your-buck breakfast in Waikiki. Dig into Portuguese sausage and fluffy pancakes topped with honey or guava or coconut syrup.

② SANS SOUCI BEACH PARK (p108) Hop on TheBus down to the southern edge of Waikiki to this seldom-crowded beach park, which may feel like your own private paradise. Snorkeling in the calm waters is a joy.

③ WAIKIKI AQUARIUM (p109) Figure out what all those fish you just snorkeled by actually are at this eco-conscious educational center. Don't miss seeing the moon jellyfish, Paluan chambered nautiluses or the Hawaiian monk seals out back.

④ KUHIO BEACH PARK (p107) Stroll or cycle back towards Waikiki's most popular strand of sand. Take the kids on an **outrigger canoe ride (p110)** or just laze the hours away until the **torch lighting and hula show (p137)** starts.

⑤ CATAMARAN CRUISE (p114) If Hawaiian music and hula dancing aren't your thing, jump aboard a catamaran that pulls up right on the beach for sunset mai tais shaken by the waves.

⑥ ROY'S – WAIKIKI BEACH (p119) After dark, Waikiki Beach Walk is the most glam place to be. Shine your shoes and treat yourself to cocktails and stellar Hawaii Regional cuisine at this star chef's newest island restaurant.

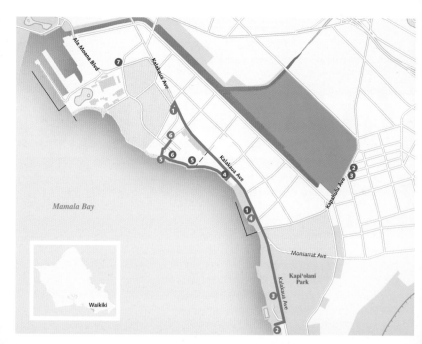

FOR VINTAGE LOVERS

❶ KUHIO BEACH PARK (p107) Pay your respects to iconic surfer **Duke Kahanamoku's statue (p109)** before taking a morning **surf lesson (p110)** from one of Waikiki's famed beachboys.

❷ BAILEY'S ANTIQUES & ALOHA SHIRTS (p123) Shrug off those heavy, sweaty clothes you brought from home and get yourself a stylin' aloha shirt at this virtual museum of vintage wear worth an inland detour.

❸ RAINBOW DRIVE-IN (p120) Join the local surfers and working folks on their lunch break at this authentic local diner, dishing up mixed-plate lunches covered in gravy. For icy goodness, **Waiola Bakery & Shave Ice II (p120)** is a block away.

❹ MOANA SURFRIDER (p132) Back at the beach, take a tour of this grand dame of island tourist hotels, then stick around for

live Hawaiian music in the gracious **banyan tree courtyard (p137).**

❺ ROYAL HAWAIIAN HOTEL (p109) Mosey up the beach north toward the inimitable 'Pink Palace,' originally designed for first-class passengers arriving in the Hawaiian Islands via Matson Cruise Lines.

❻ HALEKULANI (p132) Inside another of Waikiki's early-20th-century hostelries, grab an oceanfront table at the **House Without a Key (p137)** for classy cocktails and to catch the sunset Hawaiian music and hula show.

❼ WAILANA COFFEE HOUSE (p117) Although the food is nothing to write home about, this unabashedly retro 1970s diner is an around-the-clock meeting place for locals and tourists alike. The homespun atmosphere feels more like the countryside of O'ahu than urban Honolulu.

WAIKIKI

Sans Souci Beach Park (p108)

ANN CECIL

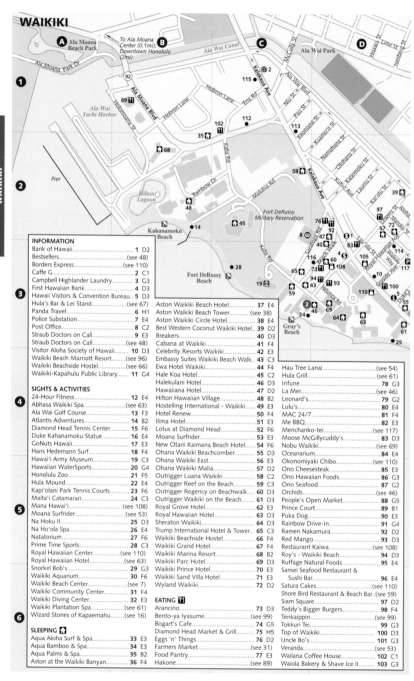

WAIKIKI

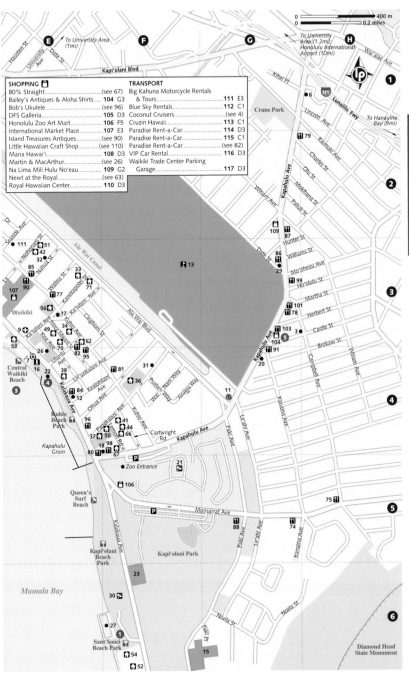

WAIKIKI

HIGHLIGHTS

❶ **BEST BEACH:** Sans Souci Beach Park (p108)
❷ **BEST VIEW:** House Without a Key (p137)
❸ **BEST ACTIVITY:** Surfing at Waikiki Beach (p110)
❹ **BEST FREE SHOW:** Kuhio Beach Torch Lighting & Hula Show (p137)
❺ **BEST ALOHA WEAR:** Bailey's Antiques & Aloha Shirts (p123)

Highlights are numbered on the map on pp102–3.

pop 27,507

HISTORY

Looking at Waikiki today, it's hard to imagine that just 125 years ago this tourist mecca was almost entirely wetlands filled with fishponds and *kalo lo'i* (taro fields). Fed by mountain streams from the Manoa Valley, Waikiki (Spouting Water) was once one of O'ahu's most fertile farming areas.

In 1795 Kamehameha I became the first *ali'i* (chief) to successfully unite the Hawaiian Islands under one sovereign's rule, and he built his royal court here. For almost the next century, Waikiki was a privileged royal retreat. By the 1880s, Honolulu's more well-to-do citizens had started building gingerbread-trimmed cottages along the narrow beachfront and at Kapi'olani Park, named after a Hawaiian queen.

Tourism started booming in 1901 when the Moana opened its doors as Waikiki's first luxury hotel, built on a former royal compound. A tram line was built to connect Waikiki with downtown Honolulu, and city folk crowded aboard for weekend beach outings. Tiring quickly of the pesky mosquitoes that thrived in Waikiki's wetlands, early beachgoers petitioned to have the 'swamps' brought under control. In 1922 the Ala Wai Canal was dug to divert the streams that flowed into Waikiki and to dry out the wetlands. Water buffaloes were quickly replaced by tourists, and within five years the Royal Hawaiian Hotel opened to serve passengers arriving on luxury ocean liners from San Francisco. Dubbed the Pink Palace, its guest list reads like a who's-who of A-list celebrities – royalty and Rockefellers, Charlie Chaplin and Babe Ruth.

The Depression and WWII put a damper on tourism, as the Royal Hawaiian Hotel was turned into an R&R playground for sailors on shore leave. From 1935 to 1975, the classic radio show *Hawaii Calls*, broadcast from the Moana Hotel, continued bringing dreams of a tropical paradise to the US mainland and the world. As late as 1950, surfers could still drive their cars right up to Waikiki Beach and park on the sand. By then, passenger jets had started making regularly scheduled flights to Hawaii, and tourism boomed after WWII. Only a lack of available land finally halted Waikiki's expansion in the late 1980s. The only place left to go was up, which is why so many high-rises are clustered here today.

ORIENTATION

Technically, Waikiki is a district of the city of Honolulu. It's bounded on two sides by Ala Wai Canal, on another by the ocean and on the fourth by Kapi'olani Park. Three parallel roads cross Waikiki: one-way Kalakaua Ave alongside the beach; Kuhio Ave, the main drag inland for buses; and Ala Wai Blvd, which borders Ala Wai Canal. Walking along the beach is an alternative to overcrowded sidewalks, since it's possible to walk the full length of Waikiki along the sand and seaside footpaths. See p133 for more information about getting around Waikiki.

INFORMATION
Bookstores

Bestsellers (☎ 953-2378; Rainbow Bazaar, Hilton Hawaiian Village, 2005 Kalia Rd; ☼ 8am-10pm) Hawaiiana books, travel guides and maps.
Borders Express (☎ 922-4154; Royal Hawaiian Center, 2201 Kalakaua Ave; ☼ 9:30am-9:30pm) A smaller but well-stocked version of Borders bookstores.

Emergency

Police, Fire & Ambulance (☎ 911) For all emergencies.

Police Substation (☎ 529-3801; 2405 Kalakaua Ave; ☺ 24hr) If you need help, or just friendly directions, stop here next to Kuhio Beach Park.

Internet Access

Dozens of shops on Kuhio and Kalakaua Aves provide pay-as-you-go internet terminals, charging $6 to $12 per hour, but few places offer wi-fi. Most Waikiki hotels have wired internet connections in guest rooms (for which a surcharge may apply), with wi-fi only in the lobby or poolside.

Caffe G (☎ 979-2299; 1888 Kalakaua Ave; per hr $6; ☺ 8am-10pm Mon-Fri, 10am-10pm Sat, 8:30am-10pm Sun) High-speed internet terminals with ethernet cables for laptops.

Hula's Bar & Lei Stand (☎ 923-0669; 2nd fl, Waikiki Grand Hotel, 134 Kapahulu Ave; ☺ 10am-2am; ☞) Free wi-fi and internet terminals inside the bar (p123).

Waikiki Beachside Hostel (☎ 923-9566; 2556 Lemon Rd; per hr $6; ☺ 24hr) Internet room available to nonguests.

Waikiki-Kapahulu Public Library (☎ 733-8488; www.librarieshawaii.org; 400 Kapahulu Ave; ☺ 10am-5pm Tue, Wed, Fri & Sat, noon-7pm Thu; ☞) Free wi-fi and internet terminals available by reservation (see p279).

Laundry

Most accommodations have coin-operated laundry facilities for guests.

Campbell Highlander Laundry (☎ 732-5630; 3340-B Campbell Ave; ☺ 6:30am-9pm) Self-serve washers and dryers available. Same-day laundry service costs $1 per pound.

Waikiki Beach Marriott Resort (☎ 922-6611; 2nd fl, 2552 Kalakaua Ave; ☺ 7am-10pm) Self-serve laundromat upstairs with teak lounge chairs, magazines and air-con.

Medical Services

For 24-hour pharmacies and hospitals with 24-hour emergency rooms in Honolulu, see p57.

Straub Doctors on Call (www.straubhealth.org) South Waikiki (☎ 971-6000; Sheraton Princess Kaiulani, 120 Ka'iulani Ave; ☺ 24hr); North Waikiki (☎ 973-5250; 2nd fl, Rainbow Bazaar, Hilton Hawaiian Village, 2005 Kalia Rd; ☺ 8:30am-4:30pm Mon-Fri) For nonemergencies; currently accepts Blue Cross/Blue Shield, Medicare and some travel health insurance policies.

Money

There are ATMs all over Waikiki, including at these full-service banks:

Bank of Hawaii (☎ 543-6900; 2155 Kalakaua Ave; ☺ 8:30am-4pm Mon-Thu, 8:30am-6pm Fri, 9am-1pm Sat)

First Hawaiian Bank (☎ 943-4670; 2181 Kalakaua Ave; ☺ 8:30am-4pm Mon-Thu, 8:30am-6pm Fri) Lobby displays Hawaii history murals by French artist Jean Charlot; get a free brochure describing the artwork at the bank's information desk.

Post

Post Office (☎ 800-275-8777; 330 Saratoga Rd; ☺ 8am-4:30pm Mon-Fri, 9am-1pm Sat) Offers free parking for customers.

Tourist Information

The **Hawaii Visitors & Convention Bureau** (HVCB; ☎ 923-1811, 800-464-2924; www.gohawaii.com; ste 801, Waikiki Business Plaza, 2270 Kalakaua Ave; ☺ 8am-4:30pm Mon-Fri) has free maps and meager tourist brochures.

DANGERS & ANNOYANCES

Don't leave your valuables unattended on the beach. It can be risky to walk the beach or along Ala Wai Canal at night. After sunset, prostitutes stroll the streets hunting for wealthy looking tourists. There's been a clampdown on the hustlers who once pushed time-shares and con deals on Waikiki street corners. They're not totally gone – some have deceptively metamorphized into 'activity centers' where time-share salespeople will offer you all sorts of deals, from a free luau and sunset cruises to $5-a-day car rentals, if you'll just come to hear their 'no obligation' pitch. Caveat emptor.

BEACHES

The 2-mile stretch of white sand commonly referred to as Waikiki Beach runs from Hilton Hawaiian Village in the west to Kapi'olani Beach Park in the east. Along the way, the beach changes names and personalities. In the early morning, the quiet beach belongs to walkers and joggers. Strolling down the beach towards Diamond Head at dawn can be a meditative experience. By midmorning it looks like a normal resort

Island Insights

beach – bodyboard, surfboard and catamaran concessionaires and lots of bronzed bodies. By noon it's a challenge to walk along the packed beach without stepping on anyone.

Waikiki is good for swimming, bodyboarding, surfing, sailing and other beach activities most of the year, and there are lifeguards and showers scattered along the oceanfront. Between May and September, summer swells make the water a little rough for swimming, but great for surfing. The best snorkeling is found towards Diamond Head at Sans Souci Beach. For windsurfing, go to Fort DeRussy Beach.

The following beaches run from northwest to southeast.

KAHANAMOKU BEACH

Fronting the Hilton Hawaiian Village, Kahanamoku Beach is Waikiki's westernmost beach. It takes its name from Duke Kahanamoku (1890–1968), whose family once owned the land where the Hilton now stands. Hawaii's legendary surfer and Olympic gold-medal winner learned to swim right here, and the beach is still a great place for kids to take the plunge. Protected by a breakwater and a coral reef, it offers calm swimming conditions and a sandy bottom that slopes gradually.

FORT DERUSSY BEACH

Seldom crowded, this overlooked beauty extends along the shore of a military reservation. Like all beaches in Hawaii, it's public; the only area off-limits to civvies is Hale Koa, a military hotel backing onto the beach, although the hotel's poolside snack bar sells to beachgoers. The water is typically calm and good for swimming, but at low tide it can be shallow. When conditions are right, this is a good place for windsurfers, bodyboarders and board surfers. Beach huts here rent windsurfing equipment, bodyboards, kayaks, snorkel sets, aqua cycles and pedal boats. Along with lifeguards and showers, you'll find a grassy lawn with picnic tables and palm trees offering sparse shade, an alternative to frying on the sand.

Step into a postcard at Kuhio Beach Park

ANN CECIL

CATCH A WAVE WITH THE DUKE

OK, so why *are* all those people standing in front of the **statue of Duke Kahanamoku** (p109) and waving wildly up at the sky? Could it be they're hip to the location of Waikiki's most popular webcam? If you want to show your friends that you've made it to Hawaii, have them log onto the Duke's live streaming webcam at www.honolulu.gov/multimed/waikiki.asp. Prearrange a time when they can be online and you can be at the Duke's statue – then wave the *shaka* (Hawaiian hand greeting) sign to all the folks back home.

Statue of Duke Kahanamoku   MERTEN SNIJDERS

GRAY'S BEACH

Near the Halekulani, Gray's Beach has suffered some of the strip's worst erosion. It was named after Gray's-by-the-Sea, a boarding house that stood here in the 1920s. Because the seawall in front of the Halekulani is so close to the waterline, the beach sand fronting the hotel is often totally submerged by the surf, but the offshore waters are shallow and calm, offering decent swimming conditions.

CENTRAL WAIKIKI BEACH

The generous stretch of beach between the Royal Hawaiian Hotel and the Moana Surfrider is Waikiki's busiest section of sand and surf, and great for sunbathing, swimming and people watching. Most of the beach has a shallow bottom with a gradual slope. The only drawback for swimmers is the beach's popularity with beginning surfers and the occasional catamaran. **Queens** and **Canoes**, Waikiki's best-known surf breaks, are just offshore, and on a good day there can be hundreds of surfers lined up on the horizon waiting to catch a wave. A longer paddle offshore, and over a lagoon, is **Populars** (aka 'Pops'), a favorite of long-boarders. The **Waikiki Beach Center** offers restrooms, showers, a snack bar, surfboard lockers and rental stands.

KUHIO BEACH PARK

This central beach park offers everything from protected swimming to outrigger canoe rides (p110) and hula shows (p137).

The beach is marked on its eastern end by **Kapahulu Groin**, a walled storm drain with a walkway on top that juts out into the ocean. A low stone breakwater, called the Wall, runs out from Kapahulu Groin, parallel to the beach. It was built to control sand erosion and, in the process, two nearly enclosed swimming pools were formed.

Local kids walk out on the Wall, but it can be dangerous due to a slippery surface and breaking surf. The pool closest to Kapahulu Groin is best for swimming, with the water near the breakwater reaching overhead depths. However, because circulation is limited, the water gets murky with a noticeable film of suntan oil. The 'Watch Out Deep Holes' sign refers to holes in the pool's sandy bottom created by swirling currents, so waders should be cautious in the deeper part of the pool.

Kapahulu Groin is one of Waikiki's hottest bodyboarding spots. If the surf's right, you can find a few dozen bodyboarders, mostly teenagers, riding the waves. The kids ride straight for the groin's cement wall and then veer away at the last moment, thrilling the tourists watching them from the little pier above.

Island Insights

The distinguished statesman Prince Jonah Kuhio Kalaniana'ole (1877–1922), who fought for Hawaiian rights his entire life, maintained his residence on Kuhio Beach, which is named after him. His house, Pualeilani (Wreath of Heaven), was torn down in 1936 to expand the public beach. Between the old-timers who gather each afternoon to play chess at sidewalk pavilions and the kids who race down here after school to bodyboard off Kapahulu Groin, this Waikiki beach has tons of local color. It's a real people's park, which definitely would've made Prince Kuhio proud.

KAPI'OLANI BEACH PARK

From Kapahulu Groin to the Natatorium, this stretch of beach, backed by a green space of banyan trees and grassy lawns, offers a relaxing niche with none of the frenzied activity found on the beaches fronting the Waikiki hotel strip. It's a popular weekend picnicking spot for local families. Facilities include restrooms and showers.

Queen's Surf Beach is the name given to the northern end of Kapi'olani Beach. The stretch in front of the pavilion is popular with the gay community, and its sandy bottom offers decent swimming. The beach between Queen's Surf Beach and The Wall is shallow and has broken coral. Offshore from lifeguard stand 2F, the left-handed surf break **Publics** is popular with longboarders in summer high tides.

At the Diamond Head end of Kapi'olani Beach Park is the 1920s **Natatorium** (http://natatorium.org), now on the National Register of Historic Places. This 100m-long saltwater swimming pool was constructed as a memorial for soldiers who died in WWI. Two Olympic gold medalists – Johnny Weissmuller and Duke Kahanamoku – trained in the tide-fed pool. For now, it remains closed to the public, awaiting renovation.

SANS SOUCI BEACH PARK

** our pick** Bordered by the New Otani Kaimana Beach Hotel, on the Diamond Head edge of Waikiki, Sans Souci (aka Kaimana Beach) is a prime sandy stretch of oceanfront away from the tourist scene. Local residents come here for their daily swims. Facilities include lifeguards and showers. A shallow reef close to shore makes for calm, protected waters and provides good snorkeling. Strong swimmers and snorkelers can follow the Kapua Channel that cuts through the reef. Be aware that currents can pick up in the channel. Check conditions with the lifeguard before heading out.

SIGHTS

Almost all of Honolulu's important museums and historic sites are outside Waikiki, so you won't find much besides the beach to occupy your time here. As you walk past public parks and landmarks, look for small interpretive signboards, part of the **Waikiki Historic Trail** (www.waikikihistorictrail.com), pointing out tidbits of Waikiki's royal and modern history.

MOANA SURFRIDER

☎ 922-3111; www.moana-surfrider.com; 2365 Kalakaua Ave; admission & tour free; ⓧ 1hr tours usually 11am & 5pm Mon, Wed & Fri

Christened the Moana Hotel in 1901, this beaux-arts, plantation-style inn was once the

KAPI'OLANI PARK: THEN & NOW

In its early days, horse racing and band concerts were the biggest attractions at Waikiki's favorite green space. Although the racetrack is long gone, this park, named after a Hawaiian queen, is still a favorite local venue for live music and community activities, from farmers markets to art-and-crafts fairs. The tree-shaded Kapi'olani Bandstand is the perfect venue for the time-honored **Royal Hawaiian Band** (☎ 922-5331; www.co.honolulu.hi.us/rhb), which performs classics from the monarchy era usually every Sunday afternoon from 2pm to 3pm, except during August. Not many tourists come down this way. It's a quintessential island scene that caps off with the audience joining hands and singing Queen Lili'uokalani's 'Aloha 'Oe' in Hawaiian.

The Royal Hawaiian Hotel   ANN CECIL

haunt of Hollywood movie stars, aristocrats and business tycoons. The hotel embraces a seaside courtyard with a big banyan tree and a wraparound veranda, where island musicians and hula dancers perform in the evenings. Upstairs from the lobby, you'll find displays of memorabilia from the early days; everything from scripts of the famed *Hawaii Calls* radio show and woolen bathing suits to period photographs and a short video of Waikiki back in the days when this was the only hotel on the horizon.

ROYAL HAWAIIAN HOTEL

☎ 923-7311; www.royal-hawaiian.com; 2259 Kalakaua Ave; admission & tour free; ⌚ 1hr tours usually 2pm Mon, Wed & Fri

With its unmissable Moorish architecture, this 1927 art deco landmark, nicknamed the Pink Palace, is a throwback to the era when Rudolph Valentino was *the* romantic idol and travel to Hawaii was by luxury liner. This historic hotel site was once a royal co-

conut grove with around 10,000 trees, and it was in this very spot that Kamehameha the Great camped before beginning his battle to conquer O'ahu in 1795. A few coconut trees can still be found in the small tropical flowering gardens at the rear of the hotel; ask the concierge for a self-guided garden walking-tour brochure.

WIZARD STONES & DUKE KAHANAMOKU STATUE

On the Diamond Head side of Central Waikiki Beach (p107) police substation, between Ka'iulani and Uluniu Aves, you'll see four boulders known as the **Wizard Stones of Kapaemahu**, which are said to contain the secrets and healing powers of 16th-century Tahitian sorcerers. Just east of the stones is a **bronze statue of Duke Kahanamoku**, standing with one of his long-boards. Considered the father of modern surfing, Duke made his home in Waikiki. Many local surfers have taken issue with the placement of the statue, which has Duke standing with his back to the sea – a position they argue he never would have taken in real life.

🏄 WAIKIKI AQUARIUM

our pick ☎ 923-9741; www.waquarium.org; 2777 Kalakaua Ave; admission & self-guided audio tour adult $9, child 4-13yr $2, youth 14-17yr $4, student with ID $6; ⌚ 9am-5pm, last entry 4:30pm; 🚌 2

Located on Waikiki's shoreline, this modern university-run aquarium features an impressive shark gallery and tanks that re-create

Don't Miss

- Making your friends back home jealous with the **Duke Kahanamoku statue's live webcam** (p107)
- Hopping aboard a catamaran that hauls up right on the beach for a **sunset cruise** (p114)
- Rocking on the lanai of the historic **Moana Surfrider** (opposite), then viewing the memorabilia galleries upstairs
- Learning how to string flower lei and dance the hula at the **Waikiki Community Center** (p114)
- Pigging out and partying at the April **Waikiki Spam Jam** (p115)

various tropical Pacific reef habitats. You'll see rare Hawaiian fish, such as the bearded armorhead, along with moon jellies and flashlight fish that host bioluminescent bacteria. This ecologically conscious aquarium was the first to breed the Palauan chambered nautilus in captivity, and you can see these creatures, with their unique spiral chambered shells, in the South Pacific section. An outdoor tank is home to a pair of rare, beautiful Hawaiian monk seals (p47), endangered marine mammals that frequent the remote Northwestern Hawaiian Islands.

HONOLULU ZOO

☎ 971-7171; www.honoluluzoo.org; 151 Kapahulu Ave; adult $6, child 6-12yr $1; ⏱ 9am-4:30pm; 🚌 4, 18, 19, 20, 22, 23 & 42

On the north side of Kapi'olani Park, this respectable zoo makes species conservation efforts for sun bears and Sumatran tigers, among others. Although small, it showcases over 300 species spread across 40-plus acres of tropical greenery. The largest exhibit is the African Savanna section, near a small petting zoo for nā keiki (children). Hawaii has no endemic land mammals, but in the aviary near the entrance you can see some native birds, including the ae'o (Hawaiian stilt), the nene (Hawaiian goose) and 'apapane, a bright-red Hawaiian honeycreeper. The zoo is accessible to baby strollers and wheelchairs.

HAWAI'I ARMY MUSEUM

☎ 955-9552; www.hiarmymuseumsoc.org; Kalia Rd; admission by donation; ⏱ 10am-4:15pm Tue-Sun; 🅿

At Fort DeRussy, this museum showcases an almost mind-numbing array of military paraphernalia as it relates to Hawaii's history, starting with shark-tooth clubs that Kamehameha the Great used to win control of the island over two centuries ago. Concentrating on the US military presence in Hawaii, extensive exhibits include displays on the 442nd, the Japanese American regiment that became the most decorated regiment in WWII, and on Kaua'i-born Eric Shinseki, a retired four-star army general who spoke out against the US invasion of Iraq in 2003 and is currently serving as President Barack Obama's Secretary of Veterans Affairs.

ACTIVITIES

Although Waikiki's beaches (p105) steal the spotlight, landlubbers can find plenty of fun in the sun. Kapi'olani Park has sports fields for soccer and softball, even cricket. For an indoor workout, there's 24-Hour Fitness (☎ 923-9090; 2490 Kalakaua Ave; daily/weekly pass $25/69; ⏱ 24hr), a gym that has cardio and weight machines and group fitness classes.

Surfing & Outrigger Canoe Rides

Waikiki has good surfing year-round, with the largest waves rolling in during summer; gentler winter breaks are suited for beginners. Surfing lessons ($75 to $100 for a two-hour group class) can be arranged at the

---

WAIKIKI GIMMICKS

There's no denying it, Waikiki is tourist central with all the attendant drawbacks: overpriced hotel meals, weak alcoholic fruity drinks and coconut bikini tops. Of the many entertainment gimmicks that line the strip, there are two standouts.

At the **Oceanarium** (☎ 921-6111; Pacific Beach Hotel, 2490 Kalakaua Ave; buffet $18-35; ⏱ 5:30am-10pm) you can dine with the fish at a hotel restaurant that wraps around a three-story aquarium brimming with colorful tropical fish and more pensive sharks and rays. The occupants of the tank are only for decoration, not for consumption. There's no need to eat here, because you can gaze at the aquarium from the lobby. Divers feed the tropical fish at noon, 1pm, 6:15pm and 8pm.

The revolving **Top of Waikiki** (☎ 923-3877; www.topofwaikiki.com; 18th fl, Waikiki Business Plaza, 2270 Kalakaua Ave; sunset special before 6pm dinner $16; ⏱ 5-9:30pm) restaurant was first introduced at a world's fair in the 1960s and has since become a retro relic. Rotating lazily at one revolution per hour, this tower-top restaurant takes in a 360-degree view. There's food involved, but the novelty is the slow-motion sit-and-spin. Sunset cocktails are tempting.

SPA ME, BABY

What's a beach vacation without a little pampering? Always call ahead for spa appointments.

- **Abhasa Waikiki Spa** (☎ 922-8200; www.abhasa.com; Royal Hawaiian Hotel, 2259 Kalakaua Ave; 50min massage from $125; 9am-9pm) A soothing island glow emanates from the cabana massage rooms surrounded by a tropical garden. Local treatments include Hawaiian-style lomilomi (loving hands) and *pohaku* (hot stone) massage.

- **Waikiki Plantation Spa** (☎ 926-2880, 866-926-2880; www.waikikiplantationspa.com; Outrigger Waikiki on the Beach, 2335 Kalakaua Ave; 50min massage from $110; 8am-7pm) Penthouse spa specializes in holistic Hawaiian therapies, including massage. Some therapists incorporate a spiritual aspect with a concluding chant or prayer. Afterwards, unwind on an ocean-view deck.

- **Na Ho'ola Spa** (☎ 923-1234; http://waikiki.hyatt.com; Hyatt Regency Waikiki Beach Resort & Spa, 2424 Kalakaua Ave; 50min massage from $130; 8am-8pm) *Limu* (seaweed) wraps detoxify, *kele-kele* (mud) wraps soothe sore muscles and *ti* leaf wraps heal sun-ravaged skin, while macadamia-nut oil exfoliates your skin and coconut extracts moisturize it – ah, bliss.

- **AquaSPA** (☎ 924-2782; www.aquaresorts.com; 50min massage from $95; 9am-7pm) Occasionally offers deep online discounts for delightfully personalized massage inside poolside cabanas at Waikiki's multiple Aqua boutique hotels; healing *noni* (Indian mulberry), papaya and pineapple body scrub add-ons available.

The **Halekulani** (p132) and **Moana Surfrider** (p132) resort hotels have top-notch spas too.

---

concession stands at **Kuhio Beach Park** (p107), which rent surfboards for $15 to $20 per hour. Some also offer $25 outrigger canoe rides that take off from the beach and ride the tossin' waves home – kids love it.

Just up the street from Kapahulu Groin, **Hans Hedemann Surf** (☎ 924-7778; www.hhsurf .com; 2586 Kapahulu Ave; 9am-5pm) and **Hawaiian WaterSports** (☎ 739-5483; www.hawaiianwatersports .com; 415 Kapahulu Ave; 9am-5pm), further inland, offer surfing lessons. Rates for a two-hour group/private lesson start at $80/160, while surfboard rental costs about $20 per day. **GoNuts Hawaii** (☎ 926-3367; www.gonuts-hawaii .com; 159 Ka'iulani Ave; 8am-9pm) offers cheaper private lessons (from $100) and charges $99 for three-day surfboard rentals. **Hawaii Surfboard Rentals** (☎ 672-5055; www.hawaiisurfboardren tals.com) offers free surfboard delivery and pick-up with a two-day minimum rental; weekly rental rates are $90 to $140.

Bodyboarding

Waikiki's top bodyboarding spot is Kapahulu Groin at Kuhio Beach Park (p107). You can rent boards from several places right on the beach, but if you're going to be riding the waves for more than a few hours, consider buying your own from one of Waikiki's ubiquitous ABC Stores.

Alternatively, **Snorkel Bob's** (☎ 735-7944; www .snorkelbob.com; 702 Kapahulu Ave; 8am-5pm) rents bodyboards for $7/26 per day/week, but it's about 1 mile inland from the beach.

Snorkeling & Diving

Waikiki's overcrowded beach is not particularly good for snorkeling, so you'll need to pick your spot carefully. The best two choices are **Sans Souci Beach Park** (p108) and **Queen's Surf Beach** (p108), at the north end of Kapi'olani Park, where you'll find some live coral and a decent variety of tropical fish. To really see the gorgeous stuff – coral gardens, manta rays and more exotic fish – go out on a boat dive.

For equipment rentals and boat dives, try the following:
GoNuts Hawaii (☎ 926-3367; 159 Ka'iulani Ave; snorkel-set rental per day/week $5/30; 8am-9pm)
Snorkel Bob's (☎ 735-7944; www.snorkelbob.com; 702 Kapahulu Ave; snorkel-set rental per day $2-11, per week $9-44, flotation devices per day/week $5/20; 8am-5pm) Rates vary depending on the quality of the gear and accessories packages.
Waikiki Diving Center (☎ 922-2121; www.waikiki diving.com; 424 Nahua St; snorkel boat trip $35, 2-tank/ wreck dive $115/125; 7am-5pm) Reliable full-service dive shop offers small-group boat dives and open-water PADI certification courses ($350).

WAIKIKI

Kayaking & Windsurfing

Waikiki's main windsurfing spot, **Fort DeRussy Beach** (p106) has fewer swimmers and catamarans to share the water with than Waikiki's central beach strip, which also makes it a better bet for kayaking. Two beach concession stands run by **Prime Time Sports** (☎ 949-8952; s/d kayak rental per hr from $12/25, windsurfing equipment rental per 1/5hr $25/75, 1hr group/private windsurfing lesson $65/85) rents sit-upon kayaks and windsurfing equipment at Fort DeRussy Beach and also can arrange windsurfing lessons.

Running

If you're into jogging, you're in good company: statistics estimate that Honolulu has more joggers per capita than any other city on the planet. Two of the best places to break out your running shoes are along Ala Wai Canal and at Kapi'olani Park. The **Honolulu Marathon Clinic** (http://honolulumarathonclinic.org)

Kayaking off Waikiki Beach   ANN CECIL

Island Insights

Built in the 1920s to drain rainwater away from the marshy wetlands of Waikiki by diverting it out to sea via the Kapahulu Groin and Ala Wai Yacht Harbor, the Ala Wai Canal resembles a giant moat. Every day from dawn till dusk Honolulu residents go out jogging along the canal, which forms the northern boundary of Waikiki. Late in the afternoon, outrigger canoe teams paddle along the canal and out to the harbor – a memorable photo op for tourists. Incidentally, those black fish that school in the canal and blow bubbles are tilapia, which thrive in brackish waters.

meets in Kapi'olani Park at 3833 Paki Ave at 7:30am most Sundays from early March until the marathon (p116) in mid-December; it's free and open to everyone, with runners allowed to join groups of their own speed.

Golf

With views of Diamond Head, the 18-hole, par-70 **Ala Wai Golf Course** (☎ 733-7387; 404 Kapahulu Ave; green fees $50) scores a Guinness World Record for being the busiest golf course in the world. Local golfers are allowed to book earlier in the week and grab all the starting times, leaving none for visitors. But there is a way to get onto this green haven. Get there early in the day and put yourself on the waiting list, and as long as your entire golfing party waits at the course, you'll probably get playing time. A driving range and club and hand-cart rental are available.

Tennis

If you've brought your own racquets, the **Diamond Head Tennis Center**, at the Diamond Head end of Kapi'olani Park, has 10 poorly maintained courts. For night play, go to the **Kapi'olani Park Tennis Courts**, opposite the Waikiki Aquarium; all four courts are lit. These public courts are all free and first-come, first-served. A few Waikiki resort hotels offer tennis courts and equipment rental for guests.

WALKING TOUR

You can walk the full length of Waikiki right along the sand. Although the beach gets crowded at noon, at other times it's less packed than the sidewalks along Kalakaua Ave.

❶ KAPAHULU GROIN (p107) Start from this people-watching hot spot, where Waikiki's daredevil bodyboarders thrill crowds of onlookers.

❷ WAIKIKI AQUARIUM (p109) Stroll down beside the shady trees of Kapi'olani Park to this aquatic museum, filled with South Pacific coral, chambered nautiluses, jellyfish and more.

❸ KUHIO BEACH PARK (p107) Trek north up the beach, through this park, with its landmark hula mound. You'll see people lining up to snap photos in front of the **Duke Kahanamoku statue (p109)** and endless racks of surfboards belonging to Waikiki's current-day wave riders.

WALK FACTS

Start Kapahulu Groin
End Royal Hawaiian Center
Distance 3 miles
Duration Two to four hours

❹ MOANA SURFRIDER (p108) Take a load off your feet in the rocking chairs on the front lanai, then duck inside to check out this historic hotel's memorabilia displays upstairs or take **afternoon high tea (p117)** on the ocean-view veranda.

❺ ROYAL HAWAIIAN HOTEL (p109) Amble north along the sand to see another grand dame among Waikiki's historic hotels, the Royal Hawaiian, which recently reopened after a $110 million makeover – ooh, la la.

❻ HALEKULANI (p132) Continue along the beach until you reach this even more genteel historic hotel with its alfresco beachfront bar, known as the **House Without**

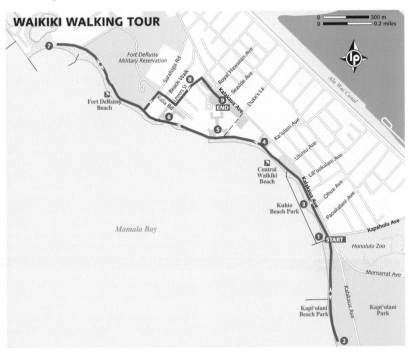

WAIKIKI

a Key (p137) – Charlie Chan fans will want to stop for a frosty drink.

❼ **KAHANAMOKU BEACH (p106)** Back on the beach, it's just a 10-minute walk north to this beautiful stretch of golden sand outside the Hilton Hawaiian Village resort hotel. On Friday nights, catch the big-deal **fireworks show (opposite)**.

❽ **WAIKIKI BEACH WALK (p123)** After dark, head back down the beach and inland to Waikiki Beach Walk, where spanking-new hotels and shops keep adding to the city's skyline.

❾ **ROYAL HAWAIIAN CENTER (p125)** If you're not shopped out yet, head inside this mammoth multistory mall, which also offers free **Hawaiian cultural classes and demonstrations (below)** and **Hawaiian music and hula shows (p138)**.

COURSES

Mana Hawai'i (☎ 923-2220; www.waikikibeach walk.com; 226 Lewers St) Book, music and gift shop (p124) organizes free weekly classes in Hawaiian language, hula dancing, ukulele playing and *lauhala* leaf-weaving, as well as workshops on traditional Hawaiian spiritual practices.

Royal Hawaiian Center (☎ 922-2299; www .royalhawaiiancenter.com; 2201 Kalakaua Ave) Shopping mall offers free cultural classes and demonstrations in Hawaiian arts and crafts, including Hawaiian quilting, flower-lei making, coconut-leaf weaving, *kapa* bark cloth making, hula dancing, ukulele playing and even lomilomi massage; check the website or call ahead for schedules.

our pick **Waikiki Community Center** (☎ 923-1802; www.waikikicommunitycenter.org; 310 Pa'oakalani Ave) Try your hand at mah-jongg, the ukulele, hula, tai chi or a variety of island arts and crafts. Instructors at this home-spun community center are brimming with aloha. Although most of the students are islanders, drop-in visitors are welcome. Lesson fees range from $3 to $15, depending on the class. Most classes happen on weekdays; call or go online for schedules.

WAIKIKI FOR KIDS

Start at the **beach** (p105). In just an hour kids can learn how to stand up on a board and **surf** (p110) or rent a **bodyboard** (p111) and ride on their bellies. Another fun way to ride the waves is to take an **outrigger canoe ride** (p110) and paddle back into shore.

Want to see the world from beneath the waves? Don a snorkel and take a look at the colorful fish at **Queen's Surf Beach** (p111) or take a ride on the **Atlantis Adventures submarine** (opposite) and see it all through a porthole.

At the beach at the north end of Kapi'olani Park, the **Waikiki Aquarium** (p109), with its kaleidoscopic array of tropical fish and reef sharks, has lots of fun things just for *nā keiki*. Ask about the current schedule of family programs with names like 'Small Fry' and 'Aquarium After Dark.'

The **Honolulu Zoo** (p110) offers several activities just for kids, including a petting zoo where children can get eye-to-eye with tamer creatures and special 'twilight tours' geared for children aged five and older from 5:30pm to 7:30pm on Friday and Saturday. Buy tickets in advance, including for 'snooze in the zoo' overnight campouts and 'breakfast with a keeper' events.

Then there are Waikiki's hula shows, all with a lively drum beat and dancing. Families sprawl on the grass to watch the nightly **torch lighting and free hula show** (p137) in Kuhio Beach Park. Head to the Hilton Hawaiian Village on Friday at 5:30pm to get tickets ($20 per person) for a poolside Polynesian song and dance show topped off with a grand **fireworks display** (opposite), visible from the beach for free. Showtime is 6:30pm (7pm April to September), with fireworks at 7:30pm (8pm from April to September).

TOURS

Forget the tour-bus scene! Several catamaran cruises leave right from Waikiki Beach – just walk down to the beach, step into the surf and hop aboard.

Atlantis Adventures (☎ 973-9811, 800-548-6262; www.atlantisadventures.com; 90min tour adult $89, child under 13yr & taller than 36in $45) See the world from a porthole aboard the sub that dives to a depth of 100ft near a reef off Waikiki, offering views of exotic sea life otherwise reserved for divers. There are several sailings daily; check-in is at the Hilton Hawaiian Village inside the Aliʻi Tower.

our pick Maitaʻi Catamaran (☎ 922-5665, 800-462-7975; www.leahi.com) Look for the white catamaran with green sails pulling up on the beach between the Halekulani and Sheraton Waikiki hotels. This company offers the biggest variety of trips, from 90-minute pleasure cruises (adult from $23, child 3 to 12yr from $12) to a sunset booze cruise (adult/child $34/17) and moonlight sails during the Friday fireworks show (by advance reservation only). Looking for something a bit different? An underwater adventure sail (adult/child $45/27) includes reef snorkeling and an onboard picnic.

Na Hoku II (www.nahokuii.com; 90min cruise incl unlimited drinks $25-30) With its unmistakable yellow-and-red striped sails, this frat boy–friendly catamaran departs five times between 9:30am and 5:30pm daily, shoving off from in front of Duke's Waikiki. No reservations necessary.

FESTIVALS & EVENTS

Waikiki loves to party. Every Friday night at 7:30pm from October to March (8pm April to September), the Hilton Hawaiian Village shoots off a big ol' fireworks display, visible from the beach and sounding like thunder inside hotel rooms across Waikiki. For more island-wide festivals and events, see p272.

Ala Wai Challenge (☎ 923-1802; www.waikikicommunitycenter.com) Held the last Sunday in January, this Hawaiian cultural festival includes outrigger canoe races on the Ala Wai Canal and Hawaiian food, games and entertainment at Ala Wai Park.

Honolulu Festival (p81) Features myriad cultural performances at Waikiki Beach Walk and a festive parade along Kalakaua Ave in mid-March.

St Patrick's Day (www.webtaylor.com/fsons) March 17 is celebrated with a parade of bagpipers and marching bands from Fort DeRussy down Kalakaua Ave to Kapiʻolani Park.

Waikiki Spam Jam (www.spamjamhawaii.com) Join thousands of Spam aficionados celebrating Hawaii's favorite tinned meat product at this street festival held on a Saturday in late April.

our pick Pan-Pacific Festival (☎ 926-8177; www.pan-pacific-festival.com) Over a weekend in early June, this Japanese, Hawaiian and South Pacific cultural festival celebrates with hula dancing, *taiko* drumming and an arts-and-crafts fair at the Royal Hawaiian Center, plus a huge *hoʻolauleʻa* (celebration) block party and parade along Kalakaua Ave.

Obon This Japanese festival of the dead with traditional dances is usually marked by an evening floating-lantern ceremony along the Ala Wai Canal in mid-August.

Hawaiian Slack Key Guitar Festival (☎ 226-2697; www.slackkeyfestival.com) Day-long celebration of traditional Hawaiian slack key guitar and ukulele music is held at Kapiʻolani Park in mid-August.

Aloha Festivals (http://alohafestivals.com) Waikiki is famous for its huge evening block party along Kalakaua Ave on the second Friday in September, with food vendors, craft demonstrations, live Hawaiian music and hula dancing on the beach.

WAIKIKI

Crafts courses can teach you how to weave flowered leis

LINDA CHING

Na Wahine o Ke Kai (www.nawahineokekai.com) Hawaii's major annual women's outrigger canoe race, held near the end of September, starts at sunrise on the island of Moloka'i and ends 40 miles later at Waikiki's Kahanamoku Beach.

Moloka'i Hoe (http://molokaihoe.org) Held in mid-October, the men's outrigger canoe world-championship race starts after sunrise on Moloka'i and finishes at Waikiki's Kahanamoku Beach about five hours later.

Honolulu Marathon (☎ 734-7200; www.honolulu marathon.org) The third-largest marathon in the USA finishes at Kapi'olani Park on the second Sunday of December (see also p82).

EATING

Waikiki is chock-full of places to eat, from unpretentious local eateries and drive-ins to some of Hawaii's most acclaimed restaurants. That's not to say there are many bargains found here – often you'll end up overpaying for so-so food. But at least some restaurants are right on the beach, offering ocean views and unforgettable sunsets. Reservations are always a good idea. For a more interesting cuisine scene, leave Waikiki and check out downtown Honolulu, Chinatown and the neighborhoods around the Ala Moana Center and University of Hawai'i campus (see p82).

By the Beach

Kalakaua Ave is stuffed with US mainland chains like the Cheesecake Factory. One block inland, Kuhio Ave has cheaper eats, from breakfast spots to all-night joints.

Top Picks

BREAKFAST BITES

- Bogart's Café (p121)
- Eggs 'n Things (below)
- Hau Tree Lanai (p119)
- LuLu's (p118)
- MAC 24/7 (opposite)

For Sunday brunch buffets, see opposite.

RUFFAGE NATURAL FOODS   Eclectic/Vegetarian $
☎ 922-2042; 2443 Kuhio Ave; items $4-8;
🕑 9am-6pm
Run by super friendly folks, this pint-size health-food store cooks up made-to-order sandwiches, taro burgers, veggie burritos, vegan chili and real-fruit smoothies that will revitalize your whole body. The shop, which also sells protein bars and cookies, shares space with a tiny, budget-friendly nighttime sushi bar run by a Japanese chef.

EGGS 'N THINGS   Diner $
☎ 949-0820; 343 Saratoga Rd; mains $4-10;
🕑 6am-10pm
Never empty, this bustling diner dishes up reliable breakfast fare, from banana–mac nut pancakes topped with tropical syrups (including guava, honey or coconut) to fluffy omelettes with Portuguese sausage on the side. You'll fit right in with the early-

A touch of tiki at the Royal Hawaiian Center (p125)

ANN CECIL

SUNDAY BRUNCH & AFTERNOON TEA

O'ahu's most elegant Sunday brunch buffet is at **Orchids** (☎ 923-2311; Halekulani, 2199 Kalia Rd; buffet $52; 🕑 9:30am-2:30pm Sun). The spread includes an omelette station, a varying array of *poke* (cubed raw tuna) and salads, and a decadent dessert bar. But don't come for the just-OK food – it's the glorious ocean view, tropical flowers and live harp and flute music that set the mood. Make reservations.

For colonial atmosphere, the **Veranda** (☎ 921-4600; Moana Surfrider, 2365 Kalakaua Ave; afternoon tea $33-43; 🕑 1-4pm) is Waikiki's top choice for afternoon tea, complete with finger sandwiches, scones with Devonshire cream and island-flavored pastries. Portions are small, but the ocean-front setting and house-blended teas are memorable. Valet parking is complimentary (don't forget to tip).

For something more casual, **Brunch on the Beach** (☎ 923-1094; www.waikikiimprovement.com; 🕑 usually 9am-1:30pm) usually takes place on the third Sunday of the month, when oceanfront Kalakaua Ave is lined with umbrella-shaded tables and transformed into a huge outdoor cafe. Chefs from some of Honolulu's top restaurants set up food stands and Hawaiian musicians perform along the beach. Most items cost just a couple of dollars; you can easily eat your fill for under $20.

morning crowd of jet-lagged tourists and post-clubbers.

ME BBQ
Korean/American $

☎ 926-9717; 151 Uluniu Ave; meals $4-12; 🕑 7am-9pm Mon-Sat

This streetside takeout counter may have zero atmosphere, but service is lightning-fast and there are a few rickety plastic sidewalk tables where you can chow down in the sunshine. Korean standards like kimchi and *kalbi* ribs are the house specialty, but the wall-sized picture menu also offers island-style mixed-plate combos including chicken *katsu* (deep-fried chicken), shrimp tempura or Portuguese sausage and eggs.

MOOSE MCGILLYCUDDY'S
American $

☎ 923-0751; 310 Lewers St; mains $5-15; 🕑 7am-10pm

This 1980s time-warped dance club rakes in a breakfast crowd with huge omelettes plus *loco moco*, French toast, *huevos rancheros* (rice, fried egg and hamburger patty) and fluffy banana muffins. At night, a hard-drinkin' crowd swings by for cheap-ass burgers, Mexican fare and steaks.

WAILANA COFFEE HOUSE
American $

☎ 955-1764; 1860 Ala Moana Blvd; mains $5-15; 🕑 24hr

Opposite the Hilton Hawaiian Village, this all-night coffee shop is stuck in the 1970s (just like the karaoke singers in the attached cocktail lounge). Wait staff call the senior citizens and graveyard-shift workers sitting at counter stools and in Naugahyde booths by name. The food ain't great, but Salisbury steak dinners including a salad bar, or the all-you-can-eat pancake special with fried Spam on the side, are bargains.

MAC 24/7
American $$

☎ 921-5564; Hilton Waikiki Prince Kuhio, 2500 Kuhio Ave; mains $6-30; 🕑 24hr

A mod *Jetsons*-style diner, with bold colors, space-age counter stools and loopy service, this ambitious hotel kitchen does classic American cooking with a twist: cinnamon streusel pancakes, mac-nut Cobb salad and chicken pot pie with island-grown vegetables. Plates are enormous, although quality varies. The full bar is closed from 4am to 6am – sorry, night owls. Free validated parking (don't forget to tip).

MENCHANKO-TEI
Japanese $$

☎ 924-8366; Waikiki Trade Center, 2255 Kuhio Ave; mains $8-12; 🕑 11am-11pm

Japanese expats and locals alike go to this modest kitchen for their fix of Hakata-style ramen soup with freshly made noodles, citrus pepper and a creamy broth that tastes just like it does on the island of Kyūshū in southern Japan. It also makes a mean *tonkatsu* (deep-fried pork cutlet), and the *gyōza* (fried dumplings) and Nagasaki-style *sara-udon* (fried noodles with stir-fried veggies) reign supreme. Free validated parking.

WAIKIKI

RAMEN NAKAMURA
Japanese $$

☎ 922-7960; 2141 Kalakaua Ave; mains $8-12;
⏲ 11am-11:45pm

Hit this urban connoisseur's noodle shop at lunchtime and you'll probably have to strategically elbow aside some Japanese tourists toting Gucci and Chanel bags just to sit down. Then dig into hearty bowls of oxtail or *tonkatsu* kimchi ramen soup with crunchy fried garlic slices on top. The food's not cheap, but almost always worth the wait.

LULU'S
American $$

☎ 926-5222; 2nd fl, 2586 Kalakaua Ave; mains breakfast $6-15, dinner $10-24; ⏲ 7am-1:45am

Surfboards on the wall and an awesome ocean view set the mood at this raucous open-air restaurant, bar and nightclub just opposite Kuhio Beach Park. Grab your friends and dig into enormous island-flavored *pupu* platters after a day at the beach. Some think Lulu's breakfasts, complete with omelettes, eggs Benedict and fruit bowls, are legendary, although most of what the kitchen churns out is pretty mediocre.

SIAM SQUARE
Thai $$

☎ 923-5320; 2nd fl, 408 Lewers St; mains $11-16;
⏲ 11am-11pm Mon-Sat, 11am-10pm Sun

A sister restaurant to Honolulu's Siam Garden Cafe, this is the most authentic Thai restaurant in Waikiki. You say you want it spicy? Good, because that's the only way you're going to get it here, like the *larb* pork salad or fried fish with chili sauce. Service is standoffish, but the kitchen works so fast and furiously that you probably won't mind.

Top Picks

LATE-NIGHT EATS

- Sansei Seafood Restaurant & Sushi Bar (right)
- MAC 24/7 (p117)
- LuLu's (above)
- Wailana Coffee House (p117)
- Ono Cheesesteak (p120)
- Da Big Kahuna (p140)

ARANCINO
Italian/Japanese $$

☎ 923-5557; 255 Beach Walk; mains $11-32;
⏲ lunch & dinner

Italian food just the way mama makes it – that is, if your mother hails from Tokyo. When you're sitting at one of the sidewalk tables with quaintly checked tablecloths, you can follow the lead of Japanese tourists ordering spaghetti with garlicky squid-ink sauce, or stick with back-to-basics pastas like penne gorgonzola or good ol' spaghetti and meatballs. Fresh house-made focaccia bread is complimentary.

RESTAURANT KAIWA
Japanese Fusion $$$

☎ 924-1555; 2nd fl, 226 Lewers St; mains $12-36;
⏲ 11am-2pm Mon-Fri, 5pm-midnight (last orders 10:30pm) daily

Catering to connoisseurs and Japanese tourists with Eurasian taste buds, this clean-lined, ultramodern dining room is equal parts zen (bamboo, steel and natural fibers) and baroque (kimono-cloth patterned fabric ceilings and silk-screened art). From the sushi bar and teppanyaki grill, expect a seasonal menu of high-flying concept dishes, many using fresh, island-grown ingredients. The sake menu is mighty tempting.

SHORE BIRD RESTAURANT & BEACH BAR
Steak & Seafood $$$

☎ 922-2887; Outrigger Reef on the Beach, 2169 Kalia Rd; breakfast & lunch buffet $13, mains lunch $9-15, dinner $14-27; ⏲ 7am-10pm

It may be a tourist trap, but being right on the ocean almost makes up for it. For dinner, there's live Hawaiian music and a huge smokin' grill where you barbecue your own order – fresh fish, juicy steaks or chicken – then hit the generous buffet-style salad bar, which includes island favorites like *haupia* (coconut pudding) and fresh tropical fruit.

SANSEI SEAFOOD RESTAURANT & SUSHI BAR
Japanese Fusion $$$

☎ 931-6286; 3rd fl, Waikiki Beach Marriott Resort, 2552 Kalakaua Ave; appetizers $3-18, mains $16-35; ⏲ 5:30-10pm Sun-Thu, 5:30pm-1am Fri & Sat

From the mind of one of Hawaii's hottest chefs, DK Kodama, the menu rolls out everything from traditional 'ahi sashimi to Dungeness crab ramen with a black truffle butter sauce. Tables on the torch-lit veranda enjoy prime sunset views. Line up for the early-bird special, only available before 6pm on Sunday and Monday evenings, and get 25% off everything you eat (but not drink), or show up after 10pm on Friday and Saturday nights for 50% off the food menu. It's almost too good to be true.

HULA GRILL
Steak & Seafood $$$
☎ 923-4852; 2nd fl, Outrigger Waikiki on the Beach, 2335 Kalakaua Ave; breakfast items $2-7, bar & cafe appetizers $8-14, dinner mains $17-34; ⏰ breakfast & dinner

Come early to score a table on the wraparound lanai that hangs over Waikiki Beach and watch the sun set over all the playful seaside action. You'll also be rewarded with cheap mai tais, 'wrong island' ice teas and island-style *pupu* like mango barbecued ribs, but the best deal is the gorgeous view. Simple à la carte breakfasts are expensive, but offer refreshingly healthy options like honey granola with tropical fruit and yogurt.

OKONOMIYAKI CHIBO
Japanese $$$
☎ 922-9722; 3rd fl, Royal Hawaiian Center, 2201 Kalakaua Ave; lunch $10-20, dinner mains $18-38; ⏰ lunch Mon-Sat, dinner daily

With a sleek, dark-wood interior, this high-end teppanyaki grill is a standout for its customized chef-made *okonomiyaki* (Japanese cabbage pancakes topped with a savory sauce). Go the traditional route and order one made with *buta* (pork) or *ika* (squid), or go all out with steak, scallops and prawns. For *okonomiyaki* novices and kids, the *mochi*-cheese version is pure comfort food. Lunch is a fair deal; dinner is overpriced.

HAU TREE LANAI
Island Contemporary $$$$
☎ 921-7066; New Otani Kaimana Beach Hotel, 2863 Kalakaua Ave; mains breakfast $8-15, lunch $10-18, dinner $30-44; ⏰ breakfast 7-10:45am daily, lunch 11:45am-2pm Mon-Sat & noon-2pm Sun, dinner 5:30-9pm nightly

A classic beachfront setting under an arbor of hau trees characterizes this delightful restaurant right on Sans Souci Beach. A favorite breakfast spot for islanders, here the menu abounds in local flavor with everything from poi pancakes to seafood omelettes. Surf-and-turf dinners, serenaded by the sounds of the surf and Hawaiian music

nightly except Sunday, is as romantic as it gets.

NOBU WAIKIKI
Japanese Fusion $$$$
☎ 237-6999; Waikiki Parc Hotel, 2233 Helumoa Rd; shared plates $2-48, mains $32-40, chef's tasting menu from $90; ⏰ restaurant 5:30-10pm Sun-Wed, 5:30-11pm Thu-Sat, lounge 5pm-midnight

Iron Chef Matsuhisa's Japanese fusion restaurant has made a big splash in Waikiki, where his hybrid dishes taste right at home. Broiled black cod with miso sauce, Japanese-Peruvian *tiradito* (similar to seviche) and seafood tartar are among Nobu's signature tastes. On weekdays before 7pm, the chic lounge sometimes offers a tasting trio of appetizers (vegetarians OK) for $18, including a signature 'sake-tini.'

ROY'S – WAIKIKI BEACH
Hawaii Regional $$$$
our pick ☎ 923-7697; 226 Lewers St; mains $28-40; ⏰ dinner

This contemporary incarnation of an island-born restaurant chain is perfect for a flirty date or celebrating the good life with friends. Innovative chef Roy Yamaguchi doesn't actually cook here, but his signature *misoyaki* butterfish, blackened 'ahi, macadamia nut–encrusted mahimahi and deconstructed sushi rolls are always on the menu, along with creative concoctions by the head chef. Molten chocolate soufflé for dessert is a must.

PRINCE COURT & HAKONE
Buffet $$$$
☎ 944-4494; 3rd fl, Hawaii Prince Hotel Waikiki, 100 Holomoana St; buffet breakfast $21, Sun brunch $35, dinner $44; ⏰ breakfast buffet 6-10:30am Mon-Sat & 6-8:30am Sun, brunch buffet 10am-1pm Sun, dinner buffet 5:30-9:30pm Fri-Sun

Hidden away from all the hubbub, the elegant Prince Court restaurant offers serene views of Ala Wai Yacht Harbor and fully loaded buffets of Asian and American cuisine. Weekend seafood dinner buffets feature hot and cold mains, chef-carved prime rib and a Vietnamese *pho* station, plus tropical desserts. The hotel's equally posh, if blandly designed, Hakone restaurant puts on a Japanese buffet nightly, with plentiful sushi, sashimi, tempura, *shabushabu* (hot pot) and noodle dishes.

WAIKIKI

LA MER
French $$$$

☎ 923-2311; Halekulani, 2199 Kalia Rd; 2-/3-/4-course dinner $90/120/135, 9-course tasting menu $150; ⏰ 6-10pm

The best of the best, La Mer is considered by many to be O'ahu's ultimate fine-dining restaurant, boasting a spectacular view of Diamond Head through swaying palms. A neoclassical French menu puts the emphasis on Provençal cuisine with the addition of fresh Hawaii-grown ingredients. Wines are perfectly paired. Formal is the byword: men must wear either a jacket or a collared long-sleeved shirt.

For snacks, groceries and takeout deli meals:

Food Pantry (☎ 923-9831; 2370 Kuhio Ave; ⏰ 6am-1am) Higher priced than chain supermarkets outside Waikiki, but less expensive than convenience stores; Beard Papa's cream puffs sold here.

Red Mango (☎ 922-0848; 227 Lewers St; yoghurt $3-6; ⏰ 9am-10pm Sun-Thu, 9am-11pm Fri & Sat) SoCal-style all-natural frozen yogurt topped with fresh fruit, crumbled cookie, nuts or chocolate.

Satura Cakes (☎ 537-1206; Royal Hawaiian Center, 2233 Kalakaua Ave; pastries $3-6; ⏰ 8am-10pm) Japanese-American bakery for perfect Eurasian pastries and an espresso bar.

Ono Cheesesteak (☎ 923-8080; 2310 Kuhio Ave; sandwiches $4-10; ⏰ 24hr) For a fairly authentic 'Philly cheesesteak in paradise' with seasoned curly fries on the side.

Puka Dog (☎ 924-7887; Waikiki Town Center, 2301 Kuhio Ave; items $5-8; ⏰ 10am-10pm) Tropical relishes catapulted this high-priced hot-dog stand (vegetarians OK) onto the *Food Network;* staff are lackadaisical.

Teddy's Bigger Burgers (☎ 926-3444; Waikiki Grand Hotel, 134 Kapahulu Ave; sandwiches $5-10; ⏰ 10:30am-9pm) For 1950s-style black-and-white checkered decor and hand-formed burgers, cheesy fries and milkshakes.

Inland

For everyday restaurants, detour inland along Kapahulu Ave, which is packed with affordable multi-ethnic eats, from Hawaiian soul food and shave ice to Japanese country cooking. The strip malls of Monsarrat Ave are also good grazing grounds.

LEONARD'S
Bakery $

our pick ☎ 737-5591; 933 Kapahulu Ave; items 75¢-$2; ⏰ 6am-9pm Mon-Thu, 6am-10pm Fri & Sat

It's almost impossible to drive by Leonard's 1950s neon sign without stopping in.

Malasadas **from Leonard's** LINDA CHING

This Portuguese bakery is known throughout O'ahu for its *malasadas*, a sweet fried dough rolled in sugar and served warm – like a doughnut without the hole. Order the *haupia malasada*, filled with coconut cream, and you'll be hooked.

WAIOLA BAKERY & SHAVE ICE II
Dessert $

☎ 949-2269; 525 Kapahulu Ave; items $2-4; ⏰ 7:30am-6pm

This clapboard corner shop has been serving super-fine shave ice since 1940, and many argue that it's got the formula exactly right. Ask for yours doused in one of 40 different flavors of sugar-syrup, then topped with azuki beans, *mochi* (sticky-sweet Japanese pounded-rice balls), condensed milk, chocolate syrup or even spicy Chinese-Hawaiian crack seed.

🍴 RAINBOW DRIVE-IN
Drive-In/Takeout $

☎ 737-0177; 3308 Kanaina Ave; meals $3.50-7; ⏰ 7:30am-9pm

Started by an island-born US Army cook after WWII, this classic Hawaii drive-in wrapped in rainbow-colored neon is a throwback to another era. Construction workers, surfers and gangly teens order all the local favorites like burgers, barbecue mixed-plate lunches, chili dogs and *loco moco* bowls from the takeout counter. The owners' family donates some of the profits to Hawaiian schools and local charity organizations. Factoid: US president, Barack Obama, likes to eat here.

DIAMOND HEAD MARKET & GRILL
Drive-in/Takeout $

☎ 732-0077; 3158 Monsarrat Ave; meals $4-15; 🕑 6:30am-9pm

Step inside this neighborhood market for fresh-baked goods and a gourmet deli serving up the likes of roast pork loin and citrus jicama salad, perfect for a beach picnic. Outside at the grill's takeout window, you can order anything from portobello mushroom burgers to mixed-plate meals with *char siu* (Chinese barbecued pork). Bike commuters and surfers stop by for big breakfasts of banana, coconut or blueberry pancakes.

TENKAIPPIN
Japanese $

☎ 723-1211; 617 Kapahulu Ave; mains $8-12; 🕑 11am-10pm Mon-Thu, 11am-11pm Fri & Sat

This imported Japanese chain of noodle shops definitely gives Ramen Nakamura (p118) a run for its yen. It's way less crowded here, though. For something unique, order the *kotteri*-style ramen, a thick, gelatinous chicken-broth stew with sliced *char siu*, minced garlic and pepper. Combo set meals with chewy fried pork *gyōza* are unbelievably filling.

🍴 ONO HAWAIIAN FOODS
Hawaiian $$

☎ 737-2275; 726 Kapahulu Ave; dishes $2-11, combo plates $12-16; 🕑 11am-8pm Mon-Sat

It's just a simple diner, where locals shoehorn themselves in among the crowded tables and sports paraphernalia, but at dinnertime people line up on the sidewalk waiting to get in. Real-deal Hawaiian-style favorites include *kalua* (cooked in a pot) pig, *lomilomi* salmon, *laulau* (meat wrapped in *ti* leaves and steamed), poi (fermented taro paste) and *haupia* (coconut-cream pudding).

TOKKURI TEI
Japanese $$

☎ 739-2800; 611 Kapahulu Ave; dishes $3-15; 🕑 11am-2pm Mon-Fri, 5:30pm-midnight Mon-Sat, 5-10pm Sun

This under-the-radar neighborhood *izakaya* (Japanese pub serving food) dishes out upbeat, contemporary versions of Japanese standards. Paper lanterns hang overhead, while built-in bookcases store customers' private bottles of liquor. Try the house-made spider *poke* with fish roe, grilled *kushiyaki* skewers or soft-shell crab drizzled with a sweet chili vinaigrette, all washed down with sake or *shōchū* (potato liquor).

BOGART'S CAFE
Coffee Shop $$

☎ 739-0999; 3045 Monsarrat Ave; mains $5-10; 🕑 6am-6:30pm Mon-Fri, 6am-6pm Sat & Sun

On the Diamond Head side of Kapi'olani Park, this locals' espresso bar, where surfers, artists and dot-com millionaires all get their caffeinated jolts, is a hot breakfast spot, especially for fluffy Belgian waffles and crab-and-avocado omelettes. At lunch, there are veggie wraps and salads. The baristas can be haughty and service might take forever. Next door is funky Diamond Head Cove Health Bar (p139).

IRIFUNE
Japanese $$

☎ 737-1141; 563 Kapahulu Ave; mains $12-18; 🕑 11:30am-1:30pm & 5:30-9:30pm Tue-Sat

This bustling kitchen decorated with Japanese country kitsch may look very odd, especially when they turn off the lights so you can see those glow-in-the-dark stars on the ceiling. But Irifune is locally beloved for its garlic *'ahi* stir-fry and *gyōza* stuffed with tofu and cream cheese. With such bargain-priced combo plates, you won't walk away hungry. Alcohol is not served, but you can BYOB (bring your own beer).

UNCLE BO'S
Hawaii Regional $$$

☎ 735-8311; 559 Kapahulu Ave; shared plates $6-14, mains $11-26; 🕑 5pm-2am

A surprisingly hip resto-bar inside a divey-looking storefront, this ubercool culinary outpost is home to chefs tried and tested in some of Waikiki's top restaurants. Boisterous groups of friends can devour the endless list of *pupu* crafted with tantalizing island flair, like baby-back ribs with Maui onions and chilis, or *kalua* pig nachos with wonton chips. For dinner, pastas and steaks take a back seat to market-fresh seafood like Chinese-style steamed *opakapaka* or Thai seafood coconut curry.

WAIKIKI

ISLAND VOICES

NAME: POMAIKA'I KEAWE LYMAN
OCCUPATION: VOCALIST & MUSICIAN
RESIDENCE: WAIKIKI

How did you get started playing music? It's in my family. There were instruments in the house all the time, and we were always tagging along to performances and gigs with my grandmother, Genoa Keawe. You know, when you're surrounded by something all the time, you can just pick things up.

Why did you choose to play the ukulele? It was the first instrument I learned – my grandma taught it to me. She had a tradition that when the children in the house become big enough to take care of an instrument and fit their fingers on the frets, she'd buy them a small ukulele so that they could start learning.

Why do you love playing music? Partly because it's relaxing for me. I also like the company that comes with it – the friendships, and the fun of playing. The other reason is because I grew up with Hawaiian music in my family, so I feel this *kuleana*, or responsibility, to perpetuate Hawaiiana. Some islanders grow up in hula families or working in the *kalo lo'i* (taro fields). This is my place in our culture, this is who I am.

What makes Hawaiian music unique? It's easy listening, I think. Even if you don't understand the words, you can get a feel for what the song is about through the melody. Sometimes it's tricky, though, because some slow songs can be about some pretty funny stuff, while the fast songs might actually be about love and romance. That's why we have *kaona*, the double meaning. That's where you have the literal translation of the lyrics, and then a more hidden meaning. It can be fun, if you understand the Hawaiian language.

How has Waikiki changed over the years? I grew up in a time when all of the changes were happening, and every hotel was trying new things. Part of Waikiki's modern makeover has been to incorporate more traditional Hawaiian music here. And I think that's important, because it's music that can give visitors a real sense of our culture – our songs tell the story.

What makes O'ahu different from other Hawaiian Islands? O'ahu has the most diversity and the biggest variety of people. We also have both the city and the country. If you head out from Waikiki to the North Shore or the west side, you'll feel like you're on a different island. O'ahu really is a place of extremes.

For island-fresh produce and takeout meals:
Farmers Market (☎ 923-1802; Waikiki Community Center, 310 Pa'oakalani Ave; 🕐 7am-1pm Tue & Fri) Fresh produce stands set up in the parking lot.

People's Open Market (☎ 522-7088; cnr Monsarrat & Paki Aves, Kapi'olani Park; 🕐 10-11am Wed) City-sponsored farmers market for fresh bounty from land and sea.

Ono Seafood (☎ 732-4806; 747 Kapahulu Ave; *poke* $2-12; 🕐 vary) An addictive, made-to-order *poke* shop – get there early before it runs out of fresh fish.

Bento-ya Iyasume (☎ 735-3530; 611 Kapahulu Ave; meals $6.50-9; 🕐 usually 7am-6pm) Tiny Japanese-Hawaiian takeout deli next to Dave's Hawaiian Ice Cream.

DRINKING & ENTERTAINMENT

Whether you just want to linger over one of those cool, frosty drinks with the little umbrellas or are looking for Hawaiian music and hula dancing, you're in the right place – just check out the Waikiki After Dark chapter (p135). For current schedules, pick up the free *Honolulu Weekly* tabloid or the TGIF insert in the Friday edition of the *Honolulu Advertiser* newspaper.

SHOPPING

Hundreds of shops in Waikiki are vying for your tourist dollars. Catwalk designers like Armani, Gucci and Pucci have boutiques inside the DFS Galleria at the north end of Kalakaua Ave, while some high-quality, only-in-Hawaii stores line the Waikiki Beach

Walk. Not feeling exactly flush? You'll never be far from one of Waikiki's ubiquitous ABC Stores, which stand on nearly every other street corner; they're the handiest and often cheapest place to pick up vacation goodies like beach mats, sunblock, snacks and sundries, not to mention plastic flower and shell leis, 'I got lei'd in Hawaii' T-shirts and motorized, grass-skirted hula girls for the dashboard of your car back home.

Antiques & Vintage Wear

BAILEY'S ANTIQUES & ALOHA SHIRTS

our pick ☎ 734-7628; 517 Kapahulu Ave; ☻ 10am-6pm

There's no place like Bailey's, which has without a doubt the finest aloha shirt collection on O'ahu. Rotating racks are crammed

---

GAY & LESBIAN WAIKIKI

What the Waikiki scene may lack in venues, it makes up for in aloha. Pick up the monthly magazine, *Odyssey* (www.odysseyhawaii.com), free at Waikiki's gay clubs and bars or the all-in-one convenience shop **80% Straight** (☎ 923-9996; Waikiki Grand Hotel, 134 Kapahulu Ave; ☻ 10am-11pm Mon-Thu, 10am-midnight Fri & Sat, noon-11pm Sun), which also sells beachwear, books, magazines, videos and leather gear. The free tabloid *Honolulu Weekly* also includes LGBT listings on its calendar.

If you're new to Waikiki, first stop by our pick **Hula's Bar & Lei Stand** (Map p136; ☎ 923-0669; www.hulas.com; 2nd fl, Waikiki Grand Hotel, 134 Kapahulu Ave; ☻ 10am-2am; ▢ ☎). This friendly, open-air bar, Waikiki's main gay venue, is a great place to meet, dance and have a few drinks. It also has a pool table and a noteworthy view of Diamond Head.

Angles Waikiki (Map p136; ☎ 926-9766, infoline 923-1130; www.angleswaikiki.com; 2256 Kuhio Ave; ☻ 10am-2am) is a high-energy nightclub with dancing, pool tournaments, all-male revues, BBQ nights and group catamaran cruises. Next door is the 2nd-floor bar **Fusion Waikiki** (Map p136; ☎ 924-2422; 2260 Kuhio Ave; ☻ 10pm-4am Sun-Thu, 8pm-4am Fri & Sat), a hot spot with weekend drag shows and DJs, plus karaoke on some weeknights. **In-Between** (Map p136; ☎ 926-7060; www.inbetweenonline.com; 2155 Lau'ula St; ☻ 4pm-2am Mon-Thu, noon-2am Fri & Sat, 2pm-2am Sun), a friendly neighborhood bar, attracts an older crowd with the 'happiest of happy hours.'

And then there's life in the sunshine. **Queen's Surf Beach** (p108) is the darling of the sun-worshipping gay crowd. Further afield, **Diamond Head Beach** (p153), near the lighthouse, is another popular gay gathering spot, with some (technically illegal) clothing-optional sun-bathing going on. Gay-oriented **Like Hike** (http://gayhawaii.com/likehike) organizes twice-monthly trips around O'ahu, but you must call or email the trip leader before joining up; details can be found on the website.

Where to stay? **Cabana at Waikiki** (☎ 926-5555, 877-902-2121; www.cabana-waikiki.com; 2551 Cartwright Rd; 1br incl breakfast $159-255; ▣ per day $22 ▨ ▢ ☎ ▨) shines as Waikiki's only exclusively gay hotel, and it's just minutes from Hula's, Queen's Surf Beach and **24-Hour Fitness** (p110). Each of the 15 units has a king-size bed, full-size sofa bed and either a kitchenette or full kitchen. The **Waikiki Grand Hotel** (p128), home to Hula's, and **Hotel Renew** (p129) are not exclusively gay but rank high with gay visitors. The former also offers longer-term vacation rentals.

For more background information, including LGBT community websites, special events and travel agencies, see p277.

with thousands of collector-worthy vintage aloha shirts in every conceivable color and style, from 1920s kimono-silk classics to 1970s polyester specials. Of the new generation of reproduced shirts, Bailey's only carries Hawaii-made labels like Kona Bay and RJC. Prices vary from $5 to several thousand dollars. Jimmy Buffet is Bailey's biggest fan.

NEWT AT THE ROYAL
☎ 922-0062; Royal Hawaiian Hotel, 2259 Kalakaua Ave; ☼ 9am-9pm

With stylish flair and panache, Newt specializes in Montecristi Panama hats – classic men's fedoras, plantation-style hats and women's *fino* – and fine reproductions of aloha shirts using 1940s and '50s designs. Everything's tropical, neat as a pin and top-drawer quality.

ISLAND TREASURES ANTIQUES
☎ 922-8223; 2nd fl, Waikiki Town Center, 2301 Kuhio Ave; ☼ 2-8pm Tue-Sat & 2-6pm Sun

Looking for retro and kitsch Hawaiiana? This mid-20th-century antique minimall is for you. Here you'll find everything you need to decorate your very own basement tiki bar, from hip-shaking hula dolls and old Hawaii license plates to souvenirs from yesteryear Waikiki hotels, plus 20th-century glassware, jewelry, ceramics and porcelain.

Art & Crafts

🌺 NA LIMA MILI HULU NO'EAU
☎ 732-0865; 762 Kapahulu Ave; ☼ 9am-5pm Mon-Sat

Aunty Mary Louise Kaleonahenahe Kekuewa and her daughter Paulette keep alive the ancient Hawaiian craft of feather lei-making at this homespun little shop. They also teach schoolchildren, and created the book *Feather Lei as an Art* to encourage a revival of this indigenous art. The shop's name translates as 'the skilled hands that touch the feathers,' and it can take days to produce a single lei, prized by collectors.

🌺 MANA HAWAI'I
☎ 923-2220; Ste 224, Waikiki Beach Walk; ☼ 9am-10pm

Unlike many shops on Waikiki Beach Walk, this soothing space displays authentic Hawaii-made products, including island wood carvings, fine-art photography, a diverse collection of Hawaiiana titles and classic posters. The shop also has a convenient headphone setup that lets you listen to Hawaiian-music CDs by everyone from Bruddah Iz to Jake Shimabukaro. The shop also hosts free Hawaiian cultural workshops and classes (see p114).

LITTLE HAWAIIAN CRAFT SHOP
☎ 926-2662; 3rd fl, Royal Hawaiian Center, 2201 Kalakaua Ave; ☼ 10am-10pm

With a bit of a split personality, this long-standing emporium of Hawaiiana sells trinkets like *kukui*-nut key chains alongside fine necklaces made of Ni'ihau shells and high-quality koa bowls, with most goods made by local or Polynesian artisans. Friendly staff don't mind if you just browse.

MARTIN & MACARTHUR
☎ 923-5333; Hyatt Regency Waikiki, 2424 Kalakaua Ave; ☼ 9am-11pm

With a motto like 'gracious Hawaiian living,' you can feel the nostalgia for Hawaii's plantation era here. Koa furniture takes up most of the shop, but there's also a standout selection of upmarket Hawaiiana products, including carved bowls, Hawaiian quilts and etched-glass jewelry. Some of the handmade items are museum-quality.

BOB'S UKULELE
☎ 372-9623; Waikiki Beach Marriott Resort, 2552 Kalakaua Ave; ☼ 9am-noon & 5-9pm

If you can't make it over to Kamaka Hawaii (p95), then this is the next-best place to shop for that uniquely Hawaiian instrument, the ukulele. Skip the flimsy, low-priced imports and take a look at the Hawaii-made ukes handcrafted from native woods. The knowledgeable staff welcome special orders.

HONOLULU ZOO ART MART
Kapi'olani Park, along Monsarrat Ave; ☼ 9am-4pm Sat & Sun

Dozens of artists hang their works along the fence on the southern side of the zoo (p110) every weekend, weather permitting. You'll find mostly contemporary paintings and photography, often sold by the artists themselves. Legal action by the **Kapi'olani Park Preservation Society** (www.kapiolanipark.org) may soon shut down the weekly art fair; check the website for updates.

Have some kitschy fun at Hawaiiana souvenir shops

LINDA CHING

Shopping Centers

Waikiki has several shopping centers, most chock-full of the brand-label stores you'd find in any US mainland city. For information about the Ala Moana Center, Hawaii's largest mall, and the nearby Ward Centers, see p94.

ROYAL HAWAIIAN CENTER

☎ 922-2299; 2201 Kalakaua Ave; ☼ 10am-10pm

Not to be confused with the Royal Hawaiian Hotel, Waikiki's biggest shopping center has four levels and houses more than a hundred stores selling jewelry, casual clothing and designer labels from Fendi to 7 For All Mankind, plus a few island-grown beachwear brands like Crazy Shirts and Honolua Surf Co, and a flagship Hilo Hattie store.

INTERNATIONAL MARKET PLACE

☎ 971-2080; 2330 Kalakaua Ave; ☼ 10am-10:30pm

For kitschy and trashy souvenirs, visit this market set under a sprawling banyan tree next to Waikiki Town Center mall. More than a hundred stalls sell everything from seashell necklaces to sarongs and hibiscus-print handbags, with live Hawaiian music, Polynesian dancing or steel drums almost every night. Check out Town & Country Surf Shop for quality O'ahu-made surfboards, surf-style clothing and rubbah slippahs.

SLEEPING

Waikiki's main beachfront strip, Kalakaua Ave, is lined with high-rise resort hotels. Some of them are true beauties with quiet gardens and seaside courtyards, while others are high-rise megahotels catering to the package-tour crowd. At many hotels, the rooms and amenities are the same, with only the views varying.

If you're paying extra for a view, you should know that the terms 'ocean view,' 'ocean front' and 'partial ocean view' are all liberally used. Waikiki doesn't have any truth-in-labeling laws governing when a hotel can call a room 'ocean view.' Some are mere glimpses of the water as seen through a series of high-rise buildings. 'City' or 'mountain' views are sometimes euphemisms for overlooking a parking lot.

If stepping out of your room and digging your toes in the sand isn't a must, there are inviting small hotels on Waikiki's backstreets. Some hotels near Kuhio Ave and near the Ala Wai Canal have rooms as lovely as many of the beachfront hotels, but at half the price. If you don't mind walking to the beach, you can save a bundle.

All rates listed below are standard high-season (mid-December to April) rack rates. Substantial discounts are often available online through the hotels' own websites, via

WAIKIKI

online travel discounters (Expedia, Orbitz, Travelocity etc) and for flight and rental-car package deals, especially in the off-season. For more valuable tips on finding accommodations on O'ahu, see p268.

Daily parking surcharges at your hotel may cost more than the actual daily car-rental fee, so only rent a car for those days that you'll be making excursions around the island. Increasingly, many hotels are implementing mandatory 'resort fees,' which tack on an extra $5 to $25 per day to your final bill. These fees may cover the costs of internet connections, local and toll-free phone calls and fitness-room access. If you're lucky, you'll get some free souvenir swag and a couple of mai tais too.

Waikiki has far more hotel rooms than condos. Apart from the condo hotels reviewed here, the best way to find a condo in Waikiki is to contact one of the vacation-rental agencies that handle bookings for individual condo owners, including **Pacific Islands Reservations** (☎ 808-262-8133; www.waikiki-condo-rentals .com), **Aloha Waikiki Vacation Condos** (☎ 924-0433, 800-655-6055; www.waikiki-condos.com) and **Hawaiian Beach Rentals** (☎ 800-853-0787; www.hawaiianbeach rentals.com). You can also browse listings online at **Vacation Rentals By Owner** (www.vrbo.com) and **Craigslist** (http://honolulu.craigslist.org).

HOSTELLING INTERNATIONAL – WAIKIKI
Hostel $

☎ 926-8313; www.hostelsaloha.com; 2417 Prince Edward St; dm $25-28, d $58-64; ⏰ reception 1pm-3am; Ⓟ per day $5 🖥

This friendly little hostel with single-sex dormitories occupies an aqua-painted, concrete-block converted apartment complex just a few short blocks from the beach. Unlike most other HI hostels, there's no dorm lockout or curfew. There's a self-catering kitchen, coin-op laundry, lockers, bike storage and free bodyboards to borrow. Advance reservations are essential and there's a seven-night maximum stay. No smoking, no alcohol.

WAIKIKI BEACHSIDE HOSTEL
Hostel $

☎ 923-9566, 866-478-3888; www.waikikibeach sidehostel.com; 2556 Lemon Rd; dm $26-35, semi-private r $67-76; Ⓟ per day $5 🖥

This private hostel attracts an international party crowd and offers plenty of perks, from a 24-hour internet room to cheap is-

land tours. Like most hostels on sketchy, back-alley Lemon Rd, this one occupies an older apartment complex. Each unit has a kitchen, bathroom, semiprivate room and dorm beds (either coed or female-only) and a telephone. Security, cleaning and hostel management are very lax. Expect higher rates during holidays and special events.

ROYAL GROVE HOTEL
Independent Hotel $

☎ 923-7691; www.royalgrovehotel.com; 151 Uluniu Ave; r $55-100; 🌀 🖥 🔊

No frills but plenty of aloha characterize this kitschy, candy pink–colored hotel that attracts so many returning snowbirds it's nearly impossible to get a room in winter without advance reservations. Retro motel-style rooms in the main wing are basic but do have lanai. Avoid rooms in the old Mauka Wing, which are small, noisy and lack air-con. All rooms have kitchenettes. Weekly rates available from April to November.

WAIKIKI PRINCE HOTEL
Independent Hotel $

☎ 922-1544; www.waikikiprince.com; 2431 Prince Edward St; r $65-100; Ⓟ per day $10 🌀 🛜

Forget about ocean views and never mind the cramped check-in office; this six-story, 1970s-era apartment complex is another one of Waikiki's hidden gems on an anonymous side street. Inside you'll find 24 compact yet cheery rooms that feel fresh and reasonably modern, each equipped with at least a small fridge, microwave and refrigerator; more expensive rooms have kitchenettes. Free wi-fi in lobby.

AQUA ALOHA SURF & SPA
International Hotel $$

☎ 923-0222, 866-406-2782; www.aquaresorts.com; 444 Kanekapolei St; r incl breakfast $85-175, ste $155-195; P per day $20 🅿 💻 🖥

If you don't mind a shoebox-sized room, or being next to Ala Wai Canal, this lively, youthful hotel can be a real bargain. The lobby is fun, with surf videos and hanging surfboards. Although the bland, contemporary rooms are on the small side, they do have microwaves, minifridges and coffee-makers. Request an upper floor. In-room wired high-speed internet is free. Parking lot is off-site.

CELEBRITY RESORTS WAIKIKI
Independent Hotel $$

☎ 923-7336, 866-507-1428; www.celebrityresorts.com; 431 Nohonani St; r $85-130, 1br $105-140; P per day $18 🅿 💻 🖥 📶

Impromptu pizza nights and sing-alongs by the tropical garden–shaded pool – guests at this unpretentious place act just like neighbors who've known each other for years. Set in a quieter low-rise section of Waikiki, this old-fashioned hotel offers basic but tidy motel-style rooms with rattan furnishings and kitchenettes. Just ignore those noisy air-con units. Warning: there are no elevators.

OHANA WAIKIKI MALIA
International Hotel $$

☎ 923-7621, 866-968-8744; www.ohanahotels.com; 2211 Kuhio Ave; r $89-129, 1br from $179; P per day $18 🅿 📶

Tennis with a view? There's a rooftop court (rental $10 per hour) at this clean, convenient high-rise tower. Motel-style rooms sure show their age, but one-bedroom suites have kitchenettes and enough space for a couple of kids. Ask about extended checkout times (when available, usually costing an extra $10 per hour). Free wi-fi in lobby.

WAIKIKI SAND VILLA HOTEL
International Hotel $$

☎ 922-4744, 800-247-1903; www.waikikisandvillahotel.com; 2375 Ala Wai Blvd; r $90-150; P per day $15 🅿 💻 🖥 📶

Overlooking Ala Wai Canal, this laid-back place, unusually popular with young Japanese travelers, offers comfy, if aging motel-style rooms and decent amenities, including some kitchenettes. An on-site fitness room and free internet terminals (plus free in-room wired high-speed internet access and free poolside wi-fi) are perks. Request one of the corner rooms with city views. Weekly discounts available.

OHANA WAIKIKI EAST
International Hotel $$

☎ 922-5353, 866-968-8744; www.ohanahotels.com; 150 Ka'iulani Ave; r $99-239, 1br & 2br ste available by special request; P per day $18 🅿 💻 🖥 📶 🖥

It lacks the historical charm and oceanfront setting of nearby iconic hotels but actual room quality is just as good and for much less money. Rooms are small, but some have kitchenettes. The property is entirely nonsmoking and attracts as many families as business travelers. Downstairs, a locally owned coffee shop sells Hawaii-grown and roasted coffees, pastries, snacks and focaccia sandwiches to go. In-room high-speed wired internet access and lobby and poolside wi-fi are free.

EWA HOTEL WAIKIKI
Condo Hotel $$

☎ 922-1677, 800-359-8639; www.ewahotel.com; 2555 Cartwright Rd; r $105-160, 1br daily/weekly/monthly $215/1050/2800; P per day $10 🅿 💻 🖥

Cheesy pastel and rattan decor sets the tone at this backstreet hotel at the far eastern end of Waikiki. It's mostly a younger Japanese crowd, but the place also attracts European travelers. Restaurants, the beach and bus stops are within easy walking distance, but it's only worth staying here for generously discounted off-season weekly and monthly rates.

AQUA PALMS & SPA
Boutique Hotel $$

☎ 406-2782, 866-406-2782; www.aquaresorts.com; 1850 Ala Moana Blvd; r incl breakfast $115-175; P per day $20 🅿 💻 🖥 📶 🖥

Poised for quick escapes from Waikiki, and within walking distance of the Ala Moana Center (p94), this boutique hotel may feel more functional than fun, but delivers bang for your buck. Smallish rooms don't have much tropical panache – imagine Tommy Bahama for working-class folks – but you can't fault the bed, sofa or fluffy robes for comfort. There's a postage stamp–sized swimming pool and workout room. Free in-room high-speed wired internet access.

BEST WESTERN COCONUT WAIKIKI HOTEL
Boutique Hotel $$

ourpick ☎ 923-8828, 866-406-2782; www.aquare sorts.com; 450 Lewers St; r incl breakfast $115-195; P per day $22 🌀 💻 🛜 🔲

Don't let the chain-gang name fool you: this Aqua-managed property delivers a brilliant, bold splash of style for anyone doing Waikiki on a budget. The hotel has hip, edgy decor, from the atomic-starburst, retro-fashioned mirrors in the hallways to cool, mint-green rooms with views of the Ala Wai Canal and mountains from private lanai. Designed with business travelers in mind, rooms also have ergonomic work desks, microwaves and minifridges. The exercise room is small, but well-equipped. Weekly cocktail social hours let you play Wii Sports with other guests.

AQUA BAMBOO & SPA
Boutique Hotel $$

☎ 922-7777, 866-406-2782; www.aquabamboo .com; 2425 Kuhio Ave; r $120-160, 1br with full kitchen $215-285, all incl breakfast; P per day $22 🌀 💻 🛜 🔲

There are a few hints of its less-glorious past as a down-at-heel budget hotel, but if you're looking for a meditative space in the midst of the urban jungle, this bamboo-bedecked boutique hotel with stylishly minimalist rooms won't disappoint budget travelers. Need to unwind even more? Ask about the shiatsu massage offered next to the saltwater swimming pool inside the intimate spa (p111). In-room high-speed wired internet access and wi-fi in the lobby and poolside are all complimentary.

BREAKERS
Independent Hotel $$

☎ 923-3181, 800-426-0494; www.breakers-hawaii .com; 250 Beach Walk; r $120-150; P 🌀 🛜 🔲

In a prohibitively priced neighborhood that's dominated by high-rise hotels, this Polynesian-style place is a throwback to another era. The facilities are plenty old and creaky, so don't come expecting one of those new-fangled remotes for your TV. Unassuming motel-style rooms each have a kitchenette; request a 2nd-floor unit, which adds a private lanai with Japanese-style *shōji* (sliding screens). Parking is free, but hard to come by. Erratic wi-fi in lobby and poolside areas.

HAWAIIANA HOTEL
Independent Hotel $$

☎ 923-3811, 800-367-5122; www.hawaiianahotel atwaikiki.com; 260 Beach Walk; r $125-215, 1br $235; P per day $15 🌀 🔲

Walk through the gate and it's like stepping back 60 years. Yes, the cinder-block motel-style rooms with kitchenettes may have faded furnishings and bathrooms that no longer sparkle, but the friendly Hawaiian staff at this low-key hotel shine. Just like in days past, none of the buildings on the grounds rise higher than a coconut tree. Avoid noisy west-side rooms closest to busy Saratoga Rd. Japanese and Korean spoken.

WYLAND WAIKIKI
International Hotel $$

☎ 954-4000, 877-995-2638; www.outrigger.com; 400 Royal Hawaiian Ave; r $129-355; P per day $18 🌀 💻 🛜 🔲

Surely you've heard of Wyland, the artist whose paintings and sculptures of whales adorn so many McMansion suburbs on the US mainland? Indeed, the aquatic theme is pervasive here, from the lobby aquarium to the swimming pool out back. Smallish rooms look fresh and contemporary, all equipped with flat-screen TVs and some kitchenettes, but they're only good value for less than $200 per night. In-room high-speed wired internet access and wi-fi in lobby and poolside are complimentary.

OHANA WAIKIKI BEACHCOMBER
International Hotel $$

☎ 922-4646, 866-968-8744; www.ohanahotels .com; 2300 Kalakaua Ave; r $119-229; P per day $28 🌀 💻 🛜 🔲

On the Kalakaua Ave strip, this modern hotel is remarkable for its prime location but subprime rates. Accommodations are exactly like all of those this-could-be-any-where-in-the-world hotel rooms you've seen before, but they've been recently renovated with flat-screen TVs and alarm clocks with MP3 player plug-ins. In-room wired high-speed internet access and wi-fi in the lobby are free. Parking is difficult. No smoking on-site.

WAIKIKI GRAND HOTEL
Condo Hotel $$$

☎ 923-1814, 888-336-4368; www.waikikigrand .com; 134 Kapahulu Ave; r $139-199, ste $159-350; P per day $17 🌀 🔲

This spiffy small condo hotel is best known as the home of Hula's Bar & Lei

Stand (p123), Waikiki's perennially popular gay hangout. It's just a minute's walk to Queen's Surf Beach. Rooms are compact, but have all the usual amenities, with limited kitchenettes available. Because each vacation-rental unit is individually owned, the actual quality of accommodations varies shockingly – view those online photos with some skepticism. Weekly discounts available.

WAIKIKI MARINA RESORT
Condo Hotel $$

☎ 955-7644; www.shellhospitality.com; 1777 Ala Moana Blvd; apt $150-195; P per day $25 ⚡ 🖥 🗺

On the far north side of Waikiki, not to be confused with the Aqua Waikiki Marina next door, this humble hotel is as close to the Ala Moana Center as it is to the beach. While the lobby and furnishings are faded, the spacious studio apartments with lanai are meticulously clean. Given its online booking discounts, you probably won't find a full kitchen for less in Waikiki. In-room wired high-speed internet access costs extra.

🏵 HOTEL RENEW
Boutique Hotel $$$

our pick ☎ 687-7700, 888-485-7639; www.hotel renew.com; 129 Pa'oakalani Ave; r incl breakfast $149-209; P per day $20 ⚡ 🖥 🛜

At this fabulous find, just a half-block from the beach, attentive concierge staff can be counted on to provide all the little niceties, from chilled drinks upon arrival to free beach mats and bodyboards to borrow. Design-savvy accommodations come equipped with platform beds, projection-screen TVs, spa robes, earth-toned furnishings and Japanese-style *shōji*. Ecofriendly practices include recycling, water-saving fixtures and 'green' cleaning products. Well-behaved small dogs welcome (fee $25).

ASTON WAIKIKI CIRCLE HOTEL
International Hotel $$$

☎ 923-1571, 877-997-6667; www.astonhotels.com; 2464 Kalakaua Ave; r $150-220; P per day $10 ⚡ 🖥

Tired of all those square boxes? This sweet little circular building must have been *très chic* back in the playful era of postmodernism, but today this survivor is all about value not fashion. About half of the not-exactly-roomy accommodations get

a sunset-cocktail-worthy lanai with a full view of the ocean for the same price that other hotels charge for a parking-lot view. In-room high-speed wired internet access costs extra.

OUTRIGGER LUANA WAIKIKI
Condo Hotel $$$

☎ 955-6000, 866-956-4262; www.outrigger.com; 2045 Kalakaua Ave; r $155-265, studios $175-295, 1br $259-485; P per day $18 ⚡ 🖥 🛜 🗺

Clean, well-kept studios equipped with kitchenettes and one-bedroom units with kitchens are the only digs worth booking at this handy condominium hotel, which has a gorgeous swimming pool and sundeck. It's a decent choice if you want to do your own cooking and don't mind white noise from the air-con units or passing traffic below. Some condos have surprisingly good views. Free wi-fi in lobby and poolside.

ILIMA HOTEL
Condo Hotel $$$

☎ 923-1877, 800-801-9366; www.ilima.com; 445 Nohonani St; studios $190-215, 1br $250-280; P ⚡ 🖥 🗺

Life feels less hurried at this older, island-style condo hotel, where the staff have aloha spirit and Hawaiian paintings hang in the lobby. Opt for the 10th floor or above for views of the mountains and nearby Ala Wai Canal. But book early, because the 98 kitchen-equipped suites often fill with return visitors. Online specials discount rack rates by up to 50%. In-room high-speed wired internet access is complimentary. Limited free parking.

ASTON AT THE WAIKIKI BANYAN
Condo Hotel $$$

☎ 922-0555, 877-977-6667; www.astonhotels.com; 201 Ohua Ave; 1br $190-295; **P** per day $10 ⛶ 🖳 ⬚ 🖳

Ideal for families, this all-suites high-rise hotel is a short walk from lots of kid-friendly attractions, including the aquarium, the zoo and, of course, the beach. Roomy suites have the usual island-style furnishings, with a handy extra sofa bed in the living room. Kids get a free sand pail filled with fun stuff at check-in, and the pool deck has a playground, tennis and basketball courts and a putting green. In-room high-speed wired internet and wi-fi in the lobby and by the pool costs extra.

EMBASSY SUITES WAIKIKI BEACH WALK
International Hotel $$$

☎ 921-2345, 800-362-2779; www.embassysuiteswaikiki.com; 201 Beach Walk; 1br incl breakfast $209-329; **P** per day $25 ⛶ 🖳 ⬚ 🖳

With an enviable position on Beach Walk, this new property has no-nonsense, lightly tropically inspired suites that are big enough for families. This hotel chain may not be sexy, but it's appreciably functional: all suites have microwaves, minifridges, coffeemakers, flat-screen TVs and radio/alarm clocks with MP3 input jacks. In-room high-speed wired internet access and wi-fi in public areas are both free, plus there's a small but professionally equipped fitness room.

NEW OTANI KAIMANA BEACH HOTEL
International Hotel $$$$

☎ 923-1555, 800-356-8264; www.kaimana.com; 2863 Kalakaua Ave; r $190-440; **P** per day $18 ⛶ 🖳 ⬚

Location, location, location. The staff are friendly and the airily spruced-up, but still incredibly small, rooms won't leave you wanting too much, but it's the quiet setting right on Sans Souci Beach that makes this place special. Book early because this low-key hotel is very popular with return visitors. No pool, but with a beach this gorgeous, who needs one? Limited free parking at nearby Kapi'olani Park. Japanese spoken.

OUTRIGGER REEF ON THE BEACH
International Hotel $$$$

☎ 923-3111, 866-956-4262; www.outriggerreef.com; 2169 Kalia Rd; r $209-465; **P** per day $25 ⛶ 🖳 ⬚ 🖳

Far less hoity-toity than its higher-priced beachfront neighbors, the Outrigger Reef has managed to nudge its way into a prime oceanfront location near the sands of Fort DeRussy Beach. A taste of Hawaiiana flows from the handcrafted outrigger canoe in the Polynesian-style lobby through to complimentary hula, ukulele and lei-making lessons. Rooms are modern and functional, with a crowd that's more suburban than urban. Free in-room high-speed wired internet access, and free wi-fi in the lobby and poolside.

WAIKIKI PARC HOTEL
Boutique Hotel $$$$

☎ 921-7272, 800-422-0450; www.waikikiparc.com; 2233 Helumoa Rd; r $215-415; **P** per day $20 ⛶ 🖳 ⬚

The affordably hip Parc epitomizes nouveau Waikiki, midway between vintage nostalgia and an ultramodern future. Staff are pampering and the renovated rooms bright and cool, although old-fashioned touches like plantation-shuttered windows are oddly mismatched with minimalist contemporary furnishings. The public areas are chic, with the celebrated Nobu Waikiki (p119) sushi bar and lounge downstairs. The Halekulani (p132), the Parc's more refined sister hotel, has a better beachfront setting.

OUTRIGGER WAIKIKI ON THE BEACH
International Hotel $$$$

☎ 923-0711, 800-442-7304; www.outriggerwaikikihotel.com; 2335 Kalakaua Ave; r $215-779; **P** per day $25 ⛶ 🖳 ⬚ 🖳

While not the classiest or the coolest place, it caters to those tourists who believe it is. Sprawled on a prime stretch of sand, you can hit the surf in the morning then join the party crowd at Duke's Waikiki (p137) and unwind over sunset cocktails upstairs at Hula Grill (p119). Steel yourself for thin-walled, noisy rooms and laughably outdated furnishings. In-room high-speed wired internet access and wi-fi in lobby and poolside are free.

WAIKIKI

Beachfront at the Hilton Hawaiian Village   ANN CECIL

HILTON HAWAIIAN
VILLAGE   Resort $$$$
☎ 949-4321, 800-445-8667; www.hiltonhawaiian
village.com; 2005 Kalia Rd; r $219-850; ℗ per day
$24 ⊠ ⌨ ⌘ ⚲
Hawaii's biggest hotel is practically a mini-
metropolis of nearly 3000 rooms. Nearly a
self-sufficient tourist fortress, the touristy
'village' comprises high-rise towers with
standard-issue rooms, swimming pools, restaurants, bars and shops. Lots of activities
are geared especially for families, including the thunderous Friday-night fireworks
display. Check-in lines move as slowly as
airport-security checkpoints.

ASTON WAIKIKI
BEACH HOTEL   International Hotel $$$
☎ 922-2511, 800-877-7666; www.astonhotels
.com; 2570 Kalakaua Ave; r incl breakfast $225-425;
℗ per day $20 ⊠ ⌨ ⌘ ⚲
From the surf-and-hula decor to the tiki
torch-lit rooftop bar, this contemporary
hotel is loads of fun. It sure doesn't hurt
to be opposite Kuhio Beach Park, either.

You'll also get a free souvenir soft-sided
cooler bag that you can fill with complimentary breakfast goodies and take along
to the beach. However, unless you score a
special online rate, it's still overpriced. In-
room high-speed wired internet access and
lobby and poolside wi-fi cost extra.

OUTRIGGER REGENCY
ON BEACHWALK   Condo Hotel $$$$
☎ 922-3871, 866-956-4262; www.outrigger.com;
255 Beach Walk; 1br $245-399, 2br $379-499;
℗ per day $18 ⊠ ⌨
This sleek, modern high-rise has more
than respectable rooms, with jewel and
earth-toned furnishings, marble baths
and bold, modern artwork on the walls.
All of the spacious condo-style suites have
full kitchens and some have private lanai
with partial ocean views. Step outside the
hotel lobby and you're right on Beach
Walk – the location is enviable. It's just
too bad that there's no pool on-site. In-
room wired high-speed internet access is
complimentary.

Courtyard at the Halekulani   LINDA CHING

MOANA SURFRIDER   Resort $$$$

☎ 922-3111, 866-716-8109; www.moana-surf rider.com; 2365 Kalakaua Ave; r $265-510; Ⓟ per day $20 🚫 🖳 🛜 🛋

Waikiki's original beachfront hotel, this grand, colonial-style establishment has been painstakingly restored by Westin. A line of rocking chairs beckons on the front porch, while in the bustling lobby Japanese wedding parties sweep through every five minutes. Graceful guest rooms no longer retain much of their period look, having been upgraded with 21st-century amenities and style. In-room wired high-speed internet access and wi-fi in lobby and poolside cost extra, as does valet parking. Self-parking is off-site.

SHERATON WAIKIKI   International Hotel $$$$

☎ 922-4422, 866-716-8109; www.sheraton -waikiki.com; 2255 Kalakaua Ave; r $380-735; Ⓟ per day $20 🚫 🖳 🛜 🛋

This chain high-rise looms over the historic Royal Hawaiian with modern utility and enough room to accommodate tour groups and conferences. Rooms may look bland, but kids will love the 'superpool' complex out back that's an amphibious playground. Online booking discounts of as much as 50% may be available, and that's a fair deal for this beachy property. In-room high-speed wired internet access and wi-fi in public areas costs extra.

ROYAL HAWAIIAN HOTEL   Resort $$$$

☎ 923-7311, 866-716-8110; www.royal-hawaiian .com; 2259 Kalakaua Ave; r $380-855; Ⓟ per day $20 🚫 🖳 🛜 🛋

Waikiki's original luxury hotel, this pink Spanish-Moorish-style landmark is loaded with charm, especially after a splendid, multimillion-dollar renovation finished in 2009. The historic section of the 'Pink Palace' maintains its classic appeal, although most guests prefer the modern high-rise tower for its ocean views. Spa suites are adorned with carved teak, bamboo and mosaic glass, plus soaking tubs and cabana day beds on the lanai to inspire tranquility. In-room high-speed wired internet access and limited wi-fi in public areas cost extra.

HALEKULANI   Resort $$$$

our pick ☎ 923-2311, 800-367-2343; www .halekulani.com; 2199 Kalia Rd; r $425-750; Ⓟ 🚫 🖳 🛜 🛋

Its name meaning 'The House Befitting Heaven,' this gracious resort is an experience, not just a place to crash. Meditative peace washes over you as soon as you step onto the stone tiles or rest by the century-old kiawe tree. Guest rooms have deep soaking tubs, high-tech entertainment centers and expansive lanai, and the pampering doesn't stop there – look for ultimate relaxation in the elite spa. If, by chance, your budget knows no bounds, book yourself into the luxury suite created by designer Vera Wang.

Also recommended:

Hale Koa Hotel (☎ 955-0555, 800-367-6027; www .halekoa.com; 2055 Kalia Rd; r $87-277; Ⓟ per day $7 🚫 🖳 🛋) Reserved for active and retired US military personnel; ask for renovated rooms in the Ilima Tower.
Aston Waikiki Beach Tower (☎ 926-6400, 877-997-6667; www.astonhotels.com; 2470 Kalakaua Ave; 1br & 2br $495-815; Ⓟ 🚫 🛋 🛜) Full-service apartment hotel in the heart of Waikiki is perfect for family reunions; free in-room wired high-speed internet access and lobby wi-fi.

Lotus at Diamond Head (☎ 922-1700, 800-367-5004; www.castleresorts.com; 2885 Kalakaua Ave; r $189-850; P per day $15 ⬚) Formerly the hip W Diamond Head, this boutique hotel is a mod, if somewhat worn, sanctuary by Sans Souci Beach.

Trump International Hotel & Tower (☎ 212-299-1062; www.trumpwaikikihotel.com; 223 Saratoga Rd; call for room rates; P ⬚ 💻 ⬚) Luxury high-rise boasts an infinity pool and apartment-style suites with panoramic windows, full kitchens and marble baths.

GETTING THERE & AROUND

For information on flights into Honolulu International Airport, see p284. For driving directions and details of transportation to/from the airport, see p287.

Bicycle

You can rent beach cruisers and commuter-quality mountain bikes from several places in Waikiki. For top-quality mountain and road bikes, visit the Bike Shop (p78) in central Honolulu.

Big Kahuna Motorcycle Tours & Rentals (☎ 924-2736; 407 Seaside Ave; per 4hr/9hr/24hr/week $10/15/20/100; ⬚ 8am-5:30pm) Rents commuter-style mountain bikes only.

Blue Sky Rentals (☎ 947-0101; 1920 Ala Moana Blvd; per day $20-30; ⬚ 8am-5:30pm) On the ground floor of the Inn on the Park condo hotel.

Coconut Cruisers (☎ 392-1174; cnr Kalakaua Ave & Lewers St; per day/week from $15/69; ⬚ 8am-5pm) Located behind the Bank of Hawaii.

Bus

For detailed information about O'ahu's public bus system, TheBus, see p289. Most public bus stops in Waikiki are found inland along Kuhio Ave, while the Ala Moana Center, just outside Waikiki, is the island's main transfer point. The one-way fare for adults is $2 ($1 per child aged six to 17), including a free transfer (two-hour time limit). Bring exact change (cash only).

Be careful to catch TheBus that's going in your direction. Each route can have different destinations, and buses generally keep the same number whether inbound or outbound. For instance, bus 2 can take you either to the aquarium or downtown Honolulu, so take note of both the number and the written destination before you jump on.

It's hardly worth checking timetables for these routes, which run frequently throughout the day and evening, with most operating until around 9pm:

Car, Motorcycle & Moped

Major car-rental companies (p290) have branches in Waikiki's larger hotels, but if

BUS ROUTES

Route	Destination
2	Downtown Honolulu, Chinatown, Bishop Museum; also Waikiki Aquarium
4	University of Hawai'i, Queen Emma Summer Palace, Foster Botanical Garden
8	Ala Moana Center (last bus back to Waikiki departs around 10:20pm), Ward Centers, downtown Honolulu, Chinatown
13	Downtown Honolulu, Chinatown; also Kapahulu Ave
19 & 20	Ala Moana Center, Ward Centers, Restaurant Row, Aloha Tower Marketplace, Chinatown, Honolulu International Airport
22	Diamond Head, Koko Marina, Hanauma Bay (no service Tuesday)
23	Ala Moana Center, Diamond Head, Hawai'i Kai, Sea Life Park
42	Ala Moana Center, downtown Honolulu, Chinatown
Route B City Express!	Honolulu Academy of Arts, downtown Honolulu, Chinatown, Bishop Museum
Route E Country Express!	Ala Moana Center, Aloha Tower Marketplace, downtown Honolulu

you're renting a car, you may be better off picking up at the airport where rates are usually cheaper. You can also tool around on a motorcycle or moped (p292), but don't expect to save any money that way – in fact, renting two-wheeled transport might cost more than a car.

Rental agencies in Waikiki:

Big Kahuna Motorcycle Tours & Rentals (☎ 924-2736, 888-451-5544; www.bigkahunarentals.com; 407 Seaside Ave; mopeds per 4hr/9hr/24hr/week $35/45/50/245, motorcycles from $65/80/100/420; ☽ 8am-5:30pm) Specializes in Harley-Davidson motorcycles and Yamaha scooters; rates include helmet and lock.

Blue Sky Rentals (☎ 947-0101; 1920 Ala Moana Blvd; mopeds per day $40-50; ☽ 8am-5:30pm) On the ground floor of the Inn on the Park condo hotel.

Coconut Cruisers (☎ 392-1174; www.coconutcruisers.com; cnr Kalakaua Ave & Lewers St; mopeds per day/week $35/150, scooter rental per day $100; ☽ 8am-5pm) Located behind the Bank of Hawaii.

Cruzin Hawaii (☎ 945-9595, 877-945-9595; www.cruzinhawaii.com; 1980 Kalakaua Ave; motorcycles per 8hr/24hr/week from $99/129/495; ☽ 8am-5pm) Rents mostly Harley-Davidson motorcycles.

Paradise Rent-a-Car (☎ 888-882-2277) Kalakaua Ave (☎ 946-7777; 1879 Kalakaua Ave); Royal Hawaiian Ave (☎ 924-7777; 355 Royal Hawaiian Ave); Uluniu Ave (☎ 926-7777; 151 Uluniu Ave) Rents VW bugs, jeeps, convertibles and motorcycles; drivers aged 18 to 24 accepted only with a hefty cash deposit.

VIP Car Rental (☎ 922-4605; www.vipcarrentalhawaii.com; 234 Beach Walk) Rents compacts, jeeps, convertibles, minivans and more; drivers aged 18 to 24 accepted only with a hefty cash deposit.

Parking in Waikiki can be an expensive challenge, with most hotels charging $15 to $25 per night for valet or self-parking. At the far eastern end of Waikiki, there's a large parking lot along Monsarrat Ave at Kapi'olani Park that has free parking with no time limit. Almost as remote, the parking lot on Kapahulu Ave, adjacent to the Honolulu Zoo, has Waikiki's lowest metered rates at just 25¢ an hour. The Waikiki Trade Center parking garage is more central and reasonably priced by Waikiki standards; enter from Seaside Ave. The garage charges $7 for overnight parking (5pm to 6am) from Sunday to Wednesday, or $11 Thursday to Saturday; otherwise, it's $3 per half-hour. Next door, the **Waikiki Parking Garage** (333 Seaside Ave) sometimes offers cheaper flat-rate parking specials during the day and evening until midnight (no overnight parking).

Taxi

Taxis are available at larger resort hotels and shopping malls. Elsewhere, you'll probably need to call one (see p292).

Trolley

Trolley-style buses offer connections between Waikiki and Honolulu's main tourist sights. Running mostly during the daytime, these services don't offer much in the way of value compared to TheBus, but are tailored to tourists and thus may seem more convenient.

The **Waikiki Trolley** (☎ 593-2822; www.waikikitrolley.com; 1-day pass adult $27, child 4-11yr $13, senior $20, 4-day pass $48/20/28) connects Waikiki with downtown Honolulu, the Ala Moana Center and parts of southeast O'ahu. An all-day or four-day pass allows you to jump on and off the trolley as often as you like; single-ride tickets ($2) are available only on the Pink and Yellow Lines. You can purchase passes online or at DFS Galleria, Hilton Hawaiian Village or Ala Moana Center.

Red Line (Honolulu City Line) Starts at Hilton Hawaiian Village with stops at the Honolulu Academy of Arts, 'Iolani Palace, Foster Botanical Garden, Bishop Museum, Aloha Tower Marketplace, Chinatown, Ward Centers and Ala Moana Center. Trolleys run every 40 minutes from 9:10am to 5:30pm; the entire route takes two hours.

Blue Line (Ocean Coast Line) Starts at DFS Galleria Waikiki with stops at the Duke Kahanamoku statue, Honolulu Zoo, Waikiki Aquarium, Diamond Head, Kahala Mall, Koko Marina Center, Hanauma Bay (photo stop only – no disembarking), Halona and Makapu'u Lookouts and Sea Life Park. Trolleys run hourly from 8:30am to 6:15pm; the entire route takes three hours. An express service to Diamond Head runs four times daily.

Pink Line (Ala Moana Shopping Center Shuttle) Starts at the DFS Galleria Waikiki and runs along Kalakaua Ave, then loops around Kuhio Ave past the Hilton Hawaiian Village to the Ala Moana Center. Trolleys run every 10 minutes from 9:30am to 9:45pm (to 7:45pm Sunday); the entire route takes one hour.

Yellow Line (Local Shopping and Dining Line) Loops between the Ala Moana Center and Ward Centers. Trolleys run every 45 minutes from 12:30pm to 7:45pm (to 7pm Sunday); the entire route takes 45 minutes.

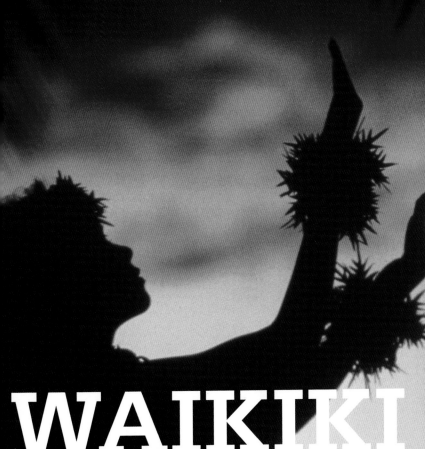

WAIKIKI
AFTER DARK

When the sun sinks below the horizon, Waikiki becomes even more of a tropical playground than it is by day. Let yourself be mesmerized by hula troupes swaying on the beach or listen to contemporary Hawaiian music icons strumming their slack key guitars and ukuleles at oceanfront hotels, all for free. Then get down with the locals, who come here to party just like tourists do, especially at bars along inland Kuhio Ave. After midnight, glam it up at a nightclub where DJs spin, or just chill in a kitschy tiki lounge with a paper umbrella in your mai tai until dawn breaks over the Pacific again.

WAIKIKI AFTER DARK

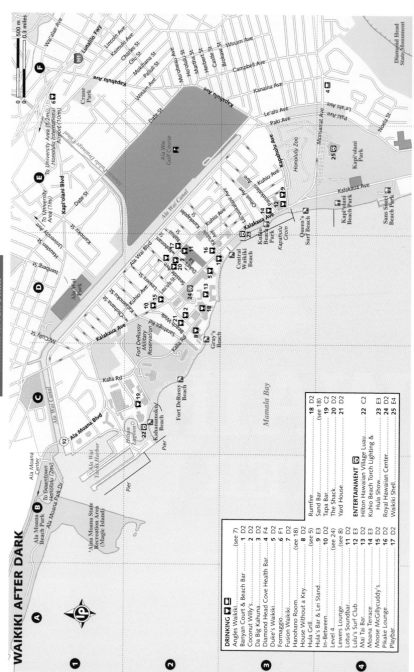

HAWAIIAN MUSIC & HULA

Island-style entertainment abounds in Waikiki, from rhythmic drums or *ipu* (gourds) and hula dancers to mellow duos and trios playing ukuleles and slack key guitars. All performances are free, unless otherwise noted. For more background on O'ahu's top musicians, see p254.

KUHIO BEACH TORCH LIGHTING & HULA SHOW

our pick ☎ 843-8002; www.honolulu.gov/moca; Kuhio Beach Park; ☾ starting around 6pm or 7pm, weather permitting

It all begins at the Duke Kahanamoku statue with the sounding of a conch shell and the lighting of streetside torches. From there, mosey on over to the nearby hula mound, lay out your beach towel and enjoy the authentic Hawaiian music and dance show. It's full of aloha, and afterwards the performers often hang around the stage to chat and take photos with visitors. The one-hour show rarely gets started until after sunset.

HOUSE WITHOUT A KEY

☎ 923-2311; Halekulani, 2199 Kalia Rd; ☾ 7am-9pm, live music 5:30-8:30pm

Named after a 1925 Charlie Chan novel set in Honolulu, this genteel outdoor lounge sprawled beneath a century-old kiawe tree simply has no doors to lock. A well-heeled crowd gathers for sunset cocktails, Hawaiian music and hula dancing by two former Miss Hawaiis. Panoramic ocean views are as intoxicating as the drinks, but skip the food.

Top Picks

SUNSET VIEWS, ISLAND RHYTHMS

- **House Without a Key** (left)
- **Banyan Court & Beach Bar** (below)
- **Mai Tai Bar** (p138)
- **Duke's Waikiki** (below)
- **Lulu's Surf Club** (p140)

BANYAN COURT & BEACH BAR

☎ 922-3111; Moana Surfrider, 2365 Kalakaua Ave; ☾ 10:30am-midnight, live music 6-10pm

Inside this historic beachfront hotel, swill cocktails while you listen to classical and contemporary Hawaiian bands play underneath the old banyan tree where the *Hawaii Calls* radio program was broadcast nationwide for four decades, starting in 1935. Today's performance schedule varies, but hula dancers usually perform on Friday, while well-known island musicians like Kelly Boy Delima take over on Saturday and Sunday nights.

DUKE'S WAIKIKI

☎ 922-2268; Outrigger Waikiki, 2335 Kalakaua Ave; ☾ 4pm-midnight

It's a crazy, tourist-filled scene, especially when weekend concerts spills over onto the beach. On weekend afternoons, the biggest names in Hawaiian music, like Henry Kapono, often appear here. Taking its name

Enjoy evening cocktails with Hawaiian music at House Without a Key

ANN CECIL

WAIKIKI AFTER DARK

from Duke Kahanamoku, the surfing theme prevails throughout. Drunken souvenir-photo taking and vacation-land camaraderie are encouraged. The upstairs Hula Grill (p119) offers more soothing live Hawaiian music with a tiki torch-lit veranda above the beach.

TAPA BAR

☎ 949-4321; Tapa Tower, Hilton Hawaiian Village, 2005 Kalia Rd; ☽ 3-11pm, live music 8-11pm

It's worth navigating the gargantuan Hilton complex to see Jerry Santos and Olomana, one of the best blended traditional and contemporary Hawaiian groups performing on O'ahu today. They usually play on Friday nights, when you can also catch the Hilton's fireworks show (p115).

MOANA TERRACE

☎ 922-6611; Waikiki Beach Marriott Resort, 2552 Kalakaua Ave; ☽ live music usually 6:30-9:30pm Thu-Mon

If you're in a mellow mood, this poolside bar overlooking Kuhio Beach features sunset happy-hour drinks and live Hawaiian music many nights of the week. If you're lucky, you'll catch slack key guitarists Martin Pahinui and George Kuo and vocalist Aaron Mahi on Sunday or the *ohana* (family) of the late, great ukulele player and vocalist Genoa Keawe (see boxed text, p122) on Thursday.

Go ahead, mai tai one on   LINDA CHING

MAI TAI BAR

☎ 923-7311; Royal Hawaiian Hotel, 2259 Kalakaua Ave; ☽ 10:30am-12:30am, live music 6-10pm

At the Royal Hawaiian's low-key bar (no preppy resort wear required) great local groups often perform Hawaiian music by the beach. If you don't dig who's playing that night, the signature Royal Mai Tai still packs a mighty wallop and the ocean views extend all the way down to Diamond Head.

RUMFIRE

☎ 922-4422, 866-952-3473; Sheraton Waikiki, 2255 Kalakaua Ave; ☽ 4pm-midnight Sun-Thu, 4pm-2am Fri & Sat

The collection of vintage rum alone is tempting at this flirty hotel bar, overlooking romantic fire pits on the beach, which also has live Hawaiian music by local musicians from 5pm to 7pm nightly. Afterwards, wander over to the circular, cabana-like Sand Bar for knockout views and more Hawaiian music poolside from 6pm to 8:30pm nightly.

PIKAKE LOUNGE

☎ 922-5811; Sheraton Princess Kaiulani, 120 Ka'iulani Ave; ☽ 11am-11:30pm, live music usually 6:15-11:30pm

While it lacks the ocean horizons of Waikiki's beachfront hotels, the good ol' PK has a small poolside lounge under the stars where some of O'ahu's best acts play, including Sam Kapu III. Classic kitschy tropical cocktails like the Blue Hawaii are served.

ROYAL HAWAIIAN CENTER

☎ 922-2299; 2201 Kalakaua Ave; ☽ schedule varies

The shopping-mall setting may not be as attractive as a beachfront bar, but it nevertheless garners some top talent. Hawaiian musicians and hula troupes perform many nights of the week, starting around 6pm. The center is also the venue for morning minishows by performers from the Polynesian Cultural Center (p192).

WAIKIKI SHELL

Kapi'olani Park; ☽ schedules varies

With Diamond Head as a backdrop, this outdoor amphitheater in Kapi'olani Park hosts twilight concerts by megastars like ukulele-playin' rocker Jake Shimabukuro. Concerts feature classical and contemporary Hawaiian music. Tickets are handled by the **Neal S Blaisdell Center** (☎ box office 591-2211; www.blaisdellcenter.com; 777 Ward Ave) in downtown Honolulu; contact its box office for the latest schedules.

LUAU & DINNER SHOWS

If your Hawaiian vacation just won't be complete without taking in a luau (feast), you can choose from a Waikiki resort-hotel production right on the beach or a big bash outside town, for which guests are picked up at select Waikiki hotels and taken by bus to Kapolei (about one hour each way). Just don't expect anything too authentic – this fanfare is strictly for tourists. For more background on authentic traditional and contemporary Hawaiian luaus, see p260.

HILTON HAWAIIAN VILLAGE LUAU

☎ 949-4321, 800-862-5335; 2005 Kalia Rd; adult $95, child 4-11yr $45; ⏰ 5:30-8:30pm Wed & Sun

This beachside luau, the only one currently happening in Waikiki, features a buffet-style dinner of Hawaiian food and a complimentary mai tai. The enthusiastic pan-Polynesian show, with Samoan fire dancing and mid-20th-century-style Hawaiian hula, is a real crowd-pleaser, especially for families. Make reservations in advance.

Commercial luaus outside Waikiki:
Germaine's Luau (☎ 949-6626, 800-367-5655; www .germainesluau.com; 91-119 Olai St, Kapolei; adult $75, youth 14-20yr $65, child 6-13yr $55; ⏰ 5:15-9pm) Nightly dinner buffet and Polynesian-style show on the beach.
Paradise Cove (☎ 842-5911, 800-775-2683; www .paradisecove.com; 92-1089 Ali'inui Dr, Kapolei; adult $80, youth 13-18yr $70, child 3-12yr $60; ⏰ 5-9pm) Adds demonstrations of traditional Hawaiian games and art and crafts.

BARS & LOUNGES

If you crave spring break–style dance clubs and kitschy tiki bars, just stroll down Kuhio Ave after dark. For details about Waikiki's gay and lesbian nightlife scene, see p123.

❀ DIAMOND HEAD COVE HEALTH BAR

☎ 732-8744; 3045 Monsarrat Ave; ⏰ 10am-8pm Mon, Fri & Sat, 10am-midnight Tue-Thu & Sun

Why rot your guts with the devil's brew when you can chill out with a coconut-husk bowl of 'awa (kava), Polynesia's spicy,

SUNSET ON THE BEACH

On some lucky weekends, on both Saturday and Sunday evenings, Queen's Surf Beach turns into a festive scene. Dubbed Sunset on the Beach, it's more fun than a luau and almost everything is free – except for the food, and even that's a bargain. Tables and chairs are set up and Hawaiian bands perform on a beachside stage for about two hours before showtime. When darkness falls, a huge screen is unscrolled above the stage and a feature movie is shown, starting around 7pm. Sometimes it's a film with island connections, like *Blue Hawaii* (the 1961 classic starring Elvis Presley), while on other nights it's a new Hollywood blockbuster.

mildly intoxicating elixir made from the *Piper methysticum* plant? A relaxed vibe and a respect for the herb's roots in Hawaiian culture set the tone. Local musicians jam some nights.

LEWERS LOUNGE

☎ 923-2311; Halekulani, 2199 Kalia Rd; ⏰ 7:30pm-1am

The dream of Waikiki as an aristocratic playground is kept alive at this sophisticated lounge. Cocktails designed by Dale DeGroff, formerly of NYC's Rainbow Room, are made from scratch using fresh (not canned) juices, including tropical flavors like lychee and ginger. Smooth jazz combos serenade most nights.

THE SHACK

☎ 921-2255; Waikiki Trade Center, 2255 Kuhio Ave; cover free-$10; ⏰ 11am-4am

If you're wondering where Waikiki's resort-hotel bartenders go when they get off shift, check out this tiki-style sports bar, with huge TVs, a waterfall and live music most Wednesday to Saturday nights. Occasionally there's homegrown Jawaiian and island reggae groups like the Ka'ala Boys.

YARD HOUSE

☎ 923-9273; 226 Lewers St; ⏰ 11am-1am

The busiest bar on Beach Walk, this mini chain with big-screen sports TVs pulls in raucous groups with its gigantic glasses of

WAIKIKI AFTER DARK

microbrewed draft beer from the US mainland, Europe and all around the Hawaiian Islands – Maui Brewing Big Swell IPA or Mehana Volcano Red, anyone? It's pricey and loud, with a classic-rock soundtrack that never dies.

HANOHANO ROOM
☎ 922-4422; Sheraton Waikiki, 2255 Kalakaua Ave; ☺ 5:30-10pm
Your head will spin here, even before you pick up an overpriced cocktail. Reached via a glass elevator, this trussed-up, 30th-floor hotel bar offers nighttime views almost as good as from the Top of Waikiki (p110). Expect a snobby attitude, especially if you show up dressed for the beach.

DA BIG KAHUNA
☎ 923-0333; 2299 Kuhio Ave; ☺ 7am-4am
Do you dream of a kitschy tiki bar where fruity, Kool-Aid–colored drinks are poured into ceramic mugs carved with the faces of Polynesian gods? To get soused fast, order Da Fish Bowl – just don't try playing pool after you've drained it. Full menu served till 3am.

FORMAGGIO
☎ 739-7719; Market City Shopping Center, 2919 Kapi'olani Blvd; ☺ 5:30-11pm Mon, 5:30-11:30pm Tue-Thu, 5:30pm-1am Fri, 6pm-1am Sat
Resembling a tiny European wine cellar, this hard-to-find hangout for chic urbanites pours everything from sparkling Japanese sake and French champagne to Californian late-harvest cabernet sauvignon by the glass. Smooth live jazz is usually heard Thursday to Saturday night.

NIGHTCLUBS
The cool club scene has migrated toward downtown Honolulu (p91), but if you don't feel like making the trek to Chinatown or the Ala Moana Center, these places have dance floors for getting your yayas out. To join the DJ party circuit, with weekly and monthly events that rotate between various venues, surf to **Metromix Honolulu** (http://honolulu.metromix.com).

LOTUS SOUNDBAR
our pick ☎ 924-1688; Waikiki Town Center, 2301 Kuhio Ave; cover $10-20; ☺ 9pm-2am Sun-Wed, 9pm-4am Thu-Sat

Top Picks
RUBBAH-SLIPPAH NIGHTSPOTS
- **Kuhio Beach Torch Lighting & Hula Show** (p137)
- **Duke's Waikiki** (p137)
- **Diamond Head Cove Health Bar** (p139)
- **The Shack** (p139)
- **Yard House** (p139)

Cutting-edge DJs imported from the mainland often spin at this tri-level club, where you can get down to soulful hip-hop, chill-out grooves, drum 'n' bass and pure house sounds, courtesy of a killer sound system. Plush, dark decor fits the after-midnight crowd that hangs here.

LEVEL 4
☎ 926-4441; Royal Hawaiian Center, 2201 Kalakaua Ave; cover $15-20; ☺ 11pm-4am Wed-Sat
Overpriced and overhyped to the max, this Vegas-style club and ultra lounge at least rises above the skanky hangouts on Kuhio Ave. Go-go dancers, catwalks and a theater-style space with a small dance floor lets the beautiful people strut and pose. Strict dress code and over-21 door policy.

PLAYBAR
☎ 923-9530; 2310 Kuhio Ave; cover $5-20; ☺ 9pm-4am
Formerly called Scruples (ironically enough, because folks here don't have any of those), this down-and-dirty dance floor is infamous for doling out cheap shots, drink specials and an over-18 door policy. DJs spin house, hip-hop and mash-ups for a no-holds-barred crowd.

Restaurants by day, dance clubs by night:
Coconut Willy's (☎ 921-9000; 227 Lewers St; ☺ 11am-4am) Live bands, dancing and drinkin' on Beach Walk.
Lulu's Surf Club (☎ 926-5222; 2586 Kalakaua Ave; ☺ 24hr) DJs spin after 10pm on weekends for a late-night, beach-party crowd.
Moose McGillycuddy's (☎ 923-0751; 310 Lewers St; ☺ 7pm-4am) Laid-back nightspot with pool tables; DJs and dancing rev up after 11pm.

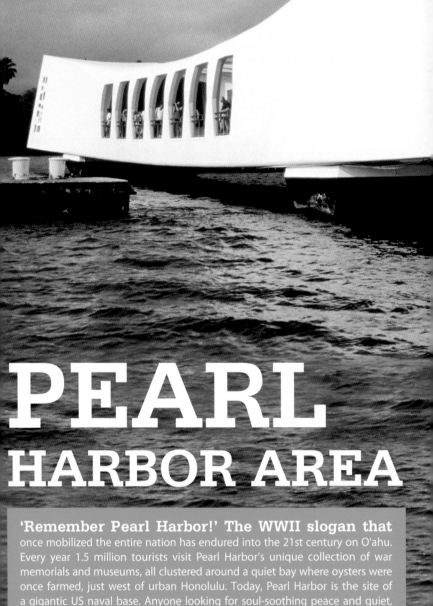

PEARL
HARBOR AREA

'Remember Pearl Harbor!' The WWII slogan that once mobilized the entire nation has endured into the 21st century on O'ahu. Every year 1.5 million tourists visit Pearl Harbor's unique collection of war memorials and museums, all clustered around a quiet bay where oysters were once farmed, just west of urban Honolulu. Today, Pearl Harbor is the site of a gigantic US naval base. Anyone looking for soul-soothing peace and quiet, especially after a deeply moving visit to the USS *Arizona* Memorial, can head up into the mountains where an ancient Hawaiian medicinal temple and forested hiking trails await at Kea'iwa Heiau State Recreation Area.

PEARL HARBOR AREA

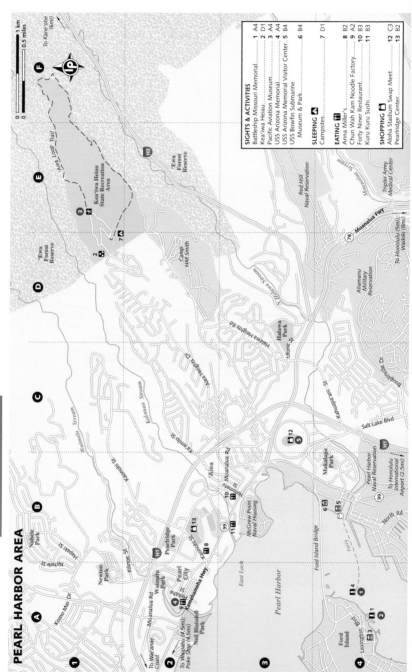

PEARL HARBOR

Once a sleepy harbor best known for its lustrous pearl oysters, Pearl Harbor was thrust into the world history books on December 7, 1941, with the surprise Japanese military attack that launched the US into WWII. Twenty-one US ships were sunk or seriously damaged and 347 airplanes were destroyed in the attack. President Roosevelt declared it a date that would live in infamy, and indeed it has – not only for the tragedy that occurred here, but also for the war that followed in its wake. Today, more tourists visit Pearl Harbor than any other sight in Hawaii.

A visit to the USS *Arizona* Memorial, the sunken ship that still holds the remains of the sailors who died during the attack, can be an emotional experience. A dramatic sense of the fateful sweep of history, and of the people whose lives were sacrificed, permeates the memorial with a poignancy that time has not erased.

But this memorial alone doesn't tell the whole story. For that, visit a trio of nearby WWII sites: the USS *Bowfin* submarine, aka the 'Pearl Harbor Avenger'; the battleship USS *Missouri,* on whose deck General Douglas MacArthur accepted the Japanese surrender marking the end of WWII; and the Pacific Aviation Museum of military history, still a work in progress.

HIGHLIGHTS

❶ **BEST HISTORY LESSON:** USS *Arizona* Memorial (p144)
❷ **BEST VIEW:** Battleship Missouri Memorial (p145)
❸ **BEST ACTIVITY:** 'Aiea Loop Trail (p148)
❹ **BEST MANAPUA:** Chun Wah Kam Noodle Factory (p147)
❺ **BEST BARGAINS:** Aloha Stadium Swap Meet (p148)

Highlights are numbered on the map on p142.

Information

You are not allowed to bring into any of the memorials, museums or visitor centers *any* items that allow concealment, including purses, camera bags, fanny packs, backpacks, diaper bags etc; only personal cameras and camcorders are allowed. Do not lock any valuables in your car. Instead use the **baggage storage facility** (per item $3; ⏲ 6:30am-5:30pm) at the Bowfin Park entrance.

All Pearl Harbor tourist attractions are closed on Thanksgiving, Christmas and New Year's Day. To visit all four sites, dedicate at least a half-day, preferably in

PEARL HARBOR AREA

The USS *Arizona* Memorial, seen from the deck of the USS *Missouri*   ANN CECIL

the morning when it's less crowded. All facilities are accessible to travelers with disabilities, including the shuttle buses (p146) over to Ford Island, where the USS *Missouri* Memorial and Pacific Aviation Museum are located.

Sights

USS ARIZONA MEMORIAL

☎ 422-0561; www.nps.gov/usar; 1 Arizona Memorial Dr, 'Aiea; admission free; ☺ visitor center & museum 7:30am-5pm (last boat tour 3pm)

One of the USA's most significant WWII sites, this somber memorial narrates the history of the Pearl Harbor attack and commemorates fallen service members. Run by the National Park Service, the memorial comprises a mainland visitor center and an offshore shrine. Inside the visitor center is a museum that displays WWII memorabilia, a model of the battleship and shrine, and photos from Japanese and US military archives showing Pearl Harbor before, during and after the attack.

The offshore shrine was built directly over the USS *Arizona*, which sank only nine minutes after the initial attack. The shrine's deliberate geometry represents initial defeat, ultimate victory and eternal serenity. Inside the far chamber is a marble wall inscribed with the names of the 1177 servicemen who perished during the attack – the average age of the enlisted men was just 19. Some tour groups and their loud-mouthed guides often break the respectful silence that all visitors are asked to maintain. Please don't follow their example.

In the central chamber of the shrine are cutaway sections through which you can see the skeleton of the sunken ship, which even today oozes about a quart of oil each day into the ocean. In the rush to recover from the attack and prepare for war, the navy exercised its option to leave the bodies of the servicemen inside the sunken ship. They remain entombed in its hull, buried at sea. The sense of tragedy feels fathomless here.

All in all, the 75-minute tour program includes a documentary film on the attack and a boat ride out to the shrine and back. Weather permitting, these programs run every 15 minutes from 7:45am to 3pm. Tickets are available on a first-come, first-served basis inside the visitor center. The shortest waits are generally in the morning, when you may only wait half an hour; however, waits of a couple of hours are not uncommon. Summer months are busiest, with an average of 4500 people taking the tour daily, and the day's allotment of tickets is often gone by noon.

PEARL HARBOR AREA

USS *Bowfin* Submarine Museum & Park   JOHN ELK III

USS BOWFIN SUBMARINE MUSEUM & PARK

☎ 423-1341; www.bowfin.org; 11 Arizona Memorial Dr, 'Aiea; park admission free, museum & self-guided submarine tour adult $10, child 4-12yr $3, senior $7; ☺ 8am-5pm (last entry 4:30pm)

This small memorial park holds the moored WWII submarine the USS *Bowfin* and a niche museum that traces the development of submarines from their early origins to the nuclear age, where a minitheater shows footage from sub patrols. The highlight is taking the fascinating self-guided audio tour aboard the USS *Bowfin* – just watch your head below deck! (Children under four years of age are not allowed on the submarine.) As you stroll around the park, you can peer through periscopes and inspect a Japanese *kaiten* (suicide torpedo), the marine equivalent of a kamikaze pilot and his plane.

BATTLESHIP MISSOURI MEMORIAL

☎ 455-1600, 877-644-4896; www.ussmissouri .com; 63 Cowpens St, Ford Island; adult $16, child 4-12yr $8, incl guided tour from $23/15; ☺ 9am-5pm (last entry 4pm)

The last US battleship built near the end of WWII, the 'Mighty Mo' saw action during the decisive battles of Iwo Jima and Okinawa. On September 2, 1945, the formal Japanese surrender that ended WWII took place on this flagship's deck. Today, the decommissioned battleship (it's bigger than the RMS *Titanic*) is docked off Ford Island, within view of the underwater remains of the USS *Arizona*. Today, you can walk the very decks where General Douglas MacArthur accepted the Japanese surrender, poke about the officers' quarters, browse exhibits on naval history and examine the spot where a kamikaze pilot flew into the ship. Taking a personally guided tour with a volunteer guide, some of whom served in the US military, is well worth the extra time and expense.

PACIFIC AVIATION MUSEUM

☎ 441-1000; www.pacificaviationmuseum.org; 319 Lexington Blvd, Ford Island; adult $14, child 4-12yr $7, incl guided tour $21/14; ☺ 9am-5pm (last entry 4pm)

A monumental work in progress, this museum unfolds the history of military aviation from WWII through the mid-20th-century

Island Insights

In ancient times, *kahuna lapa'au* (herbalist healers) used hundreds of medicinal plants and grew many on the grounds surrounding Hawaiian heiau. Among the plants used to cure ailments were *noni*, whose pungent yellow fruits were used to treat heart disease; *kukui*, the nuts of which are an effective laxative; and *ti* leaves, which were wrapped around a sick person to break a fever. Not only did these herbs have medicinal value, but heiau were believed to possess life-giving energy that could be channeled by *kahuna lapa'au*. Still today, people wishing to be healed will place offerings inside temple walls.

US conflicts in Korea and Vietnam. So far, only one aircraft hangar has been retrofitted with exhibits on the Pearl Harbor attack, the Doolittle Raid on mainland Japan in April 1942 and the pivotal Battle of Midway later that year, when the tides of war in the Pacific finally turned in favor of the Allies. Authentically restored planes hanging above the new exhibits include a Japanese Zero and a Dauntless navy dive bomber. Afterwards, try your own hand at piloting WWII-era aircraft inside high-tech flight simulators (a surcharge applies).

Tours

Private tours of Pearl Harbor that are advertised in Waikiki vary from bus trips that include stops at the Punchbowl (p75) and President Barack Obama's childhood home to excursions in WWII-era amphibious armored vehicles (nicknamed 'ducks'). These tours don't add much, if anything, to the experience of visiting the memorials and museums, however. Be aware that Pearl Harbor boat cruises don't stop at the visitor center and passengers are not allowed to disembark at the USS *Arizona* Memorial.

Festivals & Events

Memorial Day On the last Monday in May, this national public holiday honors military personnel killed in battle. The USS *Arizona* Memorial, dedicated on Memorial Day in 1962, has a special ceremony.

ISLAND VOICES

NAME: BILL SNIVELY
OCCUPATION: RETIRED US NAVY CHIEF & VOLUNTEER TOUR GUIDE, BATTLESHIP MISSOURI MEMORIAL
RESIDENCE: KANE'OHE

What makes Pearl Harbor unique? To me, what makes this place important is that we've got historical bookends. You can see the USS *Arizona*, representing the start of WWII, off the port bow of the USS *Missouri*, where WWII ended. I think the entire Pearl Harbor experience is our greatest asset here on O'ahu. It's a chance to relive history, especially for kids who may not know much about it.

What do you feel when you visit the USS Arizona Memorial? It's an emotionally charged place. I get choked up because I feel sorry for those guys who went down with their shipmates – things just happened so fast. I've seen visitors come here and say, 'I'm not gonna cry,' but they do anyway.

What makes O'ahu different from the other Hawaiian Islands? Why I like O'ahu is that you can have action if you want it. I live in Kane'ohe, on the quiet side of the island, but I can go into the city whenever I want. There's just more access to more going on here. But each island has its own beauty too. On O'ahu, I've never seen so many shades of green as in the Ko'olau Mountains. From my lanai, I can sit and look at the mountains all morning long.

What's your advice to first-time visitors to O'ahu? Learn something about island traditions. For example, there's a belief that if you bring pork over the Pali Hwy, you'll die before the next morning. It's one of those old Hawaiian sayings. Of course, I don't know anyone who has died that way, but then again, people just don't do it!

Veterans Day On November 11, this national public holiday honors US military veterans; the USS *Missouri* hosts a sunset ceremony and tribute.

Pearl Harbor Day On December 7, ceremonies at Pearl Harbor include a Hawaiian blessing and heartfelt accounts from survivors of the 1941 Japanese attack.

Eating

Bowfin Park has some fast-food concession stands, while the Battleship Missouri Memorial and Pacific Aviation Museum have small cafes serving average American fare. For local grinds, detour west to Pearl City (opposite) or the Poke Stop (p232).

Getting There & Around

The USS *Arizona* Memorial visitor center and Bowfin Park are off the Kamehameha Hwy (Hwy 99), southwest of Aloha Stadium. From Honolulu or Waikiki, take H-1 west to exit 15A (Arizona Memorial/Stadium), then follow the highway signs for the USS *Arizona* Memorial, not the signs for Pearl Harbor (which lead onto the US Navy base). There's plenty of free parking outside the visitor center and Bowfin Park.

On public transit from Waikiki, TheBus 42 'Ewa Beach ($2, one hour, twice hourly) offers the most direct route, making stops at the USS *Arizona* Memorial between 7:15am and 3pm. TheBus 20 Airport–Pearlridge covers the same route, but stops at the airport first, taking about 1¼ hours each way. Faster **VIP Trans** (☎ 836-0137, 866-836-0317; http://viptrans .com) shuttle vans pick up from Waikiki hotels approximately every 30 minutes, starting around 7am; a one-way/round-trip ticket costs $6/11 (reservations required).

If you're visiting the USS *Missouri* Memorial or Pacific Aviation Museum, it isn't possible to drive yourself to Ford Island because it's an active military base. Instead, free shuttle buses leave frequently from outside Bowfin Park. To board the buses, you must first buy tickets for the battleship memorial and/or aviation museum at the ticket windows inside Bowfin Park.

PEARL CITY

pop 32,050

Anchored by the ginormous Pearlridge Center shopping mall, this suburban enclave is home to military personnel and civilians who work on the nearby military bases. Although it's usually written off by tourists, Pearl City does have a handful of good restaurants. Its main artery is the Kamehameha Hwy (Hwy 99), which is all stop-and-go traffic through endless blocks of strip malls.

Eating

CHUN WAH KAM
NOODLE FACTORY Pan-Asian $
☎ 485-1107; Waimalu Shopping Center, 98-040 Kamehameha Hwy, 'Aiea; steamed buns $1-2, plate meals $5-12; ⊗ 7:30am-6:30pm Mon-Sat, 8:30am-4pm Sun

In a minimall stuffed with Korean barbecue houses, Vietnamese *pho* restaurants and local-style takeout shops, this bright, cheerful eatery reigns supreme. Fanatics line up for the enviable variety of *manapua* (steamed or baked buns) stuffed with anything from black sugar or *char siu* (Chinese barbecued) pork to taro and *kalua* pig. Generous mix-and-match plate lunches easily feed two people. Too bad the parking lot is such a snarled one-way mess at lunchtime.

KURU KURU SUSHI Japanese $
☎ 484-4596; Pearl Kai Shopping Center, 98-199 Kamehameha Hwy; most items $2-8; ⊗ 11am-9pm Sun-Thu, 11am-10pm Fri & Sat

A notch above Genki Sushi, O'ahu's ubiquitous chain of cheap sushi bars, Kuru Kuru also runs its classic *nigiri* sushi, spicy *'ahi* (tuna) poke and *kalbi* short-rib rolls, vegetable croquettes and fruit jelly desserts around a conveyor belt. Plates are color-coded by price, so staff can quickly total up your bill when you're stuffed to the gills.

Island Insights

First brought to the Hawaiian Islands by 19th-century Chinese immigrants, the *bao* (steamed bun), often filled with roast pork, is a staple of dim sum carts around the world. In Hawaii those dainty little steamed buns have evolved into *manapua*, which are bigger and fluffier than the original. It's speculated that the name *manapua* is derived from the Hawaiian words for thing *(mea)*, delicious *('ono)* and pig *(pua'a)* or, more poetically, from a combination of *mauna* and *pua'a*, roughly translated as 'mountain of pork.'

FORTY NINER
RESTAURANT Coffee Shop $
☎ 484-1940; 98-110 Honomanu St, 'Aiea; mains $3-10; ⊗ 7am-2pm daily, 5-8pm Mon-Thu, 5-9pm Fri & Sat

With the relaxed aloha atmosphere of the countryside, this little corner 1940s noodle shop may look abandoned, but it's a jewel-in-the-rough for those who crave saimin (local-style noodle soup), made here with a secret broth recipe inherited by the new owners. The garlic chicken and hamburger steaks ain't half bad. No air-con, though.

ANNA MILLER'S American $$
☎ 487-2421; Pearlridge Center, 98-115 Kaonohi St, 'Aiea; mains $7-19; ⊗ 24hr

From the long lines outside this faux-Scandinavian pancake house, you'd think it was serving up the best breakfasts on all of O'ahu. Too bad it's really just basic greasy-spoon diner fare, albeit with an island twist, such as omelettes with Portuguese sausage or the cloying *haupia* coconut and Belgian chocolate pie.

Shopping

PEARLRIDGE CENTER
☎ 488-0981; 98-1005 Moanalua Rd, 'Aiea; ⊗ 10am-9pm Mon-Sat, 10am-6pm Sun

A massive mall, Pearlridge has 170 mostly chain stores, including a large Borders bookstore, along with a handful of local clothing boutiques such as Cinnamon Girl and Local Motion, a movie theater and a minigolf course. Uptown Pearlridge and

ALOHA STADIUM SWAP MEET

OK, so where's O'ahu's happiest hunting ground for cheap aloha shirts, bamboo back scratchers and all sorts of Hawaiiana kitsch? Hands-down the honors go to the **Aloha Stadium Swap Meet** (☎ 486-6704; 99-500 Salt Lake Blvd; adult $1, child under 12yr free; ☒ 6am-3pm Wed, Sat & Sun; ☒ 20, 42), near the USS *Arizona* Memorial.

The Aloha Stadium, best known as the host to nationally televised football games and rockin' megaconcerts, transforms itself three days a week into Hawaii's biggest flea market. Flowery aloha designs prevail on everything from daypacks and car-seat covers to bikinis, board shorts and beach towels. Then there are the endless racks of T-shirts. Just don't expect to find many antiques or vintage goods here.

By car, take the H-1 west from Honolulu, get off at Stadium/Halawa exit 1E and follow signs for 'Stadium.' Private shuttle buses from Waikiki to the swap meet ($12 to $14 round-trip) operate every hour or so on meet days. For the required reservations, call **Hawaii Super Transit** (☎ 841-2928) or **Reliable Shuttle** (☎ 924-9292).

Downtown Pearlridge, the mall's two wings, are connected by a monorail (50¢, children under five travel free).

KEA'IWA HEIAU STATE RECREATION AREA

In the mountains north of Pearl Harbor, this state park (☎ 587-0300; www.hawaiistateparks.org; off 'Aiea Heights Dr, 'Aiea; admission free; ☒ 7am-7:45pm Apr-early Sep, 7am-6:45pm early Sep-Mar) protects Kea'iwa Heiau, an ancient Hawaiian stone temple used by *kahuna lapa'au* (herbalist healers). For hikers and mountain bikers, the scenic 4.5-mile 'Aiea Loop Trail starts from the top of the paved loop road and ends at the campground, about 0.3 miles below the trailhead. Along the way you'll enjoy sweeping vistas of Pearl Harbor, Diamond Head and the Ko'olau Range. About two-thirds of the way along, the wreckage of a C-47 cargo plane that crashed in 1943 can be spotted through the foliage on the east ridge.

The park has picnic tables, covered pavilions with barbecue grills, restrooms, showers, a payphone and drinking water. The park's few campsites don't have a lot of privacy. In winter, bring waterproof gear because it frequently rains at this elevation. There's a resident caretaker by the front gate, which is locked at night for security. As with all public campgrounds on O'ahu, camping is not permitted on Wednesday and Thursday nights, and permits must be obtained in advance (see p270).

From Honolulu or Waikiki, drive west on the H-1 Fwy, then merge onto Hwy 78 and take the exit 13A 'Aiea turnoff onto Moanalua Rd. Turn right onto 'Aiea Heights Dr at the second traffic light. The road winds up through a residential area 2.5 miles to the park. From downtown Honolulu, TheBus 11 'Aiea Heights ($2, 35 minutes, hourly) stops about 1.3 miles below the park entrance. From the bus stop, it's a long and boring uphill walk, especially if you're carrying camping gear.

Lest we forget: the USS *Arizona* Memorial's list of honored dead

CHRIS MELLOR

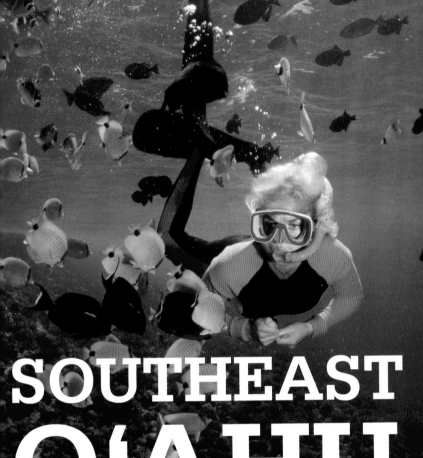

SOUTHEAST O'AHU

Be the star of your own movie, livin' large in a tropical paradise on O'ahu's most glamorous stretch of coastline – it sometimes feels like Beverly Hills by the beach. The snorkeling hot spot of Hanauma Bay, hiking trails to the top of landmark Diamond Head and the windy lighthouse at Makapu'u Point, and O'ahu's most famous bodysurfing beaches are all just a short ride east of Waikiki. Save time for the coast's more hidden delights too. Visit billionaire Doris Duke's former mansion, filled with Islamic art, or a fragrant botanical garden and a wooden stairway to the sky inside a forgotten volcano crater.

SOUTHEAST O'AHU
ITINERARIES

IN ONE DAY *This leg: 15 miles*

1 HANAUMA BAY (p158) At O'ahu's favorite snorkeling spot, get there early before the hoards of day trippers descend on the gorgeous crescent-shaped bay with its tropical fishbowl waters and coral kingdoms. Sign up for a scuba-diving trip and you'll get even more amazing underwater vistas to enjoy.

2 BLUWATER GRILL (p157) After you've dried off from the surf and sunned yourself on the beach, head inland for a smart lunch with views of Hawai'i Kai's marina. Fork into parfait glasses of seafood seviche and breezy cocktails on the back deck.

3 KOKO HEAD REGIONAL PARK (p160) In the afternoon, cruise west along the Kalaniana'ole Hwy (Hwy 72), stopping at photo-worthy roadside lookouts with panoramic views of offshore islands, the famous Halona Blowhole and stunning all-natural beaches, where bodysurfing and bodyboarding experts can test their skills against monstrous, skull-crushing waves.

4 DIAMOND HEAD STATE MONUMENT (p154) Beat the afternoon rush-hour traffic by quickly backtracking towards Waikiki, then fit in a hike to the top of this extinct volcanic crater, an O'ahu landmark. Kids of all ages and even grandparents can make the trek up to the summit just for the panoramic views.

5 HOKU'S (p156) Splash out on a feast of Hawaii Regional cuisine at Kahala's most romantic restaurant, a local favorite for special occasions – of course, your trip to Hawaii qualifies!

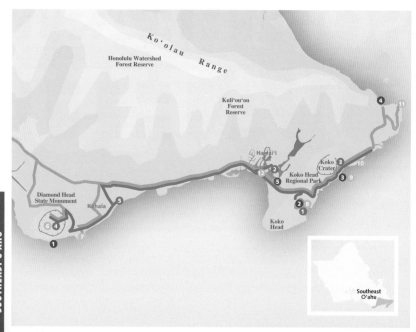

IN TWO DAYS This leg: 55 miles

6 DIAMOND HEAD STATE MONUMENT (p154) You don't necessarily have to sacrifice sleeping in late to tackle Diamond Head's summit, but it does help to get to the trailhead early: fewer crowds, less direct sunlight. If you've got two days to spend in southeast O'ahu, then we'd recommend doing things a bit differently, and starting here instead.

7 SHANGRI LA (p155) Assuming you've made reservations in advance, head back into central Honolulu to catch the last afternoon tour of Doris Duke's private mansion, a trove of Islamic art.

8 HANAUMA BAY (p158) OK, the second day of your sojourn is *really* the day to get an early start. Because if you show up at O'ahu's most popular snorkeling spot too late in the morning, water visibility will be poor and you may be turned away at the gate.

9 HALONA COVE & BLOWHOLE (p161) Bring a picnic lunch to enjoy on this gorgeous beach that starred in the classic flick *From Here to Eternity* as the famous Halona Blowhole struts its stuff.

10 SANDY BEACH PARK (p161) Even if you're not an expert bodyboarder, you can still get your thrills vicariously here, as you watch locals toss themselves into the high-powered waves.

11 MAKAPU'U POINT (p162) Trek out to the lighthouse to capture those camera shots that everyone back home will ooh and ah over. In winter, you might spot whales too.

12 ROY'S – HAWAI'I KAI (p158) Get a taste of chef Roy Yamaguchi's innovative island fusion cuisine at his original eponymous restaurant, which recently celebrated its 20th anniversary.

FOR AQUATIC ADVENTURES

1 KUILEI CLIFFS BEACH PARK (p153) When the surf's up in the morning, join the locals getting in a few waves before work at this rocky beach park in the shadow of Diamond Head. Or come when the cooling tradewinds are blowing and do a little windsurfing.

2 HANAUMA BAY (p158) Hands down, this is the best place to snorkel or dive on O'ahu's southeast coast – come to see the fish and the sea turtles, and stay to learn about ecology in the visitor center. Certified divers can have the least-trammeled nooks of the bay practically all to themselves.

3 HALONA COVE & BLOWHOLE (p161) If the surf is blasting, you're almost guaranteed a pretty good show at this lava-rock blowhole. The short cliffside trek down to Halona Cove is worth the drive, especially since it appeared in the infamous love scene in the movie *From Here to Eternity*.

4 MAKAPU'U BEACH (p162) If you're an expert bodysurfer or bodyboarder, this is the ultimate thrill – just don't say we didn't warn you that you could end up breaking your neck here!

5 KONA BREWING COMPANY (p157) Once you've dried off from all those aquatic adventures, trade surf for suds at this microbrew pub imported from the Big Island, serving draft beers and *pupu* (snack) platters big enough to feed your whole gang.

SOUTHEAST O'AHU

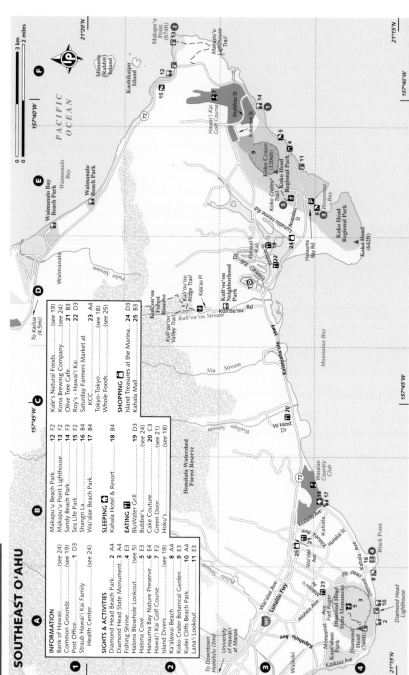

INFORMATION
Bank of Hawaii	(see 24)
Common Groundz	(see 19)
Post Office	**1** D3
Straub Hawai'i Kai Family	
Health Center	(see 24)

SIGHTS & ACTIVITIES
Diamond Head Beach Park	**2** A4
Diamond Head State Monument	**3** A4
Fishing Shrine	(see 5)
Halona Blowhole Lookout	**4** E3
Halona Cove	**5** E3
Hanauma Bay Nature Preserve	**6** E4
Hawai'i Kai Golf Course	**7** F2
Island Divers	(see 19)
Ka'alawai Beach	**8** A4
Koko Crater Botanical Garden	**9** E3
Kuilei Cliffs Beach Park	**10** A4
Lana'i Lookout	**11** E3

Makapu'u Beach Park	**12** F2
Makapu'u Point Lighthouse	**13** F2
Sandy Beach Park	**14** F3
Sea Life Park	**15** F2
Shangri La	**16** B4
Wai'alae Beach Park	**17** B4

SLEEPING
Kahala Hotel & Resort	**18** B4

EATING
BluWater Grill	**19** D3
Bubbie's	(see 24)
Cake Couture	**20** C3
Green Door	(see 21)
Hoku's	(see 18)

Kale's Natural Foods	(see 24)
Kona Brewing Company	(see 19)
Olive Tree Cafe	**21** B3
Roy's – Hawai'i Kai	**22** D3
Saturday Farmers Market at	
KCC	**23** A4
Tokyo-Tokyo	(see 18)
Whole Foods	(see 25)

SHOPPING
Island Treasures at the Marina	**24** D3
Kahala Mall	**25** B3

HIGHLIGHTS

❶ **BEST BEACH:** Sandy Beach (p161)
❷ **BEST VIEW:** Makapu'u Point (p162)
❸ **BEST ACTIVITY:** Snorkeling at Hanauma Bay (p158)
❹ **BEST HIDDEN PARADISE:** Shangri La (p155)
❺ **BEST ADVENTURE ON LAND:** Koko Crater Trail (p157)

Highlights are numbered on the map opposite.

DIAMOND HEAD

As the backdrop to Waikiki, Diamond Head is one of the best-known landmarks in Hawaii. The mountain is a tuff cone and crater formed by a violent steam explosion long after most of O'ahu's other volcanic activity had stopped. Ancient Hawaiians called it Le'ahi and at its summit they built a *luakini* heiau, a temple dedicated to the war god Ku and used for human sacrifices. But ever since 1825, when British sailors found calcite crystals sparkling in the sun and mistakenly thought they'd struck it rich, it's been called Diamond Head. In the early 1900s the US Army began building Fort Ruger at the edge of the crater. They also constructed a network of tunnels and topped the rim with cannon emplacements, bunkers and observation posts. Reinforced during WWII, the fort today is a silent sentinel whose guns have never been fired.

Beaches

From Waikiki, TheBus 14 ($2, 10 minutes, once or twice hourly) runs by the following beaches. If you're driving, follow Kalakaua Ave onto Diamond Head Rd.

DIAMOND HEAD BEACH PARK

Southwest of the lighthouse, this rocky beach occasionally draws surfers, snorkelers and tide-poolers, plus a few picnickers. The narrow strand is most popular with gay men, who pull off Diamond Head Rd onto short, dead-end Beach Rd, then walk north along the shore to find a little seclusion and (illegally) sunbathe au naturel.

KUILEI CLIFFS BEACH PARK

In the shadow of Diamond Head, this rocky beach draws experienced windsurfers when the trade winds are blowing. When the swells are up, surfers take over the waves. The little beach has showers, but no other facilities. There's a parking lot off Diamond

Diamond Head and Waikiki at twilight   ANN CECIL

Top Picks

FOR KIDS

- **Diamond Head State Monument** (right)
- **Hanauma Bay Nature Preserve** (p158)
- **Bubbie's** (p158)
- **Halona Blowhole Lookout** (p161)
- **Sea Life Park** (p162)

Head Rd, just beyond the lighthouse. Walk east past the end of the parking lot to find a paved trail down to the beach.

KA'ALAWAI BEACH

Swim in the lap of luxury at this jewel-like beach between Diamond Head and Black Point. It's in the same ritzy neighborhood as Doris Duke's former mansion, Shangri La (opposite). To get here, take Diamond Head Rd northeast along the coast past Kuilei Cliffs Beach Park and, at the point where it merges with Kahala Ave, turn right onto Kulamanu St. After about 0.2 miles you'll reach Kulamanu Pl, leading down to the beach. There's free parking on Kulamanu St.

Lookout at Diamond Head   CHRISTINA LEASE

Sights & Activities

DIAMOND HEAD STATE MONUMENT

☎ 587-0300; Diamond Head Rd; per pedestrian/vehicle $1/5; ☼ 6am-6pm (last trail entry 4:30pm); 🚌 22 & 23

The extinct crater of Diamond Head is now a state monument, with picnic tables and a hiking trail up to the 760ft-high summit. The trail was built in 1910 to service the military observation stations located along the crater rim. Although a fairly steep trail, it's fully paved and only 0.8 miles to the top, taking about an hour round-trip. Plenty of people of all ages hike up. The trail, which passes through several tunnels and up head-spinning staircases, is mostly open and hot, so wear sunscreen and pack water. The windy summit affords fantastic 360-degree views of the southeast coast to Koko Head and the leeward coast to the Wai'anae Range. The Diamond Head lighthouse, coral reefs and surfers are also visible below.

From Waikiki, take TheBus 22 or 23 ($2, 30 minutes, twice hourly). It's a 20-minute walk from the bus stop to the trailhead. By car from Waikiki, take Monsarrat Ave to Diamond Head Rd, turning right immediately after passing Kapi'olani Community College. The Waikiki trolley (p134) also stops here.

Eating

SATURDAY FARMERS MARKET AT KCC   Takeout $

☎ 848-2074; parking lot C, Kapi'olani Community College, 4303 Diamond Head Rd; ☼ 7:30am-11am Sat

O'ahu's premier gathering of farmers and their fans. Everything sold at the market is local and has a loyal following, such as 'Nalo greens, Koko Crater coffee roasters and North Shore avocados. Different restaurants are invited each week to prepare takeout meals.

KAHALA

The affluent seaside suburb of Kahala is home to many of Honolulu's wealthiest residents, the island's most exclusive resort hotel and the Waialae Country Club, a PGA

Don't Miss

- A tour of **Shangri La** (below)
- The lighthouse at **Makapu'u Point** (p162)
- Tropical-flavored or *mochi* ice cream from **Bubbie's** (p158)
- Summit views from the **Kuli'ou'ou Ridge Trail** (p157)
- Big Island microbrews at **Kona Brewing Company** (p157)
- Strolling through **Koko Crater Botanical Garden** (p161)
- Picnicking at **Wai'alae Beach Park** (below)

tournament golf course. The coastal road, Kahala Ave, is lined with expensive waterfront homes that block out virtually any ocean views.

Beaches

In between the mansions, a half-dozen shoreline access points provide public rights-of-way to the beach, but the swimming here ain't grand – it's mostly shallow, with sparse pockets of sand. One picturesque exception is **Wai'alae Beach Park**, which has a sandy beach. Surfers challenge **Razors**, a surf break off the west side of the channel. The park has picnic tables, restrooms and showers. If the parking lot is full, look for on-street parking near the bridge that crosses a stream.

Sights

SHANGRI LA

our pick ☎ 866-385-3849; www.shangrilahawaii .org; 2½hr tour $25; ◷ tours usually 8:30am, 11am & 1:30pm Wed-Sat late Sep-late Aug

Tobacco heiress Doris Duke had a lifelong passion for Islamic art and architecture, inspired by a visit to the Taj Mahal during her honeymoon voyage to India at the age of 23. During that same honeymoon in 1935, she stopped at O'ahu, fell in love with the island and decided to build Shangri La, her seasonal residence, on Black Point in the shadow of Diamond Head. Over the next 60 years she traveled the globe from Indonesia to Istanbul, collecting around 3500 priceless Islamic art objects.

Duke appreciated the finer points – the spirit more than the grand scale – of the world wonders she had seen, and she made Shangri La into an intimate sanctuary rather than an ostentatious mansion. One of the true beauties of the place is the way it harmonizes with the natural environment. Finely crafted interiors open to embrace gardens and the ocean, and one glass wall of the living room looks out at Diamond Head. Throughout the estate, courtyard fountains weave in and out of cool interiors. Collections blend with the architecture to represent a theme or region like in the Damascus Room, the restored interior of a 19th-century Syrian merchant's house. The extensive collection of Islamic art includes vivid gemstone-studded enamels, glazed ceramic paintings and silk *suzanis* (intricate Turkish needlework tapestries).

This memorable house (which is not air-conditioned, although visitors are given

THE DUKE OF SHANGRI LA

Shangri La is captivating not just for its collection but also for the unique glimpse it provides into the life of Doris Duke, once nicknamed 'the richest little girl in the world.' Like her contemporary Howard Hughes, she was eccentric, reclusive and absolutely fascinating.

Duke's immense fortune, which she inherited after her father died in 1925, when she was just 12 years old, granted her freedom to do as she pleased. Among other things, that meant two very public divorces and a scandalous marriage to an international playboy. While living in Hawaii, she became the first white woman to surf competitively and, naturally, she learned from the best: Olympic gold medalist Duke Kahanamoku and his brothers.

Curious to know more? Watch the HBO movie *Bernard and Doris* (2007), starring Susan Sarandon as Doris Duke and Ralph Fiennes as her butler Bernard Lafferty. Upon her death, Doris appointed her butler as the sole executor of her vast personal fortune, which she directed to be used to further her philanthropic projects, including in support of the arts and against cruelty to children and animals.

souvenir paper fans) can be visited only on a tour that leaves from the downtown Honolulu Academy of Arts (p67), where you'll watch a brief background video, then travel to Shangri La and back by minibus. Tours often sell out weeks ahead of time, so make your reservation as far in advance as possible. Note that children under 12 are not allowed on the tour.

Eating

At the Kahala Mall, **Whole Foods** (☎ 738-0820; 4211 Wai'alae Ave; ☺ 7am-1pm) supermarket can fill your picnic basket with organic groceries, hot and cold takeout deli items and imported cheeses and wines.

OLIVE TREE CAFE   Mediterranean $
☎ 737-0303; 4614 Kilauea Ave, cnr Pahoa Ave; mains $5-12; ☺ dinner

Hidden on the east side of Kahala Mall, this always-packed Mediterranean restaurant swears by the motto 'Mostly Greek, not so fast food.' Succulent, skewered chicken souvlaki and *dolmadakia* (stuffed grape leaves) garner rave reviews. Alcohol isn't served, but there's a Greek deli next door with a cache of imported wines for BYOB.

GREEN DOOR   Pan-Asian $$
☎ 533-0606; 4614 Kilauea Ave, cnr Pahoa Ave; mains $8-15; ☺ dinner

Leaving Chinatown behind, Betty Pang has moved her Malaysian- and Singaporean-flavored kitchen out to the ritzy 'burbs. Behind the emerald-painted door, service is infamously slow and gruff. If you dare to argue about which rice goes best with Nyonya (Straits Chinese–Malaysian) classics, the chef herself may kick you out. But the food is worth sticking around for, especially coconut chicken curry with *roti canai* (flatbread).

HOKU'S   Hawaii Regional $$$$
☎ 739-8888; Kahala Hotel & Resort, 5000 Kahala Ave; brunch buffet adult $58, child 5-12yr $29, dinner mains $32-45; ☺ 5:30-10pm Tue-Sat, 10:30am-2pm Sun

Formerly at Halekulani's Orchids in Waikiki, chef Wayne Hirabayashi has stepped up the game here. An East–West menu marries wok-fried fresh fish with Hawaiian sea salt–encrusted rack of lamb,

with a clued-in, world-ranging wine list. Sunday brunch buffet comes complete with a seafood raw bar and chocolate fountain. For top-tier sushi, sashimi and *wagyū* (Japanese marbled beef), head to the resort's Tokyo-Tokyo restaurant. Reservations are essential at both. At Hoku's, shorts and T-shirts are not allowed and collared shirts are required for men.

Shopping & Entertainment

KAHALA MALL
☎ 732-7736; 4211 Wai'alae Ave; ☺ 10am-9pm Mon-Sat, 10am-5pm Sun; 🛜; 🚌 22, 23

It's no competition for the Ala Moana Center, but this neighborhood mall contains more than 50 chain shops, including a Barnes & Noble bookstore, fast-food outlets and an eight-screen cinema that sometimes screens foreign and arthouse films. The Waikiki trolley (p134) stops here.

Sleeping

KAHALA HOTEL & RESORT   Resort $$$$
☎ 739-8888, 800-367-2525; www.kahala resort.com; 5000 Kahala Ave; r $380-845; P per day $25 🤖 🖥 🛜 🏊

On a private beach, this luxury resort is a favorite of celebs, royalty and other rich-and-famous folks who crave paparazzi-free seclusion. Elegance and class reign supreme but this grand dame maintains an appealing island-style casualness. Staff who have been working here for decades and guests who return every year know each other by name, and it's that intimacy that really separates it from the Waikiki pack. That said, some of the cheapest rooms are excruciatingly small and lack views, and if you're not an A-list star, service may not be up to par.

HAWAI'I KAI

Built around a marina and picturesque canals, and ensconced by mountains, bays and parks, this meticulously planned suburban community designed by steel tycoon Henry J Kaiser (he's the Kai in Hawai'i Kai) is an exclusive scene. Everything revolves around giant shopping centers – namely, the Koko Marina Center and Hawai'i Kai Shopping Center – off the Kalaniana'ole Hwy (Hwy 72). For anyone making their way around southeast O'ahu, it's a handy stop for a bite to eat or sunset drinks by the marina.

Information

Bank of Hawaii (☎ 397-4010; Koko Marina Center, 7192 Kalaniana'ole Hwy; ☒ 8:30am-4pm Mon-Thu, 8:30am-6pm Fri) Has a 24-hour ATM.

Common Groundz (☎ 394-8770; Hawai'i Kai Shopping Center, 377 Keahole St; ☒ 5am-9pm Mon-Sat, 7am-7pm Sun; ☎) Waterfront cafe offering free wi-fi with purchase.

Post Office (☎ 800-275-8777; 7040 Hawai'i Kai Dr; ☒ 8am-4:30pm Mon-Fri, 9am-noon Sat)

Straub Hawai'i Kai Family Health Center (☎ 396-6321; www.straubhealth.org; Koko Marina Center, 7192 Kalaniana'ole Hwy; ☒ usually 8am-5pm Mon & Fri, 8am-6pm Tue-Thu, 8am-noon Sat) Walk-in clinic for non-emergency medical services.

Activities

For sport-fishing and jet-ski outfitters, visit the Koko Marina Center. An established five-star PADI operation, **Island Divers** (☎ 423-8222, 888-844-3483; www.oahuscubadiving.com; Hawai'i Kai Shopping Center, 377 Keahole St; 2-tank dive $125-160) offers boat dives for all levels, including expert-level wreck dives. If you're a novice, staff can show you the ropes and take you to calm, relatively shallow waters. Snorkelers can also go out on the dive boats ($50 per person).

About 4 miles east of town, **Hawai'i Kai Golf Course** (☎ 395-2358; www.hawaiikaigolf.com; 8902 Kalaniana'ole Hwy; green fees incl cart $70-110) features a par-72 championship course, which has challenging greens and Koko Head views, and a par-54 executive course designed by Robert Trent Jones Sr back in the 1960s. Call ahead for tee times; club rentals are available.

Eating & Drinking

KONA BREWING COMPANY   American $$
☎ 394-5662; Koko Marina Center, 7192 Kalaniana'ole Hwy; appetizers $5-16, mains $11-25; ☒ 11am-9pm Sun-Thu, 11am-10pm Fri & Sat
Near the front of the shopping center, this brewpub has tiki torch-lit tables hanging over the marina and draft pints of Big Island brews like Longboard Lager and Pipeline Porter. Gigantic plates of just-OK appetizers, island-themed pizzas, burgers, seafood

---

DETOUR ➡

HAWAI'I KAI HIKES

Up in the mountains of the Ko'olau Range, which makes a cinematic backdrop for Hawai'i Kai, you'll find some wonderful, and often overlooked, hiking trails to get your boots on.

West of town, the 5-mile round-trip **Kuli'ou'ou Ridge Trail** is open to hikers and mountain bikers. It winds up forest switchbacks before making a stiff, but satisfying climb along a ridgeline to a windy summit offering 360-degree views of Koko Head, Makapu'u Point, the Windward Coast, Diamond Head and Honolulu. The trail is not always well maintained and may be partly overgrown with vegetation. Start from the Na Ala Hele trailhead sign at the end of Kala'au Pl, which branches right off Kuli'ou'ou Rd, just over 1 mile north of the Kalaniana'ole Hwy (Hwy 72).

East of town, the adventurous **Koko Crater Trail** leads along an abandoned wooden-tie railbed across a heart-stopping wooden bridge above a ravine to reach the summit of Pu'u Mai (1206ft) on the crater's rim. The steep, somewhat risky trail starts in Koko Head Regional Park. Use at your own risk. To get here, turn north from the Kalaniana'ole Hwy (Hwy 72) onto Lunalillo Home Rd, which borders the east side of Koko Marina Center, then turn right onto Anapalau St into the park.

---

and salads won't leave you hungry. There's live Hawaiian music on weekends, including some by big-name musicians like slack key guitar and ukulele master Led Ka'apana. Tuesday is 'Brewsday,' when souvenir-glass pints cost just $3.

BLUWATER GRILL   Seafood $$$
our pick ☎ 395-6224; Hawai'i Kai Shopping Center, 377 Keahole St; mains lunch $10-18, dinner $20-32; ☒ 11am-11pm Mon-Thu, 11am-midnight Fri & Sat, 10am-11pm Sun
Perfect for chilling out with a cocktail, this breezy, open-air restaurant overlooks the waterfront and dishes up superb kiawe-grilled

SOUTHEAST O'AHU

fare like seafood kebabs, scallops with soy-mustard butter sauce or chicken with a tropical papaya-ginger glaze. For Sunday brunch, hit the pancake bar (buttermilk blueberry, banana–chocolate chip or pineapple–mac nut) after you order a classic omelette, spicy 'ahi (Hawaiian tuna fish) Benedict or haute version of loco moco (rice, fried egg and burger patty). The crowd here looks outfitted for a supermodel runway.

ROY'S – HAWAI'I KAI Hawaii Regional $$$
☎ 396-7697; Hawai'i Kai Towne Center, 6600 Kalaniana'ole Hwy; mains $25-38, 3-course prix-fixe menu $35; ⏱ dinner

Roy Yamaguchi is one of the driving forces behind Hawaii Regional cuisine, which emphasizes fresh local ingredients and blends European, Asian and Pacific Rim influences. A pilgrimage to the chef's original outpost rarely disappoints, although it's not nearly as glitzy as his Waikiki Beach location (p119). When making reservations, request a table with a sunset view.

For quick eats and groceries:

Bubbie's (☎ 396-8722; Koko Marina Center, 7192 Kalaniana'ole Hwy; items $2-6; ⏱ 10am-11pm Sun-Thu, 10am-midnight Fri & Sat) Scoops tropical-flavored and mochi (Japanese pounded-rice cake) ice cream; there's a Foodland supermarket nearby.

Cake Couture (☎ 373-9750; Aina Haina Shopping Center, 820 W Hind Dr; items $2.50-4; ⏱ 10:30am-6:30pm Mon-Fri, 10:30am-3:30pm Sat) Divine cupcake bakery hides among Asian barbecue and island-style takeout joints.

Kale's Natural Foods (☎ 396-6993; Hawai'i Kai Shopping Center, 377 Keahole St; ⏱ 9am-8pm Mon-Fri, 9am-5pm Sat & Sun) Next to a Safeway supermarket and not far from The Shack sports bar for burgers and beer.

Shopping

ISLAND TREASURES AT THE MARINA
☎ 396-8827; Koko Marina Center, 7192 Kalaniana'ole Hwy; ⏱ 10am-6pm Mon-Thu, 10am-8pm Fri & Sat, 10am-4pm Sun

Near the waterfront, this shop collects high-quality local artisans' handiwork, including koa wood carvings and furnishings, jewelry, etched glass, pottery, painting and prints, some costing hundreds or thousands of dollars. More affordable souvenirs include

handmade soaps and lotions and Hawaiian music CDs.

Getting There & Away

From Waikiki, TheBus 22 stops at the Koko Marina Center ($2, 30 minutes, hourly) en route to Hanauma Bay (no service on Tuesday). TheBus 23 turns inland at Keahole St, stopping near Hawai'i Kai Towne Center and the Hawai'i Kai Shopping Center ($2, 30 minutes); this daily route runs less frequently. The Waikiki trolley (p134) stops at Koko Marina Center.

☘ HANAUMA BAY NATURE PRESERVE

our pick A wide, curved bay of sapphire and turquoise waters protected by a rugged volcanic ring, Hanauma is a gem. You come here for the scenery, you come here for the beach, but above all you come here to snorkel – and if you've never been snorkeling before, this is the perfect place to start.

From the overlook, you can peer into crystal waters and view the 7000-year-old coral reef that stretches across the width of the bay. You're bound to see schools of glittering silver fish, the bright-blue flash of parrotfish and perhaps sea turtles so used to snorkelers they're ready to go eyeball-to-mask with you. Feeding the fish is strictly prohibited, to preserve the delicate ecological balance of the bay. Despite its protected status, this beloved bay is still a threatened ecosystem, constantly in danger of being loved to death by the huge number of annual visitors.

Hanauma is both a county beach park and a **nature preserve** (☎ 396-4229; www.honolulu.gov/parks/facility/hanaumabay, www.soest.hawaii.edu/seagrant/education/Hanauma; adult $5, child under 13yr free; ⏱ 6am-6pm Wed-Mon Nov-Mar, 6am-7pm Wed-Mon Apr-Oct, 6am-10pm on 2nd & 4th Sat of month year-round; Ⓟ $1). There's a snack bar, lifeguards, lockers, showers and restrooms. Past the ticket windows is an award-winning educational center run by the University of Hawai'i. All visitors are required to watch a short video about the geology and ecology of the bay, but you should also take time to peruse the interesting, hands-on, family-friendly displays.

Activities

On the beach, a **concession stand** (snorkel set $6, dive light $5; 8am-5pm Nov-Mar, 8am-6pm Apr-Oct) rents snorkels, masks and fins, but you'll need to hand over $30 cash, a credit card or your car-rental keys as a deposit.

Snorkeling is fantastic year-round at Hanauma Bay. Mornings are typically better than afternoons, as crowds of swimmers haven't stirred up the sand yet. **Keyhole Lagoon**, the large, sandy opening in the middle of the coral, is the best place for novice snorkelers. It's well protected and often as calm as a swimming pool. The deepest water is 10ft, though it's very shallow over the coral – bring diving gloves, if you have them. Be very careful not to step on the coral or to accidentally knock it with your fins.

For confident snorkelers, it's better on the outside of the reef, where there are larger coral heads, bigger fish and fewer people; to get there follow the signboards or ask the lifeguard at the southern end of the beach. Because of the channel currents on either side of the bay, it's generally easier getting outside the reef than it is getting back in. Don't attempt to swim outside the reef when the water is rough or choppy. Not only are the channel currents too strong, but the sand will be stirred up and visibility poor.

If you're **scuba diving**, you'll have the whole bay to play in, with clear water, coral gardens and sea turtles. Beware of currents when the surf is up, especially surges near the shark-infested Witches Brew, on the right-hand side of the bay, and the Moloka'i Express, a treacherous current on the left-hand side of the bay's mouth.

Getting There & Away

Hanauma Bay is 10 miles east of Waikiki via the Kalaniana'ole Hwy (Hwy 72). As soon as the parking lot fills (sometimes before noon), all drivers will be turned away, so get there early. On public transit, TheBus 22, nicknamed the 'Beach Bus,' runs between Waikiki and Hanauma Bay ($2, one hour,

Picasso triggerfish at Hanauma Bay Nature Preserve

CASEY MAHANEY

SOUTHEAST O'AHU

hourly) except on Tuesday, when the park is closed. Buses leave Waikiki from approximately 8am until 4pm; the corner of Kuhio Ave and Namahana St is the first stop, and the bus often fills up shortly after. Buses back to Waikiki usually stop at Hanauma Bay between 10:45am and 5:25pm. The Waikiki trolley (p134) stops at a lookout over Hanauma Bay, but you may not disembark to visit the park.

KOKO HEAD REGIONAL PARK

With mountains on one side and a sea edged by bays and beaches on the other, the drive along this coast rates among O'ahu's best. The highway rises and falls as it winds its way around the tip of the Ko'olau Range, looking down on stratified rocks, lava sea cliffs and other fascinating geological formations. Koko Head Regional Park comprises Hanauma Bay, Koko Head, Halona Blowhole, Sandy Beach Park and Koko Crater.

Sights & Activities

LANA'I LOOKOUT

About 0.7 miles past Hanauma Bay, roadside Lana'i Lookout offers a panorama on clear days of several Hawaiian islands: Lana'i to the right, Maui in the middle and Moloka'i to the left. It's also a good vantage point for getting a look at lava-rock formations that form the sea cliffs along this coast.

FISHING SHRINE

As you drive east, keep your eye towards the ocean and, at the highest point, on a sea cliff known locally as Bamboo Ridge, you'll spot a temple-like mound of rocks surrounding a statue of Jizō, a Japanese Buddhist deity and guardian of fishers. The **fishing shrine** is often decked in lei and surrounded by sake

ISLAND VOICES

NAME: ELIZABETH KUMABE MAYNARD
OCCUPATION: EDUCATION PROGRAM LEADER, UNIVERSITY OF HAWAI'I SEA GRANT, HANAUMA BAY EDUCATION PROGRAM
RESIDENCE: HONOLULU

What makes Hanauma Bay so special? It's beautiful. Because it has been protected for over 40 years, it's almost guaranteed that you'll see fish here. It's almost like being inside an aquarium. As you swim, you'll overhear other people talking excitedly through their snorkels. Even for someone like myself, who snorkels all over O'ahu and the Neighbor Islands, it's still wonderful here because everything is so close. The more you look for marine life here, the more you'll see. The bay also has an impressive setting, being at the bottom of a volcanic crater.

What's the mission of the Hanauma Bay Education Program? To raise awareness about stewardship of the bay, with the understanding that people who come here and take our lessons to heart will take them wherever they go in the water around O'ahu. We teach 'reef etiquette' about how each of the one million visitors per year can reduce their environmental footprint when they go in the water, but still enjoy it.

What makes O'ahu different from other the Hawaiian Islands? Of course, since I'm from here, I think this island has the best weather. People from Maui are always saying 'It's so hot!' and Kaua'i residents complain 'It's always raining!', but I think O'ahu is the 'Gathering Place' for its good weather. And also for the food.

How can visitors get off the beaten path here? Get out of Waikiki, and into the country. Go hiking in the forests, which don't get as trampled as some other places on the island.

cups. There's a little roadside pull-off in front of the shrine, about 0.5 miles beyond the Lana'i Lookout.

HALONA COVE
Take your lover down for a roll in the sand at this sweet pocket cove made famous in the steamy love scene between Burt Lancaster and Deborah Kerr in the 1953 movie *From Here to Eternity*. You can peer down at the cove from the Halona Blowhole parking lot, from where you'll just be able to make out a faint path leading down to the beach. The path is steep but passable, beginning just south of the parking lot. There is no lifeguard on duty at this beach and when the surf is up, violent waves earn it the nickname Pounders, so watch out.

HALONA BLOWHOLE LOOKOUT
Just follow all the tour buses to find this one. Here, ocean waves surge through a submerged tunnel in the rock and spout up through a hole in the ledge. It's preceded by a gushing sound, created by the air that's being forced out of the tunnel by rushing water. The action depends on water conditions – sometimes it's so barely discernible you'll wonder if it's even there, while at other times it's a real showstopper. Avoid the temptation to ignore the warning signs and walk down onto the ledge, as more than a few unsuspecting people have been fatally swept off the ledge by rogue waves.

ourpick SANDY BEACH PARK
This is O'ahu's most dangerous beach: it has a punishing shorebreak, a powerful backwash and strong rip currents. Here, the ocean heaves and thrashes like a furious beast, which makes it extremely popular with bodyboarders who really know their stuff. When the swells are big, bodysurfers hit the left side of the beach, as crowds gather to watch the daredevils being tossed around in the skull-crushing waves.

Sandy Beach is wide, very long and, yes, sandy, but this is no place to frolic in the waves. Red flags flown on the beach indicate hazardous water conditions. Even if you don't see any flags, always check with the lifeguards before entering the water. There are restrooms and showers. On weekends you'll usually find a food wagon selling plate lunches and drinks.

The grassy strip next to the parking lot is utilized by people looking skyward for their thrills – it's both a hang glider landing site and a popular place for kite flying.

KOKO CRATER BOTANICAL GARDEN
☎ 522-7063; end of Kokonani St; admission free; ☾ sunrise-sunset
According to Hawaiian legend, Koko Crater is the imprint left by the magical flying vagina of Kapo, sent from the Big Island to lure the pig-god Kamapua'a away from her sister Pele, the Hawaiian goddess of volcanoes. Inside the crater today is a quiet, county-run botanical garden abloom with fragrant plumeria, oleander, cacti and other native and exotic dryland species. Connecting loop trails lead through the garden. To get here, turn inland on Kealahou St off the Kalaniana'ole Hwy (Hwy 72), opposite the north end of Sandy Beach. After around 0.5 miles, turn left onto Kokonani St. From Waikiki, TheBus 23 ($2, 55 minutes) stops at the corner of Kealahou and Kokonani Sts, about 0.3 miles from the garden entrance, but service is infrequent.

Getting There & Away
From Waikiki, TheBus 22 stops hourly at Hanauma Bay and Sandy Beach Park but makes no stops between the two, and it doesn't run at all on Tuesday, when Hanauma Bay is closed. The Waikiki trolley (p134) only stops at the Halona Blowhole Lookout.

BODYBOARDING BLUES
Sandy Beach is the bodyboarder's ultimate challenge. When the trade winds are strong, a south swell pops up a riptide with a powerful backlash. Those riding it often get upended in the shorebreak, their bodies tossed inverted and hanging upside down as the wave begins to crash back to the sand. Hundreds of people are injured at Sandy Beach each year, some with just broken arms and dislocated shoulders, but others with serious spinal injuries. The upside? For experienced shorebreak riders, the action is a thrill found nowhere else.

SOUTHEAST O'AHU

MAKAPU'U POINT & AROUND

Makapu'u Point and its coastal lighthouse mark the easternmost point of O'ahu. On the north side of the point, a roadside **lookout** affords an exhilarating view down onto Makapu'u Beach Park, its aqua-blue waters outlined by white sand and black lava. It's an even more spectacular sight when hang gliders are taking off from the cliffs above.

From the lookout you can see two offshore islands, the larger of which is **Manana Island** (aka Rabbit Island). The aging volcanic crater is populated by feral rabbits and burrowing wedge-tailed shearwaters. Curiously, the island also looks vaguely like the head of a rabbit with its ears folded back. In front is smaller **Kaohikaipu Island**, which just looks flat.

If you're going to keep driving or riding TheBus around the point to Waimanalo, see p170 for more directions and helpful information about public transit.

Sights & Activities

MAKAPU'U LIGHTHOUSE

Before reaching the lookout, there is a paved service road leading to the Makapu'u Point lighthouse on the *makai* (oceanward) side of the road. The gate is locked to keep out private vehicles, but you can park off the highway just beyond the gate and walk in for about 1 mile to the lighthouse. Although not difficult, it's an uphill walk that can be hot and windy. Along the way there are stellar coastal views of Koko Head, Hanauma Bay and, in winter, migrating whales. Note that actually climbing down the rocks to the lighthouse is illegally trespassing on federal property. From Waikiki, TheBus 22 and 23 stop near the trailhead ($2, one hour, hourly).

MAKAPU'U BEACH PARK

Opposite Sea Life Park and just barely within view of the lighthouse, Makapu'u Beach is one of O'ahu's top winter bodyboarding spots, with waves reaching 12ft and higher. It also has the island's best shorebreak. As with Sandy Beach (p161), Makapu'u is strictly the domain of expert bodyboarders who can handle rough water conditions and dangerous currents. In summer, when the wave action disappears, calmer waters afford good swimming.

SEA LIFE PARK

☎ 259-2500, 866-393-5158; www.sealifepark hawaii.com; 41-202 Kalaniana'ole Hwy; adult $29, child 3-11yr $19; ☷ 10:30am-5pm; ☐ 22, 23 & 57 Hawaii's only marine-life park offers a mixed bag of attractions that, frankly, aren't worth your time. The theme-park entertainment includes choreographed shows featuring imported Atlantic bottlenose dolphins and a pool where visitors can swim with dolphins, something that can't be recommended (see the boxed text, p43). Although the main attractions feature animals that aren't found in Hawaiian waters, the park also maintains a breeding colony of green sea turtles, releasing young hatchlings back into their natural habitat every year. Still, if you want to learn about Hawaii's marine life, you're better off visiting the Waikiki Aquarium (p109).

Makapu'u Beach Park   ANN CECIL

WINDWARD O'AHU

Welcome to O'ahu's lushest, greenest coast, where turquoise waters and white-sand beaches share a dramatic backdrop of the misty cliffs of the Ko'olau Range. Cruise through the freeway tunnels and over the mountains and you're in 'the country.' Kick back in the adventure-sports base camp of Kailua, famous for sea-kayaking and windsurfing beaches. Detour east to Waimanalo or wander north of Kane'ohe, where everything slows down. Head toward the North Shore down a two-lane coastal road, winding beside wetland taro patches, *paniolo* (Hawaiian cowboy) ranches and blissfully undeveloped beaches. Never mind all the rain, because sunshine always follows.

WINDWARD O'AHU
ITINERARIES

IN ONE DAY *This leg: 30 miles*

❶ NU'UANU PALI LOOKOUT (p167) As you climb over the mountains from Honolulu, stop at this windy viewpoint and walk a little ways down the Old Pali Hwy for panoramas of the Windward Coast. If you're inspired by the view, you can keep going along the Maunawili Trail, which winds in and out of lush, stream-fed gulches.

❷ KALAPAWAI MARKET (p175) Belly up to the espresso bar and stock your picnic basket for a morning at the beach inside this beloved 1930s grocery shop and deli.

❸ KAILUA BEACH PARK (p173) Don't miss the Windward Coast's most beautiful golden-sand beach, with gentle waves ideal for taking a dip. Swimmers, get here before

afternoon breezes kick up, to the delight of windsurfers.

❹ LANIKAI JUICE (p177) Even if you don't spot one of the TV stars of *Lost* here, this healthy-minded juice bar is still the best place to hang after surf and sun.

❺ VALLEY OF THE TEMPLES & BYŌDŌ-IN (p180) Although its location inside a cemetery is odd, this exquisite replica of an ancient Japanese temple backed by craggy *pali* (cliffs) is a rare beauty.

❻ HO'OMALUHIA BOTANICAL GARDEN (p180) If you've got time to spare before sunset, take a wander through fragrant groves of tropical trees and around an artificial reservoir on soft, grassy paths.

IN TWO DAYS This leg: 35 miles

7 CINNAMON'S RESTAURANT (p176) Follow the one-day itinerary, then rise and shine early for a drive through Windward O'ahu's 'country.' Before you hit the Kamehameha Hwy, though, stop here for breakfast.

8 KUALOA RANCH (p184) Ever wonder where the set designers for *Jurassic Park* and *Lost* found such incredible locations? Right here on O'ahu at this historic ranch, which offers adventure tours.

9 TROPICAL FARMS (p185) Get a quick pick-me-up by snacking on free samples of freshly roasted macadamia nuts flavored with honey, dark chocolate or even garlic.

10 CROUCHING LION (p186) Everyone pulls off the highway to see this natural rock formation. Of course, ancient Hawai-ians thought it looked like something very different from an African lion.

11 AHUPUA'A O KAHANA STATE PARK (p187) Stretch your legs with a gentle nature walk past an ancient fishing shrine to an overlook with knock-out bay views of Kahana Bay.

12 MALAEKAHANA STATE RECREATION AREA (p190) Don't miss northern Windward O'ahu's most inviting swimming and snorkeling beach. When the waters are calm and low, you can wade across to an offshore island.

13 KAHUKU'S SHRIMP TRUCKS (p194) Few people drive around the island without stopping to devour a dozen crustaceans here, dipped in garlic butter, doused in hot-and-spicy sauce or coconut-fried – it's your choice.

FOR BEACH LOVERS

1 WAIMANALO BAY BEACH PARK (p170) From this gorgeous beach all you see is endless sand, a sea of creamy turquoise waters and local kids hitting the surf. It's a scene right off one of those period postcards from 1930s Hawaii. Bring a board and join 'em.

2 KAILUA BEACH PARK (p173) No matter what your interest, this idyllic beach has it all. It also scores as the island's top windsurfing destination and its best place for ocean kayaking. You can rent equipment and get lessons (or do yoga!) on the beach.

3 LANIKAI BEACH (p173) Home to millionaires but accessible to all, this beach boasts the softest powdery white sand on O'ahu. Come for a walk on full-moon nights or to catch the sunrise breaking over nearshore islands.

4 MOKU NUI (p173) It's worth a little effort to find this hideaway on an island off Lanikai Beach. Pack a picnic, rent a kayak at Kailua Beach and paddle out to your own little slice of paradise.

5 KUALOA REGIONAL PARK (p184) Arguably Windward O'ahu's most purely scenic beach, Kualoa is backed by precipitous green mountains and overlooks an ancient fishpond. It's a good beach for kids, with shallow water and safe swimming.

6 MALAEKAHANA BEACH (p190) This wild, windy and larger-than-life beach has good year-round swimming, and is popular with families for all kinds of water sports.

WINDWARD OʻAHU

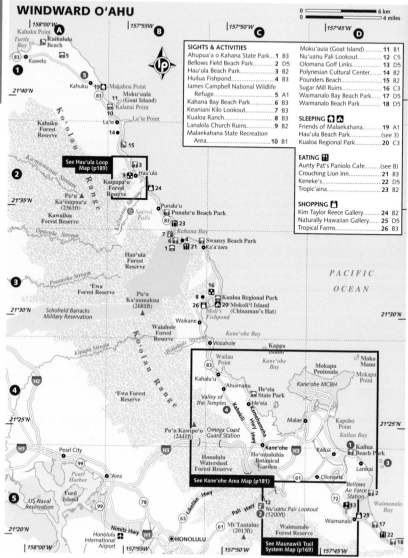

WINDWARD OʻAHU

SIGHTS & ACTIVITIES		
Ahupuaʻa o Kahana State Park...	**1**	B3
Bellows Field Beach Park..........	**2**	D5
Hauʻula Beach Park...................	**3**	B2
Huilua Fishpond.......................	**4**	B3
James Campbell National Wildlife		
Refuge..............................	**5**	A1
Kahana Bay Beach Park............	**6**	B3
Keaniani Kilo Lookout...............	**7**	B3
Kualoa Ranch.........................	**8**	B3
Lanakila Church Ruins...............	**9**	B2
Malaekahana State Recreation		
Area.................................	**10**	B1

Mokuʻauia (Goat Island)...........	**11**	B1
Nuʻuanu Pali Lookout...............	**12**	C5
Olomana Golf Links..................	**13**	D5
Polynesian Cultural Center.........	**14**	B2
Pounders Beach.......................	**15**	B2
Sugar Mill Ruins......................	**16**	C3
Waimanalo Bay Beach Park........	**17**	D5
Waimanalo Beach Park..............	**18**	D5

SLEEPING		
Friends of Malaekahana.............	**19**	A1
Hauʻula Beach Park..............(see 3)		
Kualoa Regional Park...............	**20**	C3

EATING		
Aunty Pat's Paniolo Cafe.......(see 8)		
Crouching Lion Inn..................	**21**	B3
Keneke's................................	**22**	D5
Tropic'aina.............................	**23**	B2

SHOPPING		
Kim Taylor Reece Gallery..........	**24**	B2
Naturally Hawaiian Gallery......	**25**	D5
Tropical Farms........................	**26**	B3

THE PALI HIGHWAY

Slicing through the spectacular emerald Koʻolau Range, the Pali Hwy (Hwy 61) runs between Honolulu and Kailua. If it's been raining heavily, every fold and crevice in the jagged cliffs will have an elfin waterfall streaming down it.

An ancient Hawaiian footpath once wound its way perilously over these cliffs. In 1845 the path was widened into a horse trail and later into a cobblestone carriage road. In 1898 the Old Pali Hwy (as it's now called) was built along the same route, but was abandoned in the 1950s after tunnels were blasted through the Koʻolau Range.

HIGHLIGHTS

❶ BEST BEACH: Kailua Beach Park (p173)
❷ BEST VIEW: Nu'uanu Pali Lookout (right)
❸ BEST ACTIVITY: Kayaking to offshore islands from Kailua (p173)
❹ BEST GOOD-LUCK RITUAL: Ringing the bell at Byōdō-In (p180)
❺ BEST ROAD-TRIPPIN' FOOD: Kahuku's shrimp trucks (p194)

Highlights are numbered on the map opposite.

Old Pali Hwy

You can make a scenic side trip along the Old Pali Hwy, now called Nu'uanu Pali Dr, by turning eastward off Hwy 61 about half a mile north of the Queen Emma Summer Palace. The drive runs through a cathedral of trees draped with hanging vines and philodendrons. The lush vegetation along the detour includes bamboo groves, almond trees, banyan trees with hanging aerial roots, angel's trumpets and cup of gold, a tall climbing vine with large golden flowers. This short detour returns you to the Pali Hwy just in time to exit at the Nu'uanu Pali Lookout.

Nu'uanu Pali Lookout

Follow the tour buses to the ridge-top Nu'uanu Pali Lookout (Map p166), where you'll find a sweeping vista of Windward O'ahu from a height of 1200ft. From the lookout you can see Kane'ohe straight ahead, Kailua to the right, and hat-shaped Mokoli'i Island and the coastal fishpond at Kualoa Regional Park to the far left. Remember this is *windward* O'ahu – the winds that funnel through the *pali* are so strong that you can sometimes lean against them. It's cool enough here that you'll want a jacket.

A section of the abandoned Old Pali Hwy (left) winds down from the right side of

Windward O'ahu seen from the Nu'uanu Pali Lookout, Kane'ohe ANN CECIL

THE BATTLE OF NU'UANU

O'ahu was the lynchpin conquered by Kamehameha the Great during his campaign to unite the Hawaiian Islands under his rule. In 1795, on the quiet beaches of Waikiki, Kamehameha landed his fearsome fleet of canoes to battle Kalanikupule, O'ahu's king.

Heavy fighting started around Puowaina (Punchbowl), and continued up Nu'uanu Valley. O'ahu's spear-and-stone warriors were no match for Kamehameha's troops, which included Western sharpshooters. The defenders made their last stand at the narrow ledge along the current-day Nu'uanu Pali Lookout. Hundreds were driven over the top to their deaths. A century later, during the construction of the Old Pali Hwy, more than 500 skulls were found at the base of the cliffs.

Some O'ahu warriors, including their king, escaped into the forest. When Kalanikupule surfaced a few months later, he was sacrificed by Kamehameha to the war god Ku. Kamehameha's taking of O'ahu marked the last battle ever fought between Hawaiian warriors.

the Nu'uanu Pali Lookout, ending at a barrier near the current highway about 1 mile away. Few people realize the road is here, let alone venture down it, thereby missing the magnificent views looking back up at the snaggle-toothed Ko'olau Range and out across the valley. It's worth walking even just five minutes down the trail for a photo op.

When you return to the highway, it's easy to miss the sign leading you out of the parking lot, and instinct could send you in the wrong direction. Go to the left if you're heading toward Kailua, to the right if heading toward Honolulu. TheBus travels the Pali Hwy between Honolulu and Kailua, but does not stop at the lookout.

Maunawili Trail System

our pick Winding down to coastal Waimanalo, this scenic 10-mile hiking and mountain-biking trail (Map p169) winds along the back side of Maunawili Valley, following the base of the lofty Ko'olau Range. It clambers up and down gulches,

Hiking the Maunawili Trail

ANN CECIL

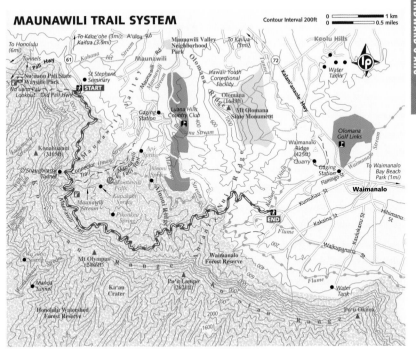

MAUNAWILI TRAIL SYSTEM

across streams and along ridges, awarding panoramic views of mountains and the Windward Coast. About 2 miles east of the Pali Hwy trailhead, watch for a connector trail that races downhill to Maunawili Falls, a small pooling waterfall alongside a muddy, mosquito-infested stream.

Hiking the Maunawili Trail in an easterly direction is less strenuous, as you will be following the trail from the mountains down to the coast. But you'll need two cars to shuttle between the trailheads, since The-Bus doesn't stop at the Pali Hwy trailhead. Or you can just hike in as far as you want, then backtrack to the trailhead. Because the trail is subject to erosion, mountain bikers should stay off the trail when it's raining or if the trail is wet. If you come across muddy sections, dismount and walk your bike.

The Maunawili Trail can be accessed by driving about 1 mile north past the Nu'uanu Pali Lookout. Pull off right at the 'scenic point' turnout at the hairpin turn just before the 7-mile marker. Walk through the break in the guardrail where a footbridge takes you over a drainage ditch. The trail

can also be picked up from the Nu'uanu Pali Lookout by walking down a mile-long stretch of the Old Pali Hwy.

To start hiking in Waimanalo, turn inland off the Kalaniana'ole Hwy (Hwy 72) at Kumuhau St, then turn right onto Waikupanaha Rd, then after 0.2 miles look for a break in the fence at a gravel pull-out and the Na Ala Hele trailhead sign.

Locals usually start the hike to Maunawili Falls from another trailhead outside Kailua, from where it's only a 2.5-mile roundtrip. Coming from Honolulu, turn right off the

Top Picks

FOR KIDS

- **Maunawili Falls Trail** (opposite)
- **Kailua Beach Park** (p173)
- **Island Snow** (p177)
- **Kualoa Regional Park** (p184)
- **Malaekahana State Recreation Area** (p190)

Pali Hwy at the second exit for A'uloa Rd, past the Kamehameha Hwy intersection. At the first fork veer left onto Maunawili Rd, which ends in a residential subdivision, then look for a gated trail-access road on your left.

WAIMANALO
pop 3600

Sprawled along gorgeous beaches, this rural Hawaiian community (Map p166) is a breadbasket of small farms. Nicknamed 'Nalo by locals, hillside farms here grow many of the fresh leafy greens served in Honolulu's top restaurants. Squeezed between the knife-edged Ko'olau Range and the crystal waters of Waimanalo Bay, this little town has O'ahu's longest continuous stretch of beach, with 5.5 miles of white sand spreading southeast all the way to Makapu'u Point (p162). A long coral reef about 1 mile offshore breaks the biggest waves, protecting much of the shore. It's practically paradise, except for the all-too-common car break-ins, vandalism and theft.

Beaches

WAIMANALO BEACH PARK
Map p166

With a seductive beach of soft white sand, tiny-tot waves here make for excellent swimming. By the side of the highway, this park has a few ironwood trees, with Manana Island and Makapu'u Point visible to

> # Don't Miss
>
> - **Waimanalo Bay beaches** (left)
> - **Ulupo Heiau** (p173)
> - **Lanikai Juice** (p177)
> - **Ho'omaluhia Botanical Garden** (p180)
> - **Sunshine Arts Gallery** (p182)
> - **Malaekahana State Recreation Area** (p190)

the south. Facilities include a grassy picnic area, restrooms, showers, lifeguards, ball-sports courts, a playground and a 22-site campground that doesn't look inviting.

WAIMANALO BAY BEACH PARK
Map p166

About 1 mile north of Waimanalo Beach Park, this county park has Waimanalo Bay's biggest waves and is popular with board surfers and bodyboarders. Even if you're not planning to hit the water, just take a walk along the beautiful broad sandy beach backed by ironwoods – not an iota of development in sight, just the feeling of old Hawaii. There are lifeguards, barbecue grills, showers, restrooms and 10 campsites.

BELLOWS FIELD BEACH PARK
Map p166

Fronting Bellows Air Force Station, the park is open to civilian beachgoers and campers only on national holidays and weekends, usually from noon Friday until 8am Mon-

Waimanalo Bay Beach Park

KARL LEHMANN

day. The long beach has fine sand and a natural setting backed by ironwood trees. The small shorebreak waves are good for beginning bodyboarders and board surfers. There are lifeguards, showers, restrooms, drinking water and 60 campsites set among the trees or by the beach. The park entrance is just north of Waimanalo Bay Beach Park. TheBus stops in front of the entrance road, about 1.5 miles from the beach itself.

Activities

Barack Obama played at Olomana Golf Links (Map p166; ☎ 259-7926; 41-1801 Kalaniana'ole Hwy; club rental $35, green fees incl cart rental from $90) just before taking up the presidency, and this is where LPGA star Michelle Wie got her start. With the dramatic backdrop of the Ko'olau Range, the two challenging nine-hole courses are played together as a regulation 18-hole course. Facilities include a driving range and the Sakura restaurant, serving beer and local grinds.

Eating

KENEKE'S   Drive-In $
Map p166; ☎ 259-9811; 41-857 Kalaniana'ole Hwy; mains $4-8; ⏰ 9:30am-5:30pm
Past the convenience shops and fast-food eateries in Waimanalo town, this red-and-white checked roadside shack ropes in locals with its plate lunches (try the *mochiko* fried chicken, *laulau* or *kalua* pig), island-style barbecue, pineapple smoothies and shave ice. Despite the Christian scripture written on the walls, cleanliness isn't necessarily next to godliness here.

Shopping

NATURALLY HAWAIIAN GALLERY
Map p166; ☎ 259-5354; www.naturallyhawaiian .com; 41-1025 Kalaniana'ole Hwy; ⏰ usually 10am-6pm
Inside a converted gas station, this outstanding gallery and gift shop displays art and handmade crafts by O'ahu artists, including wooden koa bowls, carved bone fish-hook pendants and other jewelry. It's owned by genial Patrick Ching, a former park ranger and cowboy, who also sells his own landscape and wildlife paintings, prints and illustrated naturalist books here.

Farming in Waimanalo   LINDA CHING

Sleeping

The best and safest place to camp is at Bellows Field Beach Park (opposite), which is open to the public on weekends only. For more information about camping at county parks, including getting the required permits in advance, see p270. For private house and apartment-suite vacation rentals around Waimanalo, contact Beach House Hawaii (☎ 866-625-6946; www.beachhousehawaii.com) or any of the agencies listed on p269.

Getting There & Away

Starting from the Ala Moana Shopping Center and downtown Honolulu, TheBus 57 passes through Waimanalo along the Kalaniana'ole Hwy (Hwy 72) on its way between Kailua and Sea Life Park. This route runs every 30 to 60 minutes, taking about an hour to reach Waimanalo from the Ala Moana Center or 25 minutes from Kailua ($2).

WINDWARD O'AHU

KAILUA

pop 49,250

Kailua is Windward O'ahu's largest town, though that's not saying a lot if you've just driven over the *pali* from Honolulu or Waikiki. Still, this is the one place that you would really kick yourself for missing later on your drive around the island. For starters, the shores of Kailua Bay are lined by beaches with velvety, golden sands. Kailua Beach has long been the hottest place on the island for windsurfers and kayakers, and these days you'll see kitesurfers too. Not surprisingly, the influx of adrenaline-charged visitors has given rise to surf shops and plenty of laid-back, low-profile accommodations. In fact, some people base their entire trip here – not a bad idea, given all the juice and java bars, yoga studios and endless outdoor adventures. A caveat: this bedroom suburb often feels more like the mainland than Hawaii, with Middle America retirees snapping up beach cottages and skater punks on every other corner.

Island Insights

In ancient times Kailua (meaning 'two seas') was a place of legends. It was home to a giant who turned into a mountain ridge, as well as the island's first *menehune* (the 'little people' who, according to legend, built many of Hawaii's fishponds and stonework). Kamehameha the Great lived here briefly after conquering O'ahu.

Information

Bank of Hawaii (Map p172; ☎ 266-4600; 636 Kailua Rd; ☼ 8:30am-4pm Mon-Thu, 8:30am-6pm Fri)

Bookends (Map p172; ☎ 261-1996; Kailua Shopping Center, 600 Kailua Rd; ☼ 9am-8pm Mon-Sat, 9am-5pm Sun) Independent shop sells new and used books, newspapers and maps.

Braun Urgent Care (Map p172; ☎ 261-4411; Kailua Beach Center, 130 Kailua Rd; ☼ usually 8am-8pm) Non-emergency clinic; call ahead to confirm doctors' availability.

Kailua Information Center & Chamber of Commerce (Map p172; ☎ 261-2727; www.kailuachamber.com;

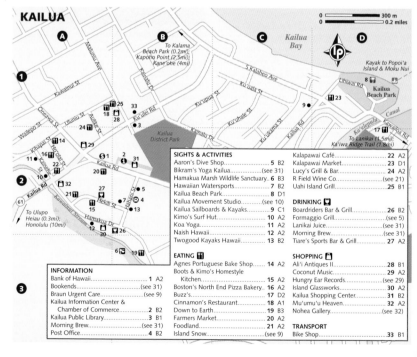

KAILUA

0 — 300 m
0 — 0.2 miles

To Kalama Beach Park (0.2mi); Kapoho Point (2.5mi); Kane'ohe (4mi)

Kailua Bay

Kayak to Popoi'a Island & Moku Nui

Kailua Beach Park

Kailua District Park

To Lanikai (1.5mi); Ka'iwa Ridge Trail (1.8mi)

To Ulupo Heiau (0.3mi); Honolulu (10mi)

SIGHTS & ACTIVITIES	
Aaron's Dive Shop	5 B2
Bikram's Yoga Kailua	(see 31)
Hamakua Marsh Wildlife Sanctuary	6 B3
Hawaiian Watersports	7 B2
Kailua Beach Park	8 D1
Kailua Movement Studio	(see 10)
Kailua Sailboards & Kayaks	9 C1
Kimo's Surf Hut	10 A2
Koa Yoga	11 A2
Naish Hawaii	12 A2
Twogood Kayaks Hawaii	13 B2

EATING	
Agnes Portuguese Bake Shop	14 A2
Boots & Kimo's Homestyle Kitchen	15 A2
Boston's North End Pizza Bakery	16 A2
Buzz's	17 D2
Cinnamon's Restaurant	18 A1
Down to Earth	19 B3
Farmers Market	20 A2
Foodland	21 A2
Island Snow	(see 9)

Kalapawai Café	22 A2
Kalapawai Market	23 D1
Lucy's Grill & Bar	24 A2
R Field Wine Co	(see 21)
Uahi Island Grill	25 B1

DRINKING	
Boardriders Bar & Grill	26 B2
Formaggio Grill	(see 5)
Lanikai Juice	(see 31)
Morning Brew	(see 31)
Tiare's Sports Bar & Grill	27 A2

SHOPPING	
Ali'i Antiques II	28 B1
Coconut Music	29 A2
Hungry Ear Records	(see 29)
Island Glassworks	30 A2
Kailua Shopping Center	31 B2
Mu'umu'u Heaven	32 A2
Nohea Gallery	(see 32)

TRANSPORT	
Bike Shop	33 B1

INFORMATION	
Bank of Hawaii	1 A2
Bookends	(see 31)
Braun Urgent Care	(see 9)
Kailua Information Center & Chamber of Commerce	2 B2
Kailua Public Library	3 B1
Morning Brew	(see 31)
Post Office	4 B2

Kailua Shopping Center, 600 Kailua Rd; ⊗ 10am-4pm Mon-Fri, 10am-2pm Sat) Hands out free maps and local information.

Kailua Public Library (Map p172; ☎ 266-9911; 239 Ku'ulei Rd; ⊗ 10am-5pm Mon, Wed, Fri & Sat, 1-8pm Tue & Thu) Free reservable internet terminals (see p279).

Morning Brew (Map p172; ☎ 262-7770; Kailua Shopping Center, 600 Kailua Rd; per hr $6; ⊗ 6am-9pm Sun-Thu, 6am-10pm Fri & Sat; ▣ ⊚) Fee-based internet terminals and free wi-fi with purchase.

Post Office (Map p172; ☎ 800-275-8777; 335 Hahani St; ⊗ 8:30am-5pm Mon-Fri, 9am-4pm Sat)

Beaches

For more beaches and water sports, see right.

KAILUA BEACH PARK

our pick **Map p172**

Curving around the southern edge of Kailua Bay, this long, broad, white-sand beach has a gently sloping sandy bottom with clear turquoise waters that are generally pacific. It's ideal for leisurely walks, family outings and all kinds of aquatic activities, including windsurfing and kayaking. Swimming conditions are excellent year-round, with gentle waves for beginning bodyboarders, but sunbathers beware: the afternoon breezes propel sand as well as windsurfers! The best time to come is on weekdays – in the mornings for swimmers and in the afternoons for windsurfers. The park has restrooms, showers, lifeguards, a volleyball court and large grassy picnic areas shaded by ironwood trees.

LANIKAI BEACH

Map p181

Lanikai is an exclusive residential neighborhood fronted by Lanikai Beach, a gorgeous stretch of powdery white sand overlooking two postcard-perfect islands. The sandy bottom slopes gently and the waters are calm, offering safe swimming conditions similar to those at Kailua. Unfortunately, the beach is shrinking, as nearly half the sand has washed away as a result of retaining walls built to protect the multimillion-dollar homes constructed on the shore. Still, it's a beauty – come see it during full-moon phases, when the beach has the most sand. Beyond Kailua Beach Park, the coastal road becomes one-way A'alapapa Dr, which loops back around

as Mokulua Dr. There are 11 narrow public beach-access walkways off Mokulua Dr. For the best stretches of sand, try the walkways furthest southeast, towards Wailea Point.

Sights

ULUPO HEIAU

Map p181; ☎ 587-0300; 1200 Kailua Rd; admission free; ⊗ sunrise-sunset

Rich in stream-fed agricultural land, abundant fishing grounds and protected canoe landings, Kailua served as a political and economic center in ancient Hawaiian times. The building of this imposing platform temple, probably a *luakini* heiau (ancient temple) dedicated to the war god Ku and used for human sacrifices, is attributed to *menehune*, the little people who myths say created much of Hawaii's stonework, finishing each project in one night. Fittingly, Ulupo means 'night inspiration.' Legends also say that nearby Kawai Nui Marsh, the largest native wetland remaining in Hawaii, was home to a *mo'o* (lizard spirit).

This state historic site is 1 mile south of Kailua, behind the YMCA. Coming down the Pali Hwy from Honolulu, take Uluoa St, the first left after passing the Kalaniana'ole Hwy (Hwy 72). Turn right onto Manu Aloha St, then right again at Manuo'o St.

Activities

KAYAKING & SNORKELING

Kailua Beach, with its pretty little uninhabited islands within the reef, is the perfect place to pick up a paddle. Landings are allowed on Popoi'a Island (Flat Island), directly off the south end of Kailua Beach Park. The magical twin Mokulua Islands, Moku Nui and Moku Iki, are directly off Lanikai Beach. It's possible to kayak over to Moku Nui, which has a beautiful beach for sunbathing and snorkeling, but landings are prohibited on Moku Iki, the smaller of the islands.

The following companies can suggest itineraries to match all skill levels and offer guided kayak tours (from $119) that last four hours, include a picnic lunch, and give you time for snorkeling and swimming.

Hawaiian Watersports (Map p172; ☎ 262-5483; www.hawaiianwatersports.com; 354 Hahani St; s/d kayak rental per half-day $49/59, incl snorkel set $54/64; ⊗ 9am-5pm) Gives discounts for online bookings.

Kailua Sailboards & Kayaks (Map p172; ☎ 262-2555, 888-457-5737; www.kailuasailboards.com; Kailua Beach Center, 130 Kailua Rd; s/d kayak rental per half-day $39/49, incl snorkel set $51/61; ☻ 8:30am-5pm) A short walk from the beach.

Twogood Kayaks Hawaii (Map p172; ☎ 262-5656; www.twogoodkayaks.com; 345 Hahani St; s/d kayak rental per half-day $39/49, incl snorkel set $47/57; ☻ 9am-6pm Mon-Fri, 8am-6pm Sat & Sun) Free delivery next to Kailua Beach Park.

WINDSURFING

Thanks to strong onshore winds, windsurfers can sail year-round here. Summer trade winds average 10 to 15 mph, with stronger bursts in spring. Different parts of the bay have different water conditions, some good for jumps and wave surfing, others for flat-water sails. Both companies listed here have shops in Kailua and give lessons and rent gear at Kailua Beach Park.

Owned by windsurfing champion Robbie Naish, **Naish Hawaii** (Map p172; ☎ 262-6068; www.naish.com; 155 Hamakua Dr; ☻ 9am-5:30pm) is top dog. Rental rates vary with the board and rig, ranging from $45 to $55 per day. Three-hour introductory group lessons cost $45 per person, or pay $100 for a private lesson for two people. Expect to spend half the time learning the basics with an instructor and half sailing on your own.

Kailua Sailboards & Kayaks (Map p172; ☎ 262-2555, 888-457-5737; www.kailuasailboards.com; Kailua Beach Center, 130 Kailua Rd; ☻ 8:30am-5pm) also rents windsurfing equipment ($69 to $89 per day), gives four-hour beginner group lessons ($129) and offers DIY advanced windsurfing tours ($99) that include equipment rental, lunch and a hotel pick-up in Waikiki.

KITESURFING

Kitesurfing (also called kiteboarding) was popularized here by windsurfing legend Robbie Naish. It helps if you know how to wakeboard or windsurf, but all you really need to start is the ability to swim. It does take a lot of muscle, stamina and coordination. **Hawaiian Watersports** (Map p172; ☎ 262-5483; www.hawaiianwatersports.com; 354 Hahani St; 6hr beginners lesson package $479; ☻ 9am-5pm) gives beginner and intermediate-level lessons on Kailua Beach. Kitesurfing doesn't come as easy as windsurfing – expect to take about six hours to learn enough to kitesurf on your own. About half of that will be lectures and learning techniques on land before you even hit the water.

If you already know how to windsurf, you can rent gear – a board, trainer kite and harness rental costs from $75 per day – at **Kailua Sailboards & Kayaks** (Map p172; ☎ 262-2555, 888-457-5737; www.kailuasailboards.com; Kailua Beach Center, 130 Kailua Rd; ☻ 8:30am-5pm) or **Naish Hawaii** (Map p172; ☎ 262-6068; www.naish.com; 155 Hamakua Dr; ☻ 9am-5:30pm), which also rents gear at Kailua Beach Park.

Kailua is the perfect place for kayaking (p173)

ANN CECIL

SURFING

On the north side of Kailua Bay, Kalama Beach Park (Map p181) has one of the largest shorebreaks in the bay. When the waves are up, board surfers and bodyboarders can find decent conditions there. Board surfers also head to the northern end of Kailua Bay to Kapoho Point (Map p181), which has a decent break during swells. Boards can be rented all over town for about $20/30 per half-/full day (up to $50/60 for stand up paddlesurfing boards), including at the following.

Hawaiian Watersports (Map p172; ☎ 262-5483; www.hawaiianwatersports.com; 354 Hahani St; 2hr group traditional or stand up paddlesurfing lesson $99; ☼ 9am-5pm) Discounts available for online bookings of rentals and lessons.

Kailua Sailboards & Kayaks (Map p172; ☎ 262-2555, 888-457-5737; www.kailuasailboards.com; Kailua Beach Center, 130 Kailua Rd; 90min group surfing lesson $89, 1hr private lesson $109; ☼ 8:30am-5pm) Rents boards and gives traditional and stand up paddle-surfing lessons.

Kimo's Surf Hut (Map p172; ☎ 262-1644; 776 Kailua Rd; ☼ 10am-6pm Mon-Sat) Sells new and used surfboards, including cool vintage models; rentals available.

Naish Hawaii (Map p172; ☎ 262-6068; www.naish.com; 155 Hamakua Dr; ☼ 9am-5:30pm) Rents basic surfboards and stand up paddlesurfing boards.

DIVING

Sea caves, lava tubes, coral gardens and WWII-era shipwrecks can all be explored with Aaron's Dive Shop (Map p172; ☎ 262-2333, 888-847-2822; www.hawaii-scuba.com; 307 Hahani St; 2-tank dive $115-125, 3-day open-water course $450; ☼ 7am-7pm Mon-Fri, 7am-6pm Sat, 7am-5pm Sun), a five-star PADI operation that offers free pick-ups from Waikiki hotels. Discounts are sometimes available for booking online.

BIRD-WATCHING

When water levels rise, birders flock to Hamakua Marsh Wildlife Sanctuary (Map p172; http://hamakuamarsh.com; admission free; ☼ sunrise-sunset). This 23-acre sanctuary borders the back side of the Down to Earth natural-foods store parking lot. If it has been raining recently, you can readily spot rare waterbirds in their natural habitat, including the *koloa maoli* (Hawaiian duck), *ae'o* (Hawaiian stilt), *'alae kea* (Hawaiian coot) and *kolea* (Pacific golden plover).

HIKING

Taking under an hour roundtrip, the mile-long Ka'iwa Ridge Trail (Map p181) offers head-spinning views of Kailua, Lanikai and the Ko'olau Range. It's best as a fair-weather trail, as it starts off steeply and can be a total mud slide after it rains. Wear shoes with traction. To get here, turn right off A'alapapa Dr in Lanikai onto Ka'elepulu Dr and continue uphill towards the country club, then park just beyond it. Walk up the side road across the street and opposite the yellow water hydrant; look for a dirt trail beginning between two chain-link fences.

YOGA & PILATES

For sunrise or starlight yoga on the sand, check out the rotating schedule of classes, styles and teachers through Kailua Beach Yoga (Map p172; ☎ 722-8923; www.kailuabeachyoga.com), which schedules sessions at Kailua, Lanikai and Kalama Beaches. Beginners are welcome – just bring a mat. The indoor Kailua Movement Studio (Map p172; ☎ 262-1933; www.kailua movementstudio.com; 776 Kailua Rd) offers classes in yoga, Pilates, belly dancing, capoeira, ecstatic dance and even martial arts.

Other recommended studios:

Aloha Yoga Kula (Map p181; ☎ 772-3520; www.alohayogakula.com; Windward United Church of Christ, 38 Kane'ohe Bay Dr) Ashtanga, vinyasa and gentle yoga in a garden setting.

Bikram's Yoga Kailua (Map p172; ☎ 262-6886; www.bikramyoga.com; Kailua Shopping Center, 600 Kailua Rd) Holds several bikram-style yoga classes daily.

Koa Yoga (Map p172; ☎ 780-8544; www.koayoga.com; 35 Kainehe St) Teaches modern yoga styles, including kundalini and vinyasa flow.

As a drop-in visitor, expect to pay about $10 to $15 per group class.

Eating

Kailua has dozens of fast-food eateries and upmarket restaurants, most serving just OK fare. Following are some notably great exceptions.

KALAPAWAI MARKET   Deli $

Map p172; ☎ 262-4359; 306 S Kalaheo Ave; snacks $1-8; ☼ store 6am-9pm, deli 7am-6pm

Everyone stops at this 1930s green-painted landmark on their way to the beach. Whether you're itching for a java fix and

WINDWARD O'AHU

a sesame-seed bagel, or stocking a picnic basket full of hot and cold deli sandwiches, market-fresh salads, fresh pizzas and wine, just ask the friendly staff for help.

BOSTON'S NORTH END PIZZA BAKERY
American $

Map p172; ☎ 263-8005; 31 Ho'olai St; slices $4-6, pies $21-29; ⏱ 11am-8pm Sun-Thu, 11am-9pm Fri & Sat

Some say it's Windward O'ahu's best pizza, and who are we to argue? Along with enormous handmade pies, this place dishes up piping-hot, super-sized pizza slices with thick, chewy crusts that are equal in size to a quarter of a pizza – truly big enough to fuel an afternoon of surfing.

CINNAMON'S RESTAURANT
Eclectic $

Map p172; ☎ 261-8724; 315 Uluniu St; mains $5-12; ⏱ 7am-2pm

Locals pack this humble little family-friendly cafe for standouts like guava chiffon pancakes, Portuguese sweet-bread French toast, eggs Benedict mahimahi, curried chicken-and-papaya salad and frittatas with sun-dried tomato pesto artichoke hearts. Takeout meals are packaged in ecofriendly biodegradable containers.

UAHI ISLAND GRILL
Island Contemporary $

Map p172; ☎ 266-4646; 307 Uluniu St; meals $6-11; ⏱ 10:30am-8pm Mon & Wed-Sat, 10:30am-2:30pm Tue

If you've been to Lanikai Juice (opposite) then you've already met the yoga-lovin', windsurfin' crowd that gets its fresh, flavorful and healthy plate-lunch fix at this under-the-radar spot. *Furikake* (a type of Japanese seasoning) tofu *poke,* red fish curry, garlic chicken, brown rice and vegan desserts all come packaged in biodegradable containers, so it's a 100% guilt-free adventure for your taste buds.

BOOTS & KIMO'S HOMESTYLE KITCHEN
Breakfast $

Map p172; ☎ 263-7929; 131 Hekili St; mains $7-10; ⏱ 7am-2pm Mon-Fri, 6:30am-2pm Sat & Sun

Expect to cool your heels out on the sidewalk for quite a while as locals and tourists alike devour fluffy banana pancakes drowned in Boots & Kimo's famous macnut syrup – too sweet for some, heaven for others. The grilled short ribs ain't bad,

Top Picks

LOCAL GRINDS

- Keneke's (p171)
- Uahi Island Grill (left)
- Waiahole Poi Factory (p184)
- Hukilau Cafe (p192)
- Kahuku's shrimp trucks (p194)

but the rest of the menu is missable. Cash only.

KALAPAWAI CAFÉ
Eclectic $$$

Map p172; ☎ 262-3354; 750 Kailua Rd; dinner mains $15-26; ⏱ 6am-9pm Sun-Thu, 6am-10pm Fri & Sat

For gourmet dinners like free-range lamb tagine with saffron couscous, citrus-brined pork chops or ranch steaks and burgers, this elegant little bistro and wine bar fits the bill. Share bruschetta and other small plates with a wine flight (a series of tasting-sized pours) out on the streetside lanai, or drop by to pick up a deli meal and knock-out slice of cake to go.

BUZZ'S
Steakhouse $$$

Map p172; ☎ 261-4661; 413 Kawailoa Rd; mains lunch $9-15, dinner $15-36; ⏱ 11am-3pm & 4:30-9:30pm

Across from the beach, old-school Buzz's pulls in sun-kissed crowds of Lanikai millionaires, especially with its tiki torch-lit lanai that has a tree growing through it. Show up for charbroiled burgers and fish sandwiches at lunch or for sunset drinks and dinner, when various cuts of kiawe-grilled steak shore up the surf-and-turf menu. Service can be lousy; waits are long. Cash only.

LUCY'S GRILL 'N BAR
Island Contemporary $$$

Map p172; ☎ 230-8188; 33 Aulike St; mains $16-32; ⏱ dinner

Decorated with surfboards and saltwater fish tanks, this casual bistro encapsulates the laid-back, moneyed Kailua vibe. Tastes of Pacific Rim and old and new worlds meet in dishes such as *'ahi*-crab cakes with chipotle aioli, Moloka'i sweet-potato mash and fresh fish sauced with wasabi-miso or lemongrass-curry glazes. Be prepared for absent-minded service. Come on Wednesday night, when a bottle of wine is half-price with dinner.

For groceries and snacks:

Down To Earth (Map p172; ☎ 262-3838; 201 Hamakua Dr; 🕑 8am-10pm) Natural-foods grocery store with a takeout deli and salad-and-hot-entree bar.

Farmers Market (Map p172; ☎ 848-2074; 591 Kailua Rd; 🕑 5-7:30pm Thu) Artisan breads, organic fruit and veggies, snacks and plate meals. In the parking garage behind Longs.

Foodland (Map p172; ☎ 261-3211; 108 Hekili St; 🕑 24hr) An R Field Wine Co specialty store stocks gourmet picnic fare inside this supermarket.

Agnes Portuguese Bake Shop (Map p172; ☎ 262-5367; 46 Ho'olai St; snacks from 75¢; 🕑 6am-6pm Tue-Sat, 6am-2pm Sun) Sweet breads, choco-mac nut logs and *malasadas* (doughnuts) made fresh and served hot (you can call ahead to pre-order).

Island Snow (Map p172; ☎ 263-6339; Kailua Beach Center, 130 Kailua Rd; shave ice $2.50-5; 🕑 10am-6pm Mon-Fri, 10am-7pm Sat & Sun) Cool off with a Lanikai Lime or a Banzai Banana shave ice.

Drinking & Entertainment

LANIKAI JUICE

our pick Map p172; ☎ 262-2383; Kailua Shopping Center, 600 Kailua Rd; items $3-8; 🕑 6am-8pm Mon-Fri, 7am-7pm Sat & Sun

With fresh fruit gathered from local farmers, this addictive juice bar blends a tantalizing assortment of smoothies with names like Ginger 'Ono or Kailua Monkey. Early in the morning, local yoga fanatics hang out at sunny sidewalk tables with overflowing bowls of granola topped with açaí berries, bananas, blueberries and grated coconut. Biodegradable cups made from sugarcane and corn cost 10¢ extra.

MORNING BREW

Map p172; ☎ 262-7770; Kailua Shopping Center, 600 Kailua Rd; items $2-7.50; 🕑 6am-9pm Sun-Thu, 6am-10pm Fri & Sat; 🖳 📶

Baristas at this bustling espresso bar and cafe cup everything from chai tea to 'Jump Start' espresso dunked in regular ol' joe and 'Funky Monkey' mochas with banana syrup. Swing by for bagel breakfasts or fresh salads and panini sandwiches at lunch.

BOARDRIDERS BAR & GRILL

Map p172; ☎ 261-4600; 201 Hamakua Dr; 🕑 noon-2am

During the day, this sports bar is just another one of Kailua's neighborhood dives, where you can order up pitchers of beer and *pupu* (snack) platters. But after dark, it's Windward O'ahu's most happening place to party, especially when live bands take the stage on weekends after 10pm and everybody gets down on the dance floor.

For a little more nightlife:

Formaggio Grill (Map p172; ☎ 263-2633; 305 Hahani St; 🕑 bar till 11pm Sun-Wed, to midnight Thu-Sat, to 1am Fri & Sat) Aspirational wine bar usually with live music Wednesday to Saturday evenings.

Tiare's Sports Bar & Grill (Map p172; ☎ 230-8911; 120 Hekili St; 🕑 2pm-4am) Karaoke, pool, live bands and sports TVs next to Pali Lanes bowling alley.

Find out what's abuzz at Buzz's   ANN CECIL

Shopping

Downtown Kailua has antiques, thrift and island gift stores aplenty, especially at the **Kailua Shopping Center** (600 Kailua Rd). Various art galleries are best visited on the second Sunday afternoon on the month during the **Kailua Art Walk**.

❀ MU'UMU'U HEAVEN
Map p172; ☎ 263-3366; Davis Bldg, 767 Kailua Rd; ⏱ 10am-6pm Mon-Sat, 11am-4pm Sun
Behind the fine-arts Nohea Gallery, this chic, contemporary boutique is nothing like its name suggests. Instead of dowdy sack-like muumuus sagging on the hangers, you'll find flowing, feminine, tropical-print dresses, skirts and tops, all handmade from vintage muumuus. Each creation is unique, as featured in fashion and style mags like *Lucky*.

ISLAND GLASSWORKS
Map p172; ☎ 263-4527; 171-A Hamakua Dr; ⏱ usually 9am-4pm Mon-Wed & Fri, 10am-4pm Sat
Part glassblowing workshop, part art gallery, this shop utilizes Italian techniques to craft one-of-a-kind pieces like gorgeously striped sake sets or the 'elements' series of calabash-shaped vases and bowls with fire, water, earth and air color palettes. Call ahead for directions (it's opposite a Midas garage) and to make sure it's open. Classes available.

ALI'I ANTIQUES II
Map p172; ☎ 261-1705; 21 Maluniu Ave; ⏱ 10:30am-4:30pm Mon-Sat
Inside the second shop of this mini antiques empire, you'll find an amazing mishmash of Hawaiiana – vintage postcards and prints, hats with feather lei, tiki barware, carved wooden bowls – and other island collectibles in wobbly stacks that tower above your head.

COCONUT MUSIC
Map p172; ☎ 262-9977; 418 Ku'ulei Rd; ⏱ 10am-6pm Mon-Sat
Small downtown guitar shop carries name-brand ukuleles – including Kamaka, handmade in Honolulu (see p95) – and vintage ukes from the early 20th century. Next-door, Hungry Ear Records stocks new, used and collectible Hawaiian music CDs and, yes, old-school vinyl records too.

Sleeping

A soul-soothing alternative to hectic Waikiki, Kailua has no hotels, but what it does have is O'ahu's biggest selection of vacation-rental houses, cottages, apartment suites and B&B-style rooms in private homes. Most are non-smoking, do not accept credit cards, require a multinight minimum stay, add a cleaning-fee surcharge and are handled exclusively by rental agencies (see p269) or listed through **Vacation Rentals by Owner** (www.vrbo.com). All of the following properties require advance reservations (which is why we haven't placed them on maps in this book), so don't just call ahead from the airport or the road. The closest campgrounds are in Waimanalo (see p171) and Kane'ohe (see p182).

MANU MELE
BED & BREAKFAST   B&B $$
☎ 262-0016; www.pixi.com/~manumele; 153 Kailuana Pl; d $100-120; ✖ ▩
A little out of the way, on the northwest edge of town, but just steps from the beach, these simply decorated, but spotlessly clean guest rooms in the contemporary home of English-born host Carol Isaacs are appealing. Each has a private entrance, refrigerator, microwave, coffeemaker and cable TV. A basket of fruit and baked goods is provided on the first morning only. Smoking is allowed in the garden.

SHEFFIELD HOUSE   B&B $$
☎ 262-0721; www.hawaiisheffieldhouse.com; 131 Ku'ulei Rd; d $105-125; 🛜
Around the corner from Kailua Beach, this kid-friendly place has tastefully designed kitchenette units. The smaller guest room is a studio with a wheelchair-accessible bathroom and built-in bookshelves full of beach reading. The one-bedroom suite has a fold-out futon and a peaceful garden lanai with a barbecue grill. A basket of pastries and fruit is provided on the first day.

BEACH LANE B&B   B&B $$
☎ 262-8286; www.beachlane.com; mailing address 111 Hekili St; d $95-135; ▱
Enjoy an ocean view at this sweet B&B just two minutes' walk from the beach. Breezy guest rooms, each handsomely renovated in tropical style, share the upper floor of a contemporary home. Out back are a pair

of airy studios with kitchenettes. All units have queen beds, fans and cable TV. Bodyboards, beach chairs and towels, and fuzzy bathrobes await. German, Danish, Swedish and Norwegian spoken.

PARADISE PALMS
BED AND BREAKFAST   B&B $$

☎ 254-4234; www.paradisepalmshawaii.com; 804 Mokapu Rd; d $110-120; ⊠

At the northwestern end of Kailua, these modern studios inside a suburban home pack a lot of comfort for the money. They all have a private entrance, kitchenette and ceiling fans, but they're relatively small, with comfy beds taking up most of the room. Fruit, coffee and fresh bread is provided by the hospitable hosts upon arrival.

PAPAYA PARADISE
BED & BREAKFAST   B&B $$

☎ 261-0316; www.kailuaoahuhawaii.com; 395 Auwinala Rd; d from $125; ⛱

A half-mile from the beach, this suburban home with backyard views of Mt Olomana rents out two simple rooms. Each has two beds, a private entrance, ceiling fan and cable TV. The atmosphere is better suited to more mature travelers. Rates include high-speed internet access and a light breakfast, but you're welcome to stash groceries and snacks in a shared refrigerator and microwave. Bodyboards, coolers and beach chairs are free to borrow.

KAILUA GUESTHOUSE   B&B $$

☎ 261-2637, 888-249-5848; www.kailuaguest house.com; d $129-159; ⛱

Near downtown Kailua, this beautifully maintained contemporary home rents out two blissfully quiet apartment-style suites where you'll find handmade Hawaiian quilts on the beds, rice cookers and Kona Blue Sky estate coffee in the kitchenettes, and open-air lanai overhung with plumeria blossoms. Modern amenities include flat-screen TVs with DVD players, digital in-room safes and shared washer and dryer access. Japanese spoken.

TEE'S AT KAILUA   B&B $$$

☎ 261-0771; www.teesinn.com; 771 Wana'ao Rd; d $215; ⊠ ⛱

This pampering, Japanese-owned getaway is a standout among Kailua's home-style

B&Bs. There's just one guest room, with tropical hardwood furnishings including a king-size sleigh bed and Aveda products in the bathroom. Breakfasts of organic tropical fruit, fresh bread and the owner's home-grown teas are served on the garden-side lanai. Paddlers can launch their kayaks in the canal nearby.

For no-fuss vacation rentals:

Auntie Barbara's Vacation Rentals (☎ 262-7420; http://hawaiibjvacations.com; 516-A N Kainalu Dr; kitchenette studios $75, 1br incl full kitchen $110; ⊠ ⛱) Good value for families, this suburban home lies northwest of downtown.

Kailua Beach Vacation Accommodations (☎ 262-5409, 800-484-1036 ext 7912; www.hawaiibestrentals .com; studios & 1br $125-179, 2br $189-209) Contemporary homes offer spacious options with kitchens; German and French spoken.

Lanikai Beach Rentals (☎ 261-7895; www .lanikaibeachrentals.com; 1277 Mokulua Dr; d $145-160, q $165-250) Beautiful, island-style contemporary studio and multibedroom apartments, many near the beach.

Getting There & Away

Many Kailua residents commute to work over the Pali Hwy, so Honolulu-bound traffic is heavy in the morning and there are outbound traffic jams in the evening. Otherwise, it's normally a 30-minute drive along the Pali Hwy (Hwy 61) between Honolulu and Kailua. For Kailua Beach Park, stay on Kailua Rd, which begins where the Pali Hwy ends and becomes the main drag through town before reaching the coast.

From Honolulu's Ala Moana Center, TheBus 56 and 57 run to downtown Kailua ($2, 45 minutes, every 15 minutes). To get to Kailua Beach Park or Lanikai, get off in downtown Kailua at the corner of Kailua Rd and Oneawa St and transfer to TheBus 70 Lanikai, which only runs every one to 1½ hours.

Avoid parking headaches and traffic jams by cycling around town:

Bike Shop (Map p172; ☎ 261-1553; www.bikeshop hawaii.com; 270 Ku'ulei Rd; per day/week from $20/100; ⏰ 10am-7pm Mon-Fri, 9am-5pm Sat, 10am-5pm Sun) For top-quality rentals, repairs and cycling gear.

Kailua Sailboards & Kayaks (Map p172; ☎ 262-2555, 888-457-5737; www.kailuasailboards.com; Kailua Beach Center, 130 Kailua Rd; per half-day/full day/week $15/25/85; ⏰ 8:30am-5pm) Rents single-speed beach cruisers.

KANE'OHE

pop 37,070

The state's largest bay and reef-sheltered lagoon, Kane'ohe Bay stretches from the Mokapu Peninsula north to Kualoa Point. It's largely silted and bad for swimming, although near-constant trade winds that sweep across the bay offer some great sailing opportunities. Kane'ohe offers a couple of interesting sights, but the town itself is largely a bedroom suburb that just doesn't pack the appeal of neighboring Kailua.

Orientation & Information

Two highways run north-south through Kane'ohe. The slower, but more scenic Kamehameha Hwy (Hwy 836) hugs the coast. Further inland, the Kahekili Hwy (Hwy 83) intersects the Likelike Hwy (Hwy 63) and continues north past Valley of the Temples. Kane'ohe Marine Corps Base Hawaii (MCBH) occupies the entire Mokapu Peninsula; the H-3 Fwy terminates at its gate. The tiny enclave of Kahulu'u, at the north side of Kane'ohe Bay, marks the real start of the Windward Coast drive.

Bank of Hawaii (☎ 233-4670; 45-1001 Kamehameha Hwy; ⏰ 8:30am-4pm Mon-Thu, 8:30am-6pm Fri, 9am-1pm Sat) Has a 24hr ATM.

Borders (☎ 235-8803; Windward Mall, 46-056 Kamehameha Hwy; ⏰ 9am-10pm Sun-Thu, 9am-11pm Fri & Sat) Stocks Hawaii-related books and maps and some international newspapers.

Kane'ohe Public Library (☎ 233-5676; 45-829 Kamehameha Hwy; ⏰ 10am-8pm Mon & Wed, 10am-5pm Tue, Thu & Sun, 1-5pm Fri; 🖥 📶) Free wi-fi and reservable internet terminals (see p279).

Post Office (☎ 800-275-8777; 46-036 Kamehameha Hwy; ⏰ 8:30am-5pm Mon-Fri, 8:30am-2pm Sat) Just south of the Windward Mall.

Sights

VALLEY OF THE TEMPLES & BYŌDŌ-IN

our pick Map p181; ☎ 239-8811; 47-200 Kahekili Hwy; adult $3, senior & child under 13yr $2; ⏰ 9am-5pm

The Valley of the Temples, an interdenominational cemetery, is home to Byōdō-In, a replica of a 900-year-old temple in Uji, Japan. Its symmetry is a classic example of Japanese Heian architecture, with rich ver-

million walls set against the verdant fluted cliffs of the Ko'olau Range. In the main hall, a 9ft-tall Lotus Buddha covered in gold leaf is positioned to catch the first rays of morning sunlight. Outside, wild peacocks roam beside a carp pond. Nearby, a 3-ton brass bell is said to bring peace and good fortune to anyone who rings it. TheBus 65 stops near the cemetery entrance on Kahekili Hwy, from where it's a 0.7-mile walk winding uphill to the temple.

HO'OMALUHIA BOTANICAL GARDEN

Map p181; ☎ 233-7323; www.co.honolulu.hi.us/parks/hbg; 45-680 Luluku Rd; admission free; ⏰ 9am-4pm

Set against a dramatic backdrop of *pali* at the foot of the Ko'olau Range, O'ahu's largest botanical garden encompasses 400 acres of trees and shrubs from tropical regions around the world. A little nature center has aging displays on Hawaiian ethnobotany and the history of the park, which was built to provide flood protection for the valley below. A network of largely unmarked grassy paths wind throughout the park and around the shores of a reservoir (alas, no swimming). The trails can get muddy, so hiking shoes are recommended. Call ahead to register for free two-hour guided nature walks, usually given at 10am Saturday and 1pm Sunday. The park is located at the end of Luluku Rd, over 1 mile *mauka* (inland) from the Kamehameha Hwy. TheBus 55 stops at the Windward City Shopping Center, opposite the start of Luluku Rd, from where the visitor center is a 2-mile walk uphill.

SENATOR FONG'S PLANTATION & GARDENS

Map p181; ☎ 239-6775; www.fonggarden.net; 47-285 Pulama Rd; adult $14.50, child 5-12yr $9, senior $13; ⏰ 10am-2pm, tours usually 10:30am & 1pm

Names like Eisenhower Plateau and Kennedy Valley are a hint at the background of these gardens, a labor of love of Hiram Fong, the first Asian-American elected to the US Senate, where he served until 1977. He dedicated the next decades of his life to preserving Hawaii's flora for future generations. Since Fong's death in 2004 at age 97, his family has taken over the lush 700-acre grounds and offers informal lei-making classes ($6.50) and

KANE'OHE AREA

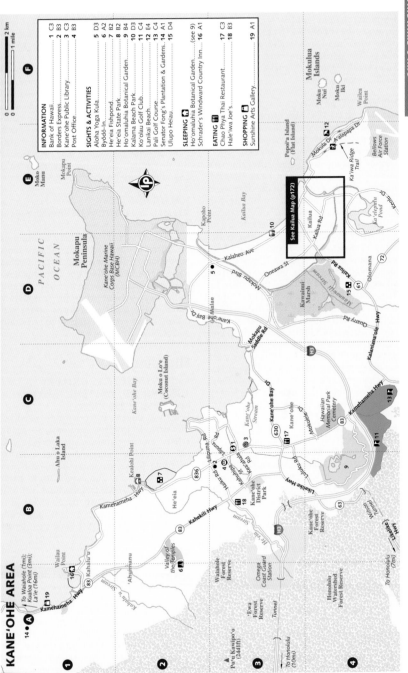

INFORMATION	
Bank of Hawaii	1 C3
Borders Express	2 B3
Kane'ohe Public Library	3 C3
Post Office	4 B3

SIGHTS & ACTIVITIES	
Aloha Yoga Kula	5 D3
Byōdō-In	6 A2
He'eia Fishpond	7 B2
He'eia State Park	8 B2
Ho'omaluhia Botanical Garden	9 B4
Kalama Beach Park	10 D3
Ko'olau Golf Club	11 C4
Lanikai Beach	12 E4
Pali Golf Course	13 C4
Senator Fong's Plantation & Gardens	14 A1
Ulupo Heiau	15 D4

SLEEPING	
Ho'omaluhia Botanical Garden	(see 9)
Schrader's Windward Country Inn	16 A1

EATING	
Chao Phya Thai Restaurant	17 C3
Hale'iwa Joe's	18 B3

SHOPPING	
Sunshine Arts Gallery	19 A1

1½-hour, 1-mile guided walking tours through the bountiful tropical flowers, palm trees, sandalwood and other native plants. The gardens are located about 0.8 miles *mauka* from the Kamehameha Hwy – just look for the sign.

HE'EIA STATE PARK
Map p181; ☎ 247-3156; www.hawaiistateparks .org, www.friendsofheeia.com; 46-465 Kamehameha Hwy; admission free; ⏰ 7am-6:45pm early Sep-Mar, 7am-7:45pm Apr-early Sep

Despite looking abandoned, this little park offers picturesque views of He'eia Fishpond, an impressive survivor from the days when stone-walled ponds used for raising fish for royalty were common on Hawaiian shores. The pond remains largely intact despite the invasive mangrove that grows along its walls. Coconut Island (Moku o Lo'e), just offshore to the southeast, was a royal playground, named for the coconut trees planted there in the mid-19th century by Princess Bernice Pauahi Bishop. During WWII, the US military used it for R&R. Today the Hawai'i Institute of Marine Biology occupies much of the island, which you might recognize from the opening scenes of the *Gilligan's Island* TV series. Back near the park entrance, there's a traditional Hawaiian outrigger canoe shed and workshop, where you might be able to chat with a master carver.

Activities

It's no contest: Ko'olau Golf Club (Map p181; ☎ 247-7088; www.koolaugolfclub.com; 45-550 Kionaole Rd; green fees $59-145) has *the* toughest golf course on O'ahu. Its par-73 tournament course is scenically nestled beneath the Ko'olau Range. For practice, there's a driving range and both chipping and putting greens. Nearby, the municipal par-72 hillside Pali Golf Course (Map p181; ☎ 266-7612; www .co.honolulu.hi.us/des/golf; 45-050 Kamehameha Hwy; green fees $21-42) also has some stunning views, stretching from the mountains to Kane'ohe Bay. Golf-club and hand-cart rentals are available.

Eating

There are more places to eat nearby in Kailua (p175).

CHAO PHYA THAI RESTAURANT   Thai $
Map p181; ☎ 235-3555; Windward Coast Shopping Center, 45-480 Kane'ohe Bay Dr; mains $7-11; ⏰ lunch Mon-Sat, dinner daily

In a humble strip mall, this family-run eatery can be a little hit or miss, but usually serves decent northeastern Thai food, including green papaya salad and sticky rice, along with spicy curries and, for an only-in-Hawaii twist, basil mahimahi. No liquor, but you can bring your own. A Hawaiian guitarist and singer often play on Saturday nights, while on Sundays there's often a complimentary dessert bar.

HALE'IWA JOE'S   Pacific Rim $$$
Map p181; ☎ 247-6671; 46-336 Haiku Rd; mains $14-33; ⏰ dinner

The floodlit Haiku Gardens location is the attraction here, with an open-air lanai overlooking a lily pond beneath the Ko'olau Range. The likes of coconut shrimp tempura and chicken satay aren't as memorable as the juicy slabs of prime rib or signature Paradise Pie made with Kona coffee ice-cream. Better yet, just stop by for cocktails and *pupu* during happy hour.

Shopping

🌺 SUNSHINE ARTS GALLERY
our pick Map p181; ☎ 239-2992; 47-653 Kamehameha Hwy; ⏰ 9am-5:30pm

With the slogan 'artwork from paradise,' this notable gallery represents 60 island artists, mostly painters, printmakers and photographers. But some of the most irresistible works are made of hand-blown glass, potter's clay and carved stone, bamboo and koa wood. Despite bold, colorful murals emblazoned on the exterior, this gallery is easy to miss; it's a half-mile south of the turn-off to Senator Fong's gardens.

Sleeping

The nearby town of Kailua (p178) offers a better choice of accommodations.

HO'OMALUHIA BOTANICAL GARDEN   Campground $
Map p181; ☎ 233-7323; www.co.honolulu.hi.us /parks/hbg; 45-680 Luluku Rd; campsites free

A prime choice for campers who don't need to be right on the beach, these grassy sites rest at the base of the Ko'olau Range. With an overnight guard and gates that open for entry after hours only for preregistered campers, it's among O'ahu's safest campgrounds. Camping is allowed from 9am on Friday to 4pm on Monday only. Free permits are issued at the visitor center only during regular park hours (see p180). No alcohol.

ALI'I BLUFFS WINDWARD
BED & BREAKFAST   B&B $
☎ 235-1124, 800-235-1151; www.hawaiiscene
.com/aliibluffs; 46-251 Iki'iki St; r incl breakfast
$70-80; 🖼
Hospitality is the attraction at this quaint island home filled with old-world Victorian furnishings, oil paintings and collectibles. The gay-friendly hosts give guests the run of the house, along with a breakfast of home-baked banana bread and tropical fruit. There's a great view of Kane'ohe Bay, although it's a bit of a drive to the beach.

SCHRADER'S WINDWARD
COUNTRY INN   Inn $$
Map p181; ☎ 239-5711, 800-735-5071; www
.schradersinn.com; 47-039 Lihikai Dr; studios & 1br
$100-185, 2/3/4/5br from $220/300/385/545, all
incl breakfast; 🖼
This low-rise bay-view place feels like staying with island relatives, as many of the time-worn accommodations will attest. For more than 30 years, Schrader's has catered to military families, family reunions and weddings. All suites have either a kitchenette or full kitchen. Rates include free Wednesday dinners with live entertainment, twice-weekly reef-kayaking trips and Saturday boat cruises, weather permitting.

Getting There & Away
By car, the main route from Honolulu is the Likelike Hwy (Hwy 63), which leads into Kane'ohe's commercial strip. A more scenic route follows the Pali Hwy (Hwy 61), turning north onto the Kamehameha Hwy before reaching Kailua. Either way the trip takes at least 30 minutes, and much longer during morning and afternoon rush hours.

Kane'ohe is also connected to Honolulu by TheBus 55 and 65, which leave from the Ala Moana Center ($2, 50 minutes, every 20 minutes). TheBus 56 connects Kailua with Kane'ohe ($2, 35 minutes, every 30 to 60 minutes). From Kane'ohe, TheBus 55 trundles north along the Kamehameha Hwy to Kawela (p199), taking less than an hour to reach the Polynesian Cultural Center in La'ie. This route runs approximately every 30 minutes from before 5am until after 6pm, then approximately hourly until 10:45pm.

Mountainside camping at Ho'omaluhia Botanical Garden LINDA CHING

WHOSE LAND IS IT ANYWAY?

Less than 10 miles north of Kane'ohe, the quintessential farming towns of Waiahole and Waikane abound with orchid nurseries, small, family-run farms of *kalo lo'i* (taro fields) and groves of coconuts, banana and papaya trees. You'll see many of these homegrown operations right along the main road, but if you want an even closer look take the inland drive up Waia-hole Valley Rd. The road starts on the north side of the historic **Waiahole Poi Factory** (48-140 Kamehameha Hwy), which opens a couple of days a week to sell bags of fermented taro and *'ono* Hawaiian plate lunches.

Not everything in these parts is as peaceful as the taro patches, however. Large tracts of Waikane Valley were taken over by the military during WWII for training and target practice, a use that continued until the 1960s. The government now claims the land has so much live ordnance it can't be returned to the families it was leased from, a source of ongoing contention with locals who are upset that much of the inner valley remains off-limits. Not surprisingly, you'll encounter quite a few Hawaiian sovereignty activists here.

In 1998, the City and County of Honolulu purchased 500 acres of the Waikane *ahupua'a* (a traditional Hawaiian pie-shaped land division that runs from the mountains to the sea), not just to stop construction of a Japanese golf course, but also to eventually create a nature park that would restore the watershed's natural ecosystem and Native Hawaiian archaeological sites. The park is currently stalled in the planning stages.

As you drive along the coast, you'll see antidevelopment signs and bumper stickers with slogans like 'Keep the Country Country' everywhere you look. At the time of writing, residents of Waiahole Valley were protesting a plan to build million-dollar homes in their rural farming community. Further north in the Kahana Valley, six Hawaiian families who had been squatting without leases on state-park property were facing eviction by Hawaii's legislature. The future of O'ahu's countryside looks to be still up for grabs.

KUALOA

Although nowadays there is not a lot to see, in ancient times Kualoa was one of the most sacred places on O'ahu. When a chief stood on Kualoa Point, passing canoes lowered their sails in respect. The children of chiefs were brought here to be raised, and it may have been a place of refuge where *kapu* (taboo) breakers and fallen warriors could seek reprieve from the law. Because of its rich significance to Native Hawaiians, Kualoa is listed in the National Register of Historic Places.

Beaches

KUALOA REGIONAL PARK
☎ 237-8525; 49-479 Kamehameha Hwy; admission free

Backed by magnificent mountain scenery, palm trees shade a narrow white-sand beach that offers safe swimming, but watch out for jellyfish in summer. The park has picnic areas, barbecue grills, restrooms, showers and a lifeguard on weekends and daily during summer. Birders can stroll south along the beach to 'Apua Pond, a 3-acre brackish salt marsh on

Kualoa Point that's a nesting area for the endangered *ae'o* (Hawaiian stilt). Further down the beach, you can spy Moli'i Fishpond, its rock walls covered with mangroves.

Activities

KUALOA RANCH
Map p166; ☎ 237-7321, 800-231-7321; www .kualoa.com; 49-560 Kamehameha Hwy; tours $21-145; ☺ 9am-3pm

Island Insights

That eye-catching peaked islet you see offshore from Kualoa Regional Park is called Mokoli'i (Little Lizard). In ancient Hawaiian legend, Mokoli'i is said to be the tail of a *mo'o* (lizard spirit) slain by the goddess Hi'iaka and thrown into the ocean. Following the immigration of Chinese laborers to Hawaii, this cone-shaped island also came to be called Chinaman's Hat, a nickname that persists today, regardless of any considerations of political incorrectness.

The horses grazing on the green slopes across the road from Kualoa Regional Park belong to O'ahu's largest cattle ranch. This irresistibly scenic dude ranch may look familiar, as it's been the setting for scores of movies and TV shows. Most of the activities are packaged for Japanese tourists who are shuttled in from Waikiki. But you might want to see where Hurley built his *Lost* golf course, Godzilla left his footprints and the *Jurassic Park* kids hid from dinosaurs on a jeep or ATV tour of the movie-set sites. Forget the ranch's horseback trail rides, which lack much giddy up.

Eating

AUNTY PAT'S
PANIOLO CAFE   Cafeteria $
Map p166; ☎ 237-7321; 49-560 Kamehameha Hwy; light meals $6-10, buffet $16; ☺ 9am-3pm
Located inside the Kualoa Ranch visitor center and gift shop, this simple cafeteria-style eatery has so-so sandwiches, salads and plate lunches. Show up between 10:30am and 1:30pm for the supersized lunch buffet, which includes sticky barbecue ribs, chili, potatoes and a salad bar, plus a few island faves like pineapples and guava juice.

TROPICAL FARMS
Map p166; ☎ 237-1960, 877-505-6887; 49-227 Kamehameha Hwy; ☺ 9am-5pm
Never mind the traffic jam of tour buses out front, because everything here is homegrown Hawaiian. You can pick up a bag of dark chocolate, honey, garlic or wasabi-flavored macadamia nuts (or just try the free samples!). If you've ever wondered what guava trees and pineapple plants look like as they grow, you can pay a whopping $15 for a guided bus-and-boat tour that visits the farm's flowering gardens, fruit and coconut groves, a Hawaiian fishpond and a couple of famous TV and movie locations.

Island Insights

In 1850 Kamehameha III leased over 600 acres of ranch land to a missionary doctor who became one of the king's advisers. Dr Judd planted the land with sugarcane, built flumes to transport it and recruited Chinese laborers to work the fields, although drought ended the business venture in 1870. You can still see the stone stack ruins of the island's first sugar mill and a bit of its crumbling walls alongside the highway, about a half-mile north of the beach park.

The islet of Mokoli'i   ANN CECIL

Sleeping

KUALOA REGIONAL PARK   Campground $
Map p166; ☎ **237-8525; 49-479 Kamehameha
Hwy; sites free;** 🚌 **55**
Pitch your tent and spend the night on a
white-sand beach where Hawaiian royalty
once slept. Just don't expect much privacy,
as this roadside park is often a local hangout
for drinking and carousing at night. As with
all public campgrounds on O'ahu, camping
is not permitted on Wednesday and Thursday nights, and county-park permits must
be obtained in advance (see p270).

KA'A'AWA
pop 1395
Here the road tightly hugs the coast and the
pali move right on in, with barely enough
space to squeeze a few houses between the
base of the cliffs and the highway. A narrow
neighborhood beach used mainly by fishers,
Swanzy Beach Park has a grassy lawn fronted
by a shore wall. Roadside camping is uninviting, but allowed on weekends; for details

about county-park permits, which must be
obtained in advance, see p270. Across the
road from the beach is a convenience store,
gas station and postage stamp–sized post
office – pretty much the center of town,
such as it is.

A natural rock formation resembling a
lion sits on a cliff behind the Crouching
Lion Inn, just north of the 27-mile marker.
According to legend, the rock is a demigod from Tahiti who was cemented to the
mountain during a jealous struggle between
Pele, the volcano goddess, and her sister
Hi'iaka. When he tried to free himself by
crouching, he was turned to stone. To see
him, stand at the restaurant sign with your
back to the ocean and look straight up to
the left of the coconut tree.

Eating
UNCLE BOBO'S   Drive-In $
☎ **237-1000; 51-480 Kamehameha Hwy; mains
$7-12;** 🕙 **10:30am-7pm Tue-Sun**
Across the street from the beach, next to
the post office, this place will satisfy your

Kualoa Regional Park

MERTEN SNIJDERS

cravings for dry-rubbed, slow hickory-smoked beef and pork, with all the traditional barbecue fixin's on the side. It also serves OK island-style plate lunches, burgers and hot dogs with chili fries, and sticky-sweet shave ice.

CROUCHING LION INN American $$$
Map p166; ☎ 237-8981; 51-666 Kamehameha Hwy; mains $11-24; 11am-10pm
With roosters parading around the parking lot, this freshly renovated restaurant attracts the lion's share of day-trippers. Lunch is pretty much predictable sandwiches and salads, while dinner offers decent surf-and-turf platters. The ocean views are gob stopping, but be prepared for a tour bus in the picture or, better yet, come in the evening when the buses are gone, the lanai tiki torches are lit and the sunset unfolds.

KAHANA VALLEY

A repository of ancient Hawaiian sites, Kahana Valley was once thickly planted with wetland taro, which thrived in this rainy valley. Archaeologists have identified the overgrown remnants of more than 130 agricultural terraces and irrigation canals, as well as the remains of a heiau, fishing shrines and numerous house sites.

In the early 20th century the area was planted with sugarcane, which was hauled north to the Kahuku Mill via a small railroad. During WWII the upper part of Kahana Valley was taken over by the military and used to train soldiers in jungle warfare. In 1969, the state bought the last remaining *ahupua'a* on O'ahu in order to preserve it from development.

When the state purchased Kahana Valley, it also acquired tenants, many of whom had lived in the valley for a long time. Rather than evict a struggling rural population, the state agreed to let the residents stay on the land, hoping to eventually incorporate all the families into a 'living park,' with the residents acting as interpretive guides to share Kahana's history and rural lifestyle with the public.

That long-term plan failed, according to local sentiment and a 2001 governmental report. At the time of writing, the state legislature was preparing to vote on whether the last remaining families, some of whom have been living here illegally without leases, should be evicted. The upper Kahana Valley is still undeveloped and mostly used by local hunters who come on weekends to hunt pigs.

Beaches

KAHANA BAY BEACH PARK
Map p166
This community hangout offers mostly safe swimming, with a gently sloping sandy bottom. Watch out for the riptide near the reef break at the south end of the beach. The park has restrooms, showers, drinking water, picnic tables, a payphone and 10 roadside campsites that aren't necessarily safe. As with all public campgrounds on O'ahu, camping is not permitted on Wednesday and Thursday nights, and state-park permits must be obtained in advance (see p270).

Sights & Activities

While many of Kahana's archaeological sites are hidden inaccessibly deep in the valley, Kahana's most impressive site, **Huilua Fishpond** (Map p166) on Kahana Bay, is readily visible from the main road and can be visited simply by going down to the beach.

AHUPUA'A O KAHANA STATE PARK
Map p166; ☎ 237-7766; www.hawaiistateparks.org; Kamehameha Hwy; admission free; sunrise-sunset
In spite of political controversy, this state park is currently open to hikers, although wandering around here often feels like intruding on someone's private home. Look for the signposted park entrance about 1 mile north of Crouching Lion Inn. Starting from the orientation center, the gentle, 1.2-mile **Kapa'ele'ele Trail** runs along a former railbed and visits a fishing shrine and the bay-view **Keaniani Kilo lookout**, then follows the highway back to the park entrance. Starting another 1.3 miles up the rough, dirt valley road, the park's **Nakoa Trail** is a 2.5-mile rainforest loop that crisscrosses Kahana Stream, passing by a swimming hole near an artificial dam. Both trails can be very slippery when wet.

PUNALU'U

pop 895

This scattered little seaside community doesn't draw much attention. **Punalu'u Beach Park** has a long, narrow beach that offers good swimming, as the offshore reef protects the shallow inshore waters in all but stormy weather. Be cautious of strong currents near the mouth of the stream and in the channel leading out from it, especially during high surf.

Eating

SHRIMP SHACK
Takeout $

☎ 256-5589; 53-352 Kamehameha Hwy; meals $8-16; ⓘ 11am-5pm

You'll find this sunny, yellow-painted food truck parked outside landmark Ching's general store. The shrimp are imported from Kaua'i then fried in garlic and dipped in butter, or you could order mussels or snow crab legs, then step inside Ching's market and deli for some *mochi* (Japanese

pounded-rice cakes) for dessert. There's much less of a wait here than at more-famous shrimp trucks in Kahuku (p194).

TROPIC'AINA
Grill $$

Map p166; ☎ 237-8688; 53-138 Kamehameha Hwy; mains $6-15; ⓘ usually 11am-8pm

With the jungle lovingly closing in around it, this sprawling plantation-style house huddles beneath the misty mountains. The cook here seems to change as often as the restaurant's name, so all bets are off when it comes to the mostly deep-fried food. Desserts from Ted's Bakery (p203) are delish. It's just north of the 25-mile marker, on the *mauka* side of the highway.

Shopping

KIM TAYLOR REECE GALLERY

Map p166; ☎ 293-2000, 800-657-7966; 53-866 Kamehameha Hwy; ⓘ noon-5pm Thu-Sat

This airy, light-filled white house on the *mauka* side of the highway is foremost

It's all in the name: the Shrimp Shack food truck

ANN CECIL

among Punalu'u's handful of art galleries. Reece's sepia-toned photographs of traditional Hawaiian *hula kahiko* dancers in motion are widely recognized in Hawaii, but it's his images of Kalaupapa, a place of exile on Moloka'i, that will haunt you.

Sleeping

PUNALU'U GUESTHOUSE   Hostel $
☎ 946-0591; 53-504 Kamehameha Hwy;
dm $20-23
Cheap without being a flophouse, this three-bedroom house in the middle of Punalu'u has been converted into an informal hostel. Because it's a cozy situation, the hostel screens potential guests, so most people come here after a stay at HI-Honolulu (p97), and walk-ins are not accepted. There's a communal kitchen and an onsite house 'parent.'

PAT'S AT PUNALU'U   Condo $$
☎ 255-9840; http://patsatpunaluu.org;
53-567 Kamehameha Hwy; rates vary; 🛋
Largely residential and looking a bit neglected, this waterfront condominium complex houses spacious, if well-worn, high-rise and cottage units, all with knock-out ocean views that you can't get at this price in Waikiki. There's no front desk; instead, privately owned rentals are posted on the bulletin board and online, including at **Vacation Rentals by Owner** (www.vrbo.com). For condo rentals at Pat's, try **Paul Comeau Condo Rentals** (☎ 293-2624, 800-467-6215; www.patsinpunaluu.com; studios $100, 1/2br $150/250, plus cleaning fee $50-150; 🛋), which has three-day minimum stay, with weekly and monthly discounts available; or **Papaya Paradise** (☎ 261-0316, 262-1008; http://kailuaoahuhawaii.com; studio d $125, plus cleaning fee $75; 🛋), Kailua B&B owners (see p179) who rent two studio condos at Pat's.

HAU'ULA

pop 3690
This small coastal town sits against a scenic backdrop of hills and majestic Norfolk pines. Aside from a couple of gas pumps, a general store and a 7-Eleven store, the only point of interest is the stone ruins of **Lanakila Church** (c 1853; Map p166), perched on a hill next to newer Hau'ula Congregational Church.

Beaches

HAU'ULA BEACH PARK
Across the road from the middle of town and shaded by ironwood trees, this beach has a shallow, rocky bottom that isn't too appealing for swimming but does occasionally get waves big enough for local kids to ride. It's popular for family picnics on weekends.

Activities

Kaipapa'u Forest Reserve offers secluded hiking trails with ocean vistas that head deeper into the Ko'olau Range. The signposted trailhead is at a bend in Hau'ula Homestead Rd, just 0.25 miles above the highway. Follow the paved access road inland, past the hunter/hiker check-in station that marks the start of the forest reserve.

HAU'ULA LOOP TRAIL
Open to hikers and mountain bikers, this tranquil 2.5-mile trail clambers through Waipilopilo Gulch and climbs along a ridge with broad views deep into Kaipapa'u Valley. It takes about 1½ hours to hike the whole loop. The trail forks off to the right immediately after the road enters the forest reserve, rising quickly through a forest of ohia and hala (screwpine) trees, as well as sweet-smelling guava and bizarre octopus trees, with their spreading, tentacle-like branches of reddish-pink flowers. Ocean

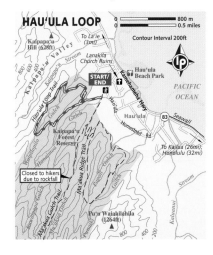

vistas open up as the trail climbs through shaggy ironwood trees, then splits into a loop about a half-mile in; it's easier to follow the trail by going left. Always stay on the trail and wear bright colors to avoid accidental run-ins with local hunters.

Sleeping

Hau'ula Beach Park (p189) has 15 roadside campsites that won't give you a good night's sleep. As with all public campgrounds on O'ahu, camping is not permitted on Wednesday and Thursday nights, and permits must be obtained in advance (see p270).

LA'IE

pop 4640

More bustling than most other seaside communities along the Windward Coast, life in La'ie revolves around Brigham Young University (BYU)–Hawaii, where scholarship programs recruit students from islands throughout the Pacific. Many students help pay for their living expenses by working as guides at the Polynesian Cultural Center (PCC), a mega tourist complex that draws nearly a million visitors here each year.

Information

Restaurants, shops and services are all clustered together in the Lai'e Shopping Center, about half a mile north of the Polynesian Cultural Center.

Bank of Hawaii (☎ 293-9238; 55-510 Kamehameha Hwy; 🕑 8:30am-4pm Mon-Thu, 8:30am-6pm Fri) Has a 24-hour ATM.

Post Office (☎ 800-275-8777; 55-510 Kamehameha Hwy; 🕑 9am-3:30pm Mon-Fri, 9:30-11:30am Sat)

Beaches

The beaches around Lai'e are a lot more attractive than those to the immediate south.

POUNDERS BEACH

Map p166

Half a mile south of the main entrance to the PCC, this is an excellent bodyboarding beach, but the shorebreak, as the name of the beach implies, can be brutal. Summer swimming is generally good, though there's a strong winter current. The area around the old landing is usually the calmest.

A PLACE OF REFUGE

La'ie is thought to have been the site of an ancient Hawaiian *pu'uhonua* – a place where *kapu* (taboo) breakers could escape being put to death. Today, La'ie is the center of the Mormon community in Hawaii.

The first Mormon missionaries to Hawaii arrived in 1850. After an attempt to establish a Hawaiian 'City of Joseph' on the island of Lanai failed amid a land scandal, the Mormons moved to La'ie. In 1865 they purchased a 6000-acre plantation here and slowly expanded their influence.

In 1919 the Mormons constructed a smaller, yet still showy version of their Salt Lake City, Utah temple here at the foot of the Ko'olau Range. This dazzling white temple at the end of a wide boulevard may be the most incongruous sight on O'ahu.

MALAEKAHANA STATE RECREATION AREA

Map p166

You'll feel all sorts of intrepid pride when you discover this wild and rugged beach, just north of town. A long, narrow strip of sand stretches between Makahoa Point to the north and Kalanai Point to the south with a thick inland barrier of ironwoods. Swimming is generally good year-round, although there are occasionally strong currents in winter. This popular family beach is also good for bodyboarding, board surfing and windsurfing. Kalanai Point, the main section of the park, about 0.6 miles north of town, has picnic tables, barbecue grills, camping, restrooms and showers.

MOKU'AUIA (GOAT ISLAND)

Map p166

This state bird sanctuary just offshore from Malaekahana Beach has a small, sandy cove with good swimming and snorkeling. It's possible to wade over to the island when the tide is low and the water's calm, but be careful of the shallow coral and spiny sea urchins. When the water is deeper, you

ISLAND VOICES

NAME: ELLEN GAY DELA ROSA
OCCUPATION: THEATER DIRECTOR, POLYNESIAN CULTURAL CENTER
RESIDENCE: HONOLULU

What's the mission of the Polynesian Cultural Center? It's a unique treasure, created to share with the world the culture, arts and crafts of the diverse peoples of Polynesia. We give you a hands-on experience, rather than just reading it in a book.

Tell me about the diversity of BYU–Hawaii students who work here. On this stage, we have people from all across Polynesia. What's interesting to me is that a lot of our students may never have learned much about their culture until coming here. They might never have danced or learned their own traditions before.

What makes O'ahu unique among the Hawaiian Islands? Living on the borderline between the country and the city, whenever we want to go to the city, we can just jump in the car. When I come back through the highway tunnels, I know that I'm coming home to the country.

O'ahu is also a true melting pot of cultures, with new people constantly making their homes here. On this island, you can choose to step backward in time or into the future. You can feel the transition between old and new Hawaii here.

What makes the Windward Coast special? This side of the island is probably the most beautiful. Sometimes I take a drive to look at the mountains on one side, the ocean on the other, with the sun coming up or setting – I just love it.

What's your advice for first-time visitors to O'ahu? Keep an open mind. Don't get too fixed on your own agenda. Every stop you make on this island can be a monumental memory. The genuine spirit of this island lives in the people.

Dancers at the Polynesian Cultural Center (p192)

MARK NEWMAN

can swim across, but beware of a rip current that's sometimes present off the windward end of the island. Before going out, be sure to ask the lifeguard about water conditions and the advisability of crossing.

Sights

There's a visitor center at the Mormon temple, where volunteers will witness to you about their faith, but nonbelievers are not allowed inside the temple itself.

Hawaiian tiki statue   KARL LEHMANN

POLYNESIAN CULTURAL CENTER

Map p166; PCC; ☎ 293-3333, 800-367-7060; www.polynesia.com; 55-370 Kamehameha Hwy; park admission & evening show adult $60, child 3-11yr $45; ⏰ 11am-9pm (villages noon-6pm) Mon-Sat

A nonprofit venture by the Mormon church, this private cultural park is continually overrun by tour buses. The centerpiece is seven re-created theme villages representing Samoa, Aotearoa (New Zealand), Fiji, Tahiti, Tonga, the Marquesas and Hawaii. Each village has authentic-looking huts and ceremonial houses, many elaborately built with twisted sennit ropes and hand-carved posts. BYU–Hawaii students demonstrate dances, games, handicrafts, poi pounding and the like. The student interpreters are amiable enough, but their talents vary. The incredibly steep admission price includes canoe rides along a waterway winding through the park, an IMAX movie and an enthusiastically received Polynesian song-and-dance revue that's partly authentic, partly Bollywood-style with creative sets and costumes.

LA'IE POINT
Eating

HUKILAU CAFE   Cafe $

☎ 293-8616; 55-662 Wahinepe'e St; mains $4-8; ⏰ usually 7am-2pm Tue-Fri, 7-11:30am Sat

Off the Kamehameha Hwy, on the north side of town, this is one of those country places that locals prefer to keep to themselves, so don't expect smiling service. The local grinds – like sweet-bread French toast, a teriyaki beef-burger lunch and good ol' *loco moco* – are mostly right on. Portions are huge and prices modest. Hours are erratic. (And if you're wondering, no this isn't the same restaurant featured in the movie *50 First Dates*.)

LA'IE CHOP SUEY   Chinese/American $

☎ 293-8022; La'ie Shopping Center, 55-510 Kamehameha Hwy; mains $7-10; ⏰ 10am-8:45pm Mon-Sat

In a busy strip mall, this little family-run Chinese dining room is packed every day at lunchtime. On a very long menu of hybrid Chinese-American concoctions, the lemon chicken is a reliable pick, along with locally flavored dishes like pot-roast pork. For faster takeout, the L&L Drive-Inn nearby serves Hawaii-style barbecue.

For quick snacks and groceries:

Angel's Ice Cream, Shave Ice & Smoothies (☎ 293-8260; La'ie Shopping Center, 55-510 Kamehameha Hwy; items $3-6; ☻ 10am-10pm Mon-Thu, 10am-11pm Fri & Sat) Cool off with a triple-flavored Angel's Halo shave ice or real-fruit smoothie.

Foodland (☎ 293-4443; La'ie Shopping Center, 55-510 Kamehameha Hwy; ☻ 6am-11pm) Supermarket with a bakery and deli; no alcohol sold (this is Mormon country).

Sleeping

Malaekahana State Recreation Area (p190) offers the best public camping at this end of the coast; you can pitch a tent near Kalanai Point as long as you get a state-park permit in advance (see p270). As with all public campgrounds on O'ahu, camping is not permitted on Wednesday and Thursday nights.

FRIENDS OF MALAEKAHANA   Campground $
our pick ☎ 293-1736; www.malaekahana@hawaii .rr.com; 56-335 Kamehameha Hwy; tent sites per person $8.50, cabins $50-150; ☻ office 10am-4pm Mon-Fri
Let the surf be your lullaby inside your tent or a 'little grass shack' or furnished 'ecocabin' in the Makahoa Point section of Malaekahana State Recreation Area. It has a separate entrance off the Kamehameha

'Little grass shack' at Malaekahana   LINDA CHING

DETOUR ➡

Crashing surf, a lava arch and a slice of Hawaiian folk history await at the lookout at La'ie Point. The nearshore island with the hole in it is Kukuiho'olua (Puka Rock). In Hawaiian legend, this island was once part of a giant lizard chopped into pieces by a demigod to stop its deadly attack on O'ahu. From the Kamehameha Hwy, head seaward on 'Anemoku St, opposite La'ie Shopping Center, then turn right onto Naupaka St.

Hwy, about 0.7 miles north of the main park entrance. A local nonprofit group maintains this area of the park and offers hot showers and 24-hour security. Try to make reservations at least two weeks in advance; there's a two-night minimum stay. Gates are locked after 7pm.

LA'IE INN   Independent Hotel $
☎ 293-9282, 800-526-4562; www.laieinnhawaii .com; 55-109 Laniloa St; d incl breakfast $75-85;
Let's be clear about one thing: there is no good reason to linger in La'ie overnight. But if you find yourself stranded, this bedraggled two-story motel right outside the gates of the Polynesian Cultural Center surrounds a courtyard swimming pool. It offers badly maintained rooms, each with a lanai, TV and minifridge. At the time of writing, there were plans to demolish the motel and build a Courtyard by Marriott chain hotel here in 2010.

KAHUKU
pop 1780
Kahuku is a former sugar-plantation town, its roads lined with wooden cane houses. Most of the old **sugar mill** (Map p166) that operated here until 1996 has been knocked down, but the remnants of the smokestack and the old iron gears can be seen behind the post office. The rest of the former mill grounds have been transformed into a small shopping center containing the town's bank, post office, gas station and grocery store.

WINDWARD O'AHU

Live or cooked shrimp for sale in Kahuku

KARL LEHMANN

Sights & Activities

JAMES CAMPBELL NATIONAL WILDLIFE REFUGE

Map p166; ☎ 637-6330; www.fws.gov/james
campbell; admission free; ☼ schedule varies

Signposted about 2 miles north of Kahuku, this currently expanding preserve

---

CRUSTACEAN CRAWL

In Kahuku, locals are looking back to the land, or more accurately the marsh, for their livelihoods. Shrimp ponds at the north side of town supply O'ahu's top restaurants, while colorful lunch trucks that cook up the crustaceans are thick along the highway. These critters aren't cheap: expect to pay at least $12 per dozen shrimp with two-scoop rice. Order your shrimp or prawns sweet-and-spicy, or fried with butter and garlic, then chow down at outdoor picnic tables. Expect to queue at famous places like **Romy's** (☎ 232-2202; 56-781 Kamehameha Hwy), just north of town, or **Giovanni's** (☎ 293-1839), near the old sugar mill. Next to Giovanni's, **Famous Kahuku Shrimp** (☎ 389-1173; 56-580 Kamehameha Hwy) offers a few more menu choices, like hot-'n'-spicy squid. All of these shrimp trucks are usually open 10am to 6pm daily, depending upon supply and demand.

---

encompasses a rare freshwater wetland that provides a habitat for four of Hawaii's six endangered waterbirds – 'alae kea (Hawaiian coot), ae'o (Hawaiian stilt), koloa maoli (Hawaiian duck) and 'alae 'ula (Hawaiian moorhen). During stilt nesting season, usually from mid-February to mid-October, the refuge is off-limits to visitors. The rest of the year, you can access the preserve by taking a free guided tour, usually offered twice weekly (reservations required).

Eating & Sleeping

Just outside town, several roadside stands sell Kahuku corn on the cob, a famously sweet variety that gets name-brand billing on Honolulu restaurant menus. The only hotel and condos in the area are at Turtle Bay Resort (p201), just beyond the north end of Kahuku. The resort also has a few decent restaurants (p200).

KAHUKU GRILL   Cafe $

☎ 293-2110; 55-565 Kamehameha Hwy; mains $5-12; ☼ 8am-7pm

Looking like a tidy little farmhouse kitchen, this cafe at the back of the town's shopping center has real aloha spirit. The pancakes are fluffy, the handmade beef burgers juicy and the island-style plate lunches piled high. It's well worth the wait, especially for coconut-encrusted shrimp.

NORTH SHORE

It's so synonymous with world-class surfing that
you don't even have to say *which* North Shore you're talking about. Don't be
fooled; there's much more to this coast than just big waves. In summer the
swells calm right down and these same beaches have great swimming and
snorkeling. Year-round the sand is golden and warm, with acres of space for sun
worshippers to invade. Like a land that time forgot, it's a struggle to find the
trappings of tourism or development here. There are few places to stay and even
fewer posh restaurants – the star attraction is the beach. Outside developers
wring their hands in frustration, but the locals like it just the way it is.

NORTH SHORE
ITINERARIES

IN ONE DAY *8 miles*

① TED'S BAKERY (p203) Grab a late breakfast at this uberclassic North Shore eatery. If you're starving, nestle into one of the tables out front, or head down to Sunset Beach (p201) and chow down on the sand. Keen surfers should wax up their boards and go for a session if the waves are looking good.

② PIPELINE (p202) Keep heading west and stop in to see if the surf is up. This classic break is a great venue to watch some big wave surfing. If you know your way around a thruster, a gun or a fish, then you'll fit in just fine here.

③ WAIMEA (p203) Go for a walk on the beach and try to take it all in – this beautiful bay is home to some of the biggest waves in surfing and, in summer, some of the best snorkeling on the North Shore.

④ PU'U O MAHUKA HEIAU STATE MONUMENT (p205) Just up the hill from Waimea, this historic site offers an interesting insight and also a great view of the bay and the surrounding area.

⑤ HALE'IWA (p207) As the largest town on the North Shore, this is the center of the urban action. Finish your day by checking out the shops, galleries and having a meal at one of the many delicious restaurants.

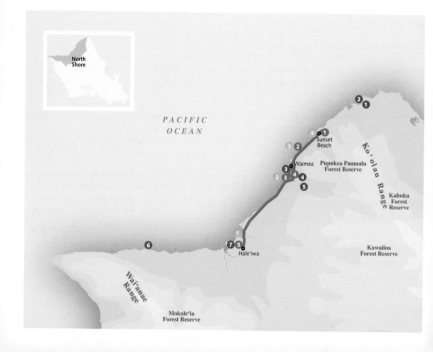

FOR SURFERS

The North Shore is all about surfing in the winter – here is a classic surfing itinerary to hit all the good spots.

① HALE'IWA ALI'I BEACH PARK (p208) It's quite fitting to begin at the first stop of the Triple Crown of Surfing. You might not be ready for the tour quite yet, but there's no reason why you can't try out their break.

② WAIMEA BAY (p203) Just 4 miles down the road from Hale'iwa and home to some of the biggest waves on the North Shore – on a big day you'll be sitting in the lineup with the worlds' best – this bay can be a fickle wave. It needs a lot of swell to actually break, but when it does – look out!

③ PIPELINE (p202) It's time for one of the most recognizable barrels in all of surfing – not for the inexperienced, the reef is only inches below the surface. The pristine, almond-shaped tubes are some of the best around. Expect crowds both in the lineup and on the beach – but who cares, you're surfing Pipeline.

④ SUNSET BEACH (p201) One of the classic breaks on the North Shore and a must-do. Sunset can be a little quieter, so when the crowds get to be a bit much at the other hot spots, head here.

FOR LANDLUBBERS

① TURTLE BAY GOLF (p200) Get your golf on with a round by the sea. It's a PGA-level course, so don't be too hard on yourself.

② TURTLE BAY RESORT TRAIL RIDES (p200) Grab your noble steed and go for a horseback ride. You can mosey along or gallop on the beach – it's up to you.

③ WAIMEA BAY (p203) Hike into the hills and discover **Pu'u O Mahuka Heiau State Monument (p205)** – take in the great views and get in touch with the Hawaiian heritage of the North Shore.

④ SHARKS COVE GRILL (p207) A great place for a lazy lunch. You can see the beach from the picnic tables out front and smell the salty air as you dig into your mixed plate.

⑤ WAIMEA VALLEY (p205) Continue the nature trend and go for a hike. The solitude is great and so is the stunning flora.

⑥ MOKULE'IA (p212) Head to the far corner of the island and go for a skydive or a glider ride for the best view going. Don't forget your camera, or to pull the chute.

⑦ HALE'IWA (p207) The final stop for a nice post-plummet meal. Check out the shops and don't forget to have a look at the **North Shore Surf & Cultural Museum (p209)** for some good history of the North Shore.

North Shore Surf & Cultural Museum LINDA CHING

NORTH SHORE

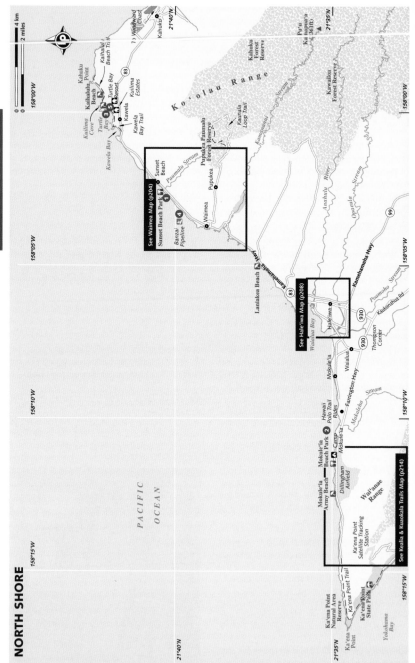

HIGHLIGHTS

❶ **BEST BEACH:** Sunset Beach (p201)
❷ **BEST VIEW:** From 10,000ft up –
courtesy of a tandem skydiving rig
(p213)
❸ **BEST ACTIVITY:** Turtle Bay Resort
Trail Rides (p200)
❹ **BEST PLACE TO WATCH MONSTER
SURF:** Pipeline (p202)
❺ **BEST ROOM WITH A VIEW:** Turtle Bay
Resort (p201)

**Highlights are numbered on the map
opposite.**

KAWELA
pop 410
Where the east meets the north and forms
the northern tip of O'ahu, the tiny settlement of Kawela sits, though it's less a town
than a map marker for the imposing Turtle
Bay Resort. This lone resort is the largest
development on the North Shore and the
only real stamp of tourism on the region.
As you head down the road towards Sunset Beach there is little more than the odd
fruit stall to grab a refreshment and the
expansive line of sand to entice you in for a
session in the surf or on the beach.

Beaches
KUILIMA COVE
This cove with a beautiful little beach
(known as Bay View Beach) is a stunner.
Like a good beach should, there is something for everyone here, including plenty of
sand to stretch out on, keeping the placid
placated. There's an outer reef that not only
knocks down the waves but facilitates some
great snorkeling. In winter there is some
nice moderate surf to be found on the right-
hand side of the bay. Add to that the prox-
imity of restaurants and beach toy-rentals
(snorkel sets $14 per day, bodyboards $15
per day) and you've got a great mix.

Parking at Turtle Bay Resort costs $5 per
day, but the cost will be waived when you
purchase anything from the resort – you
just have to ask.

Activities
HIKING
Turtle Bay Resort has several miles of
oceanfront hikes offering a good variety of
scenery.

The **Kaihalulu Beach Trail** goes in an easterly
direction from the resort to reach Kaihalulu Beach, a beautiful, curved white-sand
beach backed by ironwoods. Although a
shoreline lava shelf and rocky bottom make
the beach poor for swimming, it's a fun
place for beachcombing and you can walk
east 1 mile to Kahuku Point and then another half-mile along the beach. To get
to the trail, start from Turtle Bay Resort
beach; just walk east on the footpath that
begins at the field adjacent to the parking
lot. Alternatively, you could begin the hike
at Kuilima Cove by walking east along the
shore.

For good swimming and to visit an awesome thicket of banyan trees, walk west 1.5
miles on the shoreline trail that runs from
the resort to **Kawela Bay**. The hike begins
behind the resort's tennis courts and skirts
Turtle Bay. In winter you can sometimes
see whales cavorting offshore to the north.
After walking about 15 minutes you'll reach
the western point of Turtle Bay, which is
known as Protection Point for the WWII

HEADING NORTH
There are two main routes to get to the
North Shore – either up the center of the
island or up the Windward (east) Coast.
Along the Windward Coast, take Hwy 61
from Honolulu to Kane'ohe, then proceed
northwest along Kamehameha Hwy
(Hwy 83).

If you're starting from Waikiki, the
quickest route to get to the North Shore
is to take the H-1 Fwy west and then
exit north onto the H-2 Fwy to Wahiawa,
where you can continue north along the
Kamehameha Hwy.

TheBus 52 ($2) is the main route serv-
ing the North Shore. It runs twice hourly
from the Ala Moana Center in Honolulu
and makes numerous stops, including
Hale'iwa (90 minutes), Waimea (1¾ hours)
and Sunset Beach (1 hour 50 minutes) before terminating at Turtle Bay (2¼ hours).

NORTH SHORE

Don't Miss

- Shave ice at Matsumoto's (p210)
- A lunchtime mixed plate at Sharks Cove Grill (p207)
- Sunset at Sunset Beach (opposite)
- A mid-afternoon snooze at Waimea Bay (p204)

bunker there. Once you've walked around the point you're at Kawela Bay. Continue your hike to the middle of the bay, where you'll find the best conditions for swimming and snorkeling.

GOLF

Turtle Bay Golf (☎ 293-8574; 57-049 Kuilima Dr; Fazio/Palmer course $160/195; ☉ 6:30am-6:30pm) features two top-rate par-72 courses abounding in water views. The more challenging is the Palmer Course, which was designed by golf pro Arnold Palmer and is the site of the PGA Championship Tour. The Fazio Course, designed by George Fazio, has generous fairways, deep bunkers and is host of the LPGA Tour's SBS Open. There are handsome discounts for twilight play and hotel guests.

HORSEBACK RIDING

Imagine galloping along the beach with the warm wind blowing through your hair, the surf pounding harder than the hooves of your steed and the sun shining on your shoulders. **Turtle Bay Resort Trail Rides** (☎ 293-8811; 57-091 Kamehameha Hwy; 45min ride $55) will accommodate all ages and abilities and has five scheduled rides per day starting from 8:30am. It's best to call ahead – giddy up.

TENNIS

If you'd rather serve then surf, the 10 courts at **Turtle Bay Tennis** (☎ 293-8811; 57-091 Kame-

Top Picks

FOR KIDS

- Turtle Bay Resort Trail Rides (above)
- Matsumoto's shave ice (p210)
- Kealia Trail (p214)

hameha Hwy; per person per day $12; ☉ 8am-6pm) are the best places on the North Shore to play. There is a pro shop, instructors and even a ball machine if you don't have any friends.

Eating

BAYCLUB   Comfort Food $$
☎ 293-8811; Turtle Bay Resort, 57-091 Kamehameha Hwy; mains $7-16; ☉ noon-8:30pm
Yet another eating option in Turtle Bay Resort, this is a quick stop off the lobby for a basic meal. Burgers, sandwiches, the usual suspects are all presented here. The food is nothing to write home about but the ocean views will stop you in your tracks.

LEI LEI'S BAR & GRILL   Eclectic $$
☎ 293-8811; Turtle Bay Resort, 57-091 Kamehameha Hwy; mains $6-24; ☉ 7am-10pm
Adjacent to the golf course, the food here is above par. Japanese accents help to diversify a menu filled with golf-course stalwarts like sandwiches and prime rib. Good views of the greens and good post-play nosh.

OLA   Surf & Turf $$$
☎ 293-0801; Turtle Bay Resort, 57-091 Kamehameha Hwy; meals $25-48; ☉ lunch & dinner
Right next door to Turtle Bay Resort, this beach cabana sports raw timber ceilings and an unparalleled position right on the beach. The usual mix of surf and turf is on offer without the resort overtones found next door.

21 DEGREES NORTH   Fine Dining $$$$
☎ 293-8811; Turtle Bay Resort, 57-091 Kamehameha Hwy; mains $28-40; ☉ dinner Tue-Sat
Big windows filled with views of the ocean are the hallmark of this fine-dining establishment. Pressed white linen, polished silver and a good list of wine are all present and accounted for. Well-prepared seafood with a local infusion of flavor makes for a memorable dining experience.

Drinking & Entertainment

HANG TEN BAR
☎ 293-8811; Turtle Bay Resort, 57-091 Kamehameha Hwy; ☉ 11am-9pm
Every resort needs a pool bar, and this is a good one. Frozen margaritas and mai tais fly outta here like they're on the house.

There's a great view of the bay and, if the surf's up, the local crew will be catching waves right in front of you. There's a decent cultural show here every Wednesday and Friday at 5:30pm.

Sleeping

KUILIMA ESTATES
Condo $$

☎ 293-2800, 888-266-3690; www.turtlebaycondos .com; 57-101 Kuilima Dr; studio/1br/2br/3br apt from $110/135/190/240; ⚒ 🖳

There's no need to pay lofty resort prices to be in this area. Kuilima Estates, a modern condominium complex on the grounds fronting the Turtle Bay Resort, has comfortable, fully equipped units, each with a kitchen, washer/dryer, TV, phone and lanai.

TURTLE BAY RESORT
Resort $$$$

☎ 293-6000, 800-203-3650; www.turtlebayresort .com; 57-091 Kamehameha Hwy; r from $460; ⚒ 🖳 🛜 🖳

Situated on a spectacular section of coastline and spanning over 800 acres, Turtle Bay Resort is an expansive and spectacular place. It's a great location for travelers looking to sample the best of what the island has to offer, without the clutter of Waikiki. There is a great beach and associated activities, two top-shelf golf courses (opposite), spa facilities, multiple restaurants (opposite) and first-class amenities.

SUNSET BEACH

Surprise, surprise, Sunset Beach is a great place to watch the sun go down. But wait, there's more! The great waves make it a stellar surf spot – it hosts the second round of the Triple Crown of Surfing every November. For those who aren't pro surfers it's the beautiful expanse of golden sand that makes this one of the best beaches on the North Shore.

Beaches

SUNSET BEACH PARK

ourpick Like many beaches on the North Shore, Sunset Beach has a split personality depending on the time of year. In winter the big swells come in and the sand is pounded into submission by spectacularly large waves. It's a hot spot for the top wave riders and the posse of followers these rock stars of the sea attract.

In summer the waves calm down and the beach grows in size from the lack of swell. Though the water is inviting, be aware that there are still some nasty currents about.

The beach has restrooms, showers and a lifeguard tower.

BACKYARDS

A smokin' surf break off Sunset Point, at the northern end of the beach, Backyards draws top windsurfers. There's a shallow reef and strong currents to contend with, but it has the island's biggest waves for sailing.

Bodyboarding at Sunset Beach   MERTEN SNIJDERS

ISLAND VOICES

NAME: JEFF BUSHMAN
OCCUPATION: SURFBOARD SHAPER
RESIDENCE: SUNSET BEACH

Jeff Bushman is a legend in the surfboard-shaping world. He's crafted boards for some of the world's best – all from his small North Shore shaping room. With his new company, Country Feeling Surfboards, he's recently branched out into environmentally friendly ecoboards.

What's the difference between your ecoboards and regular surfboards? Well, our boards are made with hemp and organic cotton inlays and are glassed with an environmentally friendly material that cures in the sun.

How has the North Shore changed in the 20 years you've lived here? There's a lot more traffic, that's for sure. But there have been some interesting changes – we've had a lot of wealthy people move to the North Shore, mostly friends of Jack Johnson. Guys like Eddie Vedder and Kelly Slater have bought houses up here – but they are buying property to keep the North Shore the way it is. They want to keep the country 'country' and not have the developers take over.

What do you think about development here? I'm definitely antidevelopment.

Would you say that's a through-line in the community? Definitely. You get developers coming over from the mainland trying to build all sorts of stuff, but since we've been able to fight them off for so long, they've gotten discouraged and they don't even try any more.

Do you have any advice for surfers coming from overseas? Lots of surfers come over with a sense of entitlement, like they deserve good waves just because they're from wherever. You have to understand that there are people who live here year-round so we can be here when the waves are good. Show respect and treat the locals how you'd like to be treated and you're going to get plenty of good waves.

'EHUKAI BEACH PARK

'Ehukai Beach, aka Banzai Pipeline, aka Pipeline, aka Pipe – call it whatever you want, but if it's big surf you seek, this is *the* place to go. Pipeline is known the world over as one of the biggest, heaviest and closest-to-perfect barrels in all of wave riding. When the strong westerly swells kick up in winter, the waves jack up to monster size – often over 15ft – before breaking on the ultrashallow reef below. For those boardriders who know what they're doing (and no, a day at Waikiki Beach doesn't count) this could very well be the holy grail of surfing.

For the non-world-class surfer this is a great venue to watch the best do what they do – the waves break only a few yards off shore, so you really are front-row center. In summer everything is calm and there is even some decent snorkeling to be done off the beach.

The entrance to 'Ehukai Beach Park is opposite Sunset Beach Elementary School. The beach has a lifeguard, restrooms and showers.

Festivals & Events

O'Neill World Cup of Surfing (www.triplecrownofsurfing.com) The second leg of the Triple Crown of Surfing takes place in late November and early December at Sunset Beach.

Billabong Pipeline Masters (www.triplecrownofsurfing.com) The final leg of the Triple Crown of Surfing is in early to mid-December at Banzai Pipeline, with the world's top pros vying for a $275,000 purse.

Eating

TED'S BAKERY _Bakery $_

`our pick` ☎ 638-8207; 59-024 Kamehameha Hwy; snacks $1-7; ☺ 7am-4pm

World famous in Hawaii, Ted's is the place to go on the North Shore for a quick bite. The chocolate-coconut pie is legendary and there is a decent selection of savories and deli choices to satisfy every taste. Grab a seat out front and dig in.

NORTH SHORE
COUNTRY MARKET _Market $_

Sunset Beach Elementary School, Kamehameha Hwy; ☺ 8am-2pm Sat

Buy locally grown organic produce direct from farmers as well as fresh-baked goods and handicrafts at this weekly market. It's a good place to get in touch with O'ahu's rural community, stock up on tasty grub and take the pulse of the North Shore.

WAIMEA

Waimea could well be the quintessential North Shore village. In keeping with expectation, it's ultra laid-back with few services – more a string of houses along the road than a town of significance. The crowning glory is Waimea Bay, a picture-perfect beach that is a glorious marriage between snow-white sand and azure water.

The waves at Waimea can get epically huge in the winter season and play host to the annual Eddie Aikau memorial surf competition (see the boxed text, p205). These kings of the surf are not out of place; ancient Hawaiians believed the waters here were sacred, and only royalty was allowed to take long-boards out to surf Waimea's huge waves.

History

Waimea Valley was once heavily settled, the lowlands terraced in taro, the valley walls dotted with house sites and the ridges topped with heiau (stone temples). Just about every crop grown in Hawaii thrived

Surf mural on the wall of Ted's Bakery LINDA CHING

NORTH SHORE

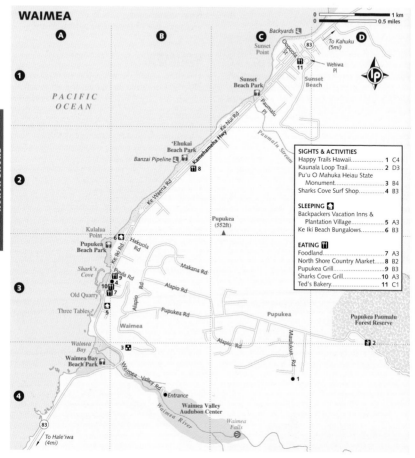

WAIMEA

0 —————— 1 km
0 —————— 0.5 miles

PACIFIC OCEAN

SIGHTS & ACTIVITIES	
Happy Trails Hawaii.....................1 C4	
Kaunala Loop Trail......................2 D3	
Pu'u O Mahuka Heiau State	
Monument.............................3 B4	
Sharks Cove Surf Shop...............4 B3	
SLEEPING	
Backpackers Vacation Inns &	
Plantation Village....................5 A3	
Ke Iki Beach Bungalows............6 B3	
EATING	
Foodland..................................7 A3	
North Shore Country Market.....8 B2	
Pupukea Grill............................9 B3	
Sharks Cove Grill......................10 A3	
Ted's Bakery............................11 C1	

in this valley, including a rare pink taro favored by the *ali'i* (royalty).

Waimea River, now blocked at the beach by a sandbar, originally emptied into the bay and served as a passage for canoes traveling to villages upstream.

In 1779, when the crew of one of Captain Cook's ships became the first Westerners to sail into Waimea Bay, an entry in the ship's log noted that the valley was uncommonly beautiful and picturesque. However, contact with the West did nothing to preserve that beauty. Logging and the clearing of land to build plantations deforested the hills above the valley, resulting in a devastating flood to Waimea in 1894. So much mud washed through the valley that it permanently al-

tered the shape of Waimea's shore, after which residents abandoned the valley and resettled elsewhere.

The **Foodland** (59-720 Kamehameha Hwy; ☼ 6am-11pm) supermarket has an ATM.

Beaches

WAIMEA BAY BEACH PARK

It may be a beauty but it's certainly a moody one. Waimea Bay changes dramatically with the seasons: it can be tranquil and flat as a lake in summer, then savage with incredible surf and the island's meanest rip currents in winter.

Winter is prime time for surfers. On winter's calmer days bodyboarders are out in

Top Picks

ICONIC NORTH SHORE EXPERIENCES

- **Shave ice in Hale'iwa** (p210)
- **Watch the surf at Pipeline** (p202)
- **Get a sunburn at Waimea Bay** (p203)
- **Have a lazy lunch at Ted's Bakery** (p203)

force, but even then sets come in hard and people get pounded. Winter water activities at this beach are not for novices. Usually the only time it's calm enough for swimming and snorkeling is from June to September.

This is the most popular North Shore beach, so parking is often tight. Don't park along the highway, even if you see others doing so; police are notorious for towing away dozens of cars at once, particularly when surf competitions are taking place. Facilities include showers, restrooms and picnic tables, and a lifeguard is on duty daily.

PUPUKEA BEACH PARK

Pupukea Beach Park is a long beach along the highway that includes Three Tables to the south, Shark's Cove to the north and Old Quarry in between. Pupukea, meaning 'white shell,' is a very scenic beach, with deep blue waters, a varied coastline, and a mix of lava and white sand. The waters off Pupukea Beach are protected as a marine-life conservation district.

There are showers and restrooms in front of Old Quarry; bus 52 stops out front.

Three Tables gets its name from the flat ledges rising above the water. In summer, when the waters are calm, Three Tables is good for snorkeling and diving. It's possible to see some action by snorkeling around the tables, but the best coral and fish, as well as some small caves, lava tubes and arches, are in deeper water further out. In winter dangerous rip currents flow between the beach and the tables. Watch for sharp rocks and coral and, as always, don't touch the reef.

Old Quarry may look like it was sculpted by human hands (thus the moniker of Old Quarry) but, rest assured, these features are natural. The tide pools are interesting micro-

habitats for sea creatures and are easily explored at low tide. Be careful when you're exploring, especially with the kiddies, because the rocks are razor sharp.

Shark's Cove is beautiful, both above and below the water's surface. The naming of the cove was done in jest – sharks aren't a particular problem. In summer, when the seas are calm, Shark's Cove has super snorkeling conditions, as well as O'ahu's most popular cavern dive.

To get to the caves, swim out of the cove and around to the right. Some of the caves are very deep and labyrinthine and there have been a number of drownings, so divers should only venture into them with a local expert.

Sights

🏛 WAIMEA VALLEY

In the perfect antithesis to the beach, this complex and endearing **park** (☎ 638-9199; 59-864 Kamehameha Hwy; adult $8, child 4-12yr $3; 🕑 9:30am-5:30pm) across from Waimea Bay Beach Park is a sanctuary of tropical tranquility. You have the option to wander through the gardens or even take a dip at the base of the 60ft waterfall. Among the foliage you'll find up to 6000 plant species and replica buildings like the ones the early Hawaiians dwelled in.

🏛 PU'U O MAHUKA HEIAU STATE MONUMENT

A stellar view of the coast and a stroll around the grounds of O'ahu's largest temple reward those who venture up to this national historical landmark, perched on a bluff above Waimea. The temple's stacked

NORTH SHORE

Island Insights

The annual Quicksilver in Memory of Eddie Aikau surf contest (generally referred to as 'the Eddie') at Waimea is only held when waves reach over 30ft. In the 23 years the event has been scheduled, it has only taken place seven times. There is no scheduled date for the competition – the bay picks the best winter day and the world's best surfers fly in for it.

DETOUR →

SUNBATHING TURTLES

Awesome green sea turtles (honu), which can weigh upwards of 200lb, like to haul up on the sand to bask in the sun. Like other beachgoers they have their favorite spots. To see these majestic creatures up close, stop at Laniakea Beach, a little strand of sand along the Kamehameha Hwy midway between the 3- and 4-mile markers, immediately south of Pohaku Loa Way. Turtles hang out right on the beach here. Loud noises and abrupt movements startle them, so approach slowly and keep a distance of at least 10 yards. Incidentally, the turtles are not permanent O'ahu residents – about once every four years they return to their ancestral nesting grounds in the remote French Frigate Shoals, 500 miles east of O'ahu, where they mate and nest.

stone construction is attributed to the legendary *menehune*, elflike people who are said to have completed their work in just one night. Pu'u O Mahuka means 'hill of escape,' and it was a *luakini* heiau, where human sacrifices took place. This was a dramatic site for a temple, and it's well worth the drive to take in the commanding view, especially at sunset.

To get there, turn inland up Pupukea Rd at the Foodland supermarket. The heiau

turnoff is half a mile up, and from there it's 0.7 miles in to the site.

Activities

WATER SPORTS

Depending on what time of year you are visiting, you'll find excellent swimming, snorkeling, diving, surfing and bodyboarding. Winter is all about surfing and summer is made for snorkeling. Surfboards, low-key beachwear, wax, leashes and fins are all jammed into tiny, roadside **Sharks Cove Surf Shop** (☎ 637-2219; Kamehameha Hwy), which has a definite local flavor. It'll rent you a board starting at $25 a day and can point you in the right direction for a lesson, if you need one.

HIKING

Little-known **Kaunala Loop Trail** sits quietly above Waimea Valley, mixing an easy valley walk with a moderate ridge climb for sweeping views of Waimea Bay. After seeing the beauty of the bay from viewpoints high atop this trail, it's easy to see why Hawaiian royalty considered its sacred.

To get to the trailhead, turn up Pupukea Rd at the Foodland supermarket and continue for 2.5 miles, where the road ends at a scout camp. From the camp parking lot, follow the Na Ala Hele signs to the trailhead. This 4.5-mile hike averages about two hours. This trail is officially open to the public only on weekends and state holidays. Hunting is also allowed in this area, so hikers should wear bright colors and avoid wandering off the trail.

Sharks Cove Surf Shop

MERTEN SNIJDERS

HORSEBACK RIDING

Two miles up Pupukea Rd from Foodland, horses from **Happy Trails Hawaii** (☎ 638-7433; www.happytrailshawaii.com; Maulukua Rd; 1½/2hr ride $62/83; ☻ 9am-5pm) take to the mountainsides, over open pasture and past orchards, offering panoramic views in all directions. The rides begin with orientation and instruction, so even if you've never been in a saddle before, you'll be up to speed before heading out. Reservations are essential.

Eating

PUPUKEA GRILL
Hawaiian Grill $

Kamehameha Hwy; mains from $8; ☻ 11am-9:30pm
Not much more than a few picnic tables in front of a permanently parked truck on the side of the highway. Shave ice, paninis, wraps, mixed plates and nachos are all served with a great outlook onto Shark's Cove.

SHARKS COVE GRILL
Hawaiian Grill $

our pick ☎ 638-8300; 712 Kamehameha Hwy; dishes $5-8; ☻ 8:30am-7pm
You can't get much more quintessential North Shore than this. The little blue shack on the roadside cranks out great breakfasts, sandwiches, mixed plates and smoothies. Pull up a ramshackle patio seat, watch the waves and dig in.

For groceries:

Foodland (☎ 638-8081; 59-720 Kamehameha Hwy; ☻ 6am-11pm) Modern supermarket opposite Pupukea Beach Park with everything you need for a beachside picnic, a quick snack or more elaborate DIY meals.

Sleeping

As with much of the North Shore, accommodation options here are thin on the ground, but here are a couple of the best.

BACKPACKERS VACATION INNS & PLANTATION VILLAGE
Hostel $

☎ 638-7838; http://backpackers-hawaii.com; 59-788 Kamehameha Hwy; dm/d/studio $30/72/120
Travelers looking for a good budget option on the North Shore are in luck. This friendly, backpacker-style accommodation is your one and only choice and thankfully it's also a groovy place to stay. In concert with the local vibe the digs are modest to the point of ramshackle. If you don't mind the odd bit

of peeling paint and an eclectic decorating style, you'll feel right at home. The location is superb and there's a variety of rooming options from bunk rooms through to private cabins on the beach. There are free scheduled pickups from the airport in Honolulu and from Waikiki. Phone ahead for pick-up times and also enquire about weekly rates if you're keen for a longer stay.

KE IKI BEACH BUNGALOWS
Boutique Cottages $$$

☎ 638-8229, toll free 866-638-8229; www .keikibeach.com; 59-579 Ke Iki Rd; 1br units $145-215, 2br units $165-230
This hideaway retreat fronts a beautiful white-sand beach just north of Pupukea Beach Park. The 11 units are comfortably furnished with tropical decor of floral prints and rattan chairs that fit the setting like a glove. Each unit has a full kitchen, TV and phone, and guests have access to a barbecue, picnic tables and hammocks strung between coconut trees. The location is an absolute gem – the beachside units are right on the sand, the others just a minute's walk from the water.

HALE'IWA

pop 2225
Hale'iwa, though small by mainland standards, is the largest port of call on the North Shore. More than just a collection of buildings, this settlement is the heart and soul of the region. With an inviting array of restaurants and a multitude of shops to wander through, it's a must-see location on your North Shore itinerary.

The Kamehameha Hwy passes through the center of town and acts as the main street. Chilled-out surfer types vagabond around while quasi-bohemian artisans peddle their wares in eclectic little shops. It's the sort of town that causes the traveler to walk slower, take a deep breath and long to stay.

If you're visiting the North Shore for one day you should aim to have at least one meal in town – the dining selection is a gastronomic delight, with multiple choices in all genres. The same goes for those on a shopping mission – whether you're seeking a new pair of board shorts or some art to remind you of O'ahu, you'll find great examples here.

Information

Coffee Gallery (☎ 637-5355; North Shore Marketplace, 66-250 Kamehameha Hwy; per 10min $1; ☷ 7am-8pm) Internet access is available at this cafe.

First Hawaiian Bank (☎ 637-5034; 66-135 Kamehameha Hwy; ☷ 8:30am-4pm Mon-Thu, to 6pm Fri) Just north of the Hale'iwa Shopping Plaza.

Post Office (☎ 637-1711; 66-437 Kamehameha Hwy; ☷ 8am-4pm Mon-Fri, 9am-noon Sat) At the south side of town.

Beaches

HALE'IWA ALI'I BEACH PARK

Hale'iwa Ali'i Beach is home to some of the best surf on the North Shore and, as a result, is a popular spot for surf contests. In late November the Triple Crown of Surfing gets underway on this break, bringing in the best surfers in the world. The waves here can be huge, with double or triple overhead tubes not uncommon.

When it's flat, the local kids rip it up with their bodyboards and mere mortals test their skills on the waves. The 20-acre

beach park has restrooms, showers, picnic tables and lifeguards. The shallow areas on the southern side of the beach are generally the calmest places to swim.

HALE'IWA BEACH PARK

On the northern side of Waialua Bay, this park is protected by a shallow shoal and breakwater so the water is usually calm and a good choice for swimming. There's little wave action, except for the occasional north swells that ripple into the bay.

Although the beach isn't as pretty as Hale'iwa's other strands, the 13-acre park has a broad range of facilities, as well as basketball and volleyball courts, an exercise area and a softball field. It also offers a good view of Ka'ena Point.

KAIAKA BAY BEACH PARK

Those wanting to get away from Hale'iwa can head a mile or so west of town to this beach. There are a few more trees here, so it's a good option when the mercury climbs and shade is necessary. The swimming is better at the other local beaches, so look

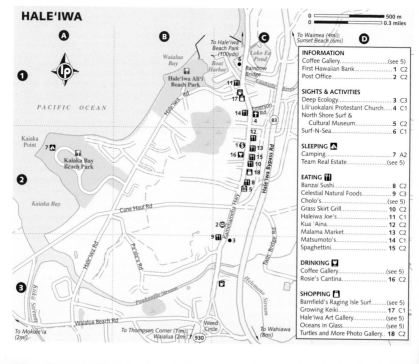

HALE'IWA

INFORMATION	
Coffee Gallery	(see 5)
First Hawaiian Bank	1 C2
Post Office	2 C2

SIGHTS & ACTIVITIES	
Deep Ecology	3 C3
Lili'uokalani Protestant Church	4 C1
North Shore Surf & Cultural Museum	5 C2
Surf-N-Sea	6 C1

SLEEPING	
Camping	7 A2
Team Real Estate	(see 5)

EATING	
Banzai Sushi	8 C2
Celestial Natural Foods	9 C3
Cholo's	(see 5)
Grass Skirt Grill	10 C2
Haleiwa Joe's	11 C1
Kua 'Aina	12 C2
Malama Market	13 C2
Matsumoto's	14 C1
Spaghettini	15 C2

DRINKING	
Coffee Gallery	(see 5)
Rosie's Cantina	16 C2

SHOPPING	
Barnfield's Raging Isle Surf	(see 5)
Growing Keiki	17 C1
Hale'iwa Art Gallery	(see 5)
Oceans in Glass	(see 5)
Turtles and More Photo Gallery	18 C2

Top Picks

AS SEEN ONSCREEN

- *Lost* – Ka'ena Point (p212)
- *Blue Crush* – Pipeline (p202)
- *Baywatch Hawaii* – Hale'iwa (p207)
- *Forgetting Sarah Marshall* – Turtle Bay Resort (p201)

elsewhere if you're looking to get wet. Kaiaka has restrooms, picnic tables, showers, drinking water and campsites.

Sights

NORTH SHORE SURF & CULTURAL MUSEUM

our pick ☎ 637-8888; North Shore Marketplace, 66-250 Kamehameha Hwy; admission by donation; 11am-5:30pm Wed-Mon

It's impossible to separate surfing from the culture of the North Shore – the best place to see how deep that connection runs is this little museum packed with vintage boards, fading photographs and some great stories. They have some cool vintage bits of memorabilia for sale, too, so it's definitely worth a wander.

LILI'UOKALANI PROTESTANT CHURCH

☎ 637-9364; 66-090 Kamehameha Hwy

Hale'iwa's historic church takes its name from Queen Lili'uokalani, who spent summers on the shores of the Anahulu River and attended services here. The church dates back to 1832, and as late as the 1940s services were held entirely in Hawaiian. The church is open only when the caretaker is in, usually in the morning.

Activities

Imagine a three-story, purpose-built surf shop stocked with all the latest and greatest gear. Then take all that stuff and squash it into an old, run-down shack – welcome to **Surf-N-Sea** (☎ 637-9887; www.surfnsea.com; 62-595 Kamehameha Hwy; 2hr beginner surfing lesson $85, 1-day surfboard/bodyboard hire $24/20; 9am-7pm). It rents gear, teaches lessons, sells new and used boards and is generally the place to go for anything water related.

If you'd rather get under the waves instead of on top of them, the folks at **Deep Ecology** (☎ 637-7946, 800-578-3992; www.deepecology hawaii.com; 66-456 Kamehameha Hwy; 2-tank dive $139; 9am-5pm Mon-Sat, to 4pm Sun) can sort you out. With a strong ecological bent to the operation, these are divers who are concerned about the ocean and lead dive trips with that in mind.

Festivals & Events

The kickoff leg of the world's premier surfing event, the **Reef Hawaiian Pro** (www.triple crownofsurfing.com), the Triple Crown of Surfing, is held at Hale'iwa Ali'i Beach Park in mid-November.

Eating

GRASS SKIRT GRILL
Hawaiian Grill $

☎ 637-4852; 66-214 Kamehameha Hwy; mains from $10; lunch & dinner

It's the micro-tiki room and there's barely room for a mini-mal let alone a long-board in this place. Retro surf decor on the walls fits right in with the traditional fare of mixed plates and seafood specialties. Popular with locals and great for a takeout meal bound for the beach.

HALE'IWA JOE'S
Surf & Turf $$

☎ 637-8005; 66-001 Kamehameha Hwy; mains lunch $9-18, dinner $16-30; 11:30am-late

With a superb location overlooking the marina, and some of the best food on the North Shore, Hale'iwa Joe's shouldn't be missed. While much of the dining in town reflects the laid-back feel of the area, the food here takes it up a notch. Brilliantly prepared seafood and hearty steaks pepper the menu. Freshness is the key ingredient, with much of the fish coming from the boats you can see out the windows.

KUA 'AINA
Takeout $

☎ 637-6067; 66-160 Kamehameha Hwy; burgers from $7; 11am-8pm

Want one of the best burgers in all of O'ahu? Look no further then this North Shore uberclassic burger joint. It has a list of burgers and sandwiches a mile long, so there will be at least a few things to tickle your fancy. The mahimahi sandwich is particularly scrummy.

SPAGHETTINI
Pizza $

☎ 637-0104; 66-200 Kamehameha Hwy; pizza slices $2.50-3, pizzas $10-$16; ☺ 11am-8pm

Don't be fooled by its unassuming looks, this place serves up the best pizza in Hale'iwa. For a quick, delicious lunch try a veggie slice loaded with spinach, olives and garlic. Forget the pasta – pizza is the real prize.

CHOLO'S
Mexican $$

☎ 637-3059; North Shore Marketplace; 66-250 Kamehameha Hwy; combination plates $8-17; ☺ 10am-9.30pm

Solid, home-style Mexican food is what attracts such a big crowd of locals and tourists alike. If you've never tried a fresh 'ahi taco or a grilled 'ahi burrito, here's your chance to get one done to perfection. It serves good fajitas and chimichangas as well.

BANZAI SUSHI
Japanese $$

☎ 637-4404; 66-246 Kamehameha Hwy; mains from $10; ☺ lunch & dinner

Hidden at the back of the Noth Shore Market Place, this sushi place does it right. It has a big menu filled with the classic rolls you'll be looking for. Try the signature dish,

---

SWEET TREATS

Having a shave ice on the North Shore is not only an essential O'ahu experience, it's also a delicious treat on a hot day. The classic place to get one is **Matsumoto's** (☎ 637-4827; 66-087 Kamehameha Hwy; shave ice $1.30-2.25; ☺ 9am-6pm), which has been turning out the tropical treats for decades and knows how it should be done.

Unlike a mainland snow cone, the shave ice here is reliant upon super-finely shaved ice that makes all the difference in the world. The toppings are a myriad of sickly sweet syrups that would send the unprepared into a diabetic coma. You can go simple with strawberry, lemon or mango, or you can go local and get an enticing combination of flavors. To really do it right, top it off with a scoop of ice cream and sweetened azuki beans. No matter how you top it off, speed is of the essence once you hit the sunshine. Even the most intrepid of eaters will end up in a sticky mess, but that's half the fun.

---

the Banzai Sushi and Sashimi set – it's the perfect postsurf scarf.

For groceries and deli items:
Celestial Natural Foods (☎ 637-6729; 66-443 Kamehameha Hwy; ☺ 9am-6pm Mon-Sat, to 5pm Sun) For those in search of karmically cool organic produce and health foods, this is the place. There is a tiny veggie-friendly deli out back for a quick meal (mains from $5).
Malama Market (☎ 637-4520; 66-190 Kamehameha Hwy; ☺ 7am-9pm) If you're looking to self-cater, get the picnic gear in order or grab a quick bite from the deli, you will find all the right ingredients at this modern supermarket.

Drinking

COFFEE GALLERY

☎ 637-5355; North Shore Marketplace, 66-250 Kamehameha Hwy; ☺ 7am-8pm; 🖥

Coffee lovers rejoice – the infrequently heard roar of the espresso machine thunders out the door at this mellow coffee house. It roasts its own beans and brews a great cup of Joe. Grab a mug and settle down to check your email on one of their computers.

ROSIE'S CANTINA

☎ 637-3538; Hale'iwa Shopping Plaza, 66-165 Kamehameha Hwy; ☺ 7am-9pm Sun-Thu, to 10pm Fri & Sat

Fruity margaritas and a cold beer are just what the doctor ordered after a day catching waves or hitting the sand. It's a friendly place, especially on Thursday when the drinks are cheap. You're bound to bump into plenty of locals here – it's the place to be for a cold drink

Shopping

Hale'iwa is the best place on the North Shore to get your dose of retail therapy – there are a whole host of shops peddling the quintessential to the quirky.

Who says glass figurines are just for Nana? The handmade fish, turtles and dolphins at **Oceans in Glass** (☎ 637-3366; North Shore Marketplace, 66-250 Kamehameha Hwy) are made before your eyes and best yet are replaced for free if you break 'em on the way home.

Hale'iwa Art Gallery (☎ 353-5763, North Shore Marketplace, 66-2250 Kamehameha Hwy) features the works of 20-plus local and regional artists, so you're sure to find something you like. There are a variety of styles on offer; everything from dreadful through to dramatic.

If your holiday snaps don't measure up, the photos in **Turtles and More Photo Gallery** (☎ 741-3510; 66-218 Kamehameha Hwy) will surely impress the gang back home. There are stunning underwater images of sea life, with some killer surfing shots thrown in too. There are various sizes for sale to suit most budgets.

Growing Keiki (☎ 637-4544; 66-051 Kamehameha Hwy) has gear for junior surf grommets and budding beach bunnies. There are mini aloha shirts, trunks and toys, all for the little ones.

Barnfield's Raging Isle Surf (☎ 637-7797; www .ragingisle.com; North Shore Marketplace, 66-250 Kamehameha Hwy; ⏱ 10am-6:30pm) is chalked full of beachwear, surfboards, skateboards and anything else you might need for life up on the North Shore.

Sleeping

Hale'iwa has no hotels or guesthouses, but there are several privately owned vacation rentals that can be booked through agents.

Hale'iwa's only camping option is at Kaiaka Bay Beach Park, where the county allows camping from Friday to Tuesday nights. For details on obtaining a permit, see p270.

**TEAM REAL
ESTATE** Vacation Rentals $$-$$$$
☎ 637-3507, 800-982-8602; www.teamrealestate
.com; North Shore Marketplace; 66-250 Kamehameha Hwy; 1br daily/weekly/monthly from
$65/455/1560
This place handles a couple dozen vacation rentals on the North Shore, including several one- and two-bedroom apartments in Hale'iwa. It will even be able to sort you out a long term rental if you're here for the season. Most budgets can be accommodated, but it's best to get in early, especially in the busy winter season.

**SANDSEA VACATION
HOMES** Vacation Rentals $$-$$$$
☎ 637-2568, 800-442-6901; www.sandsea.com;
beachfront houses $175-750
This outfit specializes in renting beachfront homes along the North Shore. It has about

> ## NO DEVELOPMENT, NO PROBLEM
> You'll notice that North Shore accommodation options are decidedly thin on the ground. With only one real resort on the entire coast it would be easy to assume that a flood of new hotels are just around the corner. The developers, however, didn't take into account the resolve of the North Shore locals. Nearly unanimously opposed to development on the Shore, they've banded together in unprecedented solidarity to rise up and stand firm against tourist infrastructure. There is a strong belief in keeping the wild and rural North Shore a steadfast part of the countryside and not an extension of Honolulu. Saying that this movement is antitourism is misplaced malice; the reality is just a desire to preserve the laid-back, simple life that makes the North Shore such a gem.

20 properties in all, ranging from places that can accommodate just two people to those that can sleep up to 20.

WAIALUA
pop 3770
This tiny town sports an eclectic history that charts boom, bust and rebirth. The Waialua Sugar Mill was once the main industry in town, but in 1996 it shut its doors and threw the settlement into a spin of future uncertainty. The energetic locals turned the disappointment into opportunity when they transformed the old mill into a pseudo-bohemian shopping complex. It's ground zero for soap makers, surfboard shapers and handicraft merchants. There's not much else to the town and you'll struggle to find any bustle or hustle – but that's just the way the locals like it.

Information
All of the following are near to each other in the town center, opposite the mill.
Post Office (☎ 800-275-8777; 67-079 Nauahi St; ⏱ 8:30am-4pm Mon-Fri)
Waialua Federal Credit Union (☎ 637-5980; 67-075 Nauahi St; ⏱ 8:30am-4pm Mon-Fri)

Waialua Public Library (☎ 637-8286; 67-068 Kealohanui St; ☷ 9am-6pm Tue-Thu, to 5pm Fri, to 2pm Sat) Free internet access – you can reserve a space up to one week in advance.

Activities

For those wanting to continue their practice while on the island, or turn over a new holistic leaf, **Jasmine Yoga** (☎ 561-9639; www .jasmineyoga.com; 67-174 Farrington Hwy; drop-in class $11; ☷ schedule varies) is the place to be. Held in the airy Weinberg Community Center, there's a variety of classes in both the vinyasa and ashtanga style – *namaste*.

Eating

If you're looking for something substantial, head to Hale'iwa (p207), just down the road, where you'll be spoiled for gastronomic choice.

Brown Bottle (☎ 637-6728; 67-292 Goodale Ave; ☷ 7am-10:30pm) The one-stop shop in town for everything you might need from bananas to beer – all under one roof.

Farmers Market (old sugar mill; ☷ 8.30am-noon Sat) Intrepid shoppers gather from all over the North Shore and beyond to get good produce, juice and flowers. It's growing every week and is quite the scene these days; get there early to get the goods before they're gone.

Shopping

The old sugar mill used to be a hive of industrial activity. Once the plant closed down, all went quiet for a while – well, the silence has been broken by a random collection of little bohemian shops that have taken up residence. Artisans, soap makers, coffee roasters and board shapers are all represented. It's a neat place to wander around for a bit.

While much of the North Shore has a distinctly rustic flavor, take one step into **Hawaiian Bath & Body** (☎ 637-8400; old sugar mill, 67-106 Kealohanui St; ☷ 9am-5pm) and you're transported into a bubble of aromatic opulence. Peek through the glass and watch the soap makers craft their bars, all made with local ingredients like *kukui* (candlenut tree) nuts.

The rambling **Island X Hawaii** (☎ 637-2624; old sugar mill, 67-106 Kealohanui St; ☷ 9am-3:30pm Mon-Fri, 8:30am-noon Sat) warehouse has everything from reasonably priced aloha shirts to wooden handicrafts and pieces of original and vintage art. Tucked in the corner is a little coffee shop that has Waialua coffee on the boil – this local brew is grown in the hills above town.

MOKULE'IA

pop 1839

Hello? Is there anybody out there? You may wonder in this desolate corner of the island. This is the least visited area of Oahu and has a real wilderness feel. The beaches are untamed, the scenery stunning and the adventurous aviation activities are plenty. The further you go down the road, the fewer people you'll see – if you're looking for solitude, Mokule'ia is your best bet to find it.

Orientation

The Farrington Hwy (Hwy 930) runs west from Thompson Corner to Dillingham Airfield and Mokule'ia Beach. Both this road and the road along the Leeward Coast are called Farrington Hwy, but they don't connect, as each side reaches a dead end about 2.5 miles short of Ka'ena Point.

Beaches

MOKULE'IA BEACH PARK

Keen windsurfers often congregate on this stretch of shore, taking advantage of the consistent winds. The beach park sports

GET LOST

Fans of the TV show *Lost* might see a few familiar sights in the Ka'ena Point area. This area is the principal location for the show's beach scenes and there are various other sets scattered amongst the trees. The sets themselves are, of course, closed to visitors but series aficionados will recognize the backdrops instantly.

When the series first started filming, tourists would be driving along the highway and see the wreckage of the crashed plane sitting on the beach. Needless to say a burned-out 747 is an alarming sight, and many called emergency services to report a downed passenger liner on the North Shore, unaware that it was all just a bit of TV magic.

Sunset over Ka'ena Point as seen from Hale'iwa Ali'i Beach Park (p208)

LINDA CHING

NORTH SHORE

a large grassy area with picnic tables, restrooms and showers. The beach itself is a nice sandy strand but the rocky seabed makes for poor swimming conditions. Come winter, the currents pick up, and entering the water isn't advisable.

MOKULE'IA ARMY BEACH
This beach, opposite the western end of Dillingham Airfield, is the widest stretch of sand on the Mokule'ia shore. Once reserved exclusively for military personnel, the beach is now open to the public, but the army no longer maintains it and there are no beach facilities. The beach is unprotected and there are very strong rip currents, especially during winter high surf.

ARMY BEACH TO KA'ENA POINT
Continuing along the coast from Army Beach the unspoiled beaches continue unabated. After about 1.5 miles the paved road abruptly ends and the sole infrastructure is a dusty parking area. The area has a distinctly remote feel and is a great place to get away from it all.

From here you can walk a further 2.5 miles to Ka'ena Point – you can also tackle this hike from the opposite end, the northern tip of the Leeward Coast. (see p240).

Activities
SKYDIVING & GLIDER RIDES
Just past Mokule'ia Beach Park, **Dillingham Airfield** (68-760 Farrington Hwy) is the jumping-off point for skydiving and glider rides.

The **Original Glider Rides** (☎ 637-0207) offers scenic glider rides that last anywhere from 10 minutes to an hour. The silent flight of the glider is a peaceful and scenic way to see the island. If that all sounds too tame, they can spice it up with some aerobatics. Prices start at $60 for 10 minutes and go up to $250 for an aerobatic hour of flight. Be sure to call ahead as flights are weather-dependent.

Skydive Hawaii (☎ 637-9700; www.hawaiiskydiving .com; jumps $225; ☯ 8am-3pm) will toss you out of a perfectly good airplane, preferably with a parachute attached. It offers tandem jumps, where you're attached to an instructor who does all the mental heavy lifting. You jump from a stomach-turning 13,000ft, free fall for one minute and pull the chute to glide down for 15 minutes. You have to be 18 years or over and weigh less than 200 pounds. If you know what you're doing, it can also sort experienced jumpers with one-way flights. Book online for some great deals.

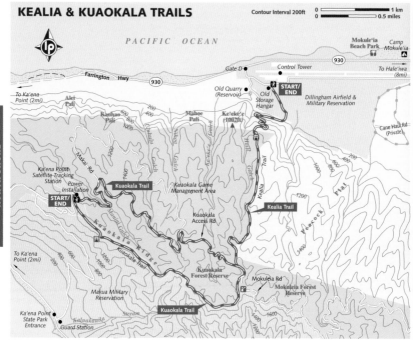

KEALIA & KUAOKALA TRAILS

HIKING

The 5-mile **Kealia Trail** ascends from Dillingham Airfield up a cliff face and through a forest of ironwoods and *kukui* trees. The snaking trail switchbacks its way up the cliff, offering ocean views along the way, but the real prize is its connection to the **Kuaokala Trail**, which brings hikers to a justly celebrated viewpoint over Makua Valley and the Wai'anae Range. The Kealia Trail is best for those wishing to avoid the hassle of securing a permit and driving up the Wai'anae Coast just to hike the Kuaokala Trail, a 5.5-mile loop trail accessible from the Ka'ena Point Satellite Tracking Station. The trailhead to Kealia Trail begins in the back of the airfield; head west 2 miles past the main airfield entrance and just before the airfield ends, take the road marked 'Gate D' and follow it inland for 0.4 miles. Just before the air control tower parking lot, there's an access road on the right. Walk around the old storage hangar to begin the trail. Give yourself about three hours to walk the Kealia Trail and back, and another three hours if you add the Kuaokala loop.

HORSEBACK RIDING

You just knew those polo fields were harboring some beauts, didn't you? **Hawaii Polo Trail Rides** (☎ 220-5153; 68-411 Farrington Hwy; 1½hr rides $65; ☑ 1pm, 3pm & sunset Tue, Thu & Sat) lets you take a thoroughbred polo horse along the beach and around its 100-acre ranch, either in a group or on your own. It also caters to special requests, such as full-moon rides and *ku'uipo* (sweetheart) dalliances.

Sleeping

CAMP MOKULE'IA   Campground $
☎ 637-6241; www.campmokuleia.com; 68-729 Farrington Hwy; campsites per person $10, r from $65, cottage from $85; ☑
Those wanting to really escape from the tourist scene can find solace here. This private, church-run camp is open to travelers as long as there isn't a prebooked group on the site. The facilities are basic with barbecue facilities, a pool, tent sites, a few rooms and a couple of cottages. It's easy to find, sitting right across the road from Dillingham Airfield.

CENTRAL O'AHU

Central O'ahu has a character all of its own. You'll find the towering peaks of the island's highest mountains standing guard over rugged rural topography, lush botanical gardens, more pineapple-based activity than you thought previously possible and a laid-back local charm. What you won't find are tourists, hotels, posh eateries, the beaches like down south or the sexy mystique of the North Shore. Most travelers view a visit to Central O'ahu as a means to an end – a necessary evil on the way through to the North Shore. But to see this region with such narrow vision is a real tragedy. It's a simple, down-to-earth place – take it or leave it.

CENTRAL O'AHU
ITINERARIES

IN ONE DAY *22 miles*

① WAHIAWA BOTANICAL GARDEN (p221) Start the day with a wander through the garden; it's a great place for a walk and the morning chirping of the birds is a great way to start the day.

② SUNNY SIDE (p224) A great place to stop for a lazy breakfast before hitting the road. The food is legendary and the pie is to die for – just don't be put off by the rustic interior.

③ DOLE PINEAPPLE PAVILION (p222) A must-stop location on the way to the North Shore. Check out the maze before it gets overrun with bus traffic in the afternoon. The kids will love it and grown-ups who are agriculturally inclined are sure to find it interesting.

④ KOLEKOLE PASS (p219) If the heat of the day is getting too much, head up to where the altitude-induced cool air is like a refreshing dip in the pool. This historic pass has been the scene of some grizzly history – both ancient and not so long ago. After taking in the view, continue along the Kunia Rd.

⑤ HAWAII COUNTRY CLUB (p219) Those keen to hit the links should stop in for a relaxed game of golf. The views of the city are great and it's a perfect way to end a big day.

CENTRAL O'AHU

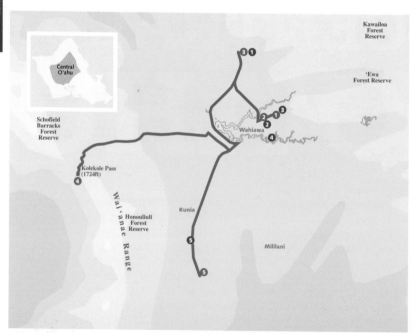

FOR GREEN THUMBS

❶ DOLE PINEAPPLE PAVILION (p222)
Start out where you can learn all about the delicious yellow fruit that put O'ahu on the map. Go for a ride on the train and a wander through the maze.

❷ SUNNY SIDE (p224) Stop in and grab a picnic lunch – don't forget the pie, it's better than mom used to make.

❸ WAHIAWA BOTANICAL GARDEN (p221) The garden is teeming with plant life, both native and introduced, and a fine location for your picnic – once you've finished lunch, go for a walk among the trees. Take the time to really explore this place – it's a lot bigger than you might first think. The massive range of plant and tree species here really make it worth the trip.

❹ WAHIAWA FRESHWATER STATE RECREATION AREA (p223) An idyllic place for a picnic beside the beautiful freshwater lake. Keen fishers will want to drop a line in here – you might just land yourself the big one!

❺ KUNIA ROAD (p218) A great way to finish the day, this drive heads down the most aesthetic road in the area, providing good views of the whole region. As you head down towards the south coast the whole island opens up beneath you. Green fields, blue sky and shimmering water fill your field of view – truly one of the best vistas on O'ahu.

CENTRAL O'AHU

Wahiawa Botanical Garden (p221)   SCOTT KENNEDY

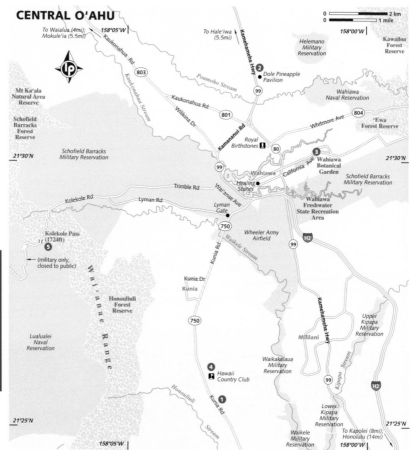

KUNIA ROAD (HIGHWAY 750)

If you're not in a hurry (and why should you be?) this slightly longer route through the center of the island is a scenic alternative. It may add a few minutes to your drive from Honolulu, but the scenery along the way is far more interesting than the H-2 speedway. Follow the H-1 from Honolulu to the Kunia/Hwy 750 exit, 3 miles west of where the H-1 and H-2 divide.

The drive starts in sprawling suburbia but soon breaks free into an expansive landscape with 360-degree views. As you gain altitude, views of Honolulu and Diamond Head emerge below you; be sure to stop off somewhere and look back at the landscape. Cornfields give way to enormous pineapple plantations, all hemmed in by the mountains to the west.

The rural landscape continues until you pass Schofield Barracks Military Reservation. This massive army base is the largest on the island and is a hive of activity – it's not uncommon to be passed on the highway by camo-painted Humvee's while Black Hawk choppers hover overhead.

The least interesting of the options across the island is the Kamehameha Hwy (Hwy 99), which catches local traffic as it runs through Mililani, a nondescript residential community.

HIGHLIGHTS

❶ **BEST VIEW:** Kunia Road (opposite)
❷ **BEST ACTIVITY:** The maze at Dole Pineapple Pavilion (p223)
❸ **BEST PLACE TO RELAX:** Wahiawa Botanical Garden (p221)
❹ **BEST AFTERNOON TEE:** Hawaii Country Club (right)
❺ **BEST SOLITUDE:** Kolekole Pass (right)

Highlights are numbered on the map opposite.

Kunia

The little town of Kunia, in the midst of the pineapple fields, is home to the field workers employed by Del Monte. If you want to see what a current-day plantation village looks like, turn west off Hwy 750 onto Kunia Dr, about 5.5 miles north of H-1.

Rows of gray-green wooden houses with corrugated tin roofs stand on low stilts. Residents take pride in their little yards, with bougainvillea and birds of paradise

adding a splash of brightness despite the wash of red dust that blows in from the surrounding pineapple fields.

The **Hawaii Country Club** (☎ 621-5654; 94-1211 Kunia Rd; 18 holes $65) is the oldest public golf course on the island. Don't let its age deter you. It's not only a challenging par-72, it also sports great views of the ocean and the city.

Kolekole Pass

This 1724ft pass occupies the gap in the Wai'anae Range that Japanese fighter planes flew through on their way to bomb Pearl Harbor. Film buffs may recognize the landscape, as the historic flight was re-created here 30 years later for the classic war film *Tora! Tora! Tora!*

Kolekole Pass, on military property above Schofield Barracks, can be visited as long as the base isn't on military alert. Access is through Lyman Gate on Hwy 750, 0.7 miles south of Hwy 750's intersection with Hwy 99. Follow Lyman Rd for 5.25 miles, passing a military golf course and bayonet assault course, to reach the pass.

A five-minute walk from the parking area leads to the top of the pass and a fine view of the Wai'anae Coast. The large, ribbed

CENTRAL O'AHU

Find fresh local produce (not just pineapples!) at the Sunday open market, Kunia   LINDA CHING

stone sitting atop the ridge here is said to have been a woman named Kolekole. According to Hawaiian legend, she took the form of this stone to become the perpetual guardian of the pass, keeping intruders from the coast from entering the sacred lands of Wahiawa.

Note the series of ridges on the stone's side. One drains down from the bowl-like depression on the top. Shaped perfectly for a guillotine, the depression has given rise to a more recent legend that Kolekole served as a sacrificial stone for the beheading of defeated warriors. The fact that military bases flank the pass has no doubt had a little influence on forming this tale.

Just west of the pass the road continues through the Lualualei Naval Reservation down to the Wai'anae Coast, but you can't take it. The reservation is a storage site for nuclear weapons and there's no public access through that side.

WAHIAWA

pop 16,714

On first inspection Wahiawa doesn't tend to inspire. It's a scruffy town that seems to have more fast-food joints and pawn shops then local population. Add to that Schofield Barracks, Hawaii's largest army base, sits immediately south of town. It would be easy to write the place off and keep the car on the highway. But don't be so quick to judge. Scratch below the surface and you'll find a few good reasons to stop.

The area around Wahiawa was long considered sacred – it was the summer home of royalty. The cooler temperatures make for serene living when the mercury climbs. Have a look at the divine botanical gardens, walk in the footsteps of history at Kolekole Pass and discover all you've ever wanted to know about pineapples at the Dole Pavilion.

Find out where pineapples come from at the Dole Pineapple Pavilion (p222)

LINDA CHING

CENTRAL O'AHU

ISLAND VOICES

NAME: GRACE DIXON
OCCUPATION: HEAD VOLUNTEER – WAHIAWA BOTANICAL GARDEN
RESIDENCE: WAHIAWA

How long have you lived on the island? We've been here for 20 years now. My husband was in the military and years ago we were stationed on O'ahu, so when he retired I said, 'let's go back!'

How did you get involved with the botanical garden? Well, when I first moved to Wahiawa I used to go for long walks and I discovered this place. It was all overgrown and I asked if I could volunteer to clean it up – I was the first-ever volunteer! And I've been here ever since. When I first started, people in the community would roll their eyes when I started talking about the gardens, but everything has changed now; people are really proud of what the gardens have become.

Have you noticed a lot of changes in Wahiawa in the 20 years that you've lived here? Now that's my next project! I want to take the idea of transforming this garden into something beautiful and do the same thing to the whole town.

Do you think locals are getting more conscious of environmental issues like sustainability? Hawaiians used to be very conscious of the environment, but as they became more acculturated with Western society they became less environmentally aware. But now everyone is getting back to the traditional ways of caring for the environment. There's a big push to plant more native plants and to plant things that require less water – it's all moving in the right direction.

Although exploring many of Central O'ahu's sights is practical only for those with their own transportation, you can get from Honolulu to Wahiawa (and onward to Hale'iwa) via TheBus 52.

The town has a **Bank of Hawaii** (☎ 622-1651; 634 California Ave) and a **post office** (☎ 800-275-8777; 115 Lehua St).

Sights

🌺 WAHIAWA BOTANICAL GARDEN

ourpick ☎ 621-7321; 1396 California Ave; admission free; 🕙 9am-4pm

While much of Wahiawa doesn't exactly impersonate anything close to aesthetic, this botanical garden, 1 mile east of Kamehameha Hwy (Hwy 80), is a slice of arboreal heaven. Nature lovers and gardeners will delight in the rollicking grounds that stretch for at least 27 acres. There is a mix of the manicured, with beautiful lawns and pruned ornamental plants, and the wild, with a gully of towering hardwoods, tropical ferns and forests of bamboo.

The garden has a long and interesting history. Started 80 years ago as an experiment by the local sugarcane farmers, it has

Top Picks

ALL PINEAPPLES ALL THE TIME

- **Dole Pineapple Pavilion** (p222)
- **Kunia Road** (p218)
- **Kunia** (p219)
- **The Royal Birthstones** (p224)

CENTRAL O'AHU

JUICY TIDBITS

- In 1901 James Dole planted O'ahu's first pineapple patch in Wahiawa.
- Dole's original 12-acre Wahiawa plot has since grown to 8000 acres.
- Each acre of a pineapple field supports about 6500 plants.
- The commercial pineapple variety grown in Hawaii is smooth cayenne.
- It takes nearly two years for a pineapple plant to reach maturity.
- Each plant produces just two pineapples, one in its second year and one in its third year.
- Pineapples are harvested year-round, but the long, sunny days of summer produce the sweetest fruit.
- The average pineapple weighs 5lb.

evolved into a striking oasis of horticultural perfection. There are several paths that weave their way through the garden, about half of which are wheelchair friendly. An enthusiastic volunteer staff is on hand to answer questions and point you in the right direction.

DOLE PINEAPPLE PAVILION

This busy **complex** (☎ 621-8408; 64-1550 Kamehameha Hwy; admission free; ☺ 9am-5:30pm) has a split personality. Outside, the maze and train are great fun for the kids and the young at heart. Inside, the gift shop is overflowing with pineapple-flavored tacky tourist crap. It's a sickly sweet overdose of everything pineapple – the final strike is that the pineapples are 20% more expensive than the grocery store in town.

Getting hopelessly lost has never been more fun than in the pavilion's **'world's larg-**

See native plants like the *hapu'u* (Hawaiian tree fern) at the Wahiawa Botanical Garden (p221)

est maze' (adult/child $6/4). It's been verified by the good folks at Guinness, so the self-proclaimed title holds true. It truly is a gigantic undertaking with over 1½ miles of pathways to lose your way in. The goal is to find six different stations before making your way out. You better be quick if you want to beat the current record of six minutes; most people take 30 minutes and the geographically challenged can take *hours*.

Thomas fans can unite at the vintage **steam train** (adult/child $7.75/5.75), which grinds a groove around the plantation, taking budding engineers and conductors for a 20-minute ride. The kids will love it and parents will have a place to sit for 20 minutes.

HEALING STONES

Among the more odd sights to be labeled with a visitors-bureau marker are the Healing Stones, caged inside a small marble 'temple' next to the Methodist church on California Ave, half a mile west of its intersection with Kamehameha Hwy.

The main stone is thought to be the gravestone of a powerful Hawaiian chief. Although the chief's original burial place was in a field 1 mile away, the stone was moved long ago to a graveyard at this site. In the 1920s people thought the stone had healing powers, and thousands made pilgrimages to it before interest waned. The housing development and church came later, taking over the graveyard and leaving the stones sitting on the sidewalk.

A local group with roots in India that sees a spiritual connection between Hawaiian and Indian beliefs now visits the temple, so you may see flowers or Ganesh statues placed around the stones.

GREG ELMS

DETOUR ➡

🌺 WAHIAWA FRESHWATER STATE RECREATION AREA

Grab some picnic grub in town and head over to this lovely freshwater **reservoir** (Walker St; ⏱ 7am-6:45pm), where you can sit on a knoll surrounded by the scent of eucalyptus trees and enjoy a view of Lake Wilson. Despite being just beyond Wahiawa center, this place has an unspoiled countryside feel and the picnic tables are oh-so inviting.

Public fishing is allowed at the reservoir, and the waters are stocked with largemouth and smallmouth bass, bluegill sunfish, channel catfish, puntat (Chinese catfish), tilapia and carp.

To get here, turn east off Kamehameha Hwy (Hwy 80) onto Avocado St at the south end of town and after 0.1 miles turn right onto Walker St. Continue 0.2 miles, turn right into the park entrance and go another 0.1 miles to the lakeside parking lot above the boat ramp.

Eating

The golden age of eating in Wahiawa has unfortunately been left to the history books. There are a few diamonds in the rough, but the overwhelming emphasis here is on chain fast-food.

SUNNY SIDE
Diner $

our pick ☎ 621-7188; 1017 Kilani Ave; mains from $2; ☻ breakfast & lunch

Delve down this side street to find one of the best eats in town. The parking lot looks like a motocross track, and the last renovations were done a half-century ago – the interior is delightfully uninviting with worn-out plastic furniture, peeling paint and faded photographs – but all is forgotten when your food arrives. It's delicious, simple and unbelievably cheap. Be sure to save room for a slice of pie; it's as good as homemade.

SEOUL INN
Korean $

☎ 621-9090; 410 California Ave; mains $5-8; ☻ 9:30am-8:30pm

This simple place lays claim to being Hawaii's oldest Korean eatery, so you can bet it has the recipes down pat. If you really want to see what warms a Korean heart, try the stir-fry kimchi – you won't regret it.

MAUI MIKE'S
Takeout $

☎ 622-5900; 96 S Kamehameha Hwy; meals $5-7; ☻ 11am-8:30pm Mon-Sat

At Mike's you have the choice of chicken, chicken or chicken. They fire-roast the birds and they're so fresh they were clucking when you woke up this morning. There are a few tables inside, but most grab the chick and run.

MOLLY'S SMOKEHOUSE
Takeout $$

☎ 621-4858; 23 S Kamehameha Hwy; meals $9-18; ☻ 11am-9pm

If you have a hankering for some Flintstone-size ribs, collard greens and some good old southern comfort soul food, come chat to Molly. You can see the giant smoker puffing away outside of Molly's from down the street. Follow your nose and don't forget your Texas-sized appetite.

THE ROYAL BIRTHSTONES

O'ahu's central uplands were once the domain of royalty, with the area so sacred that commoners were forbidden to even pass through. Kukaniloko, just north of Wahiawa, took on unique importance. As the central point on the island, Kukaniloko symbolized the human *piko* (navel) and it was at this sacred spot that divine spirits welcomed chiefly offspring into the world.

Consequently it was of great importance that a female chief reach the site in time for childbirth. And there was a very strict regimen to be followed once she arrived. A certain number of chiefs had to be present to witness the birth, and the woman needed to lean properly against the stones while giving birth for her child to be blessed by the gods. If all went according to plan, that child would be taken to a nearby temple and welcomed into the world as an *ali'i* (member of royalty). Those born at Kukaniloko were of such a high lineage that chiefs from other islands would seek to enhance their prestige by marrying a Kukaniloko-born royal.

These stones date back to the 12th century and were in use until the time of Kamehameha I, who rushed up to Kukaniloko for the birth of his son Liholiho in 1797.

Among the most sacred cultural treasures on O'ahu, these stones are one of only two documented birthstone sites in Hawaii (the other is on Kaua'i). Many of the petroglyphs you'll see on the stones are of recent origin, but the eroded circular patterns are original.

To get to the site from town, go 0.75 miles north on Kamehameha Hwy (Hwy 80) from its intersection with California Ave. Turn left onto the red dirt road directly opposite Whitmore Ave. The stones, marked with a state monument sign, are 0.25 miles down the road, through a pineapple field, among a stand of eucalypts and coconut trees.

LEEWARD O'AHU

If you're looking for big resorts, tourist-oriented shopping strips, crowded beaches and kitschy cultural encounters, don't come to Leeward O'ahu. This coast is a sanctuary of authenticity. You'll find unspoiled beaches devoid of tourists, cultural experiences that ring true and the largest Native Hawaiian population on the island. There's a rough-and-tumble feel to the place, with much of the population living at the lower end of the economic scale. Stretching from the suburban south of burgeoning 'Ewa all the way up to Makaha, with its legendary beaches and surf, this coast is ripe for discovery – and a great area for travelers looking to go beyond the main tourist track.

LEEWARD O'AHU
ITINERARIES

IN TWO DAYS This leg: 21 miles

❶ HAWAII'S PLANTATION VILLAGE (p230) Get a great sense of what the old Hawaii was like. Sugarcane plantations and rough-and-tumble settlements are all recreated and preserved.

❷ POKE STOP (p232) Tuck into a great meal at one of the best cheap eats on the island. Though it isn't much to look at, the food is divine.

❸ HAWAIIAN RAILWAY (p230) As long as it's a Sunday you can ride the old steam train that once transported sugar cane to market. The kids will love it and those with a passion for history won't want to miss this chance to ride into the past.

❹ KANE'AKI HEIAU (p238) A great place to get a real insight into what O'ahu was like before European settlement. This site is well maintained and has a wealth of information for the history-focused traveler.

❺ MAKAHA BEACH PARK (p235) Whether you're a surfer or a die-hard land lover, this beach is worth a visit. The long stretch of sand is good for lounging or wandering. If you're a wave rider, the break here can be epic when the conditions are just right.

❻ MAKAHA VALLEY (p235) This aesthetic valley is a fitting place to end your journey into the past, with only the pristine and the untouched around you.

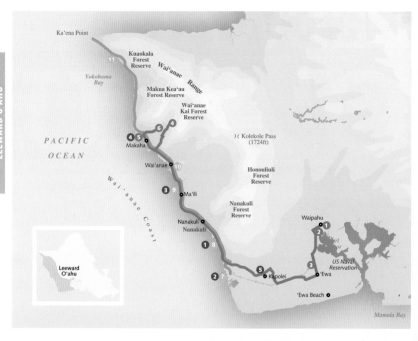

IN THREE DAYS *This leg: 20 miles*

⑦ KO OLINA RESORT (p228) Start day three at the southern end of the coast at this opulent resort. Pull up a section of sand by one of the lagoons, take a load off and relax – you deserve it. If the mood strikes, go for a snorkel and see what you can see.

⑧ TRACKS (p233) Start the journey north by hitting this underused surf break. On a good day it can have some nice swell – don't plan to spend the day here, though, because the beach isn't all that hot.

⑨ MA'ILI (p234) Another quiet beach, and if you're a bodyboarder, the shore-break here is great. If you're not a surfer, the sand is clean and expansive – great for sun worshiping.

⑩ SURFAH SMOODEEZ (p234) This is the place for a refreshing treat to kill some of that heat. The smoothies are delicious and almost nutritious. The range of flavors is inspiring, and you'll struggle to choose just one.

⑪ KA'ENA POINT TRAIL (p240) Time to go for a hike. Choose a cool afternoon to avoid the unrelenting heat of the sun and hike along to the northwest tip of the island. Take your time, look out for seabirds and, if the sea is in a friendly mood, go for a swim.

FOR SURFERS

❶ TRACKS (p233) A classic break for some good waves when the conditions are right. If the swell isn't on for the day, why not have a laugh with the skimboard – who says it's just for groms?

❷ KO OLINA RESORT (p228) When you get too tired to paddle, drop into this resort for a bite to eat and a lazy dip in the lagoon. The snorkeling is pretty good here too – it's always good to work on those breath-holding skills.

❸ MA'ILI (p234) A great bodyboarding beach with an excellent shorebreak – perfect for catching minitubes and having a good laugh. If the waves are too mellow, pull out the stand up paddle board and go for a cruise.

❹ MAKAHA (p235) If you're on the island to surf, you can't miss a day in the water at Makaha. This classic break has been the stuff of legend. In the '60s Greg Noll caught one of the biggest waves ever ridden here, and everybody else has been trying for that next biggest one ever since.

❺ HAWAIIAN WATERS ADVENTURE PARK (p230) So the surf is flat and you're dying to catch a wave – why not ride an artificial one? This wave pool and water slide complex is a big hit with the kids, but even the grown-ups will find ways to scare themselves here.

LEEWARD O'AHU

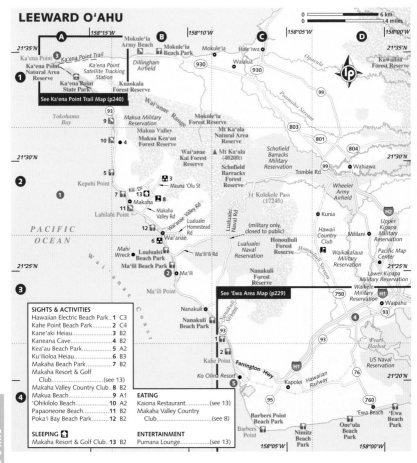

LEEWARD O'AHU

'EWA AREA

The times they are a changing in the southwest corner of O'ahu. Once the stomping ground of sugarcane plantations and the US Navy, today both of those cash cows have moved on. In their industrial wake, subdivisions, suburbia and prefab communities are popping up like spring flowers.

This corner of the island is the fastest-growing region on O'ahu, with housing and industry on the build nearly everywhere. While you'd think it would be all looking to the future, there are actually quite a few callbacks to the past. The Plantation Village and Hawaiian Railway are a throwback to the more pastoral beginnings of the area. Among it all, there is also a water park for the kids and an outlet mall for the shopaholics.

Sights

KO OLINA RESORT

No beach? No problem – all it takes is a little bit of lateral thinking and a couple of thousand tons of imported sand. When this resort was still on the drawing board it lacked the signature feature that is key for all Hawaiian resorts – a beach. A deal was struck and, in exchange for pubic access, the investors were allowed to carve out three kidney-shaped lagoons and line them

HIGHLIGHTS

❶ **BEST BEACH:** Makaha (p235)
❷ **BEST VIEW:** Ma'ili (p234)
❸ **BEST ACTIVITY:** Hike to Ka'ena Point (p240)
❹ **BEST RESTAURANT:** Poke Stop (p232)
❺ **BEST FAMILY FUN:** Ko Olina Lagoons (right)

Highlights are numbered on the map opposite.

with soft white sand. These man-made beaches are well worth a visit – the calm waters are perfect for kids. Even if you're not keen to get wet, the ample recreation opportunities make the resort a worthy stop. There's a great golf course for the energetic and a decedent spa for those in need of pampering. The road to Ko Olina Resort is off the southern side of the Farrington

Hwy. There's no bus into the resort – the bus stops along the Farrington Hwy, and from there it's a 1-mile walk to the nearest beach.

The key feature to the resort is, of course, the lagoons – four purpose-built beaches that are an indulgent treat. The largest of the bunch, at nearly 200yd across, is the lagoon in front of the JW Marriott Ihilani Resort & Spa – it's a nice little fake beach. The islands that block the open sea from the lagoons help with water circulation and are also great places for spotting fish. Keep an eye on the kiddies, though – the current picks up near the opening to the sea.

There is a wide and comfortable path that connects the lagoons, which is great for a lazy stroll. Limited free parking can be found at each of the lagoons.

The saltwater pools set amongst the grounds of the JW Marriott Ihilani Resort & Spa are home to many a captive sea creature and are like something out of Dr Evil's Lair. Reef sharks, stingrays and hammerhead sharks troll the open-topped pools. It's a great venue for those who want to get

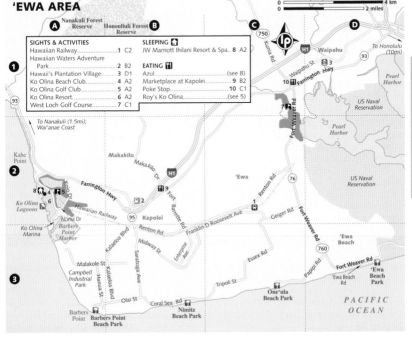

'EWA AREA

SIGHTS & ACTIVITIES		
Hawaiian Railway	1	C2
Hawaiian Waters Adventure Park	2	B2
Hawaii's Plantation Village	3	D1
Ko Olina Beach Club	4	A2
Ko Olina Golf Club	5	A2
Ko Olina Resort	6	A2
West Loch Golf Course	7	C1

SLEEPING		
JW Marriott Ihilani Resort & Spa	8	A2

EATING		
Azul	(see 8)	
Marketplace at Kapolei	9	B2
Poke Stop	10	C1
Roy's Ko Olina	(see 5)	

0 — 4 km
0 — 2 miles

up close and personal with some sea life and stay dry. All they need are laser beams attached to their heads and the scene would be complete.

❀ HAWAII'S PLANTATION VILLAGE

☎ 677-0110; www.hawaiiplantationvillage.org; 94-695 Waipahu St, Waipahu; adult $13, child 4-11yr $5; ⏱ tours on the hour 10am-2pm Mon-Sat; 🚌 42

The lives of the people who came to Hawaii to work on the sugarcane plantations are showcased at Hawaii's Plantation Village. The setting is particularly evocative, as Waipahu was one of O'ahu's last plantation towns, and its rusty sugar mill, which operated until 1995, still looms on a knoll directly above this site.

The place encompasses 30 buildings typical of an early-20th-century plantation village, including a Chinese cookhouse, a Japanese shrine and authentically replicated homes of the seven ethnic groups – Hawaiian, Japanese, Chinese, Korean, Portuguese, Puerto Rican and Filipino – that lived on the plantations.

To get there by car from Honolulu, take the H-1 Fwy to exit 7, turn left onto Paiwa St, then right onto Waipahu St, continuing past the sugar mill and turning left into the complex.

HAWAIIAN RAILWAY

☎ 681-5461; www.hawaiianrailway.com; 91-1001 Renton Rd, 'Ewa; adult/child 2-12yr $10/7; ⏱ 90min rides 1pm & 3pm Sun

If you've got a thing for rails, this is the place to be on a Sunday. For more than half a century from 1890 to 1940 this railroad carried sugarcane and passengers from Honolulu all the way through to Kahuka. The conclusion of WWII saw the boom of the automobile in Hawaii and the railway soon closed as a result. But thanks to the historical society, the trains again run for fun along 6.5 miles of restored track between 'Ewa and Nanakuli. A 1944 Whitcomb diesel locomotive pulls four cars of similar vintage. Displayed in the yard you'll find the coal engine that pulled the first O'ahu Railway and Land Company (OR&L) train in 1889.

To get there, take exit 5A off the H-1, drive south 2.5 miles on Fort Weaver Rd and turn right at the 7-Eleven onto Renton Rd.

Top Picks

FOR KIDS

- Ko Olina Lagoons (p229)
- Hawaiian Waters Adventure Park (below)
- Hawaiian Railway (left)
- Hawaii's Plantation Village (left)
- Saltwater pools (p229)

Activities

SWIMMING

Who says water parks are just for kids? The Hawaiian Waters Adventure Park (☎ 674-9283; www.hawaiianwaters.com; 400 Farrington Hwy, Kapolei; adult $38, child 3-11yr $28; ⏱ 10:30am-3:30pm Mon, Thu & Fri, to 4pm Sat & Sun) has a slide for every taste, from tame to terrifying. Covering 25 acres, it's a huge place, with a whole host of aquatic activities on offer. There is a football field–sized wave pool that can generate surfable rides and a seven-story water slide that would have Aquaman quaking in his boots. If all that sounds too scary, there is an adults-only swim-up bar, where the only thing you risk breaking is your heart.

TheBus 40 runs from the Ala Moana Center in Honolulu twice an hour, making stops in Kapolei at both Hawaiian Waters Adventure Park ($2 each way, 1¼ hours) and the shopping center.

SNORKELING

The Ko Olina Lagoons are a great place to get wet and have a look under water. The largest lagoon, near the resort, is the best of the bunch for spotting turtles, reef fish and lost room keys. Near the rocks on the side of the lagoon is the preferred location for spotting marine life. Snorkel sets can be rented right at the beach from Ko Olina Beach Club (per hr/day $8/15; ⏱ 8:30am-5pm).

GOLF

Those in the know will already know that the Ko Olina Golf Club (☎ 676-5300; www.koolinagolf .com; 92-1220 Ali'inui Dr; 18 holes $180, after 1pm $120) comes recommended by both the LPGA and the senior PGA tour – they've both held tournaments here. Mere golf mortals will enjoy it too – the course sits like an oasis of green among the barren brown hills, with frequent water hazards and abundant sand traps to entice your ball.

Golfers looking for a far more relaxed time on the links need look no further then the West Loch Golf Course (☎ 675-6076; 91-1126 Okupe St, 'Ewa Beach; 18 holes $42). Though a fraction of the price of the more posh courses on the island, this course boxes well above its weight. There are great ocean views throughout and nice wide fairways to keep the ball in play. It doesn't rent clubs, so you'll need to be packing your own.

HIKING

The Nature Conservancy (☎ 587-6220; www.nature .org/hawaii) leads monthly hikes (free, but best to book ahead) on trails in the Honouliuli Forest Reserve on the slopes of the Wai'anae Range north of Kapolei. The reserve is home to nearly 70 rare and endangered plant and animal species. The land once belonged to Hawaiian royalty and was named Honouliuli – meaning 'dark harbor' – for the dark, fertile lands that stretch from the waters of Pearl Harbor to the summit of the Wai'anae Range.

It's totally tubular at Hawaiian Waters Adventure Park

ANN CECIL

Eating

At the Marketplace at Kapolei (91-590 Farrington Hwy, Kapolei) you'll find a 24-hour Safeway supermarket and a bevy of restaurants serving pizza, Thai and Chinese fare.

POKE STOP
Takeout $

☎ 676-8100; Waipahu Town Center, 94-050 Farrington Hwy; mains $4-13; ⏲ 8am-7pm Mon-Sat, to 5pm Sun

Tucked into a sleepy corner of a nondescript mini-mall is one of the best restaurants on O'ahu. You won't believe it till you take your first bite. *Poke* (cubed raw fish) is the specialty, and you can't go wrong with it. There is a list of other delectable delights to entice you in if you come back for a second sitting. There are a couple of seats out front but most people take the fish and run – you can't get a better picnic lunch then this.

ROY'S KO OLINA
Hawaii Regional $$$

☎ 676-7697; Ko Olina Golf Club, 92-1220 Ali'inui Dr; lunch from $14, dinner from $18; ⏲ 11am-2pm & 5:30-9:30pm

Sitting like an island green, this 19th hole is a great place to end your round of golf or just sit back and enjoy the tasty fare. Miles from the sandwiches and fries that are usually found at a clubhouse, the food here is a delicious Hawaii Regional fusion. There are traditional Japanese dishes with an O'ahu flair like coconut-and-macadamia–encrusted scallops – yum!

AZUL
Seafood $$$$

☎ 679-3166; JW Marriott Ihilani Resort & Spa, Ko Olina Resort; set dinner $45; ⏲ 6-9pm Tue-Sat

With an eclectic mix of surf and turf and an emphasis on organics, this eatery is in a class of its own on this corner of the island. Crisp white linen covers the tables, which sit in a palm-shaded courtyard. Free-range foul and ultrafresh seafood populate the menu and leave you with a host of delicious choices. Be sure to reserve your space and put on your best aloha shirt.

Sleeping

JW MARRIOTT IHILANI RESORT & SPA
Resort $$$$

☎ 679-0079, 800-626-4446; www.marriotthotels.com; Ko Olina Resort, 92-1001 Olani St; r from $485; ⏲ ☒ ☐ ☐ ☐ ☒

Seated right on the beach, this aesthetic property is palatial, expansive and architecturally pleasing to the eye. It's popular with families and those wanting to avoid the Waikiki scene but still have all the trappings of mainstream luxury. If it looks a little familiar, that's because Hollywood has even checked in here – the Marriott starred in the surfer-girl movie *Blue Crush* as the hotel in which the girls worked.

No pig in this *poke*: cubed raw tuna with seaweed, green onion, chili and soy sauce

ANN CECIL

The Wai'anae Coast's beaches are stunning and often deserted   KARL LEHMANN

WAI'ANAE COAST

Charting an intriguing history, this coast is full of diversity and contradiction. In 1793 Englishman George Vancouver dropped anchor on the Wai'anae Coast and became the first European to turn up. There wasn't much here at the time, only a few scattered huts and even fewer people. A couple of years later, when Kamehameha the Great invaded the island, the population from nearly everywhere else on the island was forced to flee and many of them ended up on the Wai'anae Coast.

Since those heady days of civil war, things have quieted down considerably. The coast is now home to more Native Hawaiians then anywhere else on O'ahu and the least amount of tourist infrastructure. The beaches are stunning and often deserted and the towering peaks to the east are a beautiful backdrop. The winter surf, especially at Makaha, can be epic and the summer snorkeling is top-shelf.

The coast isn't without its shortfalls – there is a large homeless population that calls many of the beaches home and the staunch working-class communities don't exude a warm welcome to visitors. But for those looking for a more authentic O'ahu experience, this is the coast to find it.

Exploring by car couldn't be easier: just follow the Farrington Hwy (Hwy 93) up the coast, with beaches on one side and mountains on the other.

For those traveling by bus, TheBus C and 40 connect Honolulu with the Wai'anae Coast, stopping at every town as far north as Makaha.

Beaches

KAHE POINT BEACH PARK
Map p228

A hulking power plant complete with towering smoke stacks isn't the best neighbor to a beach – but, as they say, you can't pick your neighbors. Though it's called a beach park, there isn't actually a beach here, just a rocky point that's popular with anglers. There are, however, great views to the north, as well as running water, picnic tables and restrooms.

HAWAIIAN ELECTRIC BEACH PARK
Map p228

Hawaiian Electric Beach Park is what it's called on the map but all the locals refer to this stretch of sand as Tracks. This colloquial name stems from the train-transported beachgoers who frequented the beach prior to WWII. The sandy shores are good for swimming in the summer and great for surfing in the winter.

NANAKULI
pop 10,814

It's hard to find much that qualifies as aesthetic in this seaside town. It's little more then a strip of fast-food joints along the highway. The large Native Hawaiian population adds an authentic feel to town – it's just too bad there isn't more of an opportunity to experience that warm cultural embrace.

Nanakuli Beach Park is a broad, sandy beach park that lines the town, offering swimming, snorkeling and diving during the calmer summer season. In winter, high surf can create rip currents and dangerous shorebreaks. The park has a playground, sports fields and beach facilities. To get to the beach park, turn *makai* (oceanward) at the traffic lights on Nanakuli Ave.

MA'ILI

The town of Ma'ili isn't all that much to see beyond Ma'ili Beach Park. This attractive beach has the distinction of being one of the longest stretches of snow-white sand on the island. The grassy park that sits adjacent to the beach is popular with families for weekend barbecues and low-key, island-style parties. Like other places on the Wai'anae Coast, the water conditions are often treacherous in winter but usually calm enough for swimming in summer. The park has a lifeguard station, a playground, beach facilities and a few castrated coconut palms that provide limited, but safe, shade.

Sleeping

MA'ILI COVE   Condos $$

☎ 696-4186; www.mailicove.org; 87-561 Farrington Hwy; 1br unit per week from $650; 🖳 🖳
This attractive condo complex right on the beach is an often-overlooked hideaway. The two apartments for rent are clean, comfortable and eclectically decorated. There is a barbecue and the option to walk out the patio door and right onto the beach. Sitting just south of Ma'ili Beach Park, this is the quiet end of the quiet coast. One-week minimum stays.

WAI'ANAE

pop 10,525
The town that takes the name of the whole coast is also home to much of the area's infrastructure. You'll find more places to eat here then anywhere else, a nice beach and a large harbor popular with nautical folks.

Information

First Hawaiian Bank (☎ 696-7041; 86-020 Farrington Hwy; 🕑 8:30am-4pm Mon-Thu, to 6pm Fri) Just south of the post office.

Post Office (☎ 800-275-8777; 86-014 Farrington Hwy; 🕑 8am-4:15pm Mon-Fri, 9am-noon Sat) On the corner of Lualualei Homestead Rd.

Wai'anae Comprehensive Health Center (☎ 696-7081; 86-260 Farrington Hwy; 🕑 emergency room 24hr) The coast's hospital, on the corner of Maili'ili Rd.

Beaches

POKA'I BAY BEACH PARK

Map p228
This beach is a real beauty. Protected by Kane'ilio Point and a long breakwater, it has calm year-round swimming. Waves seldom break inside the bay, and the sandy beach slopes gently, making it a popular spot for families with children.

Snorkeling is fair by the breakwater, where fish gather around the rocks. The bay is also used by local canoe clubs, and you can watch them paddling if you happen by in the late afternoon. There are showers, restrooms and picnic tables, and a lifeguard is on duty daily.

To get to the beach park, turn *makai* off Farrington Hwy onto Lualualei Homestead Rd at the traffic light immediately north of the Wai'anae post office.

Eating

SURFAH SMOODEEZ   Smoothies $

☎ 478-9088; 85-979 Farrington Hwy; smoothies $5; 🕑 10:30am-7pm Mon-Fri, to 5:30pm Sat
This nondescript little shop is a hidden gem, with the smoothies a refreshing treat. The fruit is fresh and the vibe is decidedly low-key. It's just south of the highway's intersection with Wai'anae Valley Rd.

TACOS & MORE   Mexican $

☎ 697-8800; 85-993 Farrington Hwy; mains $5-10; 🕑 10am-8pm Mon-Fri, 2-8pm Sat
Great Mex made with aloha by a family that started out in Mexico City. This everexpanding eatery has retained its delicious reputation and continues to be a local favorite. The atmosphere is relaxed and the food is excellent.

BARBEQUE KAI   Comfort Food $

☎ 696-7122; 85-973 Farrington Hwy; mains $3-7; 🕑 8am-8pm
On a nice day the tables in front of this grungy little lunch bar are overflowing

DETOUR ➡

KU'ILIOLOA HEIAU

Start at the parking lot of Poka'i Bay Beach Park, walk straight across the lawn with the outrigger canoes at your right and take the path 0.1 miles out to Kane'ilio Point. Here's your reward: Ku'ilioloa Heiau, a terraced stone platform temple, and spectacular coastal views all the way to Makaha in the north. At the foot of the heiau, if the waves aren't crashing strongly, you'll find little tide pools harboring miniature marine life that can be explored.

with the local crew. Cheap-as-chips mixed plates, burgers and other local favorites populate the menu. Don't come expecting fine china or reusable silverware, but if you want a good feed for a few bucks, this is the place.

MAKAHA

pop 7750

Makaha is a town known for good surfing and gorgeous beaches. Both stereotypes are (happily) exactly right. Free of the chaotic scene that encompasses Waikiki and the gawking tourists of the North Shore, Makaha could be the best example of old-time O'ahu. It's worth a visit for the sand alone, but be sure to have a look at O'ahu's best-restored heiau. No buses run beyond Makaha; that area can only be explored with your own transportation.

Beaches

MAKAHA BEACH PARK

our pick Map p228

Makaha Beach has a long history of big-wave surfing that ranks among the richest on the island. It's a beautiful, arcing beach with a stunning stretch of sand that entices you to spread out your towel and spend the day.

Makaha jumped to fame in the 1950s when it hosted Hawaii's first international surfing competition. The long point break

at Makaha produced the waves that inspired the first generation of big-wave surfers. It's still possible to rekindle that pioneering feeling as, except on the biggest days, you're likely to have the beach and waves virtually to yourself. Winter brings big swells that preclude swimming much of the time – the golden sand, however, is a permanent feature. The beach has showers and restrooms, and lifeguards are on duty daily.

If you're going to Makaha Beach Park by bus, the express TheBus C is the most direct option, because it stays along the coast. TheBus 40 goes up Makaha Valley Rd to the golf courses and then comes down Kili Dr to the beach.

PAPAONEONE BEACH

Map p228

Most people head to Makaha Beach Park, while this smaller beauty just 1 mile to the south sees barely a soul. It's a good spot for bodysurfing, with a decent shorebreak. Protected by Lahilahi Point to the south, Papaoneone Beach seldom has rip currents unless the surf is very big, but if you've got kids with you, be cautious because the sandy bottom has a quick and steep drop-off. Access to the beach is immediately north of the Makaha Beach Cabanas condominiums.

Sights

MAKAHA VALLEY

All it takes is a turn inland to leave the arid shore behind and get lost amongst the far lusher interior. Turn inland from the Farrington Hwy onto Kili Dr opposite Makaha Beach Park. The road skirts up along scalloped cliffs into Makaha Valley.

Island Insights

In December 1969 legendary surfer Greg Noll rode what was thought to be the biggest wave in surfing history (to that point) at Makaha. Speculation still rages as to exactly how big the monster wave was, but it is commonly accepted that it was at least a 30ft face – a mountain of water for the era.

ISLAND VOICES

NAME: ANN SHAVER
OCCUPATION: ADVOCATE FOR THE HOMELESS
RESIDENCE: MAKAHA

Ann Shaver has an interesting perspective on the beaches of the Leeward Coast – she doesn't go to the beach to catch waves or get a bit of sun. Ann goes to the beach to do her bit to help the ever-growing homeless population that calls these beaches home.

How many homeless people are living on the beach on the Waiʻanae Coast? From Makaha north there are about 350 homeless people living on or around the beach.

Are most of those from the mainland or from Hawaii? Most of them are local. There was a time when many of them came from the mainland because of the weather and the benefits, but that doesn't really happen anymore. But it's impossible to generalize. There are families, educated people, there are chronic losers, there are druggies, there are religious people, nonreligious people – it's a real cross section of society. There are major problems here with affordable housing – many of the homeless people have jobs, but nowhere to live.

Are the numbers of homeless people on the coast growing? Every Wednesday we go out and serve all the homeless lunch – in the last year we've doubled the number of lunches we serve and there still isn't enough. The numbers are growing all the time.

Can you see a solution? Well, at the moment the church is in the planning stages of building 200 cabins on disused land near Makaha. It will be a sort of commune where the homeless people will have a place to live. There will be gardens where they grow their own food and be self-sustaining. It sounds pie in the sky, I know, but they are actually going to do it.

Do you see success stories? Oh yeah! All the time we go down to the beach and see that people have moved on, found housing and jobs – it's great.

Why is there such a concentration of homeless people up here? Part of it is they've all been chased out of Honolulu – it's a total not-in-my-backyard-mentality; out of sight, out of mind. These beaches aren't very popular so the state turns a blind eye to homeless people living on them. But as a community we've always been very accepting and, while we don't necessarily like living beside all of the homeless people, we know that they need a place to live, just like everyone else.

will delight in going down onto the wreck of the *Mahi*, a classic dive site in the area. Makaha Caverns, out where the waves break furthest offshore, is a popular leeward diving spot, featuring underwater caverns, arches and tunnels at depths of 30ft to 50ft.

Paradise Isle (☎ 695-8866; Makaha Marketplace, 84-1170 Farrington Hwy; body-/surf-/long-board hire per 5hr $12/20/25; ⏰ 8am-8pm), just south of Makaha

$125) prides itself as one of the best courses on the island, and a round here will more than live up to that billing. There are all sorts of challenges to deal with: slopes, traps, water – all the fun ones. With the great views everywhere you look, you'll be excused if you take your eye off the ball.

Makaha Valley Country Club (Map p228; ☎ 695-7111; 84-627 Makaha Valley Rd; 18 holes $65), tucked right up against the Wai'anae Range and with great ocean views, is a nice little course. Much more relaxed then its neighbor, the wide fairways and sand-encrusted greens get popular on the weekends. There's even a driving range if you want to bang out a bucket of balls.

Eating

MAKAHA VALLEY COUNTRY CLUB
Sandwiches $

Map p228; ☎ 695-7111; 84-627 Makaha Valley Rd; mains $5-10; ☼ 7am-2pm Mon-Fri, 6am-3pm Sat & Sun

A relaxed eatery to suit the chilled-out golf course it cohabits. You'll find the standard club sandwiches, burgers and a touch of Japanese for more eclectic eaters. The outlook is pretty and the unpretentious food is tasty; what more could you want?

KAIONA RESTAURANT
Surf & Turf $$

Map p228; ☎ 695-9544; Makaha Resort & Golf Club, 84-626 Makaha Valley Rd; mains $8-28; ☼ 7am-2pm & 5:30-9pm

If you're looking for a good feed and aren't bothered by modest furnishings and a limited menu, this is the place to be. The open-plan dining overlooks the pool, with a menu weighted towards fresh seafood and nice cuts of steak.

Entertainment

Pumana Lounge (Map p228; ☎ 695-9544; Makaha Resort & Golf Club, 84-626 Makaha Valley Rd) doesn't stray too far from the golf course–lounge stereotype. You'll find a huge TV and a nice view of the greens. Occasional live entertainment is on offer and there are always plenty of cold ones behind the bar.

Sleeping

MAKAHA RESORT & GOLF CLUB
Resort $$

Map p228; ☎ 695-9544, toll free 866-576-6447; www.makaharesort.net; 84-626 Makaha Valley Rd; r from $130; ❄ ☎ ⬛

Airlifted in from the 1970s, this decidedly retro establishment is the place to be for the sporting set. With the golf course right out the door, plus a batting cage, tennis court, pool and basketball court at your disposal,

Island Insights

You gotta get in quick – community markets, like those found on a Thursday at Kane'aki Heiau (see the boxed text, p238), are short and sweet affairs. They kick off at 11am and finish at 11.45am.

you might actually forget to relax. There are great panoramic views of the valley and the ocean, far below. The rooms are spacious and tidy. Rates can really vary – it's best to hunt for specials.

MAKAHA TO KA'ENA POINT

Farrington Hwy continues north to Ka'ena Point, but this area is solely for those with their own transportation. There are no buses beyond Makaha, nor gas stations, restaurants or towns. As you travel north of Makaha the beaches often have a large homeless population living on them. Though trouble is rarely reported, be mindful of opportunistic crime such as car break-ins and bags disappearing while you are swimming.

Beaches

KEA'AU BEACH PARK
Map p228

This beach park is a long, open, grassy strip that borders a rocky shore. It has restrooms, showers, drinking water and picnic tables, making it a good place to unpack that picnic lunch. A sandy beach begins at the very northern end of the park, although a rough reef, sharp drop and high seasonal surf make swimming uninviting.

North along the coast you'll see lava cliffs, white-sand beaches and patches of kiawe, while on the inland side you'll glimpse a run of little valleys.

'OHIKILOLO BEACH
Map p228

O'ahu is full of beaches with peculiar nicknames and this one is no different – Barking Sands. No, there isn't a rampant stray-dog population; the name refers to the sound the dry sand makes as you walk on it. Located just below Kaneana Cave this beach offers nice views of Ka'ena Point. At times there can be a large number of homeless people camping on the beach or in the surrounding area.

MAKUA BEACH

Map p228

This beach has an interesting history – way back in the day it was a canoe landing site for interisland travelers. In the late '60s it was used as the backdrop for the movie *Hawaii*, which starred Julie Andrews. These days there is little here beyond a nice stretch of sand opposite the Makua Military Reservation.

Sights

KANEANA CAVE

Map p228

Two miles north of Kea'au Beach Park sits this giant stone amphitheater, carved out by centuries of incessant waves. The waves that created the enormous cave have rescinded and now the highway sits between it and the seashore.

Hawaiian *kahuna* (priests) once performed rituals inside the cave's inner chamber. Older Hawaiians consider it a sacred place and won't enter the cave for fear that it's haunted by the spirits of deceased chiefs. From the collection of broken beer bottles

A GLIMPSE OF THE PAST

Simply no other place on O'ahu comes close to 🏵 **Kane'aki Heiau** (Map p228; ☎ 695-8174; Mauna Olu Estates; admission free; ⏱ 10am-2pm Tue-Sun) in providing a glimpse into pre-Western-contact Hawaiian culture. Restored to its original splendor and set at the base of verdant hills, the temple looks much like it did centuries ago. Because it's on restricted land, very few tourists make it up this way, and that adds a quiet, untouched element to it all. It's an awesome site to walk around and well worth working a visit into your schedule.

Built in the center of Makaha Valley, midway between the valley's wet, forested uplands and its dry, coastal lowlands, the heiau dates back to 1545 and was originally dedicated to Lono, the god of agriculture. As with many Hawaiian temples, over time it went through transformations in both its physical structure and use. In its final phase it was rededicated as a *luakini* (dedicated to Ku, the god of war) temple, and it's thought that Kamehameha the Great used Kane'aki Heiau as a place of worship after he conquered O'ahu. The heiau remained in use until his death in 1819.

The social and religious upheaval introduced by Kamehameha's successors resulted in the abandonment of Kane'aki Heiau – and all other Hawaiian temples as well. Although many of Hawaii's more accessible coastal heiau were dismantled and their stones used to build cattle fences and other structures, Kane'aki Heiau, protected by its remoteness, survived largely intact.

Constructed of stacked basalt rocks, Kane'aki Heiau has two terraced platforms and six enclosed courtyards. Its restoration, undertaken by the esteemed **Bishop Museum** (p74), took years to complete. The heiau was authentically reconstructed using ohia logs hand hewn with adzes and thatch made from native *pili* grass gathered on the Big Island. Two prayer towers, a taboo house, a drum house, an altar and several deity images were built by Hawaiian craftspeople using traditional techniques and materials.

To get to the heiau, take Kili Dr to the Makaha Valley Towers condominium complex and turn right onto Huipu Dr. A half-mile down, make a left onto Mauna Olu St, which leads 1 mile into Mauna Olu Estates and up to Kane'aki Heiau. The guard at the Mauna Olu Estates gatehouse lets visitors enter to see the heiau only during the listed hours. You might want to call the gatehouse in advance to inquire, as they can be a bit inconsistent in providing access, especially in wet weather. You'll need to show your rental-vehicle contract and driver's license at the gatehouse, so be sure to bring them.

and graffiti inside, it's obvious not everyone shares their sentiment.

MAKUA VALLEY
Map p228

Scenic Makua Valley opens up wide and grassy, backed by a fan of sharply fluted mountains. It serves as the ammunition field of the Makua Military Reservation. The seaside road opposite the southern end of the reservation leads to a little graveyard that's shaded by yellow-flowered be-still trees. This site is all that remains of the Makua Valley community that was forced to evacuate during WWII when the US military took over the entire valley for bombing practice. War games still take place in the valley, which is fenced off with barbed wire and signs that warn of stray explosives.

KA'ENA POINT STATE PARK

Running along both sides of the western-most point of O'ahu, Ka'ena Point State Park is an undeveloped 853-acre coastal strip.

Until the mid-1940s the O'ahu Railway ran up here from Honolulu and continued around the point, carrying passengers on to Hale'iwa on the North Shore. The gorgeous, mile-long sandy beach on the southern side of the point is Yokohama Bay, named for the large number of Japanese fishers who came here during the railroad days.

Like most beaches on the north and west of O'ahu, the winter brings large swells that make for either treacherous swimming or good surfing – depending on what you're after. The waves can be great but are best left to the experts as the strong currents and jagged ocean floor can be deadly for the inexperienced. Swimming is pretty much limited to summer and, even then, only during calm conditions. When the water's flat, it's possible to snorkel; the best spot with the easiest access is at the southern side of the park. Restrooms, showers and a lifeguard station are at the southern end of the park. It's best to bring food and drinks with you,

Yokohama Bay, Ka'ena Point State Park

ANN CECIL

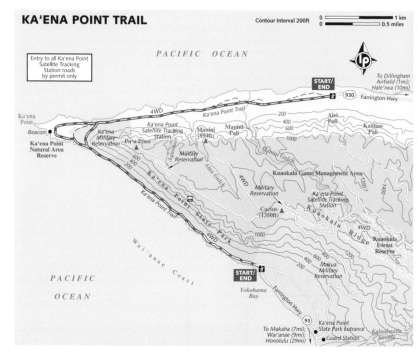

KA'ENA POINT TRAIL

Contour Interval 200ft

PACIFIC OCEAN

Entry to all Ka'ena Point Satellite Tracking Station roads by permit only

To Dillingham Airfield (1mi); Hale'iwa (10mi)

START/ END

930 Farrington Hwy

4WD

Ka'ena Point Trail

Alei Pali

Kauhao Pali

Ka'ena Point

Beacon

Ka'ena Point Satellite Tracking Station

Manini Pali

Ka'ena Military Reservation

Pu'u Pueo

Manini (893ft)

Ka'ena Point Natural Area Reserve

Military Reservation

Kuaokala Game Management Area

Military Reservation

Ka'ena Point Satellite Tracking Station

Cactus (1350ft)

Kuaokala Ridge

Kuaokala Forest Reserve

4WD

Makua Military Reservation

START/ END

PACIFIC

OCEAN

Yokohama Bay

Farrington Hwy

93

Ka'ena Point State Park Entrance

Kaluakauila Stream

To Makaha (7mi); Wai'anae (9mi); Honolulu (29mi)

Guard Station

though occasionally a lunch wagon parks here selling beef stew and smoothies.

Incidentally, those domes sitting above the park that resemble giant white golf balls belong to the air force's Ka'ena Point Satellite Tracking Station.

KA'ENA POINT TRAIL

A coastal trail runs from Yokohama Bay to Ka'ena Point, and around the point to the North Shore, utilizing the old railbed. Most hikers take the trail, which begins from the end of the paved road at Yokohama Bay, as far as the point (2.5 miles) and then come back the same way; it takes about three to four hours round-trip. This easy-to-follow hike offers fine views the entire way, with the ocean on one side and the lofty cliffs of the Wai'anae Range on the other. Along the trail there are tide pools, sea arches and a couple of lazy blowholes that occasionally come to life on high-surf days.

The trail is exposed and lacks shade (Ka'ena means 'the heat'), so take sunscreen and plenty of water. Be cautious near the shoreline, as there are strong currents, and the waves can reach extreme heights. In fact, winter waves at Ka'ena Point are the highest in Hawaii, sometimes towering in excess of 50ft.

Don't leave anything valuable in your car. Telltale mounds of shattered windshield glass litter the road-end parking area used by most hikers. Parking closer to the rest-rooms, or leaving your doors unlocked, can decrease the odds of having your car windows smashed.

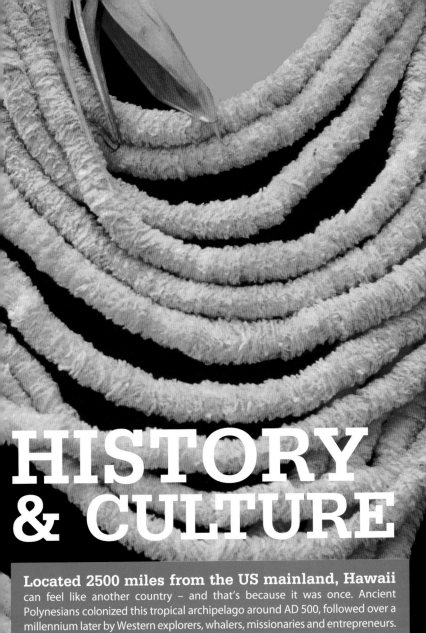

HISTORY & CULTURE

Located 2500 miles from the US mainland, Hawaii can feel like another country – and that's because it was once. Ancient Polynesians colonized this tropical archipelago around AD 500, followed over a millennium later by Western explorers, whalers, missionaries and entrepreneurs. The mid-19th century saw a melting pot of immigrants from Asia, the Americas and Europe – and an end to the Hawaiian kingdom founded by Kamehameha the Great. Today, O'ahu is a mosaic of cultures, with Honolulu a true crossroads between East and West. But underneath it all beats a Hawaiian heart, shown by a revival of the Hawaiian language, artisan crafts, music and the hula.

HISTORY

ANCIENT HAWAI'I

The first Polynesian settlers landed on this archipelago around AD 500. Not a lot is known about them, but artifacts left behind indicate they were from the Marquesas. The next wave of settlers were from Tahiti and arrived around AD 1000. Unlike the Marquesans, who sparsely settled the tiny islands northwest of O'ahu, the Tahitians arrived in great numbers and settled each of the major islands in the Hawaiian chain.

Although no one knows what set them on course for Hawaii, when they arrived in their great double-hulled canoes, they were prepared to colonize a new land, bringing with them pigs, taro roots and other crop plants. Although their discovery of Hawaii may have been accidental, subsequent journeys were not. These Tahitians were highly skilled seafarers, memorizing their route over 2400 miles of open Pacific Ocean, and repeating the journeys between Hawaii and the islands to the south for centuries. So great were the subsequent waves of Tahitian migrations that Hawaii's population probably reached a peak of approximately 250,000 by the year 1450, after which all contact between Tahiti and Hawaii seems to have stopped.

In 1976, to re-create the incredible journey of Hawaii's early settlers, the **Polynesian Voyaging Society** (www.pvs.hawaii.org) launched a modern-day reproduction of an ancient Hawaiian long-distance sailing double-hulled canoe named *Hokule'a* ('Star of Gladness'). The *Hokule'a* successfully made a 4800-mile return trip to Tahiti using only traditional Polynesian wayfaring navigational methods of observing stars, wave patterns, seabirds and clouds. Academic skeptics who had long questioned whether Hawaii's early settlers really were capable of journeying back and forth across such vast, empty ocean came to see it was indeed possible. Today, you can inspect the *Hokule'a* at Honolulu's Hawai'i Maritime Center (p64).

Ancient Hawaiian society used a class system, similar to other Polynesian island groups. In Hawai'i, the highest-ranking group was the *ali'i* (royalty), whose lineage was matriarchal. Next came the lesser chiefs, who ruled individual islands and subdistricts called *ahupua'a* (traditional pie piece–shaped divisions of land extending from the mountains to the sea). These chiefs were considered to be caretakers, not owners, of the land and people they ruled, with a sacred duty to care for the island's natural resources. The third, and largest, class of people in the social hierarchy were *maka'ainana* (commoners). *Maka'ainana* were not owned by the *ali'i,* and were free to live wherever they pleased. However, they were obligated to support the *ali'i* through taxes paid with food, goods and labor used to build temples or other important structures. Last, there was a *kaua* (outcast) class, mostly made up of slaves.

FROM 'DISCOVERY' TO MONARCHY
The First Foreigners

Hawaii was the last of the Polynesian islands to be 'discovered' by the West. This was in partly due to the fact that early European explorers who entered the Pacific

10 Million BC	AD 500	1350
Lava from an underwater volcano breaks the ocean's surface and O'ahu emerges as an island. From one million to 10,000 years ago, a period of renewed volcanism forms Le'ahi (Diamond Head).	The first human settlers – a small group of Polynesians, probably from the Marquesas Islands – arrive in the Hawaiian Islands. Later waves of immigration from Tahiti started around AD 1000 and continued into the mid-1400s.	Ma'ilikukahi, the *mo'i* (king) of O'ahu, moves the capital to Waikiki, an abundant coastal wetland known for its fertile farmlands and abundant fishing and for being a place of recreation and healing.

GODS & TEMPLES

Religion was center stage in ancient Hawaii and there was a hierarchy of gods. At the top were four main gods: Ku, Lono, Kane and Kanaloa.

Ku was the ancestor god for all generations of humankind, past, present and future. One of the most fearful of Ku's manifestations was Kukailimoku, the war god worshipped by Kamehameha the Great. At temples built for worship of Kukailimoku, sacrifices not only of food, pigs and chickens, but also of humans were offered.

Lono was the god in charge of the elements that brought rain and an abundant harvest. He was also the god of fertility and peace. Kane created the first man out of the dust of the earth and breathed life into him (the Hawaiian word for man is *kane*), and it was from him that *ali'i* (chiefs) were said to have descended.

Kanaloa often struggled against the other three gods. When heaven and earth separated, Kanaloa was placed in charge of spirits left on earth. Forbidden from drinking the intoxicating beverage *'awa* (kava), these spirits revolted and were driven to the underworld, where Kanaloa became the ruler of the dead.

To venerate their gods, ancient Hawaiians built stone temples, called heiau. Heiau were purposely built in auspicious sites, often perched on cliffs above the coast or in other places believed to have *mana* (spiritual power). Inside the terraced platforms were prayer towers, around which were placed carved wooden *ki'i* (deity images), and ceremonial houses made of ohia wood and thatched with *pili* grass.

For more about the role of religion in everyday life in ancient Hawaii, see p252.

around the tips of either Africa or South America centered their explorations in the southern hemisphere. British explorer Captain James Cook spent the better part of a decade charting most of the South Pacific before chancing upon Hawaii.

On January 18, 1778, Captain Cook sighted the islands of O'ahu, Kaua'i and Ni'ihau. Thus ended Hawaii's centuries of isolation. Cook was surprised to find that islanders had a strong Tahitian connection in their appearance, language and culture. Cook named the archipelago the Sandwich Islands in honor of his patron, the Earl of Sandwich. One legacy of Cook's 'discovery' was sexually transmitted diseases, which quickly spread from his crew throughout the islands, killing hundreds of Hawaiians.

Cook's arrival in Hawaii happened to coincide with the *makahiki*, an annual harvest festival in honor of the god Lono. He was mistaken by islanders for an earthly manifestation of the god. After stocking provisions, the expedition continued its journey. Failing to find the fabled Northwest Passage through the Arctic, Cook sailed back to Hawaii just over a year later. In a flash-mob battle spawned by growing cross-cultural tensions, including questions about why the god Lono had again returned to the islands, the captain, some of his crew and many Hawaiians were killed.

Shortly after Cook's death, the expedition's ships set sail, landing briefly on O'ahu's North Shore before finally leaving Hawaiian waters on March 15, 1779. After the ships returned to Great Britain, news of

1795	1819	1823
Kamehameha the Great conquers O'ahu, nearly completing the unification of the Hawaiian kingdom. The islands of Kaua'i and Ni'ihau, ruled by Kaumuali'i, successfully resist paying tribute until 1810.	Kamehameha the Great dies, leaving his kingdom to his son Liholiho, with his own favorite wife, Queen Ka'ahumanu, as *kuhina nui* (regent). The ancient *kapu* (taboo) system is abolished and many heiau (temples) are destroyed.	After allowing the first Christian missionaries to land on O'ahu in 1820, Kamehameha II (Liholiho) becomes the first Hawaiian king to travel abroad, dying of measles in London in 1824.

Cook's 'discovery' soon spread throughout Europe and America, opening the floodgates to other foreign explorers, traders and missionaries.

Kamehameha the Great

Meanwhile, a power struggle between Hawaiian chiefs for dominance over the entire island chain was underway. The main rivals were Kamehameha the Great, chief of the Big Island of Hawai'i, and Kahekili, the aging chief of Maui, who had taken control of O'ahu in 1783. After Kahekili died at Waikiki in 1794, his son Kalanikupule inherited O'ahu, while his half-brother Kaeokulani was given Kaua'i. The two ambitious heirs were soon battling each other over control of Maui, creating a rift for Kamehameha to exploit.

In 1795 Kamehameha swept through Maui and Moloka'i, conquering those islands before crossing the channel to O'ahu. The bloody O'ahu campaign started with a fleet of war canoes landing on the shores of Waikiki. Kamehameha then led his warriors up Nu'uanu Valley to meet the entrenched O'auhuan defenders. The O'ahuans, who were prepared for spear-and-stone warfare, panicked when they realized Kamehameha had brought in a handful of Western sharpshooters with modern firearms. What should have been the advantage of high ground turned into a death trap for O'ahuans when they found themselves wedged up into the valley.

Fleeing up the cliffs in retreat, they were forced to make a doomed last stand on a narrow, precipitous ledge, now the Nu'uanu Pali Lookout (see the boxed text, p168). Some O'ahuan warriors, including their king, escaped into the upland forests. When Kalanikupule surfaced a few months

King Kamehameha the Great   JOHN BORTHWICK

later, Kamehameha offered the fallen king as a human sacrifice to his war god Ku. Kamehameha's victory signaled the emergence of Hawai'i as a united kingdom and shifted the seat of power to O'ahu.

1843	1854	1866
Hawaii's only 'invasion' by a foreign power occurs when George Paulet, an upstart British commander upset about a petty land deal involving a British national, sails into Honolulu and seizes O'ahu for six months.	Kamehameha IV ascends to the throne. He passes a law mandating that all children be given a Christian name along with their Hawaiian name; this statute stays on the books until 1967.	The first group of patients with Hansen's disease (formerly known as leprosy) are exiled from O'ahu's Kahili Hospital to Moloka'i's Kalaupapa Peninsula. This policy of forced isolation continues until 1969.

Traders, Whalers & Soul Savers

Around the turn of the 19th century, as ever more foreign ships found their way into Honolulu, a harborside village of thatched houses sprang up. Shops selling food and other simple provisions to the sailors opened along the waterfront. The wealth of trade goods, from iron cannons to ornate furniture, that Yankee clipper ships carried was unlike anything most Hawaiians had ever seen.

In 1809 Kamehameha the Great moved his royal court from Waikiki to Honolulu to better control the growing foreign presence. As the commercial trade flowing into Honolulu grew, the king built harborside warehouses to store his acquisitions, mostly foreign weapons and luxury goods, and introduced harbor fees to fund the royal treasury. British, American, French and Russian traders all used Honolulu to reprovision their ships and to buy 'iliahi (sandalwood), which was a highly lucrative commodity in China, from the chiefs. As a result, 'iliahi was virtually decimated on the islands and remains rare today.

By 1820 whaling ships sailing the Pacific began to pull into Honolulu for supplies, liquor and women. To meet their needs, even more shops, taverns and brothels sprang up around the harbor. It was the perfect place for whalers to transfer their catch to ships heading for the USA, thus allowing them to stay in the Pacific for much longer periods of time. This in turn boosted their annual catch and, accordingly, profits. By the 1840s, Hawaii had become the whaling capital of the Pacific, with hundreds of ships and thousands of whalers stopping in port each year.

To the ire of the whalers, Hawaii's first Christian missionary ship sailed into Honolulu Harbor on April 14, 1820, carrying staunch Calvinists who were set on saving the Hawaiians from their 'heathen ways.' Their timing could not have been better, as the traditional religion that followed the strict *kapu* system had been abolished the year before after the death of Kamehameha the Great. Although both missionaries and the whalers hailed from New England, they had little else in common and were soon at odds. The missionaries were intent on saving souls, while to most sailors there was 'no God west of the Horn.'

The missionaries gained enough influence with Hawaiian royalty to have laws enacted against drunkenness and prostitution. In response, most whaling boats abandoned Honolulu, preferring to land at licentious Lahaina on Maui. By the mid-19th century, it was the sons of missionaries who became the new power brokers on O'ahu. Downtown Honolulu became the headquarters of their corporations, whose board members today read like a roster from the first mission ships.

King Sugar

Ko (sugarcane) arrived in Hawaii with the early Polynesian settlers. In 1835 a Bostonian, William Hooper, saw a business opportunity and set out to establish Hawaii's first sugar plantation. Hooper convinced Honolulu investors to put up the money for his venture and then worked out a deal with Kamehameha III to lease land on Kaua'i. Then he negotiated with *ali'i* for the right to use Hawaiian laborers.

The plantation system, which introduced the concept of growing crops for profit rather than subsistence, marked the advent of capitalism and the introduction of wage labor in Hawaii. As the sugar industry boomed, the

1881	1889	1890
Macadamia trees arrive from Australia in Hawai'i. They are initially planted in the islands as an ornamental tree. The rich, buttery nuts aren't commercially grown on O'ahu until the 1920s.	A group of 150 Hawaiian royalists attempt to overthrow the 'bayonet constitution' by occupying 'Iolani Palace. It was called the Wilcox Rebellion after its part-Hawaiian leader, who surrendered after just one day.	Captain John Kidwell plants smooth cayenne pineapples near Pearl Harbor. Just 10 years later, James Dole arrives in Wahiawa in Central O'ahu and begins large-scale commercial operations. Today, pineapples are the state's biggest crop.

Coat of arms of the Kingdom of Hawai'i, 'Iolani Palace (p59), Honolulu

LINDA CHING

Native Hawaiian population declined, largely as a result of foreign diseases. Wealthy plantation owners started to look overseas for a labor supply of immigrants accustomed to working long days in hot weather, and for whom the low wages would seem like an opportunity. In 1852, wealthy sugar-plantation owners began recruiting laborers from China, then Japan and Portugal.

During the US Civil War, sugar exports to Union states on the mainland soared, making plantation owners wealthy and powerful. After Hawaii's 1898 annexation to the USA resulted in growing restrictions on Chinese and Japanese immigration, plantation owners turned to Puerto Rico, Korea and the Philippines. Most immigrants intended to return to their homelands after their labor contracts expired, but ended up staying in the islands. For an in-depth look at plantation life on O'ahu, visit Hawaii's Plantation Village (p230) in Waipahu, a sleepy former plantation town with a now-defunct mill.

A Capital City

In 1845 Kamehameha III, Hawai'i's first Christian king, moved the capital of the kingdom from Maui to Honolulu, where he established the first national legislature and provided for a supreme court. Though still a frontier town with dusty streets and simple wooden buildings, Honolulu suddenly became the commercial and political center of the islands.

In 1848 foreign missionaries convinced the king to pass a sweeping land-reform act called the Great Mahele, which also established religious freedom and gave all male citizens the right to vote. More significantly, it permanently altered the Hawaiian concept of land rights. For the first time, land became a commodity that could be bought and sold.

Although the act was intended to turn Hawaii into a country of small farms, in the end few chiefs or commoners completed the necessary paperwork to register their holdings or

1893	1900	1901
Queen Lili'uokalani overthrown. The son of an American missionary declares himself leader of the provisional government. A contingent of US sailors comes ashore, marching on 'Iolani Palace and aiming guns at the queen's residence.	After Hawaii becomes a US territory, the Native Hawaiian population of the islands sinks to its lowest point, with fewer than 40,000 part or full-blooded Hawaiians remaining in the islands.	The Moana Hotel, Waikiki's first tourist hotel, opens to guests arriving at Honolulu Harbor on cruise ships. The resort is built atop a former royal Hawaiian compound.

paid property taxes. In 1850 purchasing land was opened to foreigners, who jumped at the opportunity, and before islanders could clearly grasp the concept of private land ownership, there was little land left to own. Native Hawaiians became a largely landless people, often drifting into Honolulu's ghettos.

Many missionaries ended up with sizable tracts of land, and more than a few left the church to devote themselves to their new estates. By then, Honolulu had a prominent foreign community composed largely of US and British expats. These foreigners opened businesses and schools, started newspapers and, more importantly, landed powerful government positions as ministry officials and consuls to the king. As the city continued to grow, Westerners wrested increasing control over island affairs from the Hawaiians, and the powers of Kamehameha the Great's successors eroded.

The Fall of the Monarchy

Known as the Merrie Monarch, King David Kalakaua nevertheless reigned in troubled times, from 1874 until 1891. An impassioned Hawaiian revivalist, Kalakaua brought back the hula, reversing decades of missionary repression and composed the national anthem 'Hawaii Pono'i,' now the state's official song. He also tried to ensure a degree of self-rule for Native Hawaiians, who had become a minority in their own land.

The king proved himself a successful diplomat by traveling to Washington DC, and persuading President Ulysses Grant to accept a treaty giving Hawaii's sugar growers tariff-free access to US markets. In so doing, he temporarily gained the support of powerful sugar-plantation owners, who controlled most of O'ahu's land. Visits with other foreign monarchs gave Kalakaua a taste for royal pageantry. He was perceived by many influential foreigners as a lavish spender, fond of all-night drinking bouts and throwing parties, including at 'Iolani Palace (p59), built in 1882.

As Kalakaua incurred huge debts, he became less popular with the sugar barons. In 1887 white businessmen formed the Hawaiian League and developed their own armies, which stood ready to overthrow Kalakaua. The league presented the king with a list of demands and forced him to accept a new 'bayonet constitution' strictly limiting his powers. It also limited voting rights to property owners, thus disenfranchising most Native Hawaiians. Kalakaua died four years later in San Francisco.

The End of a Kingdom

Kalakaua was succeeded by his sister, Lili'uokalani, wife of O'ahu's governor John O Dominis. Queen Lili'uokalani was more determined than her brother to strengthen the power of the monarchy. In January 1893, as she was preparing to proclaim a new constitution to restore royal powers, a group of armed US businessmen occupied Hawaii's Supreme Court and declared the monarchy overthrown. They announced a provisional government, led by Sanford Dole, son of a missionary family.

Opting to avoid bloodshed, the queen stepped down. The provisional government immediately requested annexation from the US, while the queen traveled to Washington DC to appeal for restoration of the monarchy. She made a favorable impression on the US media, which largely caricatured those involved in the overthrow as greedy buffoons. President Cleveland ordered that the US flag be taken down at 'Iolani Palace and the queen restored to her throne.

1912	1936	1941
Champion surfer Duke Kahanamoku wins his first gold medal in the 100m freestyle swim at the Stockholm Olympics. Afterwards, he travels to the US mainland and Australia to give surfing exhibitions.	Pan American airlines flies the first passenger flights from the US mainland to Hawaii. This aviation milestone ushers in the transpacific jet age and mass tourism on O'ahu, mainly at Waikiki Beach.	Japanese forces stage surprise attack on Pearl Harbor, catapulting the USA into WWII. Under martial law, approximately 1250 Japanese residents of Hawaii are forced into internment camps on O'ahu and the Big Island of Hawai'i.

The provisional government turned a deaf ear, declaring that President Cleveland was meddling in 'Hawaiian' affairs. On July 4, 1894, Dole stood on the steps of 'Iolani Palace and announced that Hawaii was now a republic and he was its president. In 1895 a group of Hawaiian royalists attempted a counter-revolution that was quickly quashed. Although there was no evidence that she was aware of the royalists' attempt to restore her, Lili'uokalani was accused of being a conspirator and arrested.

To humiliate her, the queen was tried in her own palace and referred to only as Mrs John O Dominis. She was fined $5000 and sentenced to five years of hard labor, later reduced to house arrest. After being pardoned in 1896, Lili'uokalani spent the rest of her life in her husband's residence, Washington Place (p63), a block from the palace. When Lili'uokalani died of a stroke in 1917, nearly all of Honolulu came out for the funeral procession. To many islanders, Lili'uokalani was still their queen.

ANNEXATION, WAR & STATEHOOD

During the Spanish-American War of 1898, the islands took on new strategic importance, being located approximately midway between the US and its newly acquired possession, the Philippines. After annexation was approved by the US Congress on July 7, 1898, Hawaii entered the 20th century as a US territory.

To the chagrin of many Hawaiians, President McKinley appointed Sanford Dole the first territorial governor. The US Navy quickly established a Pacific headquarters at Pearl Harbor and built Schofield Barracks, at that time the largest US army base in the world. The military soon became the leading sector of O'ahu's economy, followed by tourism, with commercial flights connecting Honolulu with the mainland in 1936.

On December 7, 1941, a wave of Japanese bombers attacked Pearl Harbor (p143), jolting the USA into WWII. The war brought Hawaii closer to the center stage of American culture and politics. Three decades had passed since Prince Jonah Kuhio Kalaniana'ole, Hawaii's first delegate to the US Congress, introduced a Hawaii statehood bill in 1919. It received a cool reception in Washington DC, and there were mixed feelings in Hawaii as well.

Even after the war, Hawaii was seen as too much of a racial melting pot for many US politicians to support statehood, particularly those from segregationist southern states. In March 1959 the US Congress finally passed legislation to grant Hawaii statehood. On June 27 a plebiscite was held in Hawaii, with more than 90% of the islanders voting for statehood. Hawaii became the USA's 50th state on August 21, 1959.

THE HAWAIIAN RENAISSANCE

The 1970s saw a resurgence of Hawaiian culture not seen since the reign of King Kalakaua. The retracing of ancient Polynesian migration routes by the *Hokule'a* was certainly a catalyst. So was the Protect Kaho'olawe 'Ohana (PKO), a small grassroots political activist group that began protesting the bombing of Kaho'olawe, an island off Maui taken over by the US military during WWII and used for bombing target practice for decades afterward.

A focal point of the Hawaiian renaissance has been a revival of the Hawaiian language. By the 1970s, the pool of fluent Hawaiian

1967	1971	1993
Tourism in Hawaii reaches a milestone with one million visitors arriving in a single year. Sugar production peaks at about the same time, with 1.23 million tons of raw sugarcane grown statewide.	The first Hawaiian Masters surfing competition, a precursor to the Triple Crown of Surfing, is held at Sunset Beach on O'ahu's North Shore. Legendary big-wave rider Eddie Aikau is named O'ahu's Lifeguard of the Year.	President Clinton signs 'Apology Resolution,' recognizing the illegal overthrow of the kingdom almost exactly 100 years earlier. The bill acknowledges that 'the Native Hawaiian people never directly relinquished...their claims to inherent sovereignty as a people.'

Traditional drumming at the Polynesian Cultural Center (p192), La'ie   JOHN BORTHWICK

speakers had dropped to under a thousand people statewide. Hawaiian-language immersion schools began to emerge and the University of Hawai'i started offering Hawaiian-language classes. Leading contemporary musicians also started singing in the Hawaiian language. *Hula halau* (hula schools) revived interest in Hawaiian-language chants and dances, especially among young men. Many islanders have since relearned nearly lost arts, such as the making of *kapa* (bark cloth), drums, feather lei, wooden bowls and other crafts.

In 1993, a heightened consciousness created by the centennial anniversary of Queen Lili'uokalani's overthrow served as a rallying point for a fractured Hawaiian sovereignty movement, intent on righting past wrongs. Diverse sovereignty groups exist, but a consensus on what form sovereignty should take has yet to emerge. Some seek federal recognition of Native Hawaiians as an indigenous people and a nation-within-a-nation political model similar to some Native American tribes on the US mainland.

1996	2000	2008
The last remaining sugar mill on O'ahu, built at Waialua on the North Shore in 1898, closes its doors after rising labor costs drive the sugar industry to Mexico and the Philippines.	Senator Daniel Akaka first introduces the Native Hawaiian Government Reorganization Act (Akaka Bill), which recognizes Hawaiians' indigenous status and allows limited self-governance. Subsequent revisions of the bill have repeatedly stalled in Congress.	Barack Obama, who was born and grew up in Honolulu, is elected as the 44th US President. Just before assuming office, he takes a postcampaign vacation with his family in Kailua, on O'ahu's Windward Coast.

THE CULTURE

ISLAND IDENTITY

Honolulu is 'the city,' not only for those who live on O'ahu but for all of Hawaii. It has a slower pace than its mainland counterparts, but can be surprisingly cosmopolitan. Honolulu residents see themselves as being at the center of everything. They deal with the traffic jams and high-rises because with them come the better-paying jobs, vibrant arts and cultural scenes, and hip shops and nightlife.

Honolulu's ritzier suburbs sprawl along the coast southeast of Honolulu, while many of the island's military bases are located west around Pearl Harbor and in the 'Ewa area.

If it weren't for the occasional ride into the city to pick up supplies, the lifestyle of rural O'ahuans is as 'small town' as you'll find anywhere else in Hawaii. O'ahu's Windward Coast, North Shore and Leeward Coast are considered 'the country.' Many people here take pride in their rural roots.

While many O'ahu residents see themselves as having a broader regional identity – from the North Shore, from the Wai'anae Coast – their closest connection is to their hometown. When the late Israel 'Bruddah Iz' Kamakawiwo'ole, leader of the Ni'ihau Sons of Makaha band, sang about the home he loved, he described scenes of Makaha. Back in Honolulu, locals tend to categorize one another by high school. ('Where you wen' grad?' is a standard opening line upon meeting for the first time.)

Politically, most voters are middle-of-the-road Democrats who vote along party, racial, ethnic, seniority and local/nonlocal lines. In everyday life, most people prefer to avoid heated arguments and don't jump into a controversial topic just to argue the point. At community meetings and activist rallies, the most vocal liberals are often mainland transplants. But as more mainlanders settle on O'ahu, especially around Kailua and Kane'ohe on the Windward Coast, traditional stereotypes are fading.

O'ahuans will almost never walk by somebody they know without stopping to ask how they're doing, looking like they really want to know the answer. No matter what else they may or may not have in common, people band together when one of their own vaults onto the national stage, like US President Barack Obama or golfer Michelle Wie. Win or lose, locals are usually loyal to their 'ohana (extended family).

LIFESTYLE

On O'ahu, 'ohana is central to the island lifestyle. 'Ohana includes all relatives, as well as close family friends. Growing up, the words 'auntie' and 'uncle' are used to refer to older people who are near and dear, whether by the bonds of friendship or blood. Weekends are typically set aside for family outings to beaches and parks.

O'ahuans are early risers, taking a run along the Ala Wai Canal or hitting the waves before heading to the office. The workaholic routine common elsewhere in the US is the exception here, even though

WHO ARE YOU?

- **Haole** White person (except local Portuguese). Further defined as 'mainland haole' or 'local haole.'
- **Hapa** Person of mixed ancestry, most commonly referring to *hapa haole*, who are part white and part Asian.
- **Hawaiian** Person of Native Hawaiian ancestry. It's a faux pas to call any Hawaii resident 'Hawaiian' (as you would a Californian), thus ignoring the existence of an indigenous people.
- **Kama'aina** Person who is native to a particular place (*kama'aina* literally translates to 'child of the land'). In the retail context, 'kama'aina discounts' apply to any Hawaii resident (ie anyone with a state driver's license).
- **Local** Person who grew up in Hawaii. To call a transplant 'almost local' is a compliment, despite its emphasis on the insider-outsider mentality.
- **Transplant** Person who moves to the islands as an adult; can never become 'local.'

O'ahu has more surf spots than any other Hawaiian island

RAY LASKOWITZ

wages don't measure up to the high cost of living in Hawaii. Locals tend toward conventional 'American dream' lives, meaning marriage, kids, a modest home and a stable 40-hour-per-week job with free nights and weekends. Mainland transplants are often here for other reasons: retirement; a dream B&B, art gallery or surf shop; or youthful experimentation by global nomads.

Wherever they're from, islanders appear more laid-back than their mainland cousins. For starters, they dress more casually. On weekends, Honolulu city slickers can be found hanging at Ala Moana Beach wearing a T-shirt, shorts and those ubiquitous flip-flops known as rubbah slippahs. Aloha shirts are seriously appropriate for business and social functions, but only if made of cotton or silk and, ideally, a reverse-print design. The muumuu as street attire has been outmoded for decades, but it's still fitting for hula dancers or *tutu* (grandmothers).

O'ahuans are generally accepting of other people, which helps explain the mosaic of diverse races and international cultures that make up island society. Sexual orientation is not a commonly debated issue, but tolerance is more widespread in Honolulu and Waikiki than in some tight-knit rural communities.

Traditional Hawaiian culture is an integral part of the social fabric on O'ahu. Hawaiian language classes are thriving, local artists and craftspeople are returning to traditional mediums and themes, and hula classes focus more on the nuances behind hand movements and facial expressions than on the dramatic hip shaking that sells dinner-show tickets. You'll still encounter a measure of Hawaiiana that seems almost a parody of island culture, from plastic lei to theme-park luau shows, especially in Waikiki.

A federal government crackdown on the growing of *pakalolo* (marijuana) in the 1980s successfully pushed growers underground, forcing them to abandon their fields. With the loss of the marijuana crop on the streets, crystal meth (ice) became rampant in the 1990s, where it has wreaked havoc in both the city and rural communities. Homelessness and the lack of affordable housing are other pressing social problems, with hundreds of O'ahuans taking shelter nightly on beaches, especially along the Wai'anae Coast and increasingly at Waikiki Beach. Honolulu's Chinatown still has some seedy edges, just like in the 19th-century whaling days, with skid rows of drug addicts, prostitutes and homeless panhandlers.

POPULATION

With more than 905,000 residents in the City and County of Honolulu (ie the entire island), O'ahu accounts for over 70% of Hawaii's total population. But official statistics and the number of people who are actually on O'ahu at any one time are two different realities. On any given day, there are around 80,000 tourists on O'ahu – in the tourist mecca of Waikiki, for example, there are two tourists for every resident. Another largely transient group, US military personnel and their dependents, adds approximately 90,000 more people. Add a couple of thousand more for overlaying flight crews and you begin to get a more accurate glimpse of O'ahu's population. Some locals feel inundated by O'ahu's 'unofficial residents,' and there are mixed feelings about both tourism and the military. But because tourism is concentrated in Waikiki, it's the military, which controls vast tracts of land, that tends to be the larger issue.

MULTICULTURALISM

Honolulu is the most ethnically diverse city in America. Since no one ethnic group comprises more than half of the population, everyone belongs to a minority. On average, all islanders have a 50/50 chance of marrying someone of a race different from their own, and the majority of children born here are *hapa* (of mixed blood). Don't assume an islander's racial identity by their surname, as some Native Hawaiians have European or Asian names, and vice versa.

Diversity in Hawaii means something different to on the mainland, where Latino and African American populations often predominate. Here, the major ethnic groups are rooted in history: Native Hawaiians, the indigenous people (although not officially recognized as such by the US federal government); Europeans, whose presence traces back to the early 19th-century arrival of Christian missionaries; and plantation-era immigrants, primarily from China, Japan, the Philippines and Portugal.

On Hawaii's plantations, a unique pidgin English developed, enabling different racial groups of laborers to communicate with one another. Hawaiian pidgin is still alive in the islands today (see the boxed text, p256). Another legacy of plantation life, in which wealthy owners were usually the *haole* (white) descendants of powerful missionary families, is some lingering resentment against the perceived ingrained privileges of *haole*.

Still, ethnic strife on O'ahu is minimal compared with racial tensions on the mainland. Forget political correctness too, as locals good-naturedly joke about island racial stereotypes (eg talkative Portuguese, stingy Chinese, goody-goody Japanese, know-it-all *haole*). When nonlocals enter the picture, the balance shifts. Although locals are generally warm and gracious to outsiders who show respect for island ways, be aware of the possibility of threats and violence at remote, locals-only beach parks.

RELIGION

Religion permeated every aspect of daily life in ancient Hawaiian society, which was dictated by strict religious regulations known as the *kapu* (taboo) system. *Kapu* forbade commoners from eating the same food or even walking the same ground as *ali'i*, who were representatives of the gods. For someone caught breaking a major *kapu*, the punishment could be death. For more about Hawaiian gods and heiau (temples), see p243.

Kamehameha the Great was the last king to live by the old religion. After his death many Hawaiians became willing converts to Christianity. While traditional beliefs went underground, some of the philosophy endured, often expressed as *aloha 'aina* (literally, 'love of the land'). The modern Hawaiian sovereignty movement and antidevelopment activism are rooted in *aloha 'aina,* and public ceremonies such as ground-breaking, today often include a *kahuna* (priest) to bless the land.

Almost all of O'ahu's ancient religious sites were chosen for the *mana* (power) of the land. In some places, traditionalists still perform rituals and leave offerings – a *ti* leaf wrapped around a stone and placed on a heiau wall, for example. The spirituality of old Hawaii also lives in the arts, most notably in sacred *hula kahiko.*

Today most people in Hawaii do not claim adherence to a particular faith, and the religious milieu is tolerant rather than dogmatic. Roman Catholics are the largest denomination. As mainstream Protestant Christianity struggles with declining membership, evangelical churches and the Mormon community based in Laiʻe on the Windward Coast are burgeoning. Hawaii has the highest percentage of Buddhists of any US state, with many temples functioning as lively community centers.

ARTS
Music

Tune your rental-car radio to Oʻahu's local stations and you'll hear everything from contemporary Hawaiian folk rock and country to reggae-inspired Jawaiian sounds. The most famous island musician is the late Israel Kamakawiwoʻole, whose *Facing Future* is Hawaii's all-time bestselling album. When he died in 1997, his body lay in state at the Capitol in Honolulu, an honor bestowed only on two others before him.

The guitar was first introduced to the islands by Spanish cowboys in the 1830s. Hawaiians made it their own in the late 1880s when Oʻahu-born Joseph Kekuku started experimenting with playing a guitar on his lap by sliding a pocket knife or comb across the strings, ultimately inventing the steel guitar, which lifts the strings off the fretboard using a movable steel slide, creating a signature smooth sound.

Still, the instrument most commonly associated with Hawaii is the ukulele. The ukulele is derived from the *braguinha,* a Portuguese instrument introduced to Hawaii during the late-19th-century plantation era. ʻUkulele means 'jumping flea' in Hawaiian, after the way players' deft fingers swiftly 'jump' around the strings.

Both the ukulele and the steel guitar contribute to the lighthearted *hapa haole* Hawaiian tunes with English lyrics that were popularized in Hawaii after the 1930s, of which 'My Little Grass Shack' and 'Lovely Hula Hands' are classic examples. With the *Hawaii Calls* radio show, which was broadcast worldwide for 40 years from Waikiki's Moana Hotel, this music became instantly recognizable as Hawaiian.

Since the mid-20th century, the Hawaiian steel guitar has usually been played with slack key *(ki hoʻalu)* tunings, in which the thumb plays the bass and rhythm chords, while the fingers play the melody and improvisations, in a picked style. The legendary Gabby Pahinui launched the modern slack key era with his first recording in 1946. Over the years, he played with the legendary Sons of Hawaiʻi and his home

The Hawaiian ukulele was derived from a Portuguese instrument

ANN CECIL

in Waimanalo on the Windward Coast became a mecca for backyard jam sessions. Another pioneering slack key master was Sonny Chillingworth. Today, the slack key tradition lives on in Keola Beamer, Led Ka'apana and Cyril Pahinui, among others.

Hawaiian vocalists are known for a distinctive falsetto style called *ha'i,* which stresses the breaks between lower and upper registers. Among women, the unquestioned master was the late Aunty Genoa Keawe, whose impossibly long-held notes in the song 'Alika' set the standard (and set it high). Her O'ahu-born *'ohana* still performs in Waikiki (see p138) and some say her granddaughter (see the boxed text, p122) sounds just like Genoa in her younger days.

For more contemporary Hawaiian music, check out recent winners of the **Na Hoku Hanohano Awards** (www.nahokuhanohano.org), Hawaii's version of the Grammies.

Hula

In ancient Hawaii, hula was a religious offering to the gods. Dancers used hand gestures, facial expression and rhythmic movement to illustrate historical events, legendary tales and celebrated accomplishments of *ali'i.* Dances were performed to drum beats and rhythmic chants, which served as oral history for the ancient Hawaiians, who had no written language. Hula dancers wore *kapa* (pounded-bark cloth), not the stereotypical grass skirts seen nowadays.

When Christian missionaries arrived, they viewed hula dancing as licentious and suppressed it. The hula might have been lost forever if King Kalakaua, the Merrie Monarch, had not revived it in the late 19th century. Some of today's commercial hula shows, which emphasize swaying hips and Vegas showgirl–style outfits, might be entertaining but they're not 'real' hula. Serious students join a *hula halau* (hula school),

ISLAND SOUNDS

O'ahu's leading local musicians play regular free shows at Honolulu and Waikiki hotels, restaurant lounges, bars and even shopping malls (see p137). Here are some famous names to watch out for.

- **Jake Shimabukuro** (www.jakeshimabukuro.com) The 'Jimi Hendrix of the uke' has been lured away from the islands by record companies, but occasionally comes back to play live shows in his hometown, Honolulu.
- **Brothers Cazimero** O'ahu-born, heritage-conscious duo (12-string guitar and bass) played in Peter Moon's legendary Sunday Manoa band in the early 1970s.
- **Henry Kapono** Kapahulu-born singer-songwriter Henry Kapono Ka'aihue is O'ahu's renaissance man, putting out innovative Hawaiian rock albums since the 1970s.
- **Kapena** (www.kapena.com) Kapena may not have won O'ahu's high-school battle of the bands back in the day, but founding member Kelly Boy De Lima is a ukulele star.
- **Jerry Santos and Olomana** Traditional and contemporary ukulele and falsetto performers from Windward O'ahu have been performing around the island for decades.
- **Martin Pahinui** The son of the late slack key master Gabby Pahinui is a gifted vocalist and often performs with equally talented guitarist George Kuo and former Royal Hawaiian Band leader Aaron Mahi.
- **Sam Kapu III** Part of a musical dynasty, Sam Kapu mainly performs traditional ukulele music, as well as contemporary three-part harmonies, with his trio.
- **Po'okela** Contemporary musical trio fronted by Honolulu-born slack key artist Greg Sardinha, who studied with the late, great steel-guitar player Jerry Byrd.
- **Makana** This O'ahu-born singer-songwriter, who studied guitar with Sonny Chillingworth, is a leading proponent of slack key fusion rock.
- **Ka'ala Boys** Honolulu's most popular Jawaiian island reggae group.

If you miss out on seeing these musicians live, browse their recordings at **Mountain Apple Company** (www.mountainapplecompany.com) or **Mele.com** (www.mele.com).

where they undergo rigorous training and adopt hula as a life practice. Dancers learn to control every body part, as subtle differences in gestures can entirely change the meanings.

In hula competitions, dancers vie in *kahiko* (ancient) and *'auana* (modern) categories. *Kahiko* performances are raw and primordial, accompanied only by chanting. Traditional hula instruments still used today include gourd rattles, stone castanets and sharkskin-topped drums. Accompanied by harmonious singing and stringed instruments, *'auana* is more mainstream, contemporary hula, with Western-influenced dresses and pants, sinuous arm movements and smiling faces. Waikiki is the best place to catch both kinds of hula performances, including at the Kuhio Beach Torch Lighting & Hula Show (p137).

Traditional hula dancing   LEE FOSTER

Hawaiian Art & Crafts

Woodworking is an ancient Hawaiian skill. Some of the most prized items today are native-wood bowls, often made of beautifully grained tropical hardwoods such as koa and milo. Hawaiian bowls are not decorated or ornate, but are shaped to bring out the natural beauty of the wood. The thinner and lighter the bowl, the finer the artistry and the greater the value. Don't be fooled by cheap monkeypod bowls imported from the Philippines.

Lei making is a more transitory ancient art form. Locals continue to wear leis for special events such as weddings and public ceremonies. Although the leis most visitors wear are made of fragrant flowers such as plumeria or orchids, traditional leis are made of *mokihana* berries and maile leaves. Beware that most *kukui* (candlenut) leis are cheap imports. Buy freshly made flower leis in Chinatown at Cindy's Lei Shop (p95). For intricately crafted feather leis, drop by Waikiki's Na Lima Mili Hulu No'eau (p124).

With vibrant colors and graphic patterns based on indigenous *kapa* (pounded-bark cloth) designs, Hawaiian appliqué quilts possess striking beauty. Each part has meaning and each design was once thought to contain the very spirit of the crafter. At the center of each quilt is the *piko* (navel). An open center is seen as a gateway linking the spiritual world and the physical one, while a solid core symbolizes the strength of the family. Fruits and plants have meaning, too, for example, *'ulu* (breadfruit) for abundance and *kalo* (taro) for strength. If you want to buy one of these treasures, expect to pay thousands of dollars. If prices are low, the quilts were likely made in the Philippines. To try your own hand, you can learn from experienced Hawaiian quilters during classes organized by **Poakalani & Co** (www.nvo.com/poakalani).

Many modern painters, printmakers, photographers and graphic and textile artists draw inspiration from Hawaii's rich cultural heritage, as showcased at the multimedia Hawai'i State Art Museum (p61) in downtown Honolulu. More contemporary island art galleries await in nearby Chinatown; see the boxed text, p96.

Literature

Before the Hawaiian renaissance of the 1970s, Hawaii's literary canon was dominated by foreign writers, including James Michener's historical saga *Hawaii* and Paul Theroux's *Hotel Honolulu,* about a washed-up writer who manages a run-down Waikiki hotel. For a more moving Hawaiian historical epic, try O'ahu-born Kiana Davenport's *Shark Dialogues*. For recommended travel literature, see p271.

Contemporary literature by island-born writers doesn't exoticize Hawaii, but instead examines the everyday complexities of island life. The biannual journal published by **Bamboo Ridge Press** (www.bamboo ridge.com) has launched many local writers' careers. Some have hit the national scene, such as Lois-Ann Yamanaka, author of the award-winning *Saturday Night at the Pahala Theatre* (1993), a breakthrough collection of poems written in Hawaiian pidgin. Another good introduction to the pidgin vernacular is *Growing Up Local: An Anthology of Poetry and Prose from Hawai'i*, published by **University of Hawai'i Press** (www.uhpress.hawaii.edu).

Cinema & TV

O'ahu reaps huge financial benefits from its film industry, but unless homegrown films are produced, expect to see the same island themes and stereotypes (and fake pidgin accents). The island has long captured Hollywood's imagination as a sultry, carefree paradise, as shown in *Waikiki Wedding* (1937) starring Bing Crosby, Elvis Presley's *Blue Hawaii* (1961) and WWII dramas like the classic *From Here to Eternity* (1953) or *Pearl Harbor* (2001). The kitschy 1960s, '70s and '80s TV shows *Hawaii Five-0* and *Magnum PI* were also shot here. Many Hollywood feature films and TV shows today use O'ahu to stand in for more exotic locales, like in *Jurassic Park* (1993) and the smash-hit TV series *Lost*, filmed primarily at Kualoa Ranch (p184) and at the North Shore's Mokule'ia Beach (p212). For more *Lost* filming locations, take the **Lost Virtual Tour** (www.lostvirtualtour.com).

LEARN THE LINGO

While English is the standard language used in Hawaii, you'll quickly realize that it's a far cry from mainland English. Here, locals use a combination of pidgin, Hawaiian and English (with a dose of Japanese and Chinese, too).

It sounds more challenging than it is. Local kids grow up with this hodgepodge but they're taught in public schools to use standard English in academic and professional settings. Most agree with this distinction, but a once-renegade, now-respected group called **Da Pidgin Coup at the University of Hawai'i** (www.hawaii.edu/satocenter/dapidgincoup.html) advocates recognition of pidgin (which it calls Hawai'i Creole English) as a legitimate language.

The best-known champion of pidgin use is Lee Tonouchi, a writer, playwright and lecturer at Kapi'olani Community College on O'ahu, who was hired in the English department with an application written entirely in pidgin. His books include *Da Word* (short stories), *Living Pidgin: Contemplations on Pidgin Culture* (essays) and *Da Kine Dictionary* (pictorial dictionary). In addition to Tonouchi's titles, there's Douglas Simonson's classic *Pidgin To Da Max*, a laugh-out-loud cartoon dictionary.

We offer a free downloadable *Hawaiian Language & Glossary* supplement at www.lonely planet.com/hawaiian-language. For now, here are some common words and phrases.

Hawaiian

aloha – love, hello, welcome, goodbye
hale – house
kane – man
kapu – taboo, restricted, no trespassing
mahalo – thank you
makai – a directional, toward the sea
mauka – a directional, toward the mountains (inland)
pau – finished, completed
pono – goodness, justice, responsibility
wahine – woman

Pidgin

brah – shortened form of *braddah* (brother)
chicken skin – goose bumps from cold, fear, thrill
coconut wireless – the 'grapevine', local gossip channels
da kine – whatchamacallit; used whenever you can't think of the appropriate word
fo' real? – Really? Are you kidding me?
high makamaka – stuck-up, snooty, pretentious; literally 'high eyes', meaning head in the air
howzit? – Hey, how's it going? As in 'Eh, howzit brah?'
rubbah slippahs – literally 'rubber slippers,' flip-flops
talk story – chitchat or any casual conversation
to da max – used as an adjective or adverb to add emphasis, as in 'Da waves was big to da max!'

FOOD
& DRINK

Forget about pineapple upside-down cake and blue cocktails. Honolulu is the proud culinary capital of the Hawaiian Islands, with a multicultural taste explosion rooted in the island's natural bounty. Before human contact, O'ahu's edibles were meager, just ferns and berries. The first Polynesians brought nourishing staples such as taro, sweet potato, sugarcane and coconut, plus pigs and chickens. From the 19th century, plantation immigrants added global flavors into the mix – Japanese rice, Chinese noodles, Portuguese sweet bread. Over time these cuisines fused to become simply 'local.' So, be brave and eat everything in sight. It's all *'ono grinds* (roughly, 'good eats').

STAPLES & SPECIALTIES

Native Hawaiian

With rich, earthy flavors and indigenous Polynesian ingredients, Hawaiian cuisine is an acquired taste. *Kalua* pig (traditionally roasted in an underground pit layered with hot stones, banana trunks and *ti* leaves) and starchy poi (a gooey, purplish paste pounded from cooked taro roots) are the 'meat and potatoes' of Native Hawaiian cooking. Locals describe the consistency of the latter as one-, two- or three-finger poi, indicating how many fingers are required to scoop it from bowl to mouth.

Poi is nutritious and easily digestible, but still tastes relatively bland – its purpose is to serve as a counterpoint to the stronger flavors of other dishes, such as *lomilomi* salmon (minced, salted salmon with diced tomato and green onion) or *laulau* (a bundle of pork, chicken or fish wrapped in taro and *ti* leaves and steamed). Other savory Hawaiian preparations include baked *'ulu* (breadfruit), *limu* (seaweed), *'opihi* (tiny limpet shells picked off reefs at low tide) and *pipi kaula* (beef jerky). *Haupia* is a firm dessert pudding made of coconut cream thickened with cornstarch or arrowroot.

Because it's harder to find than other ethnic cuisines, many visitors only get a taste of traditional Hawaiian food at a touristy luau (p139). But a few of O'ahu's neighborhood restaurants still specialize in Hawaiian food, including Helena's Hawaiian Food (p89) and Ono Hawaiian Foods (p121).

Hawaii Regional Cuisine

In the early 1990s, a pioneering movement dubbed Hawaii Regional cuisine took off. This type of cooking incorporates fresh island ingredients from local farmers, ranchers and fishers; borrows liberally from Hawaii's ethnic groups; and is marked by creative fusion combinations such as Peking duck in ginger-*liliko'i* (passion fruit) sauce.

Once Hawaii Regional cuisine hit the gourmet radar, some of its founding chefs, including Alan Wong, Roy Yamaguchi and Sam Choy, became celebrities. Many restaurateurs have tried to join the bandwagon, so you'll see the same catchword preparations on many menus: macadamia-crusted fish, sugarcane-skewered shrimp, pineapple-topped *anything*. These wannabes often try too hard, dousing dishes in too many sauces and competing flavors.

The best Hawaii Regional cuisine still focuses on seasonally fresh, locally grown and often organic ingredients, such as 'Nalo greens and grass-fed beef from the North Shore's free-range cattle. Keep in mind that Hawaii Regional cuisine is a regional version of Pacific Rim fusion cooking. Restaurants that still source local ingredients but de-emphasize Asian fusion are often classified as 'island contemporary,' for example, Town (p90) in Honolulu.

Local Food

Cheap, filling and tasty, local food is the stuff of cravings and comfort. Its building blocks are in the plate lunch, which includes 'two scoop rice,' a scoop of mayonnaise-laden macaroni salad and your choice of a hot protein entree such as fried mahimahi, teriyaki chicken or *kalbi* short ribs. Nonlocals might find plate lunches unbelievably calorie-laden and unhealthy, but tossed greens and brown rice are occasionally offered.

Top Picks

FOODIE FAVES

- Roy's – Waikiki Beach (p119)
- Alan Wong's Pineapple Room (p87)
- Town (p90)
- Hiroshi Eurasian Tapas (p83)
- Sansei Seafood Restaurant & Sushi Bar (p118)
- Duc's Bistro (p85)

Top Picks

O'AHU PLATE LUNCHES

- Me BBQ (p117)
- Da Spot (p85)
- Poke Stop (p232)
- Uahi Island Grill (p176)
- Waiahole Poi Factory (p184)

CRACK FOR YOUR SWEET TOOTH

Forget candy bars. The most popular snack on O'ahu is crack seed, a Chinese food that can be sweet, sour, salty, spicy or some combination of the four. Like Coca-Cola or curry, the various flavors of crack seed are impossible to describe. Just one taste, though, and you'll be hooked.

Crack seed, sold in supermarkets, convenience stores and candy shops, is often made from dried fruits such as plums, cherries, mangoes or lemons. The most popular – and most overwhelming to the uninitiated – is *li hing mui*. These days powdered *li hing mui* – sour enough to pucker the most stoic of faces – is used to spice up just about everything, from cupcakes and fried chicken to fresh-fruit smoothies and margaritas.

If your taste buds are ready, Honolulu's Ala Moana Center (see the boxed text, p94) is home to the **Crack Seed Center** (☎ 949-7200; www.crackseedcenter.com), selling an amazing variety of crack seed for more than 40 years.

Another local favorite is *poke,* which is bite-sized cubes of raw fish typically marinated in *shōyu* (soy sauce), oil, chili peppers, green onions and seaweed, though you'll find all kinds of variations on that theme. Specialty shops include the Poke Stop (p232), west of Pearl Harbor, and Ono Seafood (p122) in Waikiki.

Saimin is an island-style soup of chewy Chinese egg noodles and Japanese broth, garnished with green onion, dried nori or perhaps *kamaboko* (pureed, steamed fish cake). Gigantic *manapua,* the local version of Chinese *bao* (steamed or baked buns), feature a creative variety of fillings, from *char siu* (barbecued pork) to black sugar. Taste 'em at Chinatown's Royal Kitchen (p83) or Chun Wah Kam Noodle Factory (p147), near Pearl Harbor. Finally, you can't go home without trying *loco moco.* This local drive-in classic is a mountain of rice, eggs and usually a hamburger patty, all smothered in gravy.

Finally, on a hot day, nothing beats a mound of Hawaii shave ice, packed into a cup and drenched with sweet syrups in an eye-popping rainbow of hues. Purists stick with only ice but, for added decadence, ask for sweet azuki beans or ice cream underneath.

DRINKS

Hawaii is the only state in the USA to grow coffee. The finest coffee beans come from the Big Island's Kona district. Only 100% Kona coffee has gourmet cachet, costing up to $40 per pound. O'ahu coffee, known as Waialua coffee, is grown on the North

Shore by Dole corporation, which owns the pineapple fields of Central O'ahu.

Also on the North Shore, **Waialua Soda Works** (www.waialuasodaworks.com), a husband-and-wife operation, bottles old-fashioned soda pop that's naturally flavored with local

Hawaiian coffee is among the best RAY LASKOWITZ

ingredients like pineapple, mango, *liliko'i* and honey. It's sold in supermarkets and local-food eateries around O'ahu.

Hawaii-made fruit juices, including passion fruit, orange and guava (aka POG), can readily be found at supermarkets, but they tend to be sugary. For more pure, often organic and locally harvested juices, check out farmers markets, natural-food stores and smoothie bars like Honolulu's Vita Juice (p82) and Kailua's Lanikai Juice (p177) in Windward O'ahu.

Two traditional Hawaiian tonics are *'awa* (kava), a mild sedative, and *noni* (Indian mulberry), which some consider a cure-all. Both are pungent in smell and taste. You can find them at health-food stores, farmers markets and specialty bars and cafes, including Diamond Head Cove Health Bar (p139) in Waikiki.

Every beachside hotel bar mixes up those zany tropical cocktails topped with a fruit garnish and a little toothpick umbrella. Strictly for tourists is the legendary mai tai, a mix of rum, grenadine, orange curaçao, orgeat syrup and orange, lemon, lime and/ or pineapple juices.

From the Big Island, the state's best-known microbrewer is Kona Brewing Company, which has an outpost in Hawai'i Kai (see p157). A few more brewpubs have popped up in Honolulu (see the boxed text, p92). Wine tends to appeal to a more exclusive, urbane, professional clientele. Most top-end Honolulu and Waikiki restaurants, like Vino (p83) at Restaurant Row, offer a decent selection of imported wines. Wine bars are still scarce, with Honolulu's Formaggio (p140) the most well established.

CELEBRATIONS

Throughout Hawaii, to celebrate is to feast. Whether a 300-guest wedding or a birthday party for the *'ohana,* a massive spread is mandatory. Most gatherings are informal, held at parks, beaches or homes, featuring a potluck buffet of homemade dishes. On major American holidays, mainland dishes (eg Thanksgiving turkey) appear alongside local fare like rice (instead of mashed potatoes), sweet-potato tempura (instead of yams) and hibachi-grilled teriyaki beef (instead of roast beef).

In ancient Hawaii, a luau was held to commemorate auspicious occasions such as births and war victories. Around the autumn harvest time, the *makahiki* festival was four months of feasting, music and hula dancing, competitive games and worship of the god Lono. Luau are still commonplace in contemporary Hawaii, for example, to celebrate a baby's first birthday or a wedding. Big bashes that include extended family, coworkers and friends, these local luau are in spirit far more authentic than any touristy luau, but a short-stay visitor would be lucky to get an invitation to one. Today, commercial

SPAM CAPITAL OF THE USA

Hawaii is the Spam capital of the USA, and locals consume nearly seven million cans per year. While US food maker Hormel's Spam, a pork-based luncheon meat, is the butt of jokes almost everywhere, there's little stigma in Hawaii. Rather, Spam is a comfort food – always eaten cooked, not straight from the can.

Why Spam? No one knows exactly. Some people say it simply goes well with rice and poi, Hawaii's ubiquitous starches. Others claim it's a legacy of WWII-era cooking, when fresh meat was not always available. Even today, whenever the islands are threatened by a hurricane or dock workers' strike, locals stock up on water, batteries, toilet paper, 20lb bags of rice and…Spam.

A local favorite is Spam *musubi*, a block of rice with a slice of fried Spam on top (or in the middle), wrapped with a strip of black sushi nori. Probably originated in the 1970s, it has become a classic, and thousands of *musubi* are sold daily at supermarkets, lunch counters and convenience stores. The Spam *musubi* phenomenon has even reached Hormel, which in 2004 released a Hawaii collector's edition can with a recipe for you-know-what on the back.

You can join the official Spam Club, visit the virtual Spam museum and find more Spam recipes at www.spam.com. Die-hard Spam fans can plan their trip to O'ahu around the Waikiki Spam Jam (p272), a huge street festival in late April.

Luaus feature lavish spreads of Hawaiian foods

LINDA CHING

hotel luau offer the elaborate feast and hula dancing that many tourists expect. A $100 ticket entitles you to a choreographed Polynesian dance show and an all-you-can-eat buffet, typically including a mediocre sampling of traditional Hawaiian dishes.

Across the Hawaiian Islands, food festivals usually showcase homegrown crops, especially since organic, sustainable local produce is a growing trend. In mid-May, the **Wahiawa Pineapple Festival** (☎ 227-8229; www.hawaii pineapplefestival.com) features pineapple tastings, live entertainment and narrated tram tours through central O'ahu's pineapple plantation town (see p220). Weekly community farmers markets held all around O'ahu share much of the same festive atmosphere, drawing even more locals. Major annual events like Honolulu's Pan-Pacific Festival (p115) and Hawaii's Aloha Festivals (p115) often feature *ho'olaule'a* (block party) street festivals, during which local food vendors and top chefs cook for crowds. During **Restaurant Week Hawaii** (www.restaurant weekhawaii.com) in mid-November, dozens of restaurants around Honolulu and Waikiki offer special prix-fixe menus and other tasty incentives for dining out.

WHERE TO EAT & DRINK

Informal dining is Hawaii's forte. For takeout, head to retro drive-ins (usually serving breakfast, lunch and sometimes dinner), Japanese-style *okazuya* (takeout delicatessens, open at dawn, sold out by early afternoon) and *kaukau* wagons (lunch trucks). For sit-down meals, diners abound. Often with Formica tables, vinyl chairs and no view, they provide quick service and decent food at rock-bottom prices. If you've got an appetite, all-you-can-eat seafood, prime-rib or Sunday brunch buffets at resort hotels are your ticket.

For gourmet cuisine by star chefs like Alan Wong, Hiroshi Fukui and George Mavrothalassitis, explore Honolulu. Hawaii's cutting-edge foodie trends, such as *izakaya* (Japanese pubs serving tapas-style food), all start here. Honolulu's vibrant Chinatown provides outstanding Chinese cuisine, such as dim sum and *char siu* (barbecued pork), alongside pan-Asian noodle shops and upscale Eurasian fusion restaurants. The residential neighborhood of Kaimuki, spreading along Wai'alae Ave, beats out the city's official, but not very successful,

FOOD & DRINK

Restaurant Row, off Ala Moana Blvd near downtown Honolulu.

Touristy Waikiki is hit-or-miss when it comes to dining out. Greasy-spoon diners and coffee shops, mainland chains like McDonald's and the Cheesecake Factory, and stratospherically overpriced hotel dining rooms are lined up next to authentic Japanese hole-in-the-wall eateries and dining rooms designed by star chefs Roy Yamaguchi, Nobu Matsuhisa and DK Kodama. Oceanfront Kalakaua Ave and less-expensive Kuhio Ave attract mostly tourists, while Kapahulu Ave further inland has an eclectic collection of local drive-ins and other casual, island-style eateries.

Wherever you go on O'ahu, most bars serve tasty *pupu* (appetizers or small shared plates) such as *poke,* shrimp tempura or edamame (fresh soybeans in the pod). For groceries, head to farmers markets and locally owned supermarkets. In Hawaii, most groceries are imported from the mainland, including milk and eggs (unless labeled 'Island Fresh'), produce, chicken, pork and most beef. Thus, the everyday price of food averages 30% more than on the US mainland, so you may not save much money by self-catering during your trip.

Top Picks

LEGENDARY O'AHU SNACKS & DESSERTS

- *Malasadas* from **Leonard's** (p120) or **Agnes Portuguese Bake Shop** (p177)
- Shave ice from **Waiola Bakery & Shave Ice II** (p120) or **Matsumoto's** (p210)
- Coco puffs from **Liliha Bakery** (p89)
- *Mochi* ice cream from **Bubbie's** (p89 and p158)
- *Manapua* from **Royal Kitchen** (p83) or **Chun Wah Kam Noodle Factory** (p147)

VEGETARIANS & VEGANS

While most locals are omnivores, the Asian influence on local cuisine almost guarantees vegetable and tofu options all around the island. That said, vegetarians aren't the target market: a plate lunch without meat or fish is not quite a plate lunch. But the trend towards meatless diets is growing, especially among mainland transplants influenced by California cuisine, so whole-grain breads,

Some traditional Hawaiian dishes, including *kalua* pork and poi

LINDA CHING

grilled vegetables and brown rice aren't considered strictly for hippies anymore. Bustling farmers markets, supported by a growing, island-wide interest in sustainable agriculture, makes it easy to cater your own meals. Many restaurants have added a few vegetarian choices to their menus. When ordering, be sure to ask whether a dish is indeed meatless: soups and sauces often contain meat, chicken or fish broth, while *pupu* (appetizers) may be fried in lard.

EATING WITH KIDS

Excluding only the most formal Honolulu and Waikiki restaurants, families can eat just about anywhere on O'ahu. Most restaurants have booster seats and high chairs. Many also have special kids' menus (grilled cheese, chicken fingers etc). If restaurant dining is inconvenient, no problem: eating outdoors is among the simplest of island pleasures. Pick up fruit from a farmers market and deli takeout for a beach picnic, or devour plate lunches at open-air drive-ins. Consider renting accommodations that include a kitchen, although be aware that the high price of groceries in Hawaii means that you may not end up saving much money overall. Commercial luau (p139) might seem like cheesy Vegas shows to adults, but kids usually enjoy the flashy dances and fire tricks. For more tips on traveling with kids on O'ahu, see p274.

HABITS & CUSTOMS

Locals eat early and on the dot: typically 6am breakfast, noon lunch and 6pm dinner. Standard restaurant opening hours are: breakfast from 6am to 10am, lunch 11:30am to 2:30pm and dinner 5pm to 9:30pm. If restaurants reviewed in this book vary more than half an hour in either direction from these standard hours, we've listed the establishment's full opening hours. Because most island restaurants tend to close early in the evening, night owls will have to hunt for places to eat (see the boxed text, p82 and p118).

The casual Hawaii dress code means that T-shirts and flip-flops are ubiquitous, except at Honolulu's top-tier restaurants, such as those at Waikiki's high-end resorts. The older local generation tends toward

A local mainstay: shave ice LINDA CHING

neat, modest attire, which for men usually just means an aloha shirt and slacks. Smoking is not allowed in O'ahu's restaurants. For tipping practices, see p280.

At home, locals rarely serve formal sit-down meals with individual courses. Even when entertaining, meals are served pot-luck style with a spread of flavorful dishes and everyone usually just helps themselves. If you're invited to a local home, show up on time and bring dessert (eg a local bakery cake or pie). Remove your shoes at the door. And don't be surprised if you're forced to take home a plate or two of leftovers.

Even when eating out, locals tend to consider food quantity as important as quality – the portion sizes can be telling, especially at less-expensive island eateries such as drive-ins, cafes and plate-lunch kitchens. If you're a light eater, feel free to split a meal or take home the leftovers, as locals often do.

FOOD GLOSSARY

If someone offers you a *broke da mout malasada* or *'ono kine poke*, would you try it? Don't miss out because you're stumped by the lingo. Here's a list of common food terms; for pidgin and Hawaiian pronunciation tips, see the online Hawaiian language guide at www.lonelyplanet.com/hawaiian-language.

adobo – Filipino chicken or pork cooked in vinegar, *shōyu*, garlic and spices
arare – *shōyu*-flavored rice crackers; also called *kaki mochi*
'awa – kava, a Polynesian plant used to make an intoxicating drink
bao – Chinese-style steamed bun, usually dim sum
bentō – Japanese-style box lunch
broke da mout – delicious; literally 'broke the mouth'
char siu – Chinese barbecued pork
chawanmushi – Japanese savory egg custard
chazuke – Japanese tea-soaked rice with other toppings (eg salmon)
chirashizushi – assorted sushi and/or sashimi served over rice
crack seed – Chinese preserved fruit; a salty, sweet and/or sour snack
donburi – Japanese-style large bowl of rice topped with a protein dish
furikake – Japanese seasoning or condiment, usually dry and sprinkled atop rice; in Hawaii, often used for *poke*
grind – to eat
grinds – food
guava – green-yellow fruit with moist, pink flesh and lots of edible seeds
gyōza – Japanese grilled dumplings, usually containing minced pork or shrimp
haupia – coconut-cream pudding dessert
hijiki – Japanese seaweed
hulihuli chicken – rotisserie-cooked chicken with island-style barbecue sauce
imu – underground earthen oven used to cook *kalua* pig and other luau food
'inamona – roasted ground *kukui* (candlenut), used to flavor dishes such as *poke*
izakaya – Japanese pub serving food
kaiseki ryōri – formal Japanese meal consisting of a series of small, seasonally inspired dishes
kalbi – Korean-style grilled dishes, often marinated short ribs
kalo – taro
kalua – traditional Hawaiian method of cooking pork and other luau food in an underground pit
kamaboko – a block of pureed, steamed fish
katsu – deep-fried cutlets, usually pork or chicken; see *tonkatsu*
kaukau – food
ko – sugarcane
laulau – a bundle made of pork or chicken and salted butterfish, wrapped in taro and *ti* leaves and steamed
li hing mui – sweet-salty preserved plum; also a type of crack seed
liliko'i – passion fruit
loco moco – dish of rice, fried egg and hamburger patty topped with gravy or other condiments
lomilomi salmon – minced, salted salmon, diced tomato and green onion
luau – Hawaiian feast
mai tai – 'tiki bar' drink typically containing rum and tropical fruit juices
malasada – sugar-coated Portuguese fried doughnut (no hole), often with a creamy filling
manapua – Chinese-style steamed or baked bun with sweet or savory filling
manju – Japanese steamed or baked cake, often filled with sweet bean paste
mochi – sticky, sweet Japanese pounded-rice cake
natto – Japanese fermented soybeans
nishime – Japanese stew of root vegetables and seaweed, usually served around New Year's
noni – type of mulberry with smelly, yellow-green fruit used medicinally

nori – Japanese seaweed, usually dried
ogo – crunchy, salty seaweed, often added to *poke; limu* in Hawaiian
okonomiyaki – Japanese cabbage pancake made with meat, seafood and/or vegetables, topped with a savory sauce
'ono – delicious
'ono kine grinds – good food
'opihi – edible limpet
pho – Vietnamese soup, typically beef broth, noodles and fresh herbs
pipi kaula – Hawaiian beef jerky
poha – cape gooseberry
poi – staple Hawaiian starch made of steamed, mashed taro
poka – a fruit in the passion fruit family
poke – cubed raw fish mixed with *shōyu*, sesame oil, salt, chili pepper, *furikake, 'inamona* or other condiments
ponzu – Japanese citrus sauce
pupu – bar snack or appetizer
saimin – local Asian-style noodle soup
shave ice – cup of finely shaved ice, sweetened with colorful syrup
shōyu – Japanese soy sauce
soba – thin Japanese buckwheat-flour noodles
star fruit – translucent yellow-green fruit with five ribs like the points of a star and sweet, juicy pulp
taro – plant with edible corm used to make poi; called *kalo* in Hawaiian
teishoku – Japanese set meal
teppanyaki – Japanese style of cooking with an iron grill
tonkatsu – breaded and fried pork cutlets, also prepared as chicken *katsu*
tsukemono – pickled vegetables
tsukune – Japanese grilled meatball skewers
udon – thick Japanese wheat-flour noodles
'ulu – breadfruit, a starchy fruit prepared much like a potato
ume – Japanese pickled plum
wagyū – Japanese marbled beef, usually served as steak

NAME THAT FISH

In Hawaii, most fish go by Hawaiian and/or Japanese names.

'ahi – yellowfin or bigeye tuna, red flesh, served raw or rare
aku – skipjack tuna, red flesh, strong flavor; *katsuo* in Japanese
'ama'ama – mullet, delicate white flesh
awa – milkfish, tender white flesh
kajiki – Pacific blue marlin; *a'u* in Hawaiian
mahimahi – dolphin fish, firm pink flesh
moi – threadfish, flaky white flesh, rich flavor; traditionally reserved for *ali'i* (Hawaiian royalty)
monchong – pomfret, mild flavor, firm pinkish-white flesh
onaga – red snapper, soft and moist; *'ula'ula* in Hawaiian
ono – a white-fleshed, flaky mackerel; also called *wahoo*
opah – moonfish, firm and rich
'opakapaka – pink snapper, delicate flavor, premium quality
'opelu – mackerel scad, usually pan-fried
papio – jackfish; also called *ulua*
shutome – swordfish, succulent and meaty
tako – octopus, chewy texture; *he'e* in Hawaiian
unagi – freshwater eel, usually grilled and served with sweet sauce over *sumeshi* (sushi rice)

PLANNING YOUR TRIP

O'ahu can be a paradisiacal beach vacation for any budget, even backpackers'. If you have kids, don't worry; it's easy for families to travel here too. Hotel and car rentals typically work out better with advance planning, especially if you're traveling during peak winter season. Otherwise, you can usually get by booking things at the last minute. Most activities don't require reservations before you go. For our recommended island itineraries, see p20. For ecotravel tips, turn to p42.

WHEN TO GO

You can visit O'ahu anytime. The weather is agreeable year-round. Although it's a bit rainier in winter and a bit hotter in summer, there are no extremes because cooling trade winds blow throughout the year. For more detailed climate information, see p275.

Although the busiest tourist season is in winter (mid-December through mid-April), that has more to do with weather *elsewhere,* as many tourists are snowbirds escaping cold winters back home. June through August sees crowds of families taking summer vacations. Rooms are scarce and prices can spike around holidays, especially Thanksgiving, Christmas, New Year's and Easter, as well as during festivals and special events (see p272), when hotel and car reservations are essential. The rest of the year should pose few problems, though it's always smart to book your accommodations in advance. For bargain hunters, mid-September through mid-November, and the weeks from just after Easter until Memorial Day in late May, are the slowest times, so you're more likely to find good deals on accommodations and airfare. Everything feels more relaxed then, too.

Naturally, for certain activities there are peak seasons. For instance, if you are a board surfer, you will find the most awesome waves in winter, whereas if you are a windsurfer, optimal wind conditions arrive during summer. That said, an advantage of vacationing on O'ahu is that just about every activity can be enjoyed year-round somewhere. One exception is whale watching, with tours usually departing between January and March only.

COSTS & MONEY

How much money you need for your trip to O'ahu depends on your style. If you're a penny-pincher, you can get by on as little as $50 a day by staying in hostels, eating plate lunches and hanging out at the beach all day. For $1000 a day, you can sleep at plush oceanfront resorts, dine out on haute Hawaii Regional cuisine and shop till your credit card maxes out. Most people will opt for a middle way, spending about $150 to $200 per person per day for a hotel room, sight-

DON'T LEAVE HOME WITHOUT...

- A snorkel, mask and fins if you're planning to spend a lot of time in the water (p30)
- Dive certification cards and logbooks if you're going to take the plunge (p30)
- Driver's license, a passport and visa if necessary, and copies of your reservations for car rentals (p290) and accommodations (p268)
- A light, waterproof jacket for tropical showers (p275) and wind-whipped, cloud-shrouded *pali* (cliff or mountain) summits
- Binoculars for watching whales, dolphins and birds (p35) – and surfers too!
- Footwear with good traction – either for hitting wet, muddy trails (p37) or for jogging in Honolulu (p39)
- A flashlight for sunset and full-moon hikes (p37) or night-time snorkeling at Hanauma Bay (p158)
- A spirit of aloha and a hang-loose attitude

CLIMATE CHANGE & TRAVEL

Climate change is a serious threat to the ecosystems that humans rely upon, and air travel is the fastest-growing contributor to the problem. Lonely Planet regards travel, overall, as a global benefit, but believes we all have a responsibility to limit our personal impact on global warming.

Flying & Climate Change

Nearly every form of motorized travel generates CO_2 (the main cause of human-induced climate change), but planes are far and away the worst offenders – not just because of the sheer distances they allow us to travel, but because they release greenhouse gases high into the atmosphere. The statistics are frightening: two people taking a round-trip flight between Europe and the USA will contribute as much to climate change as an average household's gas and electricity consumption over a whole year.

Carbon Offset Schemes

Climatecare.org and other websites use 'carbon calculators' that allow travelers to offset the level of greenhouse gases they are responsible for with financial contributions to sustainable travel schemes that reduce global warming – including projects in India, Honduras, Kazakhstan and Uganda.

Lonely Planet, together with Rough Guides and other concerned partners in the travel industry, support the carbon offset scheme run by www.climatecare.org. Lonely Planet offsets all of its staff and author travel.

For more information, check out our website, www.lonelyplanet.com.

---

seeing, transportation, three square meals and a few mai tais.

Airfare is usually one of the heftiest line items on your budget. From the US mainland, fares start anywhere between $350 and $800, depending on your departure point and travel dates. Once you get here, O'ahu boasts a good, inexpensive bus system (p289), but if you really want to explore the whole island, plan on renting your own wheels for a few days. Set aside at least $55 per day to rent a compact car, keep if full of gas and pay for parking in Honolulu and Waikiki.

Waikiki Beach has the lion's share of accommodations. Other than youth hostels, which charge around $25 for dorm beds, decent budget hotels cost from just under $100. Opt for a better-class hotel or outlying B&B and you'll be looking at $100 to $200. Luxury beachfront hotels typically start around $250 but the most chic or historic properties can easily double that, especially during the peak winter travel season.

Most of O'ahu's food is shipped in, so grocery prices average at least 30% higher than on the US mainland. Tourist restaurants

Bring (or rent) snorkeling gear for a chance to see moorish idols like these   CASEY MAHANEY

HOW MUCH?

- **Shave ice with azuki beans** $2.50
- **Local plate lunch** $6
- **Vintage aloha shirt** $20
- **Weekly snorkel-set rental** $45
- **One-hour group surfing lesson** $80

See also the Lonely Planet Index inside the front cover.

typically reflect these higher prices, but food in neighborhood eateries can be better value, with prices comparable to what you'll find on the mainland. Takeout is very popular on O'ahu, and it's usually cheaper than a sit-down meal.

Families can save money by asking for children's menus at restaurants and taking advantage of discounted admission at museums and attractions. For more tips on travel with children, see p274. Everyone can use the discount coupons printed in O'ahu's free tourist magazines (see p277), which cut costs on all sorts of activities, entertainment and dining.

CHOOSING ACCOMMODATIONS

O'ahu offers a huge variety of accommodations, from hostels and homey B&Bs to fully equipped condos, deluxe hotels and oceanfront resorts. Although some places charge the same rates year-round, many put high-season rates into effect from mid-December to mid-April. When demand peaks, including from Christmas to New Year's and during special festivals and events, lodgings book up months in advance. During the off-season, finding a room is easier, and online discounts are more plentiful.

Many hotel websites regularly offer internet specials, which offer big discounts off the hotel's rack rates and aren't available over the phone. Surfing other discount travel websites can turn up even better deals. Good places to start looking online, especially for last-minute bookings:

CheapTickets (www.cheaptickets.com)
Expedia (www.expedia.com)
Hotwire (www.hotwire.com)
Kayak (www.kayak.com)
Orbitz (www.orbitz.com)
Priceline (www.priceline.com)
Travelocity (www.travelocity.com)

Reviews in this book indicate rates for single occupancy, double or simply the room when the price is the same for one or two people, as is usually the case on O'ahu. For a key to other abbreviations and icons used with accommodations reviews, see the inside front cover of this book. Reviews are listed in order of price, from lowest to highest, under the Sleeping headings in the regional chapters. Price categories are: $ (doubles under $100 per night), $$ ($100 to $170), $$$ ($170 to $260) and $$$$ (over $260). Quoted rates don't include Hawaii's

Ke Iki Beach Bungalows (p207), North Shore

ANN CECIL

steep 11.41% room tax. Unless otherwise noted, breakfast is *not* included, bathrooms are private and all lodging is open year-round.

Most room reservations require a hefty deposit in advance. There may be restrictions on getting a refund if you change your mind: many places may issue only a partial refund, and in some cases you may forfeit your entire deposit. Carefully check the cancellation policy at your hotel, condo, B&B or vacation rental before making a deposit.

B&Bs & Vacation Rentals

B&Bs are typically rooms in private homes on Oʻahu. They operate under unusual local regulations that make it difficult to establish new businesses and limit most B&Bs to renting only two guest rooms. Most cannot display signs and are not legally permitted to offer a hot breakfast. Growing tension over the proliferation of unlicensed B&Bs and vacation rentals in residential neighborhoods, such as Kailua on the Windward Coast, has resulted in proposed legislation that may place further restrictions on owners.

B&Bs discourage unannounced drop-ins and, for that reason, do not always appear on maps in this book. Because hosts are often out during the day, same-day reservations are hard to get, especially in winter, when B&Bs book up months in advance. Simple rooms start at around $75, but most average between $100 and $200. Many B&Bs and vacation rentals require a minimum stay of at least a few days.

The majority of Oʻahu's B&Bs are found around Kailua (p172) on the Windward Coast. This book reviews B&Bs that can be booked directly, but there are many more that can be booked through reservation agencies:

Affordable Paradise (☎ 261-1693; www.affordable -paradise.com) Offers the widest range of B&B rooms, apartments, bungalows and houses in the Kailua area.
All Islands Bed & Breakfast (☎ 753-3445; www.all-islands.com) A decent selection of B&B rooms, studio apartments and *ohana* (freestanding) cottages.
Bed & Breakfast Hawaii (☎ 822-7771, 800-733-1632; www.bandb-hawaii.com) Books B&B rooms, suites and cottages in Kailua, Hawaiʻi Kai and Diamond Head.

BOOK ACCOMMODATIONS ONLINE

For more accommodation reviews and recommendations by Lonely Planet authors, check out www.lonelyplanet .com/hotels. You'll find the true, insider lowdown on the best places to stay. Reviews are thorough and independent. Best of all, you can book online!

Hawaii's Best Bed & Breakfast (☎ 263-3100, 800-262-9912; www.bestbnb.com) Hand-picked, high-quality B&B rooms, condos and vacation-rental houses in Windward Oʻahu and on the North Shore.
Pat's Kailua Beach Properties (☎ 261-1653; www.patskailua.com) Over 30 options on or near Kailua Beach, ranging from small studios to large houses.
Trinity Properties (☎ 247-7521; www.trinityproper ties.com) Rents upscale multibedroom homes and luxury estates in Kailua and Lanikai.
Vacation Rentals by Owner (www.vrbo.com) Scores of vacation-rental houses, condos and cottages around Oʻahu.

Camping & Cabins

Oʻahu has no full-service campgrounds like on the US mainland. Overall, the quality of camping facilities ranges from great to not very good. Public campgrounds are spread around the island, but none of them are close to Waikiki. Most campgrounds have picnic tables, drinking water, pay-phones, restrooms and showers. Keep in mind that you can't carry stove fuel on airplanes. Local hardware stores typically sell barbecue-sized canisters of propane gas, while outdoor outfitters may carry smaller canisters of stove fuel.

Campgrounds are always busy on weekends, particularly during holidays and throughout the summer, as that's when locals like to pitch their tents. All county and state campgrounds on Oʻahu require advance permits and are closed on Wednesday and Thursday nights, ostensibly for maintenance, but also to prevent permanent encampments by homeless islanders. The private concessionaire campground and cabins at Malaekahana State Recreation Area (p193) are open daily.

Although thousands of visitors use O'ahu's public campsites each year without incident, theft and even violent assaults are not unheard of, especially at drive-up roadside campgrounds, so keep an eye on your belongings and take precautions about personal safety. Because of turf issues and an undercurrent of resentment by some locals against outsiders, camping along the Wai'anae Coast is not recommended for nonresidents. Elsewhere, some county beach-park campgrounds are known to be late-night carousing spots for drunks, drug addicts, gangs and other troublemakers.

STATE PARKS

To camp at a state park, you'll need to purchase a permit, which costs $5 per night per site. Camping is limited to five nights per month in each park. Another camping permit for the same park will not be issued until 30 days have elapsed.

Permit applications can be made no sooner than 30 days before the first camping date. Because permits are issued on a first-come, first-served basis, it's best to apply as soon as possible. If you have a change of plans, be sure to cancel so that other campers get a chance to use the space.

Applications may be made by phone, mail or in person at the **Division of State Parks** (☎ 587-0300; www.hawaiistateparks.org; 1151 Punchbowl St, PO Box 621, Honolulu, HI 96809; ⏲ 8am-3:30pm Mon-Fri).

COUNTY PARKS

County park camping permits are free. Permits can be picked up no sooner than two Fridays in advance of your intended camping dates at the **Department of Parks & Recreation** (Map pp60-1; ☎ 523-4525; www.co.honolulu.hi.us/parks/permits.htm; Frank F Fasi Municipal Bldg, 650 S King St, Honolulu; ⏲ 8am-4pm Mon-Fri). Camping permits are also available from satellite city halls, including at Honolulu's **Ala Moana Center** (Map pp68-9; ☎ 973-2600; 1450 Ala Moana Blvd, Honolulu; ⏲ 9am-5pm Mon-Fri, 8am-4pm Sat) and in **Kailua** (Map p172; ☎ 261-8575; Keolu Shopping Center, 1090 Keolu Dr; ⏲ 8am-4pm Mon-Fri).

Camping at county parks is generally allowed from 8am Friday to 8am Wednesday, except at Bellows Field Beach Park, Swanzy

HAWAII DOS & DON'TS

- Avoid honking your car horn unless absolutely necessary.
- Give a thank-you wave (or the *shaka* hand sign) if another driver lets you merge.
- Slow down – this ain't da mainland, as the bumper sticker says.
- Always act polite, respectful and 'no make waves' (ie be cool).
- Dress informally (eg T-shirt, shorts and rubbah slippahs) if you want to blend in.
- Take off your shoes before entering local homes (including most B&Bs, condos and vacation rentals).
- Don't use the term 'Hawaiian' as a catchall for local residents; Native Hawaiians are the indigenous race.
- Treat any ancient Hawaiian site or artifact you find with respect.
- Tread lightly at 'locals-only' beaches; they usually can't sustain heavy tourist traffic.
- Never drop in on a local surfer's wave.

Beach Park and most beach parks on the Wai'anae Coast, which are open only on weekends. For more information about camping at safe and scenic Ho'omaluhia Botanical Garden, see p180.

Condominiums

Most accommodations on O'ahu are found inside hotels, not condominiums. Lease-free daily, weekly and monthly condo rentals that are readily available on other Hawaiian Islands are not easily found on O'ahu. Many condos are filled with long-term local residents. You can try looking in the newspaper classified sections or browsing private ads online at **Vacation Rentals by Owner** (www.vrbo.com) or **Craigslist** (http://honolulu.craigslist.org). Honolulu is one of the most expensive housing markets in the USA, so listings can be meager, especially in winter when demand peaks. For more condo rental agencies in Waikiki, see p126.

Hostels

There are two **Hostelling International** (HI; www.hiusa.org) hostels on O'ahu: HI-Waikiki (p126) by the beach and HI-Honolulu (p97) near the University of Hawai'i at Manoa campus. Both hostels are clean, secure and well managed. A few private hostels have opened in Waikiki and on the North Shore. These places can be very unpredictable – a change in management might mean a shabby operation becomes newly respectable, or vice versa. In Waikiki most hostels occupy older apartment buildings; some have a cluster of units, while others have taken over a whole complex. These private hostels cater to backpackers and draw a fairly international crowd, but don't expect pristine digs. Some are merely crash pads that may look less inviting than the back seat of your rental car.

Hotels & Resorts

Unlike on other Hawaiian Islands, where resort hotels are scattered around multiple destinations, fewer than 10% of O'ahu's 30,000-plus hotel rooms are found outside Waikiki. Generally, the higher the floor, the higher the price, and an ocean view will commonly bump up the bill by 50% to 100%. The good news is that you should never have to pay rack rates. A few of the larger chains, such as Ohana and Outrigger, often throw in a free rental car and some hotels actually offer room/car packages for less than the standard room rate. Sometimes, all-inclusive packages are no deal at all, however, so make sure you do the math and all of your research before booking.

TRAVEL LITERATURE

Use the long flight to Honolulu to do some background reading and bone up on island history and culture, starting with these evocative nonfiction books.

Travelers Tales: Hawaii edited by Rick Carroll is a compelling anthology of quirky stories about island life – from cooking with Spam to solar eclipses – from a range of authors including literary giants, first-time visitors and Native Hawaiians.

Delve into the archipelago's singular natural history in *A World Between Waves* edited by Frank Stewart, with essays on everything from volcanoes to whales, including reflections by Diane Ackerman, Peter Matthiessen and James Houston.

In *Eddie Would Go,* Stuart Holmes Coleman combines the poetry of Oahu's monster waves on the North Shore and the inspiring life story of surfing legend and 20th-century Hawaiian folk hero Eddie Aikau (see the boxed text, p32).

In his gripping memoir *Radioman,* WWII veteran Carol Edgemon Hipperson recounts being an eyewitness to history during the surprise attack on O'ahu's Pearl Harbor and the Battle of Midway in the Northwestern Hawaiian Islands.

For a rare glimpse into the decades before the USA annexed Hawaii, read *Six Months in the Sandwich Islands* by the cantankerous and judgmental, yet still insightful, Victorian-era adventurer Isabella Bird.

Irreverent, wise and witty, Mark Twain's observations in *Letters from Hawaii*, originally printed as 19th-century newspaper dispatches to the US mainland, rhapsodize about the exoticism of Hawaiian traditions and ancient island ways.

Hawaii's Story by Hawaii's Queen, Queen Lili'uokalani's graceful autobiography, was written during the last year of her monarchy and, like the lady herself, the narrative, although somewhat long-winded, couldn't be more eloquent.

To listen to a Hawaiian king 'talk story,' read *Legends and Myths of Hawaii* by David Kalakaua, which magically mixes history with living mythology – just don't take everything the king says at face value.

INTERNET RESOURCES

Alternative Hawaii (www.alternative-hawaii.com) Ecotourism website that promotes Hawaiian culture and indie travel.

Hawaii Visitors and Convention Bureau (www.gohawaii.com) The state's official tourism website has an enormous activity database.

Honolulu Advertiser (www.honoluluadvertiser.com) Online version of the island's major daily newspaper.

Honolulu Weekly (http://honoluluweekly.com) Find out what's going on right now around O'ahu.

LonelyPlanet.com (www.lonelyplanet.com) Overviews of island travel, useful web links and chatty forums.

O'ahu Visitors Bureau (www.visit-oahu.com) In-depth tourist information only for O'ahu includes wedding tips.

FESTIVALS & EVENTS
CALENDAR

JANUARY–FEBRUARY

Chinese New Year (p81)
late January–mid-February
Firecrackers, lion dances and a parade in Honolulu's Chinatown around the second new moon after the winter solstice.

MARCH

Honolulu Festival (p81 & p115)
mid-March
Asian and South Pacific cultural celebrations of music, dance and drama in Honolulu and Waikiki.

APRIL

Waikiki Spam Jam (p115)
late April
Chow down – without shame! – on Hawaii's favorite tinned meat product at this quirky street festival.

MAY–JUNE

Lei Day
May 1
Everybody dons a lei, and lei-making competitions take place around O'ahu, including at Waikiki's Kapi'olani Park, where a lei queen is crowned.

50th State Fair
late May–late June
With carnival games and rides, exhibits and live entertainment, this family-friendly event takes place over four weekends at 'Aiea's Aloha Stadium.

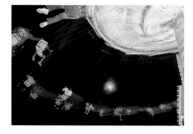

Pan-Pacific Festival (p115)
early June
Japanese and Polynesian cultural heritage is celebrated with everything from *taiko* drumming to hula and ukulele shows around Honolulu, plus a block party and parade in Waikiki.

King Kamehameha Day
June 11
On this state holiday, downtown Honolulu's statue of Kamehameha the Great (p62) is ceremoniously draped with lei, followed by a parade to Waikiki's Kapi'olani Park for music and hula shows.

JULY
Prince Lot Hula Festival (p81)
3rd Saturday of July
Top *hula halau* (hula schools) compete at Honolulu's Moanalua Gardens, a former retreat for Hawaiian royalty.

AUGUST
Hawaiian Slack Key Guitar Festival (p115)
mid-August
Lay out a picnic blanket at Waikiki's Kapi'olani Park to enjoy Hawaiian guitar and ukulele shows.

SEPTEMBER
Aloha Festivals (p115)
mid-September
A 10-day celebration of all things Hawaiian, with cultural events, parades, hula dancing and live music, plus a block party in Waikiki.

OCTOBER
Talk Story Festival (p82)
mid-October
Locals and tourists alike turn up at Honolulu's Ala Moana Beach Park for three nights of family-friendly storytelling.

Hawaii International Film Festival (p82)
late October
Ground-breaking dramas and documentary films from Polynesia and the Pacific Rim are shown in Honolulu.

NOVEMBER–DECEMBER
Triple Crown of Surfing (p203 & p209)
mid-November–December
Drawing the world's top surfers to O'ahu's North Shore, competitions kick off in mid-November and usually run through December, depending on when the surf's up. Bring binoculars!

Honolulu Marathon (p82)
2nd Sunday of December
The USA's third-largest marathon is run from downtown Honolulu's Aloha Tower to Waikiki's Kapi'olani Park.

Hula Bowl
Christmas Day
All-star collegiate football game (www.hulabowlhawaii.com) held at 'Aiea's Aloha Stadium often launches pro careers.

DIRECTORY & TRANSPORTATION

CONTENTS

PRACTICALITIES

For more about Oʻahu's outdoor activities and adventures, see p26.

BUSINESS HOURS

Unless there are variances of more than a half-hour in either direction, these standard opening hours apply throughout this book:

Banks From 8:30am to 4pm Monday to Friday; some till 6pm Friday and 9am to noon or 1pm Saturday.

Bars & Clubs To midnight daily; some clubs open till 2am Thursday to Saturday.

Businesses From 8:30am to 4:30pm Monday to Friday; some post offices open 9am to noon Saturday.

Restaurants Breakfast from 6am to 10am; lunch from 11:30am to 2:30pm; dinner from 5pm to 9:30pm.

Shops From 9am to 5pm Monday to Saturday, some also noon to 5pm Sunday; major shopping areas and malls keep extended hours.

CHILDREN

Oʻahu offers tons of beaches and outdoor activities for all ages and abilities. Many hotels have swimming pools, and malls have video-game arcades and movies. Traveling families are common, and most hotels, restaurants and local businesses are ready to welcome your kids. Just remember to keep everyone covered in sunblock, and don't overdo things by packing too much into one day. When the going gets tough, bust out the chocolate-covered macadamia nuts or stop for shave ice (see p259). Consult Lonely Planet's *Travel with Children*, which is packed full of valuable tips and interesting anecdotal stories. Also, see the Honolulu for Kids (p80) and Waikiki for Kids (p114) sections earlier in this book.

PLUGGING INTO O'AHU

- As in the rest of the USA, Hawaii's electricity is 110/120V, 60 cycles and uses a flat, two-pronged plug.
- Distances are measured in feet, yards and miles; weights in ounces, pounds and tons; liquids in cups, pints, quarts and gallons; see the Quick Reference page inside the front cover for a metric conversion chart.
- O'ahu has about 45 AM and FM radio stations. All of the major US TV networks are represented, as well as cable channels offering 24-hour tourist information.
- If you're buying videos to take home, be aware Hawaii uses the NTSC system, the same as in the rest of the USA, which is incompatible with the PAL system used in Europe and Australia. DVDs are coded for Region 1 (USA and Canada only).

Practicalities

Children under 18 often stay for free when sharing a hotel room with their parents, but only if they use existing bedding. Cots and roll-away beds are usually available for a surcharge at hotels and resorts, either upon request or with advance reservations.

Many restaurants have children's menus (eg grilled cheese sandwiches, chicken fingers) with significantly lower prices. High chairs are usually available. Most car-hire companies rent child-safety seats for around $10 per day, but don't always have enough on hand, so reserve them in advance. If you're traveling with infants and come up short, **Baby's Away** (☎ 497-2009, 800-496-6386; www.babysaway.com) rents cribs, strollers, playpens, high chairs, car seats and more.

You can find babysitters by asking your hotel's concierge, or contact **Aloha Nannies** (☎ 394-5434; www.alohanannies.com). There are some family-friendly resorts in Waikiki (see the boxed text, p126) that often have extensive children's programs and day camps, allowing parents to slip away for a day.

Baby food, infant formula, soy and cow's milk, and disposable diapers are widely available in supermarkets and drugstores. Most women choose to be discreet about breastfeeding in public. Many women's public restrooms have a baby-changing table; gender-neutral 'family' facilities are sometimes available at airports, museums, etc.

CLIMATE

O'ahu's climate is unusually pleasant for the tropics, as cooling trade winds blow year-round. There can be spells of stormy weather, particularly in winter (December through March), although most precipitation falls as short daytime showers accompanied by rainbows. Rainfall varies greatly with elevation, even within short distances. Waikiki has an average annual rainfall of only 22in, whereas the Lyon Arboretum in the upper Manoa Valley, on the north side of Honolulu, averages 153in.

The **National Weather Service** (www.prh.noaa .gov/hnl) provides recorded weather forecasts for all of **O'ahu** (☎ 973-4381) and a coastal **marine forecast** (☎ 973-4382) with detailed water conditions. Average water temperatures in Waikiki are 74°F in winter, 80°F in summer.

See also the When to Go section of Planning Your Trip (p266).

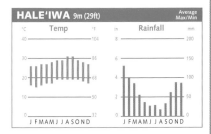

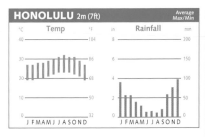

COURSES

Some resort hotels and shopping centers offer free or inexpensive workshops in hula, traditional Hawaiian crafts and the like. Aimed at tourists, these classes are often light-hearted, rather than serious – even hokey. Since schedules are unpredictable, keep your eyes and ears open. Your hotel concierge is always a good source of information. For Hawaiian craft and cultural classes in the Waikiki area, see p114.

The **University of Hawai'i at Manoa** (UHM; Map p71; ☎ 956-8111; www.hawaii.edu) offers full-time college-credit classes, including summer-school sessions. Contact **UHM Outreach College** (Map p71; ☎ 956-5666, 800-862-6628; www.outreach.hawaii.edu; Room 101, Krauss Hall, 2500 Dole St, Honolulu; ☽ 8am-5:30pm Mon-Fri) for a catalog of continuing-education classes and workshops offered year-round. For short-term campus leisure programs, see p80.

DANGERS & ANNOYANCES

For most visitors, the major concerns are car break-ins (common) and natural disasters (rare but serious). The **Visitor Aloha Society of Hawaii** (VASH; Map pp102-3; ☎ 926-8274; www.visitoralohasocietyofhawaii.org; Waikiki Shopping Plaza, Suite 403-3, 2250 Kalakaua Ave; ☽ office 8:30am-5pm Mon-Fri, on-call hours 5-9:30pm Mon-Fri, 8:30am-9:30pm Sat & Sun) provides short-term emergency (but nonmonetary) aid to tourists who are victims of crimes while vacationing on O'ahu. See also Legal Matters (p279).

Drugs

The use of 'ice' (methamphetamine, aka crystal meth) has been an ongoing social and law-enforcement issue since the 1990s, especially in rural communities. The 'ice epidemic' has abated somewhat recently, but ice-related crimes remain common and social-service agencies struggle to provide adequate treatment programs for addicts.

Earthquakes

There is a great deal of seismic activity in the Hawaiian Islands, although much of it takes place on the island of Hawai'i (the Big Island), well to the southeast of O'ahu. Should you be in an area where an earthquake occurs, there are several precautions you can take to minimize the risk of injury. If you're indoors, take cover in a doorway or under a heavy desk or table and stay clear of windows and anything that's in danger of breaking or falling, such as mirrors and bookcases. If you're outdoors, get into an open area away from buildings, trees and power lines. If you're driving in a car, pull over to the side of the road away from overpasses and power lines and stay inside the car until the shaking stops.

Scams

The main scams directed toward O'ahu tourists involve fake activity-operator booths that are really fronts for vacation timeshare realty sales. If you see a sign touting car rentals for $5 a day or a free luau, you've probably found one of these. To get the deal, you'll have to endure a high-pressure 'no obligation' sales pitch – caveat emptor.

Theft & Violence

Petty theft is one crime that ranks high on O'ahu. Watch your belongings and never leave anything unattended on the beach. Most hotels have a place where you can store your valuables, either in guest rooms or at the front desk, or both.

O'ahu is notorious for thefts from parked cars, whether locals' or tourist rentals. Thieves can pop open a trunk or pull out a door-lock assembly in seconds. They do it not only when you've left your car in a secluded area to go for a long hike, but also in crowded parking lots where you'd expect safety in numbers.

Try not to leave anything of value in your car anytime you walk away from it. If you must, pack things well out of sight *before* pulling up to park; thieves watch and wait to see what you put in your trunk. Some locals keep their cars unlocked at all times to avoid paying for broken windows.

Other than rip-offs, most hassles encountered by visitors are from drunks. You should be tuned in to the vibes on any island beaches at night, even in Waikiki where police patrol the main beach, and in places like campgrounds and roadside parks where young locals hang out to drink.

Honolulu has a lower violent crime rate than most other US cities, but like any city, crime does occur. Don't leave your street smarts at home when you visit Hawaii. In rural areas, there are some pockets of resentment against tourists and mainland transplants; this is particularly true along the more remote places on the Windward and Wai'anae Coasts.

Tsunamis

Tsunamis are generated by earthquakes or other underwater disturbances, such as volcanoes. In Hawaii, tsunamis, aka tidal waves, have occurred on average once a decade over the last century. When they do hit, they can be severe. Hawaii has installed a modern tsunami warning system aired through yellow speakers mounted on telephone poles. They're tested on the first working day of each month at 11:45am for about one minute. If you're in a low-lying coastal area when a tsunami approaches, head for higher ground immediately. The front section of the O'ahu telephone book has maps showing tsunami evacuation zones.

DISCOUNT CARDS

Free tourist magazines like *Spotlight's O'ahu Gold* and *This Week O'ahu,* packed with discount coupons, are freely available around Waikiki and at other tourist spots.

Hawaii residents *(kama'aina)* and military personnel with ID receive discounts at some sightseeing attractions. People over the age of 65 (sometimes 55, 60 or 62) often qualify for similar discounts; any ID showing your birth date should suffice as proof of age. If you have a student ID card, bring it along, as it may occasionally get you small discounts at movie theaters, museums and other attractions.

Card-carrying members of the **American Automobile Association** (AAA; www.aaa.com) and their international affiliates (eg CAA) are entitled to discounts on car rentals, hotels and many sightseeing attractions. For instance, all Outrigger hotels give discounts of up to 40% off the regular 'rack' rates for AAA/CAA members. For US citizens aged 50 years and older, membership in the nonprofit **American Association of Retired**

Persons (AARP; ☎ 843-1906, 888-687-2277; www.aarp.org) is another source of travel discounts, typically 10% to 25% off car rentals and accommodations.

The **Go Oahu Card** (☎ 866-637-8819; www.gooahucard.com) covers admission to museums and sightseeing tours and includes some beach activities, but it's pricey ($48 per day, $75/145/200/225 for two/three/five/seven days). Unless you plan on going everywhere and doing everything it's valid for, you're probably better off without it.

FOOD

Reviews in the Eating section for each island destination are broken down into four price categories: $ (for meals under $12), $$ (most main dishes cost $12 to $18), $$$ (most dinner mains cost $18 to $25) and $$$$ (most dinner mains over $25). These price estimates do not include taxes, tips or beverages. For more information about the island's cuisine scene, turn to the Food & Drink chapter (p257).

GAY & LESBIAN TRAVELERS

Hawaii is a popular vacation spot for LGBT visitors. The state has strong minority protections and a constitutional guarantee of privacy that extends to sexual behavior between consenting adults. Public hand-holding and other outward signs of affection between same-sex partners are not commonplace, however.

In terms of nightlife, the main gay club scene on O'ahu is unquestionably in Waikiki (see the boxed text, p123). Gay Pride Weekend, at the end of June, includes a beach party at Ala Moana Beach Park and a parade from Magic Island to Waikiki's Kapi'olani Beach Park.

The monthly magazine *Odyssey* (http://odysseyhawaii.com), distributed free at LGBT-friendly businesses throughout Hawaii, covers O'ahu's gay scene. The national monthly magazine *OutTraveler* (www.outtraveler.com) archives its Hawaii travel articles online, and also publishes the *Out Traveler: Hawaii* handbook ($15.95).

Helpful DIY resources for LGBT travelers include the nonprofit **Aloha Pride Center** (www.alohapridecenter.org) and the commercial **Gay Hawaii** (www.gayhawaii.com). **Pacific Ocean Holidays** (☎ 545-5252, 800-735-6599; http://gayhawaii vacations.com) arranges package vacations for gays and lesbians.

HOLIDAYS

On the following holidays, banks, schools and government offices (including post offices) are closed, and transportation and museums operate on a Sunday schedule. Holidays falling on a weekend are usually observed the following Monday. These weekends can also be busy, as residents of the Neighbor Islands often take advantage of the break to visit O'ahu. See also the Festivals & Events Calendar (p272).

New Year's Day January 1
Martin Luther King Jr Day Third Monday in January
Presidents' Day Third Monday in February
Good Friday March or April
Prince Kuhio Day March 26
Memorial Day Last Monday in May
King Kamehameha Day June 11
Independence Day July 4
Statehood Day Third Friday in August
Labor Day First Monday in September
Columbus Day Second Monday in October
Veterans Day November 11
Thanksgiving Fourth Thursday in November
Christmas Day December 25

INTERNATIONAL TRAVELERS
Entering Hawaii
PASSPORTS & VISAS

All of the following information is highly subject to change. Check the latest requirements for passports and visas online at http://travel.state.gov/visa.

For all foreign visitors, your passport must be valid for at least six months longer than your intended stay in the USA. Upon arrival, you must register with the US-VISIT program, which entails having your fingerprints scanned and a digital photo taken.

Currently under the Visa Waiver Program (VWP), citizens of 35 countries (including Australia, Austria, Belgium, the Czech Republic, Denmark, Finland, France, Germany, Hungary, Iceland, Ireland, Italy, Japan, the Netherlands, New Zealand, Norway, Portugal, Singapore, the Slovak Republic, South Korea, Spain, Sweden, Switzerland and the UK) may enter without a tourist visa for stays of 90 days or less (no extensions allowed). As of 2009, citizens of VWP countries must register with the US government online at https://esta.cbp.dhs.gov at least 72 hours before arrival. Once approved, that registration is valid for two years.

If your passport does not meet current US standards, you'll be turned back at the border, even if you belong to a VWP country and have travel authorization. If your passport was issued before October 26, 2005, it must be 'machine readable' (with two lines of letters, numbers and <<< at the bottom); if it was issued between October 26, 2005, and October 25, 2006, it must be machine-readable and include a digital photo; and if it was issued on or after October 26, 2006, it must be an e-Passport with a digital photo and an integrated chip containing biometric data.

Citizens from all non-VWP countries, as well as those whose passports are not machine-readable or otherwise don't meet the current US standards, will need to obtain a nonimmigrant visa from a US consulate or embassy abroad, preferably in your home country. The process costs at minimum a nonrefundable $100, involves a personal interview and can take several weeks, so apply as early as possible.

CUSTOMS

Each visitor is allowed to bring 1L of liquor and 200 cigarettes (ie one carton) duty-free into the USA, but you must be at least 21 years old to possess alcohol and 18 years old for tobacco. In addition, each foreign visitor can import up to $100 worth of gift merchandise duty-free.

Most fresh fruits and plants are restricted from entry into Hawaii and customs official are militant. To help prevent the spread of invasive species, it's important to clean off your hiking shoes and outdoor gear before arrival. Because Hawaii is a rabies-free state, the pet quarantine laws here are draconian. For more details, contact the **Hawaii Department of Agriculture** (☎ 973-9560; http://hawaii.gov/hdoa). See also the boxed text, p285.

Consulates

Australia (Map pp60-1; ☎ 524-5050; Penthouse, 1000 Bishop St, Honolulu)

France (Map pp60-1; ☎ 547-5852; Ali'i Place, Suite 1800, Ali'i Tower, 1099 Alakea St, Honolulu)

Italy (Map pp60-1; ☎ 531-2277; Suite 201, 735 Bishop St, Honolulu)

Japan (Map pp54-5; ☎ 543-3111; 1742 Nu'uanu Ave, Honolulu)

Korea (Map pp54-5; ☎ 595-6109; 2756 Pali Hwy, Honolulu)

Netherlands (Map pp60-1; ☎ 531-6897; Suite 702, 745 Fort St Mall, Honolulu)

New Zealand (Map p73; ☎ 595-2200; 3929 Old Pali Rd, Honolulu)

INTERNET ACCESS

O'ahu's cybercafes offer internet access for an average of $6 per hour. You'll find most of them in Waikiki and around the University of Hawai'i at Manoa campus and Ala Moana Center. Hotel business centers and **FedEx Office** (☎ 800-463-3339; www.fedex.com) branch locations offer more expensive internet access, typically for $12 to $20 per hour.

When accommodations provide internet access for those traveling without laptops, this is noted in this book with ⌨ . Only some midrange and top-end hotels have installed wireless networks for guests; for the latest info, inquire when booking. If hotels or other venues (such as cafes) provide wi-fi access, this is noted in this book with 🛜 . For hotels, when wi-fi access is available elsewhere on the property (eg in the lobby, by the swimming pool), this is also noted in the review.

Island-wide public libraries provide free online terminals for internet access, but you'll need to purchase a three-month nonresident library card ($10). Free wi-fi is available at an increasing number of public library branches, including the Hawaii State Library (p57) in downtown Honolulu.

For recommended websites, see p271.

LEGAL MATTERS

Anyone arrested in Hawaii has the right to have the representation of a lawyer, from the time of their arrest to their trial; if a person cannot afford a lawyer, the state will provide one for free. The **Hawaii State Bar Association** (☎ 537-9140) can make referrals. Foreign visitors may want to call their consulate (see left) for advice.

Bars, clubs and stores often ask for photo ID to prove you're of legal age to consume alcohol (21 years). It's illegal to have open containers of alcohol in motor vehicles, and drinking in public parks or on the beaches is also forbidden. Drunk driving is a serious offense that might incur stiff fines, jail time and other penalties. In Hawaii, anyone caught driving with an alcohol blood level of 0.08% or greater is guilty of driving under the influence (DUI) and will have their driver's license taken away on the spot.

As in most places, the possession of marijuana and nonprescription narcotics is illegal in Hawaii. Be aware that US Customs has a zero-tolerance policy for drugs; federal authorities have been known to seize boats after finding even minute quantities of marijuana on board. Tobacco smoking is prohibited in enclosed public places, including restaurants and hotel lobbies. You must be at least 18 years old to smoke.

For consumer issues, Hawaii's **Department of Commerce & Consumer Affairs** (☎ 587-3222; http://hawaii.gov/dcca) provides information on your rights and the opportunity to file complaints about car rentals, time-share contracts, etc.

MAPS

Waikiki's free tourist magazines contain elemental island maps, but if you're going to be renting a car and doing any exploring, it's worth picking up a good driving map.

The **American Automobile Association** (Map pp54-5; AAA; ☎ 808-593-2221; www.aaa.com; Suite A170, 1130 N Nimitz Hwy; ☾ 9am-5pm Mon-Fri, 9am-2pm Sat) distributes a free, reliable road map of Honolulu and O'ahu that members can pick up at its Honolulu office. You can buy a similar road map published by Rand McNally ($4.95) at convenience stores all over the island.

Don Phears' full-color, 200-plus-page *O'ahu Mapbook* ($14.95), which indexes every street on the island, is the most comprehensive and easy-to-use map atlas, though it's more detailed than most visitors will need. It's sold at bookstores.

Topographical maps of O'ahu, both full-island and detailed sectional maps, can be ordered or downloaded online from the **US Geological Survey** (USGS; ☎ 888-275-8747; www.usgs .gov). Note the dates on these maps, as some were drawn decades ago. In Honolulu, USGS maps, nautical charts and other specialty maps are sold at the **Pacific Map Center** (Map p228; ☎ 677-6277; Gentry Business Park, 94-529 Uke'e St, Waipahu; 🕑 9am-noon & 1-5pm Mon-Fri).

Franko's Maps (www.frankosmaps.com) produces a laminated, waterproof O'ahu map ($10) showing popular snorkeling and diving spots. Ask for it at dive shops, water-sports outfitters and convenience stores, especially in Waikiki.

MONEY

All prices in this book are quoted in US dollars. For an idea of how much to budget for your vacation, see Planning Your Trip (p266).

If you're carrying foreign currency, it can be exchanged for US dollars at larger banks or at the exchange booths inside Honolulu International Airport. See the Quick Reference page on the inside front cover for exchange rates.

Major banks, such as the **Bank of Hawaii** (www.boh.com) and **First Hawaiian Bank** (www.fhb .com), have extensive ATM networks throughout O'ahu that will give cash advances on major credit cards. Most ATMs accept bank cards from both the Plus and Cirrus systems, the USA's two largest ATM networks. For cash withdrawals, most ATMs charge at least $2. Besides at banks, ATMs can be found at supermarkets, convenience stores and shopping centers.

Major credit cards are widely accepted, including at car rental agencies and most hotels, restaurants, gas stations, stores and tour operators. Some B&Bs, condominiums and vacation rental agencies will not accept credit cards, preferring cash, traveler's checks or personal checks drawn on US bank accounts. Major hotels, restaurants and stores accept US dollar traveler's checks as if they're cash, although smaller businesses and fast-food chains may refuse them.

Hawaii has a 4.17% state sales tax tacked onto virtually everything, including meals, groceries, car rentals and accommodations. An additional 7.24% room tax brings the total tax for accommodations to 11.41%.

TIPPING

Tipping practices in Hawaii are the same as in the rest of the USA. Only withhold tips if you've had outrageously bad service. Here's a thumbnail tipping guide:

- **Airport & hotel porters** $2 per bag, minimum $5 per cart
- **Bartenders** 10% to 15% per round, minimum $1 per drink
- **Hotel maids** $2 to $4 per night, left in the card provided
- **Restaurant servers** 15% to 20%, unless a service charge is already on the bill
- **Taxi drivers** 10% to 15%, rounded up to the next dollar
- **Valet parking attendants** At least $2 when you get back the keys to your car

Also targeting tourists, a $3-per-day 'road use' tax is added to the cost of all car rentals.

PHOTOGRAPHY

For a short course on general photographic dos and don'ts, consult Lonely Planet's *Travel Photography*. Try not to leave your camera in direct sunlight, if possible. Don't even think about taking photos of Hawaii's military installations.

Both print and slide film are widely available on O'ahu. Disposable underwater cameras costing about $15 are sold everywhere and deliver surprisingly good snaps. Consider having your film developed in Hawaii, because the high temperature and humidity of the tropics greatly accelerate the deterioration of exposed film. Longs Drugs is one of the cheapest places for both purchasing film and having it developed. Several places in Waikiki offer one-hour photo processing and occasionally have one-stop digital-photo printing and CD-burning stations. Most cybercafes around Waikiki offer inexpensive memory-card-to-CD transfer services for digital photos.

POST

Although mail between Hawaii and the US mainland can be slow, the **US Postal Service** (USPS; ☎ 800-275-8777; www.usps.com) is reliable and inexpensive. For postal rates, post office locations and opening hours, call the 24-hour hotline or go online.

The **main post office** (Map pp54-5; 3600 Aolele St; ⏱ 7:30am-3pm Mon-Fri) is not in central Honolulu, but instead is next to Honolulu International Airport, opposite the commuter terminal. For general-delivery poste-restante service, domestic mail is usually held for 10 days, international mail for 30 days. Bring photo ID to collect your mail. Some hotels will also hold mail (but usually not packages) for incoming guests.

At the time of writing, domestic US postage rates for 1st-class mail were 42¢ for letters up to 1oz and 27¢ for postcards; international airmail rates for letters or postcards up to 1oz were 72¢ to Canada or Mexico and 94¢ to all other countries.

SHOPPING

Honolulu is a cosmopolitan city, with sophisticated stores selling designer clothing, jewelry and more. The most fashionable shops are found on Waikiki's Kalakaua Ave, alongside endless touristy Hawaiiana kitsch – usually made in China, not Hawaii.

There are many fine craftspeople living on O'ahu and choice handicrafts are easily found around the island. Ensure that what you buy is authentic Hawaiiana by shopping at respected art galleries and artists' cooperatives. For more about traditional and contemporary arts and crafts, see p255. Many of O'ahu's contemporary island potters are influenced by Japanese styles and aesthetics; skillfully made *raku* (rustic-style pottery) work, in particular, abounds in island galleries and gift shops.

Hawaii's island-style clothing is light and colorful, often with tropical flower prints. The aloha shirt is a Hawaii creation, the product of Ellery Chun, a Honolulu tailor who created the original in 1931. It was influenced by two things: the baggy checkered shirts worn by plantation workers and then-popular Japanese immigrant shirts made from colorful kimonos. Aloha shirts have been the island dress for men ever since. Today the classiest aloha shirts are made of lightweight cotton with subdued colors (like those of reverse fabric prints).

For locally made jewelry, the premium product in Hawaii is the delicate Ni'ihau shell leis. These necklaces, made from tiny seashells that wash up on the island of Ni'ihau, are one of the most prized Hawaiiana souvenirs. Ni'ihauans painstakingly string the tiny shells into finely handcrafted spiral strands with intricate patterns. The best Ni'ihau shell lei cost thousands of dollars and are sold at top-end jewelry stores.

The standard edible souvenir is macadamia nuts, either plain or covered in chocolate. But there are many other Hawaii-made food products, such as macadamia nut butters, *liliko'i* (passion fruit) preserves and lavosh flatbread crackers – all make convenient, compact gift items. O'ahu's Waialua coffee has yet to gain the gourmet cachet of 100% Kona coffee, but the latest harvest is worth sampling. Another O'ahu-grown souvenir, pineapples, are not necessarily great gifts: not only are they heavy and bulky, but they're likely to be just as cheap back home.

Be aware that all fresh produce and food products must be pre-packaged and approved for plane travel from Hawaii to the US mainland, or you'll be forced to surrender it at the airport. For details, see the boxed text, p285.

TELEPHONE

All phone numbers in Hawaii consist of a three-digit area code (☎ 808) followed by a seven-digit number. Any call made from one point on O'ahu to any other point on O'ahu is a local call. Long-distance calls from O'ahu to the Neighbor Islands require dialing the area code.

Always dial '1' before any domestic long-distance or toll-free (☎ 800, ☎ 866, ☎ 877, ☎ 888 etc) number. Some toll-free numbers may work only within Hawaii or from the US mainland, while others may work from Canada, too. For directory assistance for O'ahu phone numbers dial ☎ 411; for phone numbers elsewhere in Hawaii dial ☎ 808-555-1212.

If you're calling Hawaii from abroad, the international country code for the USA (and Canada) is ☎ 1. To make an international call direct from Hawaii, dial ☎ 011 plus the country code plus the area code plus the number. For calls to Canada, dial ☎ 1 plus the area code plus the number (international rates still apply). For international operator assistance, dial ☎ 0.

Payphones may still be found in public places such as shopping centers, beach parks and hotel lobbies. You can deposit coins, use a phonecard (sold at post offices, convenience stores, pharmacies and supermarkets), call collect or freely dial toll-free numbers from payphones. Local calls made from payphones cost 25¢ or 50¢. Most hotels tack on hefty surcharges for any calls made from in-room phones.

The only European and Asian cell (mobile) phones that will work in Hawaii are GSM tri- or quad-band models. Reception is quite good on most of O'ahu, but can be spotty in remote areas and on hiking trails. Verizon has the most extensive cellular network on the islands, but AT&T, Cingular and Sprint also have decent coverage. At the time of writing, the Verizon and Sprint networks were not GSM-compatible.

Faxes can be sent and received through the front desks of most hotels. There are also business centers that offer reasonably priced fax services, such as **FedEx Office** (☎ 800-463-3339; www.fedex.com), which has a few branches in Honolulu.

TIME

Hawaii Standard Time (HST) is 10 hours behind GMT/UMC; Hawaii does not observe daylight saving time (DST). When it's noon in Hawaii, it's 2pm in Los Angeles (3pm during DST) and 5pm in New York City (6pm during DST). In midwinter, the sun rises around 7am and sets around 6pm. In midsummer, it rises before 6am and sets after 7pm. The term 'Hawaii time' means taking things at a slow pace (it's often a euphemism for being late).

TOURIST INFORMATION

Far and away the best place to pick up information is at the airport. In the arrivals area there are staffed tourist-information desks, and while you're waiting for your bags to appear on the carousel, you can leaf through racks of tourist brochures and magazines, such as **101 Things to Do** (www.101thingstodo.com), covering everything from arts and entertainment to outdoor activities and dining.

Hawaii Visitors & Convention Bureau (HVCB; Map pp102-3; ☎ 923-1811, 800-464-2924; www.gohawaii.com; Suite 801, Waikiki Business Plaza, 2270 Kalakaua Ave, Waikiki; ⏰ 8am-4:30pm Mon-Fri)
O'ahu Visitors Bureau (Map pp60-1; ☎ 524-0722, 877-525-6248; www.visit-oahu.com; Suite 1520, 733 Bishop St, Honolulu; ⏰ 8am-4pm)

TOURS

O'ahu has an extensive public bus system (p289), so self-guided touring, even without a rental car, is a good option. However, waiting for buses and walking between bus stops and sights does take up time. You can undoubtedly pack much more into a day by joining an organized tour, which can easily be booked after arrival.

A variety of conventional sightseeing van and bus tours are offered by **Polynesian Adventure Tours** (☎ 833-3000, 800-622-3011; www.polyad.com) and **Roberts Hawaii** (☎ 954-8652, 866-898-2519; www.robertshawaii.com). For example, Polynesian Adventure Tours offers a half-day tour that includes downtown Honolulu, Punchbowl Crater and Pearl Harbor's USS *Arizona* Memorial. Another half-day tour takes in Diamond Head, Hanauma Bay, Halona Blowhole, Nu'uanu Pali Lookout and Mt Tantalus. These half-day tours cost around $30/20 per adult/child.

The mainstay for these tour companies are full-day (roughly 8am to 6pm) 'Circle Island' tours costing around $65/40 per adult/child. It typically starts with a visit to Diamond Head Crater and a drive past Southeast O'ahu sights; goes up the Windward Coast, taking in Byōdō-In temple in Kane'ohe; circles back along the North Shore, stopping at Sunset Beach and Waimea Bay; then drives past the pineapple fields of central O'ahu before returning to Waikiki.

If you want to visit another Hawaiian island but only have a day to spare, consider a mini-package tour to one of the Neighbor Islands, including round-trip airfare and a day-long sightseeing tour. Rates typically start at $300 per person, not including lunch. The largest company for island-hopping tours is Roberts Hawaii. If you'd rather not rush, weekend Neighbor Island tours offered through the University of Hawai'i's **Campus Center Leisure Programs** (Map p71; ☎ 956-6468; www.hawaii.edu/cclp; Room 101,

Hemenway Hall, 2445 Campus Center Rd; tours $334) happen monthly.

Elderhostel (☎ 800-454-5768; www.elderhostel.org) offers excellent educational programs for those aged 55 or older focusing on Hawaii's people and culture and the natural environment. One- to three-week programs cost from $1200 to $4350, including accommodations, meals and classes, but not airfare.

For specialized tours, including helicopter flights, see the Outdoor Activities & Adventures chapter (p26), as well as the Activities sections for each destination in the destination chapters. For cruises to Hawaii, see p287.

TRAVELERS WITH DISABILITIES

O'ahu is a reasonably accommodating destination for travelers with disabilities, and Waikiki is considered one of the more accessible destinations in the USA. Many larger and/or recently renovated hotels have elevators, wheelchair-accessible rooms, TDD-capable phones and other features to help ease the way. The Waikiki beachfront has been extensively renovated with dropped curbs and many low-profile ramps. The **Department of Parks and Recreation** (☎ 768-3027; www.co.honolulu.hi.us/parks/programs /beach/) provides all-terrain wheelchairs that allow those with mobility issues to wheel onto the sand at several beaches, including Ala Moana, Fort DeRussy, Hanauma Bay, Sans Souci, Kailua, Kualoa and Poka'i Bay. These wheelchairs are free of charge, but you'll need to call ahead to make arrangements in advance.

In terms of getting around O'ahu, all public buses are accessible to those with disabilities and will 'kneel' if you are unable to use the steps – just let the driver know that you need to use the lift or ramp. If you have a disability parking placard from home, bring it with you and hang it from your rental car's rearview mirror when parking in designated handicapped-parking spaces. Some major car-rental agencies (p290) offer hand-controlled vehicles at no extra charge, but you'll need to reserve these well in advance.

Hawaii's **Disability & Communication Access Board** (Map pp54–5; ☎ 586-8121; www.hawaii.gov/health /dcab/travel; Room 101, 919 Ala Moana Blvd, Honolulu) provides online 'Travel Tips' brochures with information on airport arrivals, transportation, medical equipment and supplies, and various support services. **Access Aloha Travel** (☎ 545-1143, 800-480-1143; www.accessaloha travel.com), an established local travel agency, is a great resource for finding wheelchair-accessible accommodations, sightseeing tours and rental vans.

Guide dogs and other service animals are not subject to the same animal-quarantine requirements as other pets, provided they meet certain requirements. For details, contact the **Animal Quarantine Station** (☎ 483-7151; http://hawaii.gov/hdoa) before your arrival in Hawaii.

VOLUNTEERING

A partnership network of community and nonprofit organizations, **Mālama Hawai'i** (www .malamahawaii.org) fills its online volunteer calendar with fundraising concerts, educational events, cultural workshops and outdoor field trips (eg pulling up invasive weeds, beach clean-up days). Aimed at O'ahu residents, **Volunteer Zone** (www.volunteer zone.org) also welcomes short-term visitors. For more about local volunteer opportunities, see p43.

WOMEN TRAVELERS

Women travelers are no more likely to encounter problems in O'ahu than elsewhere in the USA. Exercise extra caution walking along beaches after dark, especially alone. If you're camping (see p269), opt for secure, well-used camping areas over isolated locales. Many county parks and their campgrounds are notorious for late-night beer binges by locals; some are also known for long-term squatters, particularly on the Wai'anae Coast.

If you are sexually assaulted, it may be best to call the 24-hour, multilingual **Sex Abuse Treatment Center hotline** (☎ 524-7273) before contacting the **police** (☎ 911), or go straight to a hospital emergency room. Many police do not have as much training or experience in aiding sexual-assault survivors as do rape crisis-hotline counselors and specially trained nurses; a rape crisis center or hospital will advocate on your behalf and act as a liaison to other community services, including the police.

Planned Parenthood Hawaii (Map pp68-9; ☎ 589-1149; www.plannedparenthood.org/hawaii; 1350 S King St, Honolulu; 🕒 by appointment) operates a female-friendly medical clinic.

WORK

US citizens can seek employment in Hawaii as they would in any other state. Foreign visitors in the USA on tourist visas are not legally allowed to take up employment. To work legally, foreign citizens must apply for a nontourist visa before leaving home

Much of the economy here is tied to the minimum-wage service industry. For newcomers, the most common work is waiting tables in Waikiki, and if you're young and energetic, there are job possibilities in bars and clubs. Folks with foreign-language abilities, outdoor-sports guiding experience (such as scuba instructors) or cosmetology skills might investigate employment with hotel resorts, outdoor-activity operators and spas.

Finding more serious 'professional' employment is difficult since Hawaii has a tight labor market. Professional jobs that do open up are generally filled by established Hawaii residents. The biggest exceptions are for teachers and nurses, which are usually in short supply.

Check the classified job ads online at **Craigslist** (http://honolulu.craigslist.org) and the **Honolulu Advertiser** (www.honoluluadvertiser.com) and also at http://browsewww.jobshawaii.com and www.hirenethawaii.com. For more details about employment, contact Hawaii's **Department of Labor & Industrial Relations** (Map pp60-1; ☎ 586-8842; www.hawaii.gov/labor; 830 Punchbowl St, Honolulu; 🕒 8am-4:30pm Mon-Fri).

GETTING THERE & AWAY

Most visitors to O'ahu arrive by air. Honolulu is a major Pacific hub and intermediate stop on many flights between the US mainland and Asia, Australia, New Zealand and the South Pacific. Flights can be booked online at www.lonelyplanet.com/bookings.

AIR

To get through US airport security checkpoints, you will need a boarding pass and photo ID. Airport security measures restrict many common items (eg pocket knives) from being carried on planes. These regulations often change, so get the latest information directly from the **Transportation Security Administration** (TSA; ☎ 866-289-9673; www.tsa.gov). All checked baggage is screened for explosives, and TSA inspectors may open your suitcase for visual confirmation, breaking the lock if necessary. Either leave your bags unlocked or use a TSA-approved lock like **Travel Sentry** (www.travelsentry.org).

Airports

All flights to O'ahu arrive at **Honolulu International Airport** (Map pp54-5; HNL; ☎ 836-6413; www.honoluluairport.com), a modern facility with the usual amenities like currency-exchange booths, duty-free shops and fast-food eateries. You'll find a visitor information booth, car-rental counters and courtesy phones in the baggage claim area. Free **Wiki-Wiki shuttle buses** (🕒 6am-10pm) connect the airport's public terminals.

Airlines

Airlines flying into Honolulu (listed here with US toll-free numbers):

Air Canada (AC; ☎ 888-247-2262; www.aircanada.com)
Air New Zealand (NZ; ☎ 800-262-1234; www.air newzealand.com)

THINGS CHANGE...

The information in this chapter is particularly vulnerable to change. Check directly with the airline or a travel agent to make sure you understand how a fare (and ticket you may buy) works, and be aware of the security requirements for international travel. Shop carefully. The details given in this chapter should be regarded as pointers and are not a substitute for your own careful, up-to-date research.

AGRICULTURAL INSPECTION

All luggage and carry-on bags leaving Hawaii for the US mainland are checked by an agricultural inspector using an X-ray machine. You cannot take out gardenia, jade vine or Mauna Loa anthurium, even in leis, although most other fresh flowers and foliage are permitted. You can bring home pineapples and coconuts, but most other fresh fruits and vegetables are banned. Other things not allowed to enter mainland states include plants in soil, fresh coffee berries (roasted beans are OK), cactus and sugarcane. However, any seeds, fruits and plants that have been certified and labeled for export are allowed. For more information, call the **USDA Honolulu Inspection Office** (☎ 861-8490) or go online to http://hawaii .gov/hdoa.

Air Pacific Airways (FJ; ☎ 800-227-4446; www.air pacific.com)
Alaska Airlines (AS; ☎ 800-252-7522; www.alaska air.com)
All Nippon Airways (NH; ☎ 800-235-9262; www.fly-ana.com)
American Airlines (AA; ☎ 800-433-7300; www.aa.com)
China Airlines (CI; ☎ 808-955-0088; www.china -airlines.com)
Continental Airlines (CO; ☎ 800-523-3273; www.continental.com)
Delta Air Lines (DL; ☎ 800-221-1212; www.delta.com)
go!/Mesa Airlines (YV; ☎ 888-435-9462; www .iflygo.com)
Hawaiian Airlines (HA; ☎ 800-367-5320; www .hawaiianair.com)
Island Air (IS; ☎ O'ahu 484-2222, mainland 800-652-6541; www.islandair.com)
Japan Airlines (JL; ☎ 800-525-3663; www.japanair .com)
Korean Air (KE; ☎ 800-438-5000; www.korean air.com)
Mokulele Airlines (MW; ☎ 808-426-7070; www .mokuleleairlines.com)
Northwest-KLM (NW; ☎ 800-225-2525; www.nwa .com)
Pacific Wings (LW; ☎ 888-575-4546; www.pacific wings.com)
Philippine Airlines (PR; ☎ 800-435-9725; www .philippineairlines.com)

Qantas Airways (QF; ☎ 800-227-4500; www.qantas usa.com)
United Airlines (UA; ☎ 800-864-8331; www.united .com)
US Airways (US; ☎ 800-428-4322; www.usairways .com)

Tickets

Airfares to Hawaii vary tremendously, depending on the season and day of the week you fly and how much flexibility is allowed for flight changes and refunds. There's a lot of competition, and at any given time any airline could have the cheapest fare.

Start by checking airline websites and online travel-booking sites (eg www.expe dia.com, www.orbitz.com, www.travelocity .com). Similar sites also worth trying are www.cheaptickets.com and www.lowest fare.com. Meta-sites are good for price comparisons, but they don't provide direct booking: try www.farecast.com, www .kayak.com, www.mobissimo.com, www .qixo.com and www.sidestep.com. If you're flexible, you might be able to save a bundle with www.priceline.com, www.hotwire .com or www.skyauction.com, but read all of the fine print carefully before bidding. Click to www.biddingfortravel.com for more advice about Priceline, which can also be great for car rentals and hotels.

Once in Hawaii, you'll find discounted fares to virtually anywhere around the Pacific. Travel agencies that specialize in discount tickets, including for interisland flights, include **Panda Travel** (Map pp102-3; ☎ 738-3898, 800-303-6702; www.pandaonline.com; 1017 Kapahulu Ave, Honolulu).

Round-the-world (RTW) tickets allow you to fly in only one direction (ie east or west) on the combined routes of airline partnerships such as **Star Alliance** (www .staralliance.com) and **One World** (www.oneworld.com). RTW tickets are valid for a fixed period, usually a year. Circle Pacific tickets are similar to RTW tickets, as they allow you to keep flying in the same circular direction between destinations ranged around the Pacific Ocean.

For RTW and Circle Pacific tickets:
Air Brokers International (☎ 800-883-3273; www .airbrokers.com)
Airtreks (☎ 877-247-8735; www.airtreks.com)
JustFares (☎ 800-766-3601; http://justfares.com)

US MAINLAND

Competition is high among airlines flying to Honolulu, and fares can fluctuate wildly. Typically, round-trip fares from the US mainland to Honolulu range from $350 (from the West Coast during the off-season) to $800 (from the East Coast during peak winter months). American Airlines, Continental Airlines, Delta Air Line, Northwest Airlines and United Airlines fly to Honolulu from both the East and West Coasts. In addition, Hawaiian Airlines flies to Honolulu from several West Coast cities, including Los Angeles, Oakland, Portland, Sacramento, San Diego, San Francisco, San Jose (California) and Seattle, as well as from Las Vegas and Phoenix. US Airways flies to Honolulu from Phoenix. Alaska Airlines flies to Honolulu from Seattle and Anchorage.

If you're going to Hawaii for only a short getaway, vacation packages that include accommodations and possibly car rental might cost only a little more than airfare alone. **Pleasant Holidays** (☎ 800-742-9244; www.pleasantholidays.com) and **Sun Trips** (☎ 800-514-5194; www.suntrips.com) offer Hawaii package tours with departures from dozens of US mainland cities.

Possibly the cheapest way to fly between the West Coast and Hawaii, **AirTech** (☎ 212-219-7000; www.airtech.com) offers super deals by selling stand-by seats. If you provide them with a four-day travel window, they'll get you a seat or refund your money. Currently, AirTech flies to Honolulu from San Francisco and Los Angeles.

WITHIN HAWAII

Frequent flights between Honolulu and the major Neighbor Islands (Maui, Kaua'i and the Big Island of Hawai'i) are available with the main interisland carriers, Hawaiian Airlines and go!, a subsidiary of Mesa Airlines. Both of these airlines fly comfortable widebody jets, although Hawaiian Airlines has far more flights and reliable service. Upstart commuter airlines such as Island Air and Pacific Wings also fly between the Hawaiian Islands, including to Moloka'i and Lana'i, using smaller turboprop aircraft that almost double as sightseeing planes – seriously, it's a lot of fun!

Given the intense competition between airlines, interisland fares vary wildly. Expect to pay from around $65 to $150 one way. Round-trip fares are usually double the one-way fares without any additional discounts. The earlier you book your interisland ticket, the more likely you are to find a cheaper fare. It's usually best to buy tickets via the airlines' websites, which post internet-only deals and other promotions.

AUSTRALIA

Hawaiian Airlines and Qantas Airways, as well as Qantas' budget airline, **Jetstar** (☎ 131 538; www.jetstar.com), fly nonstop between Sydney and Honolulu. Travel agents serving Australia include **Flight Centre** (☎ 1300 133 133; www.flightcentre.com.au), **STA Travel** (☎ 1300 134 782; www.statravel.com.au) and **Zuji** (☎ 1300 888 180; www.zuji.com.au).

CANADA

Air Canada offers direct flights to Honolulu from Toronto and Vancouver, with connections via these hubs from other Canadian cities. Travel agents serving Canada include **Expedia** (☎ 888 397 3342; www.expedia.ca), **Travel Cuts** (☎ 866 246 9762; www.travelcuts.com) and **Travelocity** (☎ 800 457 8010; www.travelocity.ca).

JAPAN

Japan Airlines (JAL) flies to Honolulu from Tokyo, Osaka and Nagoya. All Nippon Airways (ANA) flies to Honolulu from Tokyo. Both JAL and ANA offer connecting flights from other Japanese cities. Northwest Airlines and United Airlines have flights to Honolulu from Tokyo; Northwest also flies from Osaka. Travel agents serving Japan include **No 1 Travel** (☎ 03 3205 6073; www.no1-travel.com) and **STA Travel** (☎ 03 5391 2922; www.statravel.co.jp).

NEW ZEALAND, MICRONESIA & SOUTH PACIFIC ISLANDS

Air New Zealand flies from Auckland to Honolulu. Continental Airlines has nonstop flights from Guam to Honolulu, sometimes allowing stops en route at the Micronesian islands of Chuuk (Truk), Pohnpei, Kosrae, Kwajalein and Majuro – a cool way to see some of the world's most remote islands. Hawaiian Airlines flies to Honolulu from Tahiti and American Samoa. Travel agents serving New Zealand include **Flight Centre** (☎ 0800 243 544; www.flightcentre.co.nz), **STA Travel** (☎ 0800 474 400; www.statravel.co.nz) and **Travelocity** (☎ 0800 451 297; www.travelocity.co.nz).

UK & CONTINENTAL EUROPE

In addition to some European carriers, American, Continental Airlines and United Airlines offer flights to Honolulu from various European cities. The most common route from Europe to Hawaii is flying west via New York, Chicago or Los Angeles. If you're heading east with stops in Asia, consider getting a RTW ticket (see p285). Travel agents serving the UK include **Flight Centre** (☎ 0870 499 0040; www.flightcentre.co.uk), **STA Travel** (☎ 0871 230 0040; www.statravel.co.uk) and **Trailfinders** (☎ 0845 058 5858; www.trailfinders.com).

SEA

Cruise Ships

Most cruises to Hawaii not only include stopovers in Honolulu, but also visit Maui, Kaua'i and the Big Island of Hawai'i. Most cruises last 10 to 15 days, with fares starting at around $100 per day per person, based on double occupancy. Airfare to and from the departure point costs extra.

Cruise lines sailing to Honolulu:

Holland America Line (☎ 877-932-4259; www.hollandamerica.com) Typically departs from San Diego, Seattle or Vancouver.

Princess Cruises (☎ 800-774-6237; www.princess.com) Offers the most cruises, with departures from Los Angeles, Vancouver, Tahiti and Australia.

Royal Caribbean Cruise Line (☎ 866-562-7625; www.royalcaribbean.com) Has departures mostly from Vancouver.

Currently, the only company running interisland cruises is **Norwegian Cruise Line** (☎ 866-234-0292; www.ncl.com). Seven-day cruises on its *Pride of America* liner originate in Honolulu, stopping at Maui, the Big Island and Kaua'i. Per-person fares range from $1250 for an inside berth (no view!) to $5050 for a suite, based on double occupancy.

Ferry

The **Hawaii Superferry** (☎ 877-443-3779; www.hawaiisuperferry.com) is a state-of-the-art, 800-passenger catamaran that carries both passengers and vehicles. At press time, the Superferry had suspended all services for the foreseeable future following a Hawaii Supreme Court ruling that it had unfairly bypassed a legally required environmental review. If the company does start making daily round trips again between Honolulu, O'ahu and Kahului, Maui, the interisland trip is usually three hours each way. Some major car-rental agencies may allow their vehicles to be taken on board. Consult the Superferry website for details, including the latest status updates, routes, schedules and fares.

GETTING AROUND

O'ahu is a relatively easy island to get around, whether you're traveling by car or public bus. Compared with US mainland cities, O'ahu's traffic is fairly manageable, although Honolulu jams up during rush

WHICH WAY?!

Directions on O'ahu are often given by using landmarks. If someone tells you to 'go 'Ewa' (an area west of Honolulu) or 'go Diamond Head' (east of Waikiki), it simply means to head in that direction. Two other commonly used directional terms are *makai*, meaning 'toward the ocean', and *mauka*, meaning 'inland' or 'toward the mountain'.

hours, usually weekdays from 7am to 9am and 3pm to 6pm. Expect heavy traffic in both directions on the H1 Fwy during this time, as well as on the Pali and Likelike Hwys headed into Honolulu in the morning and out of town in the late afternoon. If you're going to the airport during rush hour, give yourself plenty of extra time.

TO/FROM THE AIRPORT

The vast majority of visitors to O'ahu land at **Honolulu International Airport** (HNL; Map pp54–5; ☎ 836-6413; www.honoluluairport.com), the island's only commercial airport. It's on the western outskirts of Honolulu, about 9 miles northwest of Waikiki via Ala Moana Blvd/Nimitz Hwy (Hwy 92) or the H1 Fwy.

From the airport, you can get to Waikiki by airport shuttle, local bus, rental car or taxi. A taxi from the airport to Waikiki costs approximately $30 to $35, depending on your hotel. Major car-rental agencies have booths or courtesy phones in the arrivals and baggage-claim area.

Airport Shuttle

A few private companies, including **Roberts Hawaii** (☎ 954-8652, 866-898-2519), offer 24-hour shuttle service between the airport and Waikiki hotels, departing every 20 minutes. The ride averages 45 minutes, but can be longer or shorter depending on how many passengers are dropped off before reaching your hotel. Board these buses at the roadside median on the ground level, in front of the baggage-claim areas. You don't need a reservation from the airport to Waikiki but you do need to call 48 hours in advance for the return trip to the airport. If you buy a round-trip ticket upon boarding at the airport, it costs $15; otherwise each one-way ticket costs $9. Any odd-sized or excess baggage costs $4 extra ($17 per surfboard, $25 per bicycle).

Bus

Travel time between the airport and Waikiki via TheBus, O'ahu's public bus network (see opposite), takes about 70 minutes. TheBus lines 19 and 20 both depart the airport about every 20 minutes from 5am to 11:30pm daily; the fare is $2. These buses stop at the roadside median on the airport terminal's second level, near the airline counters. There are two stops, but buses sometimes fill up, so it's best to catch them at the first stop, which is in front of Lobby 4; the second stop is between Lobby 6 and 7. Luggage is limited to what you can hold on your lap or store under your seat, the latter comparable to the space under an airline seat. In Waikiki, buses stop every couple of blocks or so along Kalia Rd, Saratoga Rd and Kuhio Ave.

Car

The easiest way to drive to Waikiki from the airport is to take Hwy 92, which starts out as the Nimitz Hwy and turns into Ala Moana Blvd, leading directly into Waikiki.

Although this route joins more local traffic, it's hard to get lost on it. For life in the fast lane, take the H1 Fwy heading east, then follow the signs to Waikiki. (Incidentally, H1 is a US *interstate* freeway – an amusing designation for an island road in the middle of the Pacific.) Driving back to the airport, beware of the poorly marked interchange where H1 and Hwy 78 split; if you're not in the right-hand lane at that point, you could easily end up on Hwy 78. It takes about 20 minutes to get from Waikiki to the airport via H1 – if you don't catch heavy traffic – but give yourself at least 40 minutes during rush hour.

BICYCLE

Getting around O'ahu solely by bicycle is challenging. First, there's heavy traffic to contend with, especially in the Honolulu metro area. O'ahu has been slow to adopt pro-bike policies such as bicycle lanes. In Waikiki, the best thoroughfares for cyclists are the one-way streets of canalside Ala Wai Blvd and oceanfront Kalakaua Ave. An easier way to get into O'ahu's countryside without peddling through Honolulu traffic is to take TheBus beyond the city limits. Public buses (see opposite) are now equipped with racks that can carry two bicycles. To use the bike rack, first tell the bus driver you will be loading your bike, then secure your bicycle onto the fold-down rack, hop aboard and pay the regular fare. There's no surcharge for bringing along your bike.

Cyclists are not allowed to ride on sidewalks within a business district, such as Waikiki or downtown Honolulu. Cyclists using a roadway have all the rights and duties applicable to motor-vehicle drivers, and must travel on the right side of the road, stop at red lights etc. The state of Hawaii does not require cyclists over the age of 15 to wear helmets, but they are still recommended. Any bicycle used from 30 minutes after sunset until 30 minutes before sunrise must have a forward-facing headlight and at least one red reflector mounted on the rear. Bicycles are prohibited on all freeways.

Hawaii's Department of Transportation publishes a free *Bike O'ahu* map, available online at www.state.hi.us/dot/highways/bike/oahu, showing suggested routes for novice and experienced cyclists. You can pick up a free hard-copy map from the **Hawaii Visitors & Convention Bureau** (HVCB; Map pp102-3; ☎ 923-1811, 800-464-2924; www.gohawaii.com; Suite 801, Waikiki Business Plaza, 2270 Kalakaua Ave, Waikiki; ◷ 8am-4:30pm Mon-Fri) or at bike shops around O'ahu.

Bicycle rental rates average $15 to $20 per day for a beach cruiser and $30 to $40 per day for a mountain bike, with weekly discounts available (a hefty credit-card deposit is required). Waikiki rental shops (see p133) are ultra-convenient, but for top-notch gear and service, try this place:

Bike Shop Honolulu (Map pp68-9; ☎ 596-0588; 1149 S King St, Honolulu; ◷ 9am-7pm Mon-Fri, 9am-5pm Sat, 10am-5pm Sun); Windward Coast (Map p172; ☎ 261-1553; 270 Ku'ulei Rd, Kailua; ◷ 10am-7pm Mon-Fri, 9am-5pm Sat, 10am-5pm Sun) Rentals, sales and free weekend group rides.

BOAT

Although not many visitors know about it, a weekday commuter ferry service called TheBoat runs between the Aloha Tower (Map pp60–1) in downtown Honolulu and Kalaeloa Pier at Barbers Point Harbor (Map p229) in Leeward O'ahu. While this 149-passenger ferry is not designed for tourists, it does offer an inexpensive one-hour cruise down O'ahu's south shore. If you want to ride TheBoat in both directions, you'll probably need to catch either the first outbound boat at 6:35am or the 3:55pm afternoon departure outbound from the Aloha Tower; always call ahead to confirm schedules, as they're highly subject to change. The one-way adult fare is $2 ($1 for seniors and children); TheBus transfers can be used to get on board.

BUS

O'ahu's extensive public bus system, **TheBus** (☎ 848-5555; www.thebus.org; ◷ infoline 5:30am-10pm), is convenient and easy to use. TheBus has over a hundred routes that collectively cover most of O'ahu. You can take TheBus to watch windsurfers at Kailua or surfers at Sunset Beach, visit Chinatown or the Bishop Museum, snorkel at Hanauma Bay or hike Diamond Head. TheBus is also useful for short hops around Waikiki and Honolulu's other neighborhoods. Some of the island's prime viewpoints and hiking trails are beyond reach of TheBus, however. For instance, TheBus doesn't stop at the Nu'uanu Pali Lookout, go up into the Tantalus green belt or run as far as Ka'ena Point on the Wai'anae Coast.

Although TheBus is convenient enough, if you set your watch by it, you'll come up with Hawaii time (see p282). Besides not getting hung up on schedules, buses can sometimes bottleneck, with one packed bus after another passing right by crowded bus stops (you can't just flag a bus down anywhere along its route). Waiting for a bus between the Ala Moana Center and Waikiki on a Saturday night can be a frustrating experience.

Still, TheBus usually gets you where you want to go. As long as you don't try to cut your travel time too close or schedule too much in one day, it's a great deal. All buses are wheelchair-accessible and have front-loading racks that can accommodate two bicycles for no extra charge. One caveat: be prepared for arctic air-con; a public bus in Honolulu is probably the coldest place on O'ahu, regardless of the season.

Another bus-like alternative is the Waikiki Trolley (see p134).

Fares & Passes

The regular one-way fare is $2 for adults and $1 for children aged six to 17; children under six ride free. You can pay with coins or $1 bills, but bus drivers do not give change. Transfers, which have a two-hour time limit stamped on them, are free, and limited to one transfer per paid one-way fare.

The best deal for short-term visitors is the O'ahu Discovery Passport, which is valid for unlimited rides over four consecutive days, costs $20 and can be purchased at any of Waikiki's ubiquitous ABC stores or at **TheBus Pass Office** (Map pp54-5; ☎ 848-4444; 811 Middle St; ◷ 7:30am-4pm Mon-Fri).

A monthly bus pass is valid for unlimited rides during a calendar month, and not just any 30-day period. It costs $40 and can be purchased at TheBus Pass Office, 7-Eleven convenience stores and Foodland or Star supermarkets.

Seniors (65 years and older) and anyone with a physical disability can buy a $10 discount card that entitles them to pay $1 per one-way fare, $5 for a monthly pass or $30 for an annual pass (valid for unlimited rides during a one-year period).

Routes & Schedules

Bus schedules vary with the route. Many operate from about 5am to 9pm, although many of the busiest main routes, such as those that serve Waikiki, run until almost 11pm. The Ala Moana Center is Honolulu's central transfer point.

Each route can have different destinations, and buses generally keep the same number when inbound and outbound. For instance, TheBus 8 can take you into the heart of Waikiki or away from it toward Ala Moana, so take note of both the number and the written destination before just jumping on. If in doubt, ask the bus driver – they're used to disoriented and jet-lagged visitors.

You can get printed timetables for individual routes free from TheBus Pass Office, public libraries, satellite city halls (such as at the Ala Moana Center; see p270) and **McDonald's** (2136 Kalakaua Ave) in Waikiki. Wherever you pick up timetables, also grab one of the free island-wide bus route map brochures – these will come in handy if you're using TheBus a lot.

For more details about specific bus routes, see the regional chapters earlier; for a table of common routes around Honolulu and Waikiki, see p133.

CAR

If you really want to explore off the beaten path, a car is the way to go. Just beware that Hawaii has the most expensive gasoline in the USA, costing up to 50% more than on the mainland. At the time of writing, gas on O'ahu cost about $2.45 per US gallon.

Parking is usually plentiful, except in the Honolulu and Waikiki areas. When parking on the street, be sure to feed the meter and read all posted restrictions to avoid being towed. Don't park within 15ft of a fire hydrant and be aware of colored curbs:

Blue Parking only for those with disabilities (permit required).

Green Parking for a limited time, as painted on the curb or signposted.

Red No parking or stopping anytime.

Yellow Stopping only to load or unload passengers.

Automobile Associations

Members of the **American Automobile Association** (AAA; Map pp54-5; ☎ 808-593-2221; www .aaa.com; Suite A170, 1130 N Nimitz Hwy; ☺ 9am-5pm Mon-Fri, 9am-2pm Sat) are entitled to discounts on car rentals and at some hotels and sightseeing attractions, as well as free road maps, trip-planning tools and travel-agency services. For emergency roadside assistance and towing, members should call ☎ 800-222-4357. For information on joining AAA before arrival in Hawaii, call ☎ 800-564-6222. AAA also has reciprocal agreements with automobile associations in other countries, so bring your membership card from home.

Driver's License

International visitors can legally drive in Hawaii with a valid driver's license issued by their home country. However, car-rental companies will generally accept valid foreign driver's licenses only if they are written in English. Otherwise, be prepared to present an International Driving Permit (IDP) along with your home license. The national automobile association in your home country can provide you with one for a small fee.

Rentals

Rental cars are available at the airport and in Waikiki. Always make reservations in advance. With most companies there's little or no cancellation penalty if you change your mind. Walking up to the counter without a reservation will subject you to higher rates, and during busy periods it's not uncommon for all cars to be rented out. (Really.)

The daily rate for a standard car ranges from $30 to $60, while weekly rates are typically $200 to $275, excluding insurance, taxes and fees. Rental rates usually include unlimited mileage, though if you drop off the car at a different location than where you picked it up, there's usually a hefty surcharge. Because some promotional discounts exclude economy and compact cars, sometimes the lowest rate available may actually be for a midsize vehicle.

If you belong to an automobile club or a frequent-flyer program, you'll often be eligible for some sort of discount. You might get a better deal by booking through discount-travel websites such as www.priceline.com or www.hotwire.com, or by using online booking agents like www.expedia.com, www.orbitz.com or www.travelocity.com.

Most rental companies require you to be at least 25 years old, possess a valid driver's license and have a major credit card, *not* a debit or check card. Otherwise, some agencies simply won't rent you a vehicle, while others will require prepayment by cash or traveler's checks, a deposit of $200 per week, proof of return airfare and more. A few companies rent to drivers between the ages of 21 and 24, typically for a surcharge of around $20 per day.

When picking up your vehicle, most car-rental agencies will request the name and phone number of the place where you're staying. Some companies may be loath to rent to visitors who list a campground as their address on the island, and a few specifically add 'No Camping Permitted' to their rental contracts.

Major car-rental companies operating on O'ahu:

Alamo (☎ 800-462-5266; www.alamo.com)
Avis (☎ 800-331-1212; www.avis.com)
Budget (☎ 800-527-0700; www.budget.com)
Dollar (☎ 800-800-3665; www.dollar.com)
Enterprise (☎ 800-261-7331; www.enterprise.com)
Hertz (☎ 800-654-3131; www.hertz.com)
National (☎ 800-227-7368; www.nationalcar.com)
Thrifty (☎ 800-847-4389; www.thrifty.com)

Avis, Budget, Dollar, Enterprise, National and Hertz all have rental cars available at Honolulu International Airport. Alamo and Thrifty have their operations about a mile outside the airport, off the Nimitz Hwy (Map pp54–5). All things being equal, try to rent from a company with its lot inside the airport – it's more convenient, and on the way back to the airport, all the highway signs lead to in-airport car returns. Driving around looking for a car-rental agency lot outside the airport when you're trying to catch a flight can be stressful.

In addition to their airport facilities, most of the international companies have multiple branch locations in Waikiki, many of them in the lobbies of larger hotels. When you

ROAD DISTANCES & DRIVING TIMES

Although actual times vary depending upon traffic conditions, the average driving times and distances from Waikiki to points of interest around O'ahu are as follows:

Destination	Miles	Time
Diamond Head	2	10min
Hale'iwa	33	50min
Hanauma Bay	11	25min
Honolulu Airport	9	20min
Ka'ena Point State Park	43	70min
Kailua	15	30min
La'ie	35	65min
Makaha Beach	38	60min
Nu'uanu Pali Lookout	8	20min
Sea Life Park	15	30min
Sunset Beach	39	60min
USS *Arizona* Memorial	12	25min
Waipahu	17	30min

make your reservation, keep in mind that the best rates sometimes aren't offered at the smaller branch offices, so even if you're already in Waikiki, it might be worth your while to catch a bus to the airport and pick your car up there, especially for longer rentals or if you're planning on keeping the car until you fly out of O'ahu.

Independent car-rental agencies in Waikiki (p133) may offer lower rates, especially for one-day rentals and 4WD vehicles such as Jeeps. These agencies may also be more likely to rent to drivers between the ages of 18 and 25.

INSURANCE

Liability insurance offered by car-rental companies covers any people and property you might hit. For damage to the rental vehicle, a collision damage waiver (CDW) is available for an extra $15 to $20 per day. If you decline the CDW, you will be held liable for any damages up to the full value of the car. If damage does occur and you find yourself in a dispute with the rental company, call Hawaii's **Department of Commerce & Consumer Affairs** (☎ 587-3222; http://hawaii.gov/dcca) for recorded information on your legal rights.

If you have collision coverage on your vehicle at home, it might cover your rental car in Hawaii; check with your insurance company before departure. Additionally, some credit cards offer reimbursement for rental-car damages, if you charge the entire rental cost to the card. Even so, there are exceptions that may not be covered (eg some rental-car agencies will also charge you for the rental cost of the car during the entire time it takes to be repaired). Most credit-card coverage isn't valid for rentals over 15 days or for exotic models, such as convertibles and 4WD Jeeps.

Road Rules

On O'ahu slow, courteous driving is the rule, not the exception. Don't honk your horn unless a crash is imminent, don't follow too closely (ie tailgate) and please let other drivers pass or merge whenever it's safe to do so. When other drivers do you a favor, you can thank them by waving the *shaka* sign – fold down your three middle fingers to your palm and extend your thumb and little finger, then hold your hand out and shake it back and forth. (You might want to practice this *before* getting on the road.)

Speed limits are posted and enforced. If you are stopped for speeding, expect to get a ticket, as island police rarely just give warnings. Car pool lanes marked with a diamond symbol are reserved for high-occupancy vehicles; without the minimum number of passengers, you risk stiff fines. Driving under the influence (DUI) of alcohol and/or drugs is strictly prohibited by law (for more details, see p279).

Drivers and front-seat passengers are required to wear seat belts, as are back-seat passengers under the age of 18. State law also requires the use of child safety seats for children aged three and younger, while four-to seven-year-olds under 4ft 9in tall must be either in a safety or booster seat or secured by a lap-only belt in the back seat. Most car-rental companies rent child-safety seats for around $10 a day, but it's recommended that you reserve one in advance.

MOPED & MOTORCYCLE

Motorcycles and mopeds are available for rent in Waikiki (see p133), but you'll have to contend with heavy traffic, which can be a challenge for inexperienced riders. The minimum age for renting a moped is 16; for a motorcycle, it's 21. For either, you'll need a valid home driver's license. There are no helmet laws in Hawaii, but rental agencies often provide 'brain buckets' for free, so why not be smart and use them? State law requires mopeds to be ridden by one person only and prohibits their use on sidewalks and on freeways. Mopeds must always be driven single-file and never faster than 30mph. Rental mopeds cost around $40/175 per day/week, while motorcycles start around $100/500 per day/week, depending on the make and model.

TAXI

Taxis have meters and charge a flag-down fee of around $3, plus another $3 per mile. Because island taxis are often station wagons or minivans, they can be a good deal for groups. There's a surcharge of 50¢ for each suitcase or backpack. Remember to tip the driver 10% to 15%, rounded up to the next dollar. Taxis are readily available at the airport and larger resort hotels and shopping centers, but otherwise can be hard to find and you'll probably need to call for one. In the Honolulu metro area, including Waikiki, try **City Taxi** (☎ 524-2121), **The-Cab** (☎ 422-2222) or **Charley's** (☎ 531-1333, from payphones 877-531-1333).

BEHIND THE SCENES

SARA BENSON *Coordinating Author*

After graduating from college, Sara jumped on a plane to California with just one suitcase and $100 in her pocket. She then hopped across the Pacific to Japan, ultimately splitting the difference by living on Maui, the Big Island and O'ahu. She's an avid outdoor enthusiast who has worked for the National Park Service in California and as a volunteer at Hawai'i Volcanoes National Park. The author of 30 travel and nonfiction books, Sara has also written for Lonely Planet's *Hawaii* and *Hiking in Hawaii* guides. For this book, Sara wrote the Green O'ahu, Honolulu, Waikiki, Waikiki After Dark, Pearl Harbor Area, Southeast O'ahu, Windward O'ahu, History & Culture, Food & Drink, Planning Your Trip and Directory & Transportation chapters.

SCOTT KENNEDY

Scott Kennedy grew up in the un-tropical mountains of Western Canada – perhaps that's why he's always been drawn to warm places. A divemaster, *mojito* connoisseur and sometime surfer, Scott has had sand in his surf trunks on beaches from Aitutaki to Zanzibar. Scott's a keen mountain-biker, marathon runner, hiker and mountain guide. A decade ago, he first stepped foot on O'ahu and has been maintaining a long-distance relationship with Hawaii ever since. He now lives in Queenstown, New Zealand, where he longs for clean waves, golden beaches and raspberry shave ice. Visit Scott's website at www.adventureskope.com. For this book, Scott wrote the Outdoor Activities & Adventures, North Shore, Central O'ahu and Leeward O'ahu chapters.

LONELY PLANET AUTHORS

Why is our travel information the best in the world? It's simple: our authors are passionate, dedicated travelers. They don't take freebies in exchange for positive coverage so you can be sure the advice you're given is impartial. They travel widely to all the popular spots, and off the beaten track. They don't research using just the internet or phone. They discover new places not included in any other guidebook. They personally visit thousands of hotels, restaurants, palaces, trails, galleries, temples and more. They speak with dozens of locals every day to make sure you get the kind of insider knowledge only a local could tell you. They take pride in getting all the details right, and in telling it how it is. Think you can do it? Find out how at **lonelyplanet.com**.

THIS BOOK

This 4th edition of *Honolulu, Waikiki & O'ahu* was written by Sara Benson and Scott Kennedy. Contributions were also made by Jake Howard. The previous edition was written by Ned Friary and Glenda Bendure. This guidebook was commissioned in Lonely Planet's Oakland, California, office and produced by the following:

Hawaii Product Development Manager & Commissioning Editor Emily K Wolman
Coordinating Editor Ali Lemer
Coordinating Cartographer Anthony Phelan
Managing Editor Sasha Baskett
Managing Cartographer Alison Lyall
Assisting Editors Andrew Bain, Jessica Crouch, Victoria Harrison, Angela Tinson
Indexer Sarah Stewart
Series Designer Gerilyn Attebery
Layout Designer Vicki Beale
Managing Layout Designers Laura Jane, Indra Kilfoyle
Cover Designers & Image Researchers Nicholas Colicchia, Yukiyoshi Kamimura, Marika Kozak, Nic Lehman, Michael Ruff, Kate Slattery
Project Manager Eoin Dunlevy
Language Content Coordinator Quentin Frayne

Thanks to Lucy Birchley, Michaela Klink Caughlan, Mark Germanchis, Brice Gosnell, Bronwyn Hicks, Lauren Hunt, Abbot L Moffat III, Wayne Murphy, Paul Piaia, Raphael Richards, Julie Sheridan, Christina Tunnah, Vivek Waglé, Juan Winata

Internal photographs p244, p249, p273 John Borthwick/Lonely Planet Images; p14, p19, p37, p59, p75, p85, p90, p99, p101, p106, p109, p112, p116, p131, p135, p137, p143, p153, p162, p163, p167, p168, p174, p177, p185, p188, p195, p231, p232, p239, p242, p253, p268, p273 Ann Cecil/Lonely Planet Images; p18, p41, p44, p46, p52, p62, p64, p70, p80, p95, p97, p115, p120, p125, p132, p138, p171, p183, p193, p197, p203, p213, p219, p220, p246, p261, p262, p263, p272 Linda Ching/Lonely Planet Images; p9, p13, p215 Richard Cummins/Lonely Planet Images; p144 John Elk III/Lonely Planet Images; p222, p272 Greg Elms/Lonely Planet Images; p8, p51, p255, p257 Lee Foster/Lonely Planet Images; p272 Rick Gerharter/Lonely Planet Images; p27, p34 Richard I'Anson/Lonely Planet Images; p12, p17, p217 Scott Kennedy; p16, p251, p259 Ray Laskowitz/Lonely Planet Images; p38, p154 Christina Lease/Lonely Planet Images; p10, p35, p49, p76, p170, p192, p194, p225, p233 Karl Lehmann/Lonely Planet Images; p141 Holger Leue/Lonely Planet Images; p36 Dave Levitt/Lonely Planet Images; p7 Clint Lucas/Lonely Planet Images; p15, p45, p57, p107, p186, p201, p206 Merten Snijders/Lonely Planet Images; p149, p159, p267 Casey Mahaney/Lonely Planet Images; p148 Chris Mellor/Lonely Planet Images; p191 Mark Newman/Lonely Planet Images; p272 Lawrence Worcester/Lonely Planet Images

All images are copyright of the photographer unless otherwise indicated. Many of the images in this guide are available for licensing from Lonely Planet Images: www.lonelyplanetimages.com.

THANKS from the Authors
Sara Benson
Special thanks to all those who took the time to be my Island Voices: Ellen Gay Dela Rosa, Stephen Little, Bill Snively, Elizabeth Kumabe Maynard and the entire Keawe 'ohana. Thanks

SEND US YOUR FEEDBACK

We love to hear from travelers – your comments keep us on our toes and help make our books better. Our well-traveled team reads every word on what you loved or loathed about this book. Although we cannot reply individually to postal submissions, we always guarantee that your feedback goes straight to the appropriate authors, in time for the next edition. Each person who sends us information is thanked in the next edition – and the most useful submissions are rewarded with a free book.

To send us your updates – and find out about Lonely Planet events, newsletters and travel news – visit our award-winning website: lonelyplanet.com/contact.

Note: We may edit, reproduce and incorporate your comments in Lonely Planet products such as guidebooks, websites and digital products, so let us know if you don't want your comments reproduced or your name acknowledged. For a copy of our privacy policy visit lonelyplanet.com/privacy.

THE LONELY PLANET STORY

Fresh from an epic journey across Europe, Asia and Australia in 1972, Tony and Maureen Wheeler sat at their kitchen table stapling together notes. The first Lonely Planet guidebook, *Across Asia on the Cheap*, was born.

Travelers snapped up the guides. Inspired by their success, the Wheelers began publishing books to Southeast Asia, India and beyond. Demand was prodigious, and the Wheelers expanded the business rapidly to keep up. Over the years, Lonely Planet extended its coverage to every country and into the virtual world via lonelyplanet.com and the Thorn Tree message board.

As Lonely Planet became a globally loved brand, Tony and Maureen received several offers for the company. But it wasn't until 2007 that they found a partner whom they trusted to remain true to the company's principles of traveling widely, treading lightly and giving sustainably. In October of that year, BBC Worldwide acquired a 75% share in the company, pledging to uphold Lonely Planet's commitment to independent travel, trustworthy advice and editorial independence.

Today Lonely Planet has offices in Melbourne, London and Oakland, with over 500 staff members and 300 authors. Tony and Maureen are still actively involved with Lonely Planet. They're traveling more often than ever, and they're devoting their spare time to charitable projects. And the company is still driven by the philosophy of *Across Asia on the Cheap*: 'All you've got to do is decide to go and the hardest part is over. So go!'

also to Lesa Griffith, Lee Britos, Rebecca Pang, Bianca Mordasi, Lisa Mock and Seth Casey. Without editor Emily Wolman and all the in-house staff at LP, this book would never have come to fruition. The Pickett family graciously shared their hospitality on the Windward Coast, for which I'm grateful. Finally, big thanks to Mike Connolly Jr, who didn't mind my doing a little guidebook research during our Hawaii honeymoon.

Scott Kennedy

Much *mahalo* must go to all those that helped with this edition – first to my wonderful editor, Emily Wolman, and superstar coauthor, Sara Benson. Cheers to the many people who helped so graciously while I was on the road: Jeff Bushman, Kyle Bernhardt, Grace Dixon, Ann Shaver, Ned Myopus, Adrian Nankivell, Toby Stanton, Chase Jarvis, Celeste Brash and Kieran O'Leary. Many thanks to Jack Johnson and Eddie Vedder for providing the sound-track, and as always to my wonderful wife, Sophie – for everything. Aloha.

THANKS from Lonely Planet

Many thanks to the travelers who used the last edition and wrote to us with helpful hints, useful advice and interesting anecdotes: Barbara Brown, Stephanie Kriebel, Karl McKusic, Michelle Netrval.

INDEX

BEACHES

000 Map pages

GREENDEX

GOING GREEN

It seems like everyone's going 'green' these days, but how can you know which businesses are actually eco-friendly and which are simply jumping on the sustainability bandwagon?

The following listings have all been selected by Lonely Planet authors because they demonstrate an active sustainable-tourism policy. Some are involved in conservation or environmental education, and many are owned and operated by local and indigenous operators, thereby maintaining and preserving Hawaiian identity and culture.

We want to keep developing our sustainable-tourism content. If you think we've omitted someone who should be listed here, or if you disagree with our choices, email us at talk2us@lonelyplanet.com.au. For more information about sustainable tourism and Lonely Planet, see www.lonelyplanet.com/responsibletravel.

MAP LEGEND

ROUTES

	Primary		One-Way Street
	Secondary	→ MM29	Mile Marker
	Tertiary		Walking Tour
	Lane		Walking Trail
	Unsealed Road		Walking Path
			Track

TRANSPORT

	Ferry		Rail

HYDROGRAPHY

	River, Creek		Reef
	Intermittent River		Glacier
	Swamp		Water

BOUNDARIES

	State, Provincial		Regional, Suburb
	Marine Park		Cliff

AREA FEATURES

	Airport		Land
	Beach		Market
	Building		Park, Reserve
	Forest		Sports

POPULATION

○	CAPITAL (NATIONAL)	◉	CAPITAL (STATE)
●	Large City	●	Medium City
●	Small City	○	Town, Village

SYMBOLS

Sights/Activities
- Beach
- Bodysurfing
- Buddhist
- Canoeing, Kayaking
- Christian
- Diving
- Golf
- Monument
- Museum, Gallery
- Point of Interest
- Pool
- Ruin
- Snorkeling
- Surfing, Surf Beach
- Trail Head
- Windsurfing
- Winery, Vineyard
- Zoo, Bird Sanctuary

Eating
- Eating

Drinking
- Drinking
- Café

Entertainment
- Entertainment

Shopping
- Shopping

Sleeping
- Sleeping
- Camping

Transport
- Airport, Airfield
- Bus Station
- Cycling, Bicycle Path
- General Transport
- Parking Area
- Petrol Station
- Taxi Rank

Information
- Bank, ATM
- Hospital, Medical
- Information
- Internet Facilities
- Police Station
- Post Office, GPO

Geographic
- Lighthouse
- Lookout
- Mountain, Volcano
- National Park
- Beach Park
- Picnic Area
- Shelter, Hut
- Spot Height
- Waterfall

LONELY PLANET OFFICES

Australia
Head Office
Locked Bag 1, Footscray, Victoria 3011
☎ 03 8379 8000, fax 03 8379 8111
talk2us@lonelyplanet.com.au

USA
150 Linden St, Oakland, CA 94607
☎ 510 893 8555, toll free 800 275 8555
fax 510 893 8572, info@lonelyplanet.com

UK
2nd Fl, 186 City Rd
London EC1V 2NT
☎ 020 7106 2100, fax 020 7106 2101
go@lonelyplanet.co.uk

Published by Lonely Planet Publications Pty Ltd
ABN 36 005 607 983

© Lonely Planet 2009

© photographers as indicated (p294) 2009

Cover photographs: Mt Konahuanui, Windward O'ahu, Mark A Johnson/Corbis (front); Lei hanging from statue, Honolulu, Chris Mellor/Lonely Planet Images (back top); Bodyboarder at Sandy Beach, southeast O'ahu, Richard I'Anson/Lonely Planet Images. Many of the images in this guide are available for licensing from Lonely Planet Images: www.lonelyplanetimages.com

Printed by Hang Tai Printing Company, Hong Kong.
Printed in China.

Although the authors and Lonely Planet have taken all reasonable care in preparing this book, we make no warranty about the accuracy or completeness of its content and, to the maximum extent permitted, disclaim all liability arising from its use.

Mixed Sources
Product group from well-managed forests and other controlled sources
www.fsc.org Cert no. SGS-COC-005002
© 1996 Forest Stewardship Council
FSC